MARION BROWN'S

Southern COOK BOOK

MARION BROWN'S

Southern COOK BOOK

GRAMERCY BOOKS
NEW YORK

This 2001 edition is published by Gramercy Books™, an imprint of
Random House Value Publishing, Inc. 280 Park Avenue, New York, N.Y. 10017
by arrangement with the University of North Carolina Press.

Gramercy Books™ and design are trademarks of Random House Value Publishing, Inc.

Random House
New York • Toronto • London • Sydney • Auckland
http://www.randomhouse.com/

Library of Congress Cataloging-in-Publication Data

Brown, Marion Lea, 1906-
    Marion Brown's Southern cookbook.
        p. cm.
    Originally published: Chapel Hill : University of North Carolina Press, 1968
    Includes index.
    ISBN 0-517-21875-5 (hardcover)
        1. Cookery, American--Southern style. I. Title: Southern cookbook. II. Title: Marion
    Brown's Southern cookbook. III. Title.

TX715.2S68 B78 2001
641.5975--dc21
                                                                            2001023636

Printed and bound in the United States of America.

9 8 7 6 5 4 3 2 1

Recipes on the following pages are from the following copyright sources: 136, 141, 211, from *Charleston Receipts* ©1961 by The Junior Leagues of Charleston, Inc.; 60, 67-68, 200-201, 223-24, 231, 442 from *Coastal Cookery* © 1937 by Cassina Garden Club of St. Simon's Island, Ga.; 169, 220-21, 229, 330, 367-68, from *The Columbia Woman's Club Cook Book* © 1947 by The Woman's Club of Columbia; 58, 338-39, from *The Creole Kitchen Cook Book* © 1946 by The Naylor Company, San Antonio, Tex.; 97-98, 449, from *DAR Cook Book* © 1949 Aileen Lewers Langston; 92, *De Bonnes Choses A Manger* © 1945 by St. Matthew's Guild, Houma, La.; 29, 316, *De Virginia Hambook* © 1946 by The Dietz Press, Inc., Richmond, Va.; 49-50, 306, 377, from *Dixie Dishes* © 1941 by Marion Flexner; 173-74, from *Food Is A Four Letter Word* © 1948 by Eliot Elisofon, reprinted by permission of Rinehart & Co. Inc.; 29-30, 73, 453, from *Gay Nineties Cook Book* © 1945 by The Dietz Press, Inc., Richmond, Va.; 13, 96, 107, 148, 248, 271, 302-3, 346, 403-4 418-19, 449, from *The Junior League of Dallas Cookbook* © 1948 by The Junior League of Dallas, Inc.; 45, 163, 179, 281-82, 319, 364, 421, 442, from *Katch's Kitchen* © 1938 by the Department of Applied Education of the Women's Club, West Palm Beach, Fla.; 68, 219, 368, from *Lady Jo's Southern Recipes* © 1950 by Lady Jo Kirby Beals; 440, from *Light from the Kitchen* © 1950 by the Canadian National Institute for the Blind, Toronto; 32, 38, from *The Making of Palatable Table Wines* © 1931 by Bernard P. Chamberlain; 28, 298-99, 422, 423, from *Maryland Cooking* © 1948 by the Maryland Home Economics Association; 186, from *Modern French Culinary Art by Henri-Paul Pellaprat* © 1966 by World Publishing Co.; 150, 181, 276, 442, from *The Monticello Cook Book* © 1937 by the University of Virginia Hospital League; 184, 262, 263, 286, 385-86, from *Mt. Pleasant's Famous Recipes* © Parent-Teachers Association, Mt. Pleasant, S.C.; 60, 87, 105, 120-21, 133, 270, 348, 458, 459, 460, from *New Orleans Recipes* © 1932 by Mary Moore Bremer, reprinted by permission of Dorothea Thompson, Owner and Publisher; 63-64, 352-53, from *The Original Picayune Creole Cook Book* © 1947 by the Times-Picayune Publishing Co.; 20-21, 260, 328, 362-63, from *Out of Kentucky Kitchens* © 1949 by Marion Flexner; 64, 237-38, 393, from *The Pee Dee Pepper Pot* © 1948 by Trinity Methodist Church of Darlington, S.C.; 215, 277-78, 426, from *Puerto Rican Cook Book* © 1948 by Eliza B. K. Dooley; 260-61, from *The Purefoy Hotel Cook Book* © 1941 by Eva. B. Purefoy; 363-64, 462, from *Recipes from Old Virginia* © 1946 by Virginia Federation of Home Demonstration Clubs; 217, 232, 334, from *Recipes from Southern Kitchens* © The Junior League of Augusta, Inc.; 5, 89-90, 166, 401, 419-20, from *St. Anne's Parish Recipe Book* © 1937 by Capital-Gazette Press, Annapolis, Md.; 316, 428, from *The Savannah Cook Book* © 1933 by Harriet Ross Colquitt; 152, from *A Taste of Texas* © 1949 by Random House, inc.; 30, 32, 226-27, 282, from *200 Years of Charleston Cooking* © 1930, 1934 by Harris Smith and Robert Haas, Inc., reprinted by permission of Random House, Inc.; 91, 101, 107, 262, 349,358, from *The Williamsburg Art of Cookery* © by Colonial Williamsburg, Inc.; 157-58, 244-45, from *With a Jug of Wine* © 1949 by Morrison Wood, published by Farrar, Straus & Young, Inc. Sources that are not copyrighted appear under individual recipes.

PREFACE ∽

Cook books, like charity, usually begin at home, and *The Southern Cook Book* is no exception. When I started the adventure for the original book my first steps were to collect, test, and select an extensive collection of North Carolina recipes and cookery memorabilia which I had enlarged after having edited *Soup to Nuts* for the Woman's Auxiliary of the Episcopal Church of The Holy Comforter at Burlington. This led to a project to unearth local and regional cook books in all the Southern states in order to make a truly "all Southern" selection of the best recipes of the South. As the result of letters sent out by George Colcough, secretary of the Burlington Chamber of Commerce, important Chambers of Commerce in every Southern state furnished me names of cook books and other information leading to the location of recipes. With the co-operation of other alert organizations, through public library facilities, newspaper contacts, radio officials, and interested individuals, I found hundreds of cook books and recipes.

To these I added recipes from hotels and restaurants with a tradition for fine Southern cuisine—thus refuting the idea that good Southern cooking is found only in the home. Finally I sought out the most difficult of all recipes to obtain—the guarded treasures of the Southern household. Here I must admit that despair and indignation often followed. Many generous persons, however, gave their most cherished recipes, and others persuaded friends to contribute theirs. Some sent treasured old manuscript cook books, one of which was carried by a bride in a covered wagon trek to the West coast, but was returned several generations later by train.

The results from the research for the first *Southern Cook Book* netted files of more than 30,000 recipes. Among them were hundreds of ways to cook chicken—not all *fried*. There were, to be sure, the much publicized turnip greens (salat), hog jowl, candied yams, "chitterlins," and pecan pie, but there were also hundreds of other dishes which have long been served in the South, though little known beyond their home neighborhoods. In the years following, this research has gone on until now it would be impossible to count the recipes or data on cooking.

Now, seventeen years after the publication of *The Southern Cook Book*, another adventure has begun: the revision of the book. This has come about for several reasons. One is that the book has been widely distributed and has appealed not only to Southerners but to persons in almost every state in this country and in many foreign countries. Letters, comments, questions, and book orders have encouraged The University of North Carolina Press to urge me to extend my efforts to reach further and to give the book a "new look" as well as to offer many new recipes. Because the women of today are so much on the go, I feel that the new book should contain some simple, easy-to-prepare dishes which were not included in the original work. New prepared mixes and packaged and processed foods have made a place in today's preparations of meals. I feel these should be given a nod of approval and wish there were space for more. Also modern cooks want clear-cut measurements of ingredients and exact directions for following recipes. For this reason I have evolved a standard format for all recipes that it seemed appropriate to standardize. So, for those who look for an old favorite and do not at first recognize it, I advise a closer look. The recipe may still be there but with an "uplifted" face. The index for the new book is also completely revised and considerably easier to use.

It was my purpose in the original book to combine "the old and the new." In this book I have combined "the old with the *newer*," although I believe that those who enjoyed the charming and often quaint phraseology of many of the old recipes will find enough retained to provide an air of familiar nostalgia.

In the preface for the original book I pointed out that the art of cooking in the South has never stood still. This is worth repeating. Southern cooking during the past seventeen years has moved faster than in any preceding period. Glancing back, we find the basis for the variety of cuisines even in our early cookery.

Southern cooking is the natural result of the evolution through more than three centuries, from the indigenous foods of early Jamestown to the cosmopolitan cuisine of New Orleans. It is significant that the first cook book published in this country, *The Compleat Housewife, or Accomplish'd Gentlewoman's Companion*, by "E. Smith" (published in England in 1727), was published by William Parks in a revised edition in Williamsburg, Virginia, in 1742, thus documenting the basic influence on early Southern cookery. But even before Parks entered the cook-book field, Europeans were bringing to the South various continental dishes and merging them with such native foods as corn and yams.

Very early the French and the Spanish of New Orleans blended the cookery of the two peoples. This happy combination, touched with the magic of Negro cooks, at length gave the Deep South the inimitable Creole cookery. This cookery swept north to influence the English foods and westward to blend with the Mexican cookery of the border states. Meanwhile, Germans, Italians, and others brought exciting new dishes and different methods of preparing food. The Southern cook has always welcomed new dishes and with ingenious skill has adapted them to his or her own requirements.

Since the first noticeable amalgamations of Southern cookery took place, the evolution has moved on. Now in almost any modern Southern home or restaurant one is likely to find on the menu dishes from practically every section of the country and from almost every foreign country that has traditional good food. The result of all this is that the Southern "meal" can no longer be rigidly defined. There still are sections in the South where neither the atmosphere nor the "table" has changed; the same rich ingredients like "loads" of butter, cream, and eggs are used to make original dishes. Cakes and breads are baked from scratch with infinite care, vegetables are still boiled with salt pork or ham hock, and smoke houses hang heavy with meats. But progress is being made in every other field. It is only natural that cookery, too, should be on the move.

In this new book, as in the old, space limitations have made it necessary to omit many recipes that have been given to me. Some have been omitted because they could not be worked out to conform to a new format; others because they were similar. The line as to whether a recipe is distinctively "Southern" has been broadened to include recipes from other sections and countries. This has been done because our population now embraces so many residents (and some who are not) who are not Southern but who belong to us anyway. These good cooks should have a voice in this book, and in the end we will learn from each other.

In the preface to the original edition I said that my goal was to produce a book from which one could prepare a complete meal in the true Southern manner, a book that would help to preserve the best in a way of living suggested by a motto above the mantle of the Apollo Room of the Raleigh Tavern at Williamsburg, *Hilaritas Sapientiae et Bonae Vitae Proles,* "Jollity, the offspring of Wisdom and Good Living." The aim of this book is the same, with the hope that with the addition of new recipes and a more modern format, the scope of the cook may be given more bountiful resources.

As in the first book, I wish it were possible to acknowledge personally the help of the hundreds of enthusiastic and generous people who have made both books possible. Many who do not have a recipe in it have nevertheless contributed greatly to the makings. My sincere thanks to all who have helped to bring attention to the best in Southern, and in any, Cookery. What we would like to say is, " 'Man,' dig this new book!"

MARION BROWN

"Brownlea"
Burlington, N.C.
February, 1968

"Hilaritas Sapientiae et Bonae Vitae Proles."

—Motto in the Apollo Room of the Raleigh Tavern,
Williamsburg, Virginia

CONTENTS ∾

APPROXIMATE EQUIVALENTS—WEIGHTS AND MEASURES
(Approximate can contents, Multiple servings, etc.)

"Dash" or "Pinch" means less than ⅛ teaspoon
60 drops = 1 teaspoon
2 teaspoons = 1 dessert spoon
3 teaspoons = 1 tablespoon
4 tablespoons = 1 wineglass
2 wineglasses = 1 gill
1 pony = 1 ounce
16 tablespoons = 1 cup
2 cups = 1 pint
2 pints = 1 quart
4 quarts = 1 gallon

The Following Equal 1 Pound

2 cups liquid
2 cups butter or shortening
2 cups granulated sugar
2¾ cups powdered sugar
2¾ cups brown sugar
3 cups meal
2 cups raw rice
2 cups chopped cooked meat
4 cups sifted flour
4½ cups sifted cake flour
1 qt. sifted flour
9 average-size eggs
4 cups grated cheese
3 cups currants or raisins
4 cups cocoa

The Following Equal 1 Ounce

2 tablespoons butter
4 tablespoons flour
4 tablespoons cocoa
1 square chocolate

Size of Cans and Contents

No. 1 can = 1½ cups
No. 2 can = 2½ cups
No. 2½ can = 3½ cups
No. 10 can = 13 cups

Multiple Servings: For 50

1½ gallons brick ice cream
2½ gallons bulk ice cream
3 layer cakes
1½ lbs. shelled almonds
3 pints olives
1 pound coffee
2½ pullman loaves bread
5 chickens for salad
7 bunches celery
3 heads lettuce for serving salad
2 pounds crackers
1 quart cream for coffee

Other Equivalents

3-lb. dressed chicken makes approximately 4½ cups chopped cooked meat
2½-lb. lobster makes approximately 1 pound meat
1 cup rice makes approximately 3 cups cooked
"Butter the size of an egg" = approximately 1½ ounces

1. Hors d'Oeuvres

The hors d'oeuvre, now generally accepted as the complement of the cocktail, has within the past several decades acquired new stature and a list of subregional titles such as "appetizers," "tantalizers," "tidbits," and so on. Added to the small "finger foods," in recent years, many substantial dishes are served as the hors d'oeuvre: chafing-dish foods, casseroles, molded mixtures, pâtés, and so on. These substantial items turn many cocktail parties into buffet dinners.

The hors d'oeuvre hour is not entirely a recent innovation in the South. In Colonial Williamsburg and in other Colonial sections, "assorted relishes" were served with the midday and evening meals—a custom adhered to in many homes and establishments. In the Deep South the hors d'oeuvre is a French inheritance classified as hors d'oeuvres chauds *and* hors d'oeuvres froids, *or hot and cold side-dishes. The hot hors d'oeuvre is a recherché course more often reserved for formal entertaining, and may substitute for an entree. The cold hors d'oeuvre in many Southern sections is served daily and consists of such crisp raw vegetables as celery, tomatoes, lettuce, cucumbers, onions, radishes, and so on.*

In this section we are giving some of the light and hearty; the hot and the cold hors d'oeuvres.

DATES IN BACON
About fifty dates

1½ lbs. pasteurized dates, pitted
Halves of pecan nut meats
   (around 50)

1 lb. thin bacon

Open the dates, and insert in one date a large half of pecan. Take a second date, open it, and form it with the first date to make one large date. Continue until all dates have been used. (Dates vary in shape so it may be necessary to use 3 small dates to make 1 large one. Or, if preferred, 1 date may be stuffed with a broken piece of nut meat.)

Allow bacon to stand at room temperature until slices may be separated without tearing. Spread bacon on cookie sheets with sides; bake the bacon for 8 to 10 minutes in a preheated 325-degree oven. Pour off the fat and drain bacon on absorbent towels. As soon as bacon is cool enough to handle, cut each strip in half crosswise. Wrap each formed date in ½ strip of bacon; secure the ends with a toothpick. Arrange the dates on a cookie sheet and place on middle rack of a preheated 400-degree oven. Bake the dates for 10 minutes, or until bacon is crisp. Serve warm.

These may be made ahead of serving time and frozen or refrigerated. Before baking, however, be sure dates are thoroughly thawed and are at room temperature. The dates may be made with bacon that has not been precooked, but they are not as greasy if bacon has been precooked.

Alfred G. Lea, St. Petersburg, Fla.

PRUNE RELLENAS (*Stuffed Fried Prunes*)

Dried prunes, soaked in water, pitted
Ground cooked ham

Vegetable oil
1 egg, beaten
Fine bread crumbs

Soak the dried prunes in cold water for at least 1 hour. Remove and dry well. Slit the prunes and remove the pits. Fill the cavities with small balls of ground ham. In a deep fryer with basket, heat vegetable oil (or any frying oil) until the oil is hot enough to fry a small piece of bread brown (375 degrees). Dip the prunes in the beaten egg, then roll them in the bread crumbs. Fry until the coating is golden brown. Remove and drain on paper. Serve hot.

Mr. and Mrs. Kent Belmore, Hickory, N.C.

BARBECUE OYSTERS
Serves ten to twelve

The secret of this dish is to try to keep the oysters from being too soupy.

1 qt. large "select" oysters
1 cup Sauce Concentrate (see recipe below)

Crackers and toothpicks

Put the oysters in a saucepan over medium heat; heat just long enough to liquify the juice. Do *not* overcook. Drain oysters through a colander; discard juice. Return oysters to saucepan; carefully stir in the Sauce Concentrate. Just before serving time, reheat oysters to about boiling point, but do not boil. To serve, pour the mixture into a chafing dish and keep heated while guests help themselves.

Sauce Concentrate

⅓ cup Worcestershire sauce
⅓ cup tomato catchup
⅓ cup vinegar
2 teaspoons powdered (dry) mustard

⅛ teaspoon cayenne pepper
1½ teaspoons salt

Blend all together by beating vigorously. Pour over the oysters and stir carefully. Makes 1 cup.

Mrs. W. Clary Holt, Burlington, N.C.

BROILED OYSTERS COLLEGE INN
Twenty-four

Salt and pepper 24 **select oysters** (large); dredge in flour. Broil on lightly buttered griddle on top of stove until crisp and browned on both sides. Dress with the following sauce:

3 tablespoons melted butter
2 teaspoons lemon juice
2 tablespoons A-1 steak sauce

1 tablespoon Worcestershire sauce
1 jigger sherry or Madeira wine

Have sauce hot before dressing freshly broiled oysters.

Ernest Coker, Owner, Ye Old College Inn, Houston, Tex.

PICKLED OYSTERS
One-half gallon

Pickled oysters is an early Southern dish, the "ripe" oyster often having been served as a salad. This is an old recipe of Mrs. J. D. Murray, Acton, Maryland.

½ gal. raw oysters
1 cup vinegar
Pinch allspice

Pinch powdered cloves
Pinch stick mace, yellow
Red pepper, salt

Remove oysters from own liquor; wash oysters and put back on stove in liquor. Add vinegar, spices, etc.; let simmer until the gills just turn (curl). Take out oysters and let liquid come to a scald and pour over the oysters and set to cool. Cover them up to keep them in strength. (They may be placed in covered jar and refrigerated.) Serve on crackers or dunk in any good red sauce.

Contributed by Mrs. J. P. McComas, from St. Anne's Parish Recipe Book, *Annapolis, Md.*

MRS. POWELL'S COCKTAIL CLAM FRITTERS
About forty

Mrs. Robert J. Powell is known for specialties such as these little fritters, which she piles high on a serving platter and passes at cocktail parties.

2 cups finely ground raw clams, drained, save juice
2 cups sifted flour
1 teaspoon baking powder
½ teaspoon salt

Pepper, use generously
Milk or water
2 eggs, beaten
Minced green pepper to taste

Mix flour with dry ingredients; add enough milk or water to clam juice to make 1 cup liquid; mix liquid into flour. Add beaten eggs, clams, and minced green pepper. The batter should be thin like pancake batter. Fry on a hot griddle or in heavy frying pan in shallow hot lard. Fritters should be about the size of a silver dollar. Serve at once.

Mrs. Robert J. Powell, Fayetteville, N.C.

ROSEMARY BOLLES'S LOBSTER CELERY
Twelve stalks

This delicious hors d'oeuvre is lobster meat with cheese or mayonnaise or both. Blend the following and stuff celery stalks.

½ lb. lobster meat, flaked
1 3-oz. pkg. cream cheese
Mayonnaise or cream to make

thick mixture
Salt, cayenne pepper to taste

Mrs. Chadborne Bolles, Charlotte, N.C.

LITTLE CRAB CAKES
About twelve to fourteen

1 lb. fresh crab meat (or canned, or frozen, drained)
2 eggs
¼ teaspoon salt

½ teaspoon black pepper (fresh ground)
2 tablespoons fresh bread crumbs, finely crumbled
Butter for frying

Flake the crab meat and pick over for bones. Place crab meat in a bowl, and beat the eggs into the meat. Add the salt and pepper, and mix in the bread crumbs. Heat about ¼ inch butter in a skillet. When butter is bubbling hot, spoon in the crab meat mixture, using a teaspoon of mixture for cocktail-size cakes, or a larger amount if regular cakes are to be made. Fry until golden brown on one side; turn and brown other side. Drain on absorbent paper. Serve hot with any seafood sauce. Spear the little cakes with toothpicks; arrange them around a bowl of sauce if cakes are to be served as an hors d'oeuvre.

Mrs. Calvin Smith, Burlington, N.C.

GARLIC SUGGESTIONS

Rub cocktail toothpicks with clove of peeled garlic; stick the picks into shrimp, sausages, other cocktail "bites." A subtle flavor penetrates the food. Or, to give a garlic flavor, stick a clove of garlic on a toothpick and swish around in cheese mixtures or sauces. Or place a peeled clove of garlic in a tin container of potato chips; close the lid, and let stand several hours. Chips will have garlic flavor. Garlic clove added to hot melted butter gives seasoning when poured over popped corn.

ANNIE LEIGH'S CRAB MEAT IN CHOUX PASTE PUFFS
Thirty small puffs

This delightful little "cream puff" filled with crab meat is served by Mrs. Harden as an hors d'oeuvre or on a party plate.

1 lb. crab meat
2 teaspoons fresh horseradish
½ teaspoon prepared mustard
1 cup mayonnaise

1 teaspoon Worcestershire sauce
1 cup grated hard-boiled egg
30 little cream puffs (See Choux
    Paste recipe, p. 320)

Mix the ingredients well and heap into the hollowed-out cream puff shells. Garnish with grated egg or chopped parsley.

Mrs. Robert Harden, Burlington, N.C.

SHRIMP ERNIE
Serves eight

Ye Old College Inn, Houston, Texas, has been famous for its fine Southern cuisine since its establishment in 1920. Under Mr. Coker's direction since 1945, the Inn has received many honors. Selected several years ago by Duncan Hines in a *Saturday Evening Post* article as among the fifty-four best eating establishments in the United States, it was the first Texas restaurant to receive the noted connoisseur's rating. Mr. Coker, originator of the Inn's best dishes, gives here two of his celebrated sea food recipes. "Shrimp Ernie," named for the owner, is served as an hors d'oeuvre or an entrée.

Prepare two lbs. raw shrimp as for frying; marinate overnight in refrigerator in the following sauce:

2 cups salad oil	1 teaspoon paprika
1 level tablespoon salt	1 small garlic clove, chopped fine
4 tablespoons catchup	

Put shrimp on sides in shallow pan. Pour over some of the sauce; do not let sauce cover them. Broil at 350 degrees under flame until lightly browned on both sides, allowing 7 to 8 minutes to each side.

Ernest Coker, Owner, Ye Old College Inn, Houston, Tex.

CURLY'S BOILED SHRIMP
About 3 lbs. cooked shrimp

This recipe is a specialty of Mr. Sanders, and one he originated after years of experimenting. This is the first time anyone has been fortunate enough to persuade him to "put it on paper."

5 lbs. raw shrimp	Celery tops: 1 bunch celery cut to first joint, rinsed
3 qts. cold water	Juice of 1 lemon (squeeze lemon until no juice left), and the rind, cut up
½ cup salt	
3 teaspoons black pepper	
20 whole allspice	
1 teaspoon ground cayenne pepper	1 pod of garlic (use all the cloves in one pod), peeled
6 bay leaves	3 medium onions, peeled, sliced

Rinse the shrimp; drain. Combine all other ingredients in a large kettle. Bring to a boil and boil for 3 minutes. Put in the shrimp; cover the kettle, and boil slowly for 10 to 20 minutes depending on the size of the shrimp and the toughness. Test after 10 minutes to see if tender. When shrimp are done, run cold water into the shrimp until they sink to the bottom. Allow them to remain 3 to 5 minutes. Drain; spread the shrimp out to cool thoroughly. Peel shrimp and devein them. Serve with a sauce, with mayonnaise, or in any manner desired. They may be placed in plastic and frozen. Thaw thoroughly.

Emerson T. (Curly) Sanders, Burlington, N.C.

SHRIMP PICK-UPS

This is a miniature "turnover" pie; a delicious finger-food for a cocktail party—or any party.

Cleaned, cooked shrimp, whole or broken

Pie crust (homemade or pie crust mix)

Shrimp cocktail sauce

Preheat oven to 350 degrees.

Prepare the shrimp (or use frozen or canned shrimp, cooked). Make a pie crust dough. Roll out thin on a floured board. Cut the crust with a cutter about the size of a doughnut cutter. Place 1 to 2 shrimp (according to size) on one side of the cut out dough. Place a teaspoon or more of cocktail sauce on the shrimp. Fold the dough over the shrimp and crimp the edges to seal. Place the pies on a baking sheet and bake until brown on top. Turn and brown the other side. Total baking time is about 20 minutes. These may be kept in a warm oven, and served as needed.

If fresh shrimp are used, the unbaked pies may be frozen and then defrosted and baked as needed.

E. Z. Jones, WBBB Radio, Burlington, N.C.

MUZZIE'S GARLIC SHRIMP
Twenty to thirty shrimp

1 lb. cooked, shelled shrimp
2 garlic cloves, mashed
1 cup chili sauce
1 tablespoon Worcestershire sauce

2 dashes Tabasco sauce
1 teaspoon lemon juice
Thin bacon strips, cut in sections
Toothpicks

Dry the shrimp well with absorbent paper. In a bowl, mash the garlic cloves to a pulp. Add the sauces and lemon juice. Blend well. Dip each shrimp in the sauce mixture, being sure to coat well. Wrap each shrimp in a section of the bacon and secure the bacon with toothpicks. Fry the shrimp in a 350-degree heated skillet, turning them so the bacon will be brown on each side. Serve in a heated serving dish.

Mrs. A. F. Soutar, St. Petersburg Beach, Fla.

NOTE: These are best fried in an electric fry-pan.

SHRIMP BOWLS (Hors d'Oeuvres Froids)

The shrimp bowl, the pièce de résistance of the modern cocktail party, is a satisfying dish and needs but a few rounds of toast, crackers, or chips as accompaniment. The shrimp may be piled in a hollowed-out block of ice, a salad bowl, a cabbage head; stuck on toothpicks and arranged piggy back on an hors d'oeuvre "pig," arranged on a platter, or marinated in sauce and served from a chafing bowl. Here the imagination has full swing—the shrimp and sauce are the requisites; the serving manner is incidental.

SHRIMP IN BEER

Boil shrimp in beer to bring out a flavor similar to lobster. Use 1 lb. shrimp (not peeled), enough beer to cover. Heat beer to boiling point. Drop in shrimp; boil 10 to 15 minutes, according to size of shrimp. Let cool in beer. May be served hot or cold.

Mrs. Robert W. Messer, Burlington, N.C.

SHRIMP ARNAUD

One of the most famous shrimp bowls is Shrimp Arnaud, originated by the late Count Arnaud Cazenave, founder of Arnaud's Restaurant. The following recipe was given me by Germaine Wells, daughter of Count Cazenave. I am giving this in the original form, which does not specify proportions. One pound of shrimp will make about 4 servings.

Chop green onions, parsley, and celery very fine. Add Creole mustard, paprika, olive oil, vinegar, salt and pepper to taste. Mix well; pour over boiled shrimp.

Mrs. Germaine Wells, Arnaud's Restaurant, New Orleans, La.

SHRIMP BOWL A LA TEXAS
Serves eight to ten

Mrs. Robert Nutt, whose husband is a memory expert, has a keen memory of this shrimp bowl from Texas. The basis is shrimp and onion rings marinated in a special French dressing. Serve from large salad bowl.

2 lbs. cooked peeled shrimp	French dressing
2 Bermuda onions, sliced thin and divided into rings	

Arrange shrimp and onion rings alternately in salad bowl. Pour over the following dressing, and allow all to marinate in the refrigerator 24 hours.

French Dressing

1 cup olive oil	2 cloves garlic
2 cups vinegar	2 small onions cut in small pieces
½ bottle Worcestershire sauce	1 teaspoon paprika
1 teaspoon French's mustard	Salt, pepper to taste

Mix well; let stand until flavors are blended; strain before pouring over shrimp.

Mrs. Robert Nutt, Greensboro, N.C.

ISABEL TORREY'S SHRIMP LOUISIANA
Serves four

Isabel Torrey, of Oak Grove, Madison Heights, near Lynchburg, serves this shrimp at cocktail parties as an hors d'oeuvre from a bowl, on crackers, or as a salad on lettuce leaves.

1 lb. cooked shrimp	2 medium sized onions, sliced
About 20 bay leaves	2 cups salad oil
½ cup vinegar	¼ cup Worcestershire sauce
1 teaspoon paprika	½ teaspoon salt
Dash cayenne pepper	

Clean shrimp; remove the black vein. Rinse in cold water, and drain. Heat vinegar in a saucepan with about 10 of the bay leaves, but do not allow to boil. Remove bay leaves, and set vinegar aside to cool. In a quart-size stone crock or jar, place a layer of shrimp, a layer of onion, a few bay leaves, and so on until all shrimp have been used. Make a dressing, using the spiced vinegar, salad oil, Worcestershire, paprika, salt, and cayenne. Pour over shrimp and let stand in refrigerator 24 hours.

Mrs. Thomas T. Torrey, Madison Heights, Va.

SHRIMP MOLD
Serves eight

This may be served as an hors d'oeuvre or as a salad.

1 tablespoon plain gelatin	¼ teaspoon salt
¼ cup water	2½ cups cooked, deveined shrimp, broken fine
Juice of 1 lemon	
2 pimientos (canned) chopped fine	1 cup minced celery
	2 hard-cooked eggs, chopped
1 small onion, grated fine	Black pepper to taste, use generously
1 2-oz. bottle stuffed green olives, chopped fine	1 cup mayonnaise

Soften the gelatin in the water; stir the lemon juice into the gelatin. Heat and dissolve gelatin mixture over hot water. Mix the remaining ingredients in a large mixing bowl. Stir in the gelatin and mix well. Pour into a 1-quart mold (melon mold is pretty), or individual molds for a salad. Chill until firm. Be sure all ingredients are chopped very fine to insure easy slicing. Unmold and garnish platter as desired. Furnish crackers and knives so guests may serve themselves. A bowl of mayonnaise may accompany the shrimp mold.

Mrs. Staley P. Gordon, Burlington, N.C.

SHRIMP CANAPE A LA IRMA
About three dozen

Germaine Wells inherited Arnaud's Restaurant in 1948 from her father, Count Arnaud Cazenave. Mrs. Wells has continued to preserve the famous recipes of the establishment and has originated many dishes in the true Arnaud tradition. Canapé Irma is named for her mother.

1 lb. shrimp, boiled	2 tablespoons claret
½ bunch shallots, minced	2 egg yolks, beaten
Small clove garlic, minced	Toast cut in desired forms
2 tablespoons butter	2 hard-boiled eggs
2 tablespoons flour	Parsley
Fish broth	Bread crumbs ˈ
	Grated cheese

Mince shallots with garlic and fry in butter until browned. Add 2 tablespoons flour to make a roux. Add enough fish broth to make a thick sauce. Slice shrimp fine; add to sauce. Cook about 20 minutes. Slowly add wine mixed with beaten egg yolks to tighten dressing. Season to taste. Spread on toast forms; border with hard-boiled eggs and parsley, minced fine. Top with bread crumbs and cheese and bake in moderate (350-degree) oven until golden brown. [See "To Make a Roux," p. 430.]

Mrs. Germaine Wells, Arnaud's Restaurant, New Orleans, La.

SHRIMP COCKTAIL FRITTERS
Eighteen to twenty

1 lb. raw shrimp, peeled, minced	2 eggs, beaten
1 cup flour	Milk
1 teaspoon baking powder	1 small onion, minced
½ teaspoon salt	1 tablespoon parsley, minced
Pepper to taste	Dash Tabasco sauce

Sift together the dry ingredients; add eggs and enough milk to make a thick batter; add onion, parsley, Tabasco, and shrimp. Beat well; drop by teaspoon into deep hot lard (375 degrees). Brown until golden. Serve hot.

Mrs. Everette Rogers, Greenville, Miss.

AVOCADO MADEIRA
Serves six

This is an excellent first course for a sea food dinner.

3 ripe avocados, halved (½ for
   each serving)
2 cups seedless green grapes, fresh
   or canned

½ cup powdered sugar
⅛ teaspoon grated nutmeg (optional)
Chilled Madeira

Just before serving, slice the avocados. Wash and dry fresh grapes; drain canned ones. Roll the grapes in a mixture of sugar and nutmeg. Have everything cold. Half fill the avocado halves with the grapes. Pass the wine decanter and let each guest fill his avocado.

Mrs. Ray Taylor, Greensboro, N.C.

AVOCADO AND CHEESE CANAPE
Two dozen

1 ripe avocado
2 3-oz. pkgs. cream cheese, or 1
   3-oz. pkg. cream cheese and 3
   ozs. of Roquefort cheese
Juice of 1 lemon

½ teaspoon onion juice
1 tablespoon Worcestershire sauce
Salt to taste

Sieve the peeled, stoned avocado. Mash the cream cheese (or cheeses) and mix with the avocado; add remaining ingredients; cream to a smooth paste. Serve at once on rounds of bread, crackers, or potato chips.

Mrs. John M. McCoy, from The Junior League of Dallas
Cook Book, *Dallas, Tex.*

BENEDICTINE SANDWICH (*Canape*)
Two dozen small

This little party sandwich, or canapé, was originated by the late Miss Jennie Benedict, leading caterer of Louisville, Kentucky, for thirty-two years. When she died she left her treasured recipes as a guide for Louisville cooks. Cissy Gregg, Home Consultant for the *Courier-Journal,* says of her, "Miss Benedict's fame extended far beyond the borders of Louisville and Kentucky—her recipes have become synonymous with Kentucky and Kentucky cooking." Through the courtesy of Mrs. Gregg and others, a few of Miss Benedict's best recipes have been contributed.

Cream cheese
Onion and chopped cucumber to
taste

Homemade mayonnaise to mois-
ten
Salt to taste
Green food coloring

Mix thoroughly and spread on open-face bread or between thin slices of bread. These may be garnished or served plain.

Contributed by Mrs. Harris W. Rankin, Paducah, Ky.

GINGER-CHEESE PINWHEELS
Twenty-four

1 3-oz. pkg. cream cheese
2 tablespoons ground crystallized
ginger

Cream to make paste
Loaf bread
Softened butter

Make a smooth paste of cheese, ginger, and cream. Slice day-old bread thin, lengthwise. Spread bread with thin coating of softened butter, then with cheese mixture; roll in long slender roll; wrap in damp cloth to chill. Cut in thin sections like jelly roll. This mixture may also be spread on open-face or deck sandwiches.

Mrs. Paul Huddleston, Bowling Green, Ky.

MRS. REID'S MUSHROOM SANDWICH
Eighteen

A rolled mushroom sandwich sounds easy, but until Mrs. Reid consented to part with her recipe the right consistency and flavor were to many a coveted secret.

½ cup sweet milk
½ cup chicken stock
2 tablespoons butter
3 tablespoons flour
¼ teaspoon salt
Few grains black pepper

1 cup fresh mushrooms, chopped
Salt and pepper
1 teaspoon lemon juice
Thinly-sliced fresh bread
¼ cup creamed butter

Make a thick white sauce of the first 6 ingredients, using your preferred method. Clean mushrooms; sprinkle with salt, pepper, and lemon juice; sauté in butter until tender. Add mushrooms to white sauce. Allow mixture to cool until ready to spread. Spread slices of bread with mixture and roll sandwiches. When ready to serve, toast until bread is slightly browned. Garnish with a sprig of parsley in end of each roll. (Each sandwich may be tied with twine or held together with toothpick until ready to toast. A damp cloth spread over sandwiches helps to keep them from unrolling.)

Mrs. R. M. Reid, Burlington, N.C.

MUSHROOMS CARBEREAN (*with Caviar*)

Mrs. Hendricks, the owner of Normandy Farm (on the Great Falls Road), Maryland, and Water Gate Inn, Washington, D.C., has created numbers of wonderful dishes. Mushrooms Carberean is an original Normandy Farm creation given me by Flora G. Orr, publicity associate.

Remove stems from **large cap mushrooms** so that nice cap depressions will be available. Broil mushrooms, putting a bit of **sherry** and **butter** in each cap. When mushrooms are tender, remove from broiler. Allow to cool; then fill each with fine **caviar.**

Mushrooms Carberean are suitable for serving on toast points with lemon slices as a first course, for hors d'oeuvres on toothpicks, or for making unusual canapés.

Marjory Hendricks, Owner, Normandy Farm, Rt. 189, Rockville, Md.

CAVIAR CANAPE
About two dozen

¾ cup caviar	1 tablespoon heavy cream
1 3-oz. pkg. cream cheese	Few grains cayenne pepper
1 teaspoon onion juice	1 tablespoon minced parsley
1 teaspoon lime juice	Mayonnaise to soften

Prepare canapés from thinly sliced bread. Mix cream cheese with cream and soften to desired consistency with mayonnaise. Add cayenne pepper and spread thinly on canapés. Mix onion and lime juice with caviar. In the center of each canape place a small biscuit cutter or open mold. Into each mold pour 1 teaspoon of caviar. Remove mold. Flute edges with cream cheese mixture, using pastry tube or knife. Sprinkle parsley over cream cheese fluting. Serve at once.

Mrs. Lynwood Fowkes, Rockingham, N.C.

GORDITAS DE TORTILLA (*South-of-the-Border Cheese Balls*)
About thirty

These little Mexican fritters, with cheese and chili added, are favorite Texas cocktail party appetizers. The basis is the tortilla, a corn cake made of coarse Mexican meal not available in many sections of the South.

12 tortillas, canned or frozen
1 cup milk
3 ozs. American cheese, grated
1 mashed red chile ancho

½ cup plus 2 tablespoons flour
1 teaspoon baking powder
1 teaspoon salt

Soak tortillas in milk and mash with half the cheese and the red chili. Add the flour, baking powder, and salt, and form into little fat cakes. Fry until crisp in deep hot fat (375 degrees). Sprinkle rest of the grated cheese on top. Serve very hot.

Mrs. H. G. De Partearroyo, from La Cocina Mexicana, *by "Sally Ann," Food Editor, El Paso Herald-Post, El Paso, Tex.*

NOCHES TORRIDO (*Torrid Nights*)

These are grand with beer!

Tortillas, canned or frozen
Vegetable oil and shortening

Chile Torridos (canned), or any hot chili peppers, cut into strips or wedges
Sharp cheese

Cut the tortillas into bite-sized "pie" wedges. In a skillet heat about ⅓ inch of vegetable oil with 1 tablespoon of butter or Crisco. Fry the wedges quickly for about 1 to 2 minutes, or until they just begin to brown. Remove the tortillas to absorbent towels to drain. Place the tortilla wedges on a flat baking sheet. On each wedge lay several strips of the peppers (the more peppers the hotter the "Noche"). Place a thin slice of cheese over the peppers. Bake in a preheated 400-degree oven for about 2 to 3 minutes, or until the cheese has melted. Serve hot. These may be made hours before baking.

Alfred G. Lea, St. Petersburg, Fla.

HAM FRITTERS
Twenty-five to thirty small fritters

½ cup crushed pineapple, drained
2 cups ground cooked ham, boiled
  or baked
⅔ cup flour
1 teaspoon baking powder

⅓ cup milk
2 eggs
1 teaspoon Angostura bitters
Fat for deep frying
Sauce

Drain the pineapple. Grind ham and measure.
In a mixing bowl sift together the flour and baking powder. Add the milk,

eggs, and bitters; beat until mixture is smooth. Fold in the pineapple and ham. Let chill in refrigerator for about one hour. Heat fat in deep fryer to 350 degrees. Drop the ham mixture by teaspoons (a few at a time) into the fat. Fry until fritters are golden brown.

To serve as an hors d'oeuvre, arrange fritters around a bowl of any sauce (mustard, chili, curry, etc.).

Mrs. Robert E. Wooten, Burlington, N.C.

HAM ROLLS

Wrap slices of paper-thin boiled ham around 1 tablespoon of apricot preserves or tart conserve. Serve cold.

Mrs. E. H. Foley, Burlington, N.C.

HAM-CHEESE ROLLS

Thin slices boiled ham
Guava jelly
1 3-oz. pkg. cream cheese

½ cup finely ground pecans
Cream to moisten
Salt, pepper, and cayenne to taste

Spread the ham slices with the jelly. Combine cream cheese and pecans. Add cream to moisten; season to taste. Spread the cream cheese mixture over the ham slices and roll up.

Mrs. E. H. Foley, Burlington, N.C.

CREOLE MEAT BALLS
About one hundred

2 lbs. choice beef round, ground
½ lb. pork shoulder, ground
1 cup soft bread crumbs
1 medium onion, minced
3 garlic cloves, minced
½ green bell pepper, minced
1 egg, well beaten

Salt and pepper to taste
1 tablespoon Worcestershire sauce
2 tablespoons tomato catchup
Extra ground black pepper
Fresh parsley, minced fine, optional
Oil or shortening for frying

Meat Sauce

Have the meats ground together 3 times. In a mixing bowl combine the meat and the next 8 ingredients; mix well. Roll into little balls about the size of a hickory nut. Sprinkle black pepper on waxed paper and roll the balls in pepper. Then roll them in minced parsley if desired. (These meat balls may be wrapped in plastic and frozen and cooked later, or fried and frozen.)

Heat about ¼ inch fat in a heavy skillet. Fry a few meat balls at a time over medium heat. Turn them so all sides will brown. Cook for about 10 minutes. Remove to absorbent paper to drain; continue frying until as many as needed are fried. To serve, pile in a chafing dish and pour over any desired meat sauce (see Sauces). Keep hot. Furnish guests with toothpicks for spearing out the meat balls. Serve with rounds of bread.

NOTE: These meat balls may be added to spaghetti sauce and served over spaghetti.

FRANKS IN BOURBON SAUCE
Serves twenty

1½ cups good bourbon whiskey
1½ cups tomato catchup
¾ cup brown sugar

3 lbs. frankfurters, cut into bite-size sections
Crackers or toast rounds

In a saucepan mix the bourbon, catchup, and brown sugar. Bring to near boiling point, but do not boil. Add the frankfurters and stir. Serve in a chafing dish, or in a dish with heat under it to keep the mixture hot.

This is better if it is made the day before and franks are allowed to stand in the sauce overnight. Reheat before serving. Serve with crackers or toast rounds.

Mrs. Dana T. Moore, Omar, W. Va.

CHILIS RELLENOS (*Deep Fried Chilis*)
Serves six

1 doz. canned green chilis (peppers), roasted
Sharp Cheddar cheese (grated or cut into wedges)

Flour
1 egg, beaten
⅛ teaspoon salt
Heated oil or shortening (Crisco)

Roast the chilis in a hot oven until the skin is tender. Remove skin; rinse in cold water. Remove the seeds and stems. (Split the chilis carefully). Insert in each chili a small ball of grated cheese or a cheese wedge. Roll chilis lightly in flour; dip into the beaten egg mixed with the salt. Have about 2 inches of oil or shortening smoking hot. Fry the chilis until they are browned, turning them with a spatula so they will brown on all sides. Drain on absorbent paper. Serve with a tomato sauce.

Sauce

2 tablespoons oil (olive or any vegetable oil)
1 small onion, chopped fine
1 clove garlic, minced
1 tablespoon flour
½ teaspoon each chili powder and oregano

1 teaspoon salt
1 teaspoon sugar
1 teaspoon Worcestershire sauce
2 dashes Tabasco sauce
2 cups peeled, diced tomatoes
1 cup beef consommé

Heat the oil in heavy skillet; fry in it the onion and garlic until slightly browned. Stir in flour and seasonings. Add remaining ingredients. Stir well. Simmer the sauce until the tomatoes are tender and sauce has thickened to desired consistency. Reseason to taste.

Candalaria Cornish, from How We Cook in El Paso, *El Paso, Tex.*

DIP-SPREAD MIXTURES

The dip-spread mixtures are numerous; the same concoction often doubles for spreading sandwiches and dunking bouchées (bites) such as shrimp, cocktail sausages, oysters, celery, potato chips, etc. Here again the recipes are flexible; favorite seasonings may be added or substituted without serious injury to the original recipes.

PRAIRIE FIRE
Serves eight to ten

The recipes of Adalyn Lindley, manager of the Neiman-Marcus Tea Room, are a treasure-trove to the fortunate.

1 no. 2 can Ranch-Style Beans (put through sieve)
½ lb. butter
⅓ lb. grated sharp cheese

2 jalanpini peppers; a little of the juice
1 medium onion, grated fine
1 clove garlic, chopped fine

Heat all in double boiler until cheese is melted. Serve in a chafing dish to keep warm. Serve with crackers or as a dip for corn chips, potato chips, etc.

Adalyn Lindley, Manager, Neiman-Marcus Tea Room, Dallas, Tex.

HOT CLAM DIP
One and one-fourth cups

1 6½-oz. can minced clams
2 tablespoons minced onions
2 tablespoons butter
1 tablespoon catchup
2 to 3 dashes Tabasco sauce
1 cup sharp cheese, grated

2 tablespoons chopped ripe olives
1 teaspoon Worcestershire sauce
1 egg, beaten (the egg keeps the cheese from separating in the dip)

Drain the clams, reserving 1 tablespoon of the liquid. In a skillet, fry the onions in the butter until tender but not brown. Add the clams and reserved clam juice. Stir in remaining ingredients. Heat until the cheese is melted and mixture is hot. Pour into a chafing dish so the dip may be kept hot.

Mrs. Albert A. Stoddard, Burlington, N.C.

GUACAMOLE (*Avocado Dip*)
Serves eight

Guacamole, a Mexican dish of mashed avocado with added condiments, is popular in the South as a cocktail sandwich spread or dip for shrimp, sausages, crackers, potato chips, etc. "Sally Ann," Food Editor for El Paso's *Herald-Post*, lists a basic guacamole with the notation that the most famous salad of the country is "the inimitable guacamole." This basic recipe is adapted to conform to dipping or spreading, but it may also serve as a salad.

1 cut clove garlic
2 ripe avocados (aguacates)
1 small onion, minced
1 small ripe tomato, minced

Few canned green chilis, minced
Juice 1 lemon
Mayonnaise

Rub a salad bowl with garlic. Peel and slice ripe avocados (aguacates) and mash them to a pulp with fork, removing any fibre. Add onion, tomato, green chilis, lemon juice. Mix with enough mayonnaise to make creamy. As a salad serve on lettuce leaves with crisp tostados—pieces of deep-fried tortillas.

This dish may be varied by the addition of chili colorado (red chili sauce) to give color and added flavor. [For Chili Colorado see p. 451.]

Adapted from recipe by Mrs. Oren C. Wingfield, Santa Rita, N.M., from La Cocina Mexicana, *by "Sally Ann," El Paso Herald-Post, El Paso, Tex.*

BEER CHEESE
Two pounds

Marion Flexner, of Louisville, Kentucky, author of *Out of Kentucky Kitchens, Dixie Dishes,* and many magazine articles on cookery, has graciously permitted us to use recipes from her books. Of this beer cheese she says in part, "In the days when free lunches were served in Kentucky saloons with every 5-cent glass of beer, we were told of a wonderful Beer Cheese that decked every bar. Finally we found someone who had eaten it and who told us vaguely how to prepare it. So Dorothy Clark and I experimented until we had what proved to be a very tangy sandwich spread. It will keep for weeks in a covered jar in the icebox. . . . It makes wonderful sautéed sandwiches, or it can be dumped into a double boiler and allowed to melt, when it makes a perfect understudy for Welsh Rabbit." Mrs. Flexner usually puts the cheese jar on a tray and surrounds it with toasted crackers.

1 lb. aged Cheddar cheese (sharp)
1 lb. American or "rat" cheese (bland)
2 or 3 cloves garlic (to taste)
3 tablespoons Worcestershire sauce

1 teaspoon salt, or more to taste
1 teaspoon powdered mustard
Dash Tabasco sauce or cayenne pepper
¾ of a 12-oz. bottle of beer (about 1 cup more or less)

Grind the cheese (do not use processed cheese) with garlic cloves. Mix with this: Worcestershire sauce, salt, mustard, and Tabasco or cayenne. Put in a bowl in an electric mixer and slowly add enough beer to make a paste smooth enough to spread. Store in covered jars and keep in icebox until needed.

From Out of Kentucky Kitchens, *by Marion Flexner, Louisville, Ky.*

MRS. MESSER'S GARLIC CHEESE
One and a half pounds

1 lb. American cheese (sharp)
3 3-oz. pkgs. cream cheese
3 garlic cloves, ground

1 teaspoon lemon juice
1 teaspoon sugar
Dash salt and cayenne pepper

Blend all ingredients thoroughly (grind together American cheese and garlic; mash in the cream cheese). Divide mixture into about 6 pieces and form each into a small roll about ¾ inch in diameter. Wrap rolls separately and store in refrigerator several days. Slice thin and serve on crisp crackers.

Mrs. Robert W. Messer, Burlington, N.C.

SAUSAGE-CHEESE BALLS
One hundred balls

1 lb. lean sausage
10 ozs. grated sharp Cheddar cheese

3½ cups Bisquick mix

Break up sausage into small pieces; allow to stand at room temperature until softened. Mix in the cheese and Bisquick with your hands. Thoroughly blend the mixture until it can be formed into a large ball. Pinch off small pieces and roll between palms to form balls about the size of a large marble. Place on a baking sheet (do not let the sausage balls touch each other), and bake in a preheated 325- to 350-degree oven for around 20 minutes, or until balls are puffed and golden brown. They should be baked on a rack one notch below the middle of the oven. Serve at once with a chili or mustard sauce.

Mrs. Mary W. Umstead, Durham, N.C.

CHEESE-OLIVE PUFFS
Sixty puffs

2 cups grated natural sharp American cheese
½ cup butter, softened
1 cup sifted flour
½ teaspoon salt
1 tablespoon paprika
60 stuffed olives

In a mixing bowl blend the cheese, butter, and dry ingredients to make a stiff dough. Blending with the hand is the best method. Drain the olives until they are as dry as possible. Pinch off a small amount of dough and flatten in the palm of hand; wrap the dough around an olive so that the olive is well sealed. Place on a cookie sheet and freeze. (Freezing keeps the juice from softening the dough.) Bake in a preheated 400-degree oven for 15 minutes. Do not thaw before baking.

Mrs. Benjamin T. Wade, Jr., Burlington, N.C.

BRANDIED GORGONZOLA CHEESE
One and one-fourth pounds

1 lb. ripe Gorgonzola cheese
¼ lb. cream cheese
3 ozs. good brandy
Crushed nuts, optional

Soften both Gorgonzola and cream cheese. Crush and mix together with a fork. Add the brandy and blend well. Make into a ball or a roll and place in refrigerator for 2 to 3 days. Serve on crackers as an hors d'oeuvre, or as an accompaniment to fruits for an after-dinner course. Crushed nuts may be added if desired.

Mrs. Clarence Salzer, Cincinnati, Ohio

COCKTAIL PRESSED CHICKEN
Two to two and one-half quarts

1 large hen (6 to 7 lbs.), or 2 small ones
Juice of 6 lemons
Salt and pepper to taste
1½ tablespoons celery seed

2 pkgs. plain gelatin (2 tablespoons)
4 cups chicken broth, all fat skimmed off
12 hard-cooked eggs, ground
Pyrex loaf pans or molds

Boil the hen until the meat falls from the bones. Remove the chicken, reserve the broth. Chill and skim the broth of all fat. Remove all skin and bones from the chicken; grind the meat in a meat grinder (medium blade). Place meat in a large bowl and pour the lemon juice over. Marinate for 1 hour. Season the chicken with salt, pepper, and celery seed. The more pepper the better the flavor. Soften the gelatin in ½ cup chicken broth. Heat 3½ cups of broth and stir in the softened gelatin; stir until dissolved.

Grind the hard-cooked eggs, and season with salt, pepper, and celery seed to taste.

Use a 2- to 2½-quart mold (loaf pyrex dish) or use two 1½-quart loaf dishes or molds. In the large mold place ½ of the ground chicken; then make a layer of the eggs. Spread the remaining chicken over the eggs. Press down with the hands to pack the dish firmly. Gently pour the broth-gelatin mixture over, adding it slowly so the gelatin can seep through the layers.

Chill at least 12 hours. Unmold (garnish platter as desired) on a serving platter. Serve with mayonnaise and crackers on the side. Furnish knives for guests to slice the mold and serve themselves. This may be used as a salad or main course dish.

Mrs. Josephine Hill Carrigan, Burlington, N.C.

CHICKEN PATE AMANDINE, NEIMAN-MARCUS
Serves six

1 can minced chicken (3½ to 4 ounces)
4 tablespoons butter, softened

1 tablespoon dry sherry
Salted walnuts or almonds, coarsely chopped

Blend the chicken with the butter; blend in the wine. Put into a small earthenware crock. Sprinkle the top with the nuts.

Special permission, Adalyn Lindley, Manager, Neiman-Marcus
Tea Room, Dallas, Tex.

MOLDED FOIE GRAS MOUSSE
Serves eight to ten

2 cups chicken stock or consommé
1 envelope plain gelatin
¾ cup sliced black olives (or truffles if obtainable)
1½ cups mock foie gras purée (see p. 25)

1 envelope plain gelatin (for the mousse)
½ cup cold water
⅓ cup heavy cream, whipped

Heat 1 cup of the chicken stock in a small saucepan. Soften the gelatin in a small amount of the remaining stock. Combine the gelatin with the hot stock and stir until dissolved; add the remaining stock. Set aside. Place a pâté mold or a pyrex 1½-pint loaf pan in a pan of cracked ice. Pour in part of the chicken-gelatin mixture and roll the pan from side to side until coated. Repeat this procedure until the bottom and sides have a nice thick coating of aspic. Keep the mold refrigerated until aspic begins to set. Press slices of olives or truffles into the aspic, making any desired pattern in the pan.

Pour the foie gras purée into a bowl. Soften the envelope of gelatin in the cold water; melt it over a pan of hot water. Stir the purée; add the gelatin and stir again. Fold in the whipped cream. Pack the mousse into the aspic-lined mold or pan. Chill. Pour a layer of the remaining chicken-gelatin mixture over the mousse. Chill for at least 12 hours. Unmold on serving dish. Garnish the dish as desired. Slice to serve with crackers or bread rounds.

MEMPHIS LIVER PATE
One pound

1 lb. liver, chicken, turkey, calf's, or goose (preferred)
1 cup minced onion
4 tablespoons butter
2 to 3 tablespoons lemon juice
¼ teaspoon garlic juice

2 tablespoons brandy
Salt and pepper
2 hard-cooked eggs, sieved
Chopped mushrooms, nuts (optional)

Boil the liver in water to cover until soft, 10 to 15 minutes. Drain; grind in medium-blade food chopper or mash with fork. Sauté the onions (mushrooms also if used) in the butter until soft. Toss with the liver paste. Add lemon juice to taste, garlic, and brandy. Season to taste with salt and pepper. Chopped nuts (truffles are best if can be had) may be added. Make into a mound and chill thoroughly. Serve with the sieved egg sprinkled over. Slice and serve as salad or on toast rounds for an hors d'oeuvre. This is a favorite with the medical students at Memphis State University.

Jack Camp, Memphis, Tenn.

FOIE GRAS (*Mock Foie Gras Puree*)
About two cups

"Foie gras" literally means "fat liver." The term is commonly applied to liver from geese which have been fattened by a special feeding. Fine foie comes from Alsace and southwestern France. A few other Europeans countries import the purée to this country. The purée comes in cans and may be converted into other foie gras dishes. This is a mock foie gras made of chicken livers.

1 lb. chicken livers, big fat ones preferred	⅓ cup chopped truffles, or sliced black olives
1 cup sherry	Salt and pepper to taste
½ cup butter, softened	

Put the chicken livers and the wine into a heated skillet. Cover the vessel and bring quickly to boiling point. Reduce heat and simmer livers for about 5 to 7 minutes, according to size of the livers. Purée the livers through a food mill or sieve (or blender). Stir in the softened butter, truffles, or olives. Season to taste with salt and pepper.

This purèe may be used to cover a roast fillet of beef such as that used for Beef Wellington (see recipe). It may be molded, baked, or served cold as an hors d'oeuvre spread.

To store, pack in a small jar or jars, and cover with a layer of melted butter Makes about 1½ to 2 cups.

Mrs. W. H. May, Jr., Burlington, N.C.

EGGS STUFFED WITH CHICKEN LIVERS
Serves six

6 hard-cooked eggs	1 dash Tabasco sauce
3 large chicken livers	1 teaspoon tomato catchup
1 teaspoon minced onion	Salt and pepper
2 tablespoons butter	½ cup grated Cheddar cheese, or Parmesan cheese
1 teaspoon chopped parsley	
2 teaspoons Worcestershire sauce	Toast rounds and chili sauce

Peel and cut eggs lengthwise. Remove the yolks and press them through a sieve. Set aside. Chop the livers and mix with the minced onion. Sauté in the butter until livers are tender. Mix the livers with the egg yolks, parsley, sauces, and tomato catchup. Lightly season with salt and pepper. Blend mixture well and fill the egg whites with the mixture. Place eggs in a baking dish and sprinkle with the cheese. Bake eggs in a 350-degree oven until cheese melts. Place on small toast rounds and serve. Accompany eggs with a bowl of chili sauce, or place a small amount of sauce on top of each egg.

Mrs. Graydon Pugh, Atlanta, Ga.

CRAB- OR SHRIMP-STUFFED EGGS
Serves twelve to fourteen

12 hard-cooked eggs, peeled, cut in half lengthwise
½ cup cooked crab meat, or cooked shrimp, finely minced
¼ teaspoon sugar
1 teaspoon hot prepared mustard
Salt and white pepper to taste

1 tablespoon Durkee's dressing
Mayonnaise
Paprika
Garnishing for eggs (sliced stuffed olives, a dab of red caviar, sprig of parsley, strips of pimiento, etc.)

While eggs are still warm, cut and remove yolks. Mash the yolks in a bowl. Mix in the crab meat or shrimp, sugar, mustard, salt, pepper, and Durkee's dressing. Fold in enough mayonnaise to make a thick mixture. Fill the egg whites with the egg paste. Sprinkle with paprika and garnish as desired.

They may be made a day before serving time if kept well wrapped and refrigerated in very cold compartment. Do not freeze.

Mrs. John F. Schoonmaker, Freeport, Grand Bahama

SHRIMP PASTE
Serves four to six

This is often called "Shrimp Butter." It is for spreading canapés or it may be molded and served as a salad.

1 qt. boiled and picked shrimp
Seasoning to taste

3 tablespoons butter

Grind shrimp; place in a saucepan with butter and any desired seasoning (salt, pepper, etc.). Heat thoroughly; pack in molds, pressing down hard with a spoon, and pour melted butter on top. Place in refrigerator to chill. An excellent hors d'oeuvre or, sliced, an addition to a salad. [I sometimes add ½ cup minced celery, 1 teaspoonful Worcestershire sauce, 1 teaspoonful minced onion to the recipe.—M.B.]

Mrs. Joseph Brennan, from The Cotton Blossom Cook Book, *Atlanta, Ga.*

THELMA THOMPSON'S SEA FOOD COCKTAIL
Serves two

Thelma Thompson, author of *Give Us This Night, Dr. Red,* and *Bright Ramparts,* extends her talents to cookery. This sauce may be served over crab, oysters, lobster, or other sea food.

½ cup catchup

2 tablespoons vinegar from canned chilis

1 tablespoon fresh horseradish

5 drops garlic juice

Mix well, chill, and serve.

Thelma Thompson (Mrs. Walter Slayden), Raleigh, N.C.

CANTALOUPE-MELON COCKTAIL

Kitty Knox does the unusual with fruits. Following is a special cocktail:

½ cup sugar
½ cup water
3 tablespoons chopped mint leaves

Juice 1 lemon
Juice 1 orange
Melon balls

Boil sugar and water together for 5 minutes. Pour syrup over mint leaves; cool and strain. Add fruit juices; chill. Cut balls of melon, honey-dew, or cantaloupe. Chill. Place a combination of balls (or one variety) in cocktail glasses. Pour syrup over and garnish with a sprig of mint.

Mrs. James W. Knox, from The Cotton Blossom Cook Book,
Atlanta, Ga.

PAWPAW COCKTAIL
Serves four

1 pawpaw
Juice of 4 oranges
2 teaspoons sugar

Pinch salt
2 oz. maraschino juice
4 maraschino cherries

Chill a pawpaw; peel and dice. Add the juice of oranges, sugar, salt, and cherry juice. Serve in chilled cocktail glasses garnished by a cherry.

From The Key West Cook Book, *Key West, Fla.*

HENTAILS
About forty

¼ lb. old Cheddar cheese
¼ lb. butter
1 cup flour

¼ teaspoon cayenne
¼ teaspoon salt

Mix all together with hands; roll out and cut into 1-inch squares (or other shapes). Bake in 375-degree oven for about 10 minutes.

Mrs. George Adams, from The Cotton Blossom Cook Book, *Atlanta, Ga.*

COCKTAIL CRACKERS
About thirty

⅔ cup flour
½ teaspoon salt
6 tablespoons grated sharp cheese

2 tablespoons butter
3 tablespoons milk
6 oz. deviled ham

Sift flour and salt. Cut in grated cheese and butter. Add milk and mix. Roll for pastry. Spread with deviled ham. Roll like jelly roll. Chill in refrigerator. Slice thin. Bake on cookie sheet about 10 minutes at 400 degrees.

Mrs. Alfred E. Kemp, Baltimore, Md., from Maryland Cooking,
Maryland Home Economics Assoc.

2. Beverages

PUNCHES

From the Gay Nineties Cook Book, *comes the following general rule to make a good punch:*

> "A little water to make it weak,
> A little sugar to make it sweet;
> A little lemon to make it sour,
> A little whiskey to give it power."

"The proportion of water should ordinarily be two-thirds to one-third of the whiskey or rum, with a very little of the thin, yellow rind of lemon, and sugar to suit the taste."

From the same book is the following famous Virginia Punch.

SUGAR SYRUP FOR PUNCHES

"Always sweeten a punch with syrup, not sugar." The proportions are 1 cup sugar to 1 cup water, boiled till clear.

From De Virginia Hambook, *by F. Meredith Dietz, Richmond, Va.*

JEFF DAVIS PUNCH (*for Receptions*)
Five gallons

"President of the Confederate States of America Punch is said to have been served in the 'White House of the Confederacy' before supplies ran short.

1½ pts. lemon juice
3½ lbs. sugar dissolved in
Water (just enough to dissolve sugar)
12 bottles claret
1½ bottles sherry
½ bottle brandy
¼ bottle rum
1 cup maraschino
3 qt. bottles ginger ale
6 qt. bottles Apollinaris or soda
2 lemons, sliced thin
½ cucumber sliced with peel
1 orange, sliced

"If too strong, water may be added till the quantity reaches 5 gallons. Best if made twenty-four hours before using, adding the ginger ale and Apollinaris just before serving. Serve with plenty of ice."

From Gay Nineties Cook Book, *by F. Meredith and*
August Dietz, Jr., Richmond, Va.

ST. CECILIA PUNCH
About ten and one-half quarts

"This recipe was given by one of the Board of Managers of the St. Cecilia Society, and has often been used at those famous balls [of the Society.]

6 lemons
1 qt. brandy
1 pineapple
1½ lbs sugar (3 cups)
1 qt. green tea

1 pt. Jamaica rum
1 qt. brandy (peach preferred)
4 qts. champagne
2 qts. Apollinaris

"Cut the lemon in thin slices and cover with brandy. Allow to steep for 24 hours. Several hours before ready to serve, slice the pineapple into the bowl with the lemon slices; then add the sugar, tea, rum, and peach brandy. Stir well. When ready to serve, add the champagne and Apollinaris."

From 200 Years of Charleston Cooking, *by Blanche S. Rhett,*
Lettie Gay, and Helen Woodward

THE ORIGINAL CAPE FEAR PUNCH
About eleven and one-half quarts

The formula for Cape Fear Punch has for generations been a guarded secret. This is the first time that it has been given for publication.

6 tablespoons sugar
1 pt. lemon juice
1 qt. strong green tea
4 full qts. straight rye or bourbon
    whiskey

1 qt. West Indian rum
1 full qt. French brandy

Mix; let the above mixture stand for 30 to 90 days, the longer the better. When stock is made, seal it until ready for use. It is better if put into 1 gallon bottles so that it may be used as wanted.

When ready to serve, to ½ gallon of stock add:

2 bottles of sparkling water
2 bottles of champagne

2 oranges, sliced
2 lemons, sliced

Serve in large punch bowl with 1 large lump of ice.

From an original Cape Fear recipe

PENDENNIS CLUB CHAMPAGNE PUNCH
One gallon

A famous Louisville beverage associated with the Christmas holidays.

3 qts. champagne
1 pony maraschino
3 ponies brandy
2 ponies curaçao
Juice 4 lemons

Sugar to taste
Fruit to taste
Block of ice
2 qts. sparkling Canada Dry water

Mix all; pour into punch bowl with block of ice, and add sparkling water last.

Fred H. Crawford, Manager, Pendennis Club, Louisville, Ky.

RALEIGH WHISKEY PUNCH
About one gallon

This punch is a favorite in the North Carolina State Capital, and in many other places.

1 cup brandy
Sugar to taste
1 qt. bourbon

1 qt. sauterne wine
2 large bottles sparkling water

Make a base of the brandy mixed with sugar to taste. Put large piece of ice in punch bowl; add other ingredients, pouring in sparkling water last. Serve in punch cups.

Mrs. Louis E. Wootten, Raleigh, N.C.

REGIMENTAL PUNCHES

A number of army regiments, both American and English, have named their favorite punches for their regiments. Bernard P. Chamberlain, recognized authority on "the making of palatable table wines" and other beverages, says that the most famous early American regimental punches were "The Seventh Regiment National Guard" punch and the "Sixty-ninth Regiment" punch. The American punches were traditionally mixed in individual glasses, while the English beverage was more often given in larger quantities. The best known English regimental punches (known and long served in the South) are the "Chatham Artillery" and "The Light Guard." Here are Mr. Chamberlain's recipes for the "Seventh Regiment National Guard" and the "Chatham Artillery" punches.

SEVENTH REGIMENT NATIONAL GUARD PUNCH
For one serving

Dissolve one teaspoon of sugar in a little water in a large bar-glass; pour in 1 wineglassful of brandy, 1 wineglassful of sherry, and the juice of ¼ of a lemon; flavor with raspberry syrup; fill the glass with shaved ice and shake it thoroughly; dress the glass with pieces of orange, pineapple, and berries in season; add a dash of Jamaica rum, and serve with a straw.

From The Making of Palatable Table Wines, *by Bernard P. Chamberlain, Charlottesville, Va.*

CHATHAM ARTILLERY PUNCH
For about twenty persons

1 bottle Catawba wine
1¼ bottles Jamaica rum
1¼ bottles rye whiskey

1½ pineapples, sliced
Strawberries to color and flavor
3 bottles champagne

Mix all except champagne in a punch bowl. Let stand overnight under seal. When ready to serve, add the champagne.

From The Making of Palatable Table Wines, *by Bernard P. Chamberlain, Charlottesville, Va.*

CHARLESTON LIGHT DRAGOON'S PUNCH
Eleven and one-half quarts

"The astounding quantities of this recipe seem to fit well with its hard-riding title. It is just as good made in less terrifying portions. This recipe used to be made before the Civil War when the cotton buyers from England and France and the North came to Charleston. This is distinctively a Charleston punch and was popular at the Jockey Club balls, at weddings and it is still the most popular punch at parties.

4 cups granulated sugar
Juice 2 doz. lemons
4 qts. black tea
4 qts. California brandy
1 qt. Jamaica rum

1 cup peach brandy
Peel of 6 lemons, cut in very thin
    slivers or curls
Carbonated water (1 qt.)

"Mix in the order given. Add sparkling water before serving."

Captain Lionel Legge, from 200 Years of Charleston Cooking, *by Blanche S. Rhett, Lettie Gay, and Helen Woodward*

SAMUEL STONEY'S PLANTER'S PUNCH
Serves one

1 teaspoon orange marmalade
3 dashes of angostura bitters
1 jigger of best black rum from a
    British Isle

1 jigger of unassertive whiskey
Ice to fill glass
Slice of orange, cherry, etc., etc.

"Put last mentioned articles into the garbage can before serving the punch instead of afterwards. This saves time.

"Supply drinkers with spoons. Instruct them to stir the marmalade if they like it sweet, and leave it lie if they like it dry. If they stir too much they can always ask for more rum to remedy over-sweetness. This gives a polite letout for Oliver Twistings."

Samuel Gaillard Stoney, Charleston, S.C.

SOUFRIERE LIME PUNCH

The night before, you peel **Persian** limes thin, adding **1 teaspoon of sugar for each skin.** Crush together to extract oil. Cover with **rum** and let steep. Squeeze **lime juice** and add **¼ part honey.** (Don't keep up the steeping more than 24 hours or the stuff will taste like citronella.)

When the time comes, draw the rum off the skins; mix with the juice, and add **rum to double the quantity;** 2 dashes of Angostura Bitters, crushed ice to fill glass. Use only good black rum from a British Island.

A Soufrière in the West Indies is a semi-extinct volcano. Key limes are good for this if you can get them.

Samuel Gaillard Stoney, Charleston, S.C.

PINK ROSE-PETAL WINE
One gallon

This unusual and delicately flavored wine is a recipe brought by Mrs. Durham from South Carolina. She makes this wine and bottles it in any soft-drink bottle with tight-fitting cap. It is very potent and when ripe has a pale pink color.

1 qt. pink rose petals, packed
    down tightly
1 gal. boiling water

3 lbs. sugar
2 cakes yeast, or equivalent in dry
    yeast

Pick only sweet pink rose petals—the sweeter the rose, the better the wine. Pack petals down tightly in large glass or enameled container until it makes 1 qt.

of packed petals. Pour the boiling water over and let stand 24 hours. Drain off the liquid, squeezing as much juice as possible from the petals, and add sugar and yeast. Let work in stone crock about 6 weeks; strain and bottle.

Mrs. A. L. Durham, Burlington, N.C.

"CREOLE SPECIAL"
Serves one

Leon "Creole" Delaune is a famous Louisiana former bartender who on very special occasions officiates at the mixing of drinks for Glenwood Plantation guests. This is one of his original creations which he serves with great ceremony and aplomb.

1 teaspoon simple syrup
Lemon peel
1 part bourbon whiskey

¼ part French vermouth
2 dashes Peychaud bitters

Put simple syrup and lemon peel into glass with ice. Stir until glass is well chilled. Add whiskey, vermouth, and bitters. Stir again briskly. Make each glass separately.

Contributed by Mrs. Edward P. Munson,
Glenwood Plantation House, Napoleonville, La.

SAZERAC
Serves one

Sazerac was a famous hero of historic New Orleans. This cocktail was named for him.

1 jigger bourbon whiskey (Scotch
      may be used)
1 dash absinthe

1 dash Italian vermouth
Dash or two of bitters

Shake with cracked ice. Strain; serve in cocktail glasses, with cherry.

MARGARITA
Serves one

1½ ozs. tequila
½ oz. lime juice
½ teaspoon sugar

Cracked ice
Wedges of fresh lime
Salt

Shake the tequila, lime juice, sugar, and cracked ice in a cocktail shaker. Rub the rim of a cocktail glass with the lime wedge; then invert the glass into salt to lightly frost the rim of glass. Strain the mixed drink into glass.

Ricardo Montes de Oca, Leon, GTO, Mexico

TWENTY-FOUR HOUR COCKTAIL
Two and one-half quarts

A "Whiskey Sour" type of cocktail.

1 doz. lemons, ground	4 cups whiskey
4 cups water	1 cup sugar

Combine all ingredients. Let stand 24 hours, stirring often. Strain; serve chilled.

Mrs. Spencer Longshore, from
Southern Recipes, Montgomery, Ala.

PENDENNIS OLD FASHIONED COCKTAIL
Serves one

In Kentucky's famous Pendennis Club, many fine dishes and drinks have originated. Here, according to Irvin S. Cobb, the internationally known Old Fashioned was conceived.

"Using an Old Fashioned glass, crush small lump of sugar in just enough water to dissolve thoroughly. Add 1 dash of Angostura and 2 dashes of Orange Bitters. Add large cube of ice and 1 jigger of whiskey. Twist and drop in lemon peel, and stir until mixed thoroughly. Remove ice and garnish with cherry."

Fred H. Crawford, Manager, Pendennis Club, Louisville, Ky.

HOTEL ROOSEVELT'S RAMOS GIN FIZZ
Serves one

Ramos was one of Old New Orleans' most colorful characters and renowned bartenders. The recipe for his Ramos Gin Fizz comes from the Hotel Roosevelt, New Orleans.

1 jigger sweet gin	3 dashes Orange Flower water
3 dashes lime juice	3 ozs. milk or cream
3 dashes lemon juice	Ice (cracked)
1 tablespoon powdered sugar	Seltzer water
½ egg white	

Ice and shake well; add 1 dash of Seltzer water when completed. [We use cracked ice, shake all in a cocktail shaker until very foamy, pour into tall glasses and add dash of Seltzer water.—M. B.]

Seymour Weiss, President and Managing Director,
The Roosevelt, New Orleans, La.

BEN THIELEN'S "SOUTHERNMOST SWILL"

Serves one

"As reluctantly served by its inventor," the well-known writer.

Gin, preferably a reputable brand   ½ Key lime
1 young green coconut

"Fill a tall glass with ice. Add practically any amount of gin. Cut off the top of the coconut. (In doing this the end of your finger will probably be sliced off too. Some connoisseurs claim the resultant pink color of the drink adds to the effect.) Add the coconut water. Cautiously squeeze in the lime juice, tasting constantly. Too much lime kills the taste of the coconut water. There should be a precise balance of the two. In the spring, it is customary—in fact inevitable—to leave a termite wing or two floating on the surface."

From The Key West Cook Book, *Key West, Fla.*

ABOUT THE MINT JULEP

Few people agree on the way in which a "proper" mint julep should be made. The argument is periodically revived by the indignation of those who contend that theirs is the one and only way the drink should be concocted. Not wishing to become involved in a controversy which after centuries shows no signs of abating, I shall let a few of the best known authorities speak for themselves.

HENRY CLAY'S MINT JULEP

Henry Clay preferred his mint julep the way his body servant, Nelson, made it. This is his recipe from a diary:

"The mint leaves, fresh and tender, should be pressed against the goblet with the back of a silver spoon. Only bruise the leaves gently and then remove them from the goblet. Half fill with cracked ice. Mellow Bourbon, aged in oaken barrels, is poured from the jigger and allowed to slide slowly through the cracked ice. In another receptacle, granulated sugar is slowly mixed into chilled limestone water to make a silvery mixture as smooth as some rare Egyptian oil, then poured on top of the ice. While beads of moisture gather on the burnished exterior of the silver goblet, garnish the brim of the goblet with choicest sprigs of mint."

HENRY WATTERSON'S MINT JULEP

Henry Watterson, editor of the *Courier-Journal*, had very definite ideas about how a mint julep should be mixed. Here is the method:

"Take a silver goblet—one that holds a pint—and dissolve a lump of loaf sugar in it with not more than a tablespoon of water. Take one mint leaf, no more, and crush it gently between the thumb and forefinger before dropping it into the dissolved sugar. Then fill the goblet nearly full to the brim with shaved ice. Pour into it all the bourbon whiskey the goblet will hold. Take a few sprigs of mint leaves and use for decorating the top of the mixture, after it has been frappéd with a spoon. Then sip, but don't use a straw."

Recipes from "The Real Kentucky Julep," by Cissy Gregg,
Courier-Journal, Louisville, Ky.

IRVIN COBB'S RECIPE FOR MINT JULEP

Irvin S. Cobb pulled no punches either in his writing or in the crushing of mint leaves in his julep. A copy of his famous signed recipe is given here:

"Take from the cold spring, some water, pure as the angels are; mix it with sugar till it seems like oil. Then take a glass and crush your mint in it with a spoon—crush it around the border of the glass and leave no place untouched. Then throw the mint away—it is a sacrifice. Fill with cracked ice the glass; pour in the quantity of Bourbon you want. It trickles slowly through the ice. Let it have time to cool, then pour your sugared water over it. No spoon is needed, no stirring allowed. Just let it stand a moment. Then around the brim place sprigs of mint, so that one who drinks may find taste and odor at one draught.

" 'And that, my friend, is one hell of a fine mint julep.' "

Irvin S. Cobb. Special permission, J. T. Theobald, Manager,
The Hotel Irvin Cobb, Paducah, Ky.

ALABAMA MINT JULEP

A crusader for the Alabama Mint Julep gives us this recipe:

"Take a double handful of mint leaves and crush them well until bruised. Drop leaves into a saucepan of boiling water—about 1½ cups. Add 1 cup of sugar and let boil until a thick syrup is formed. Pack julep glasses full of crushed ice. Pour 1 teaspoon of the mint syrup over the ice. Add enough whiskey to fill glasses. Serve with a sprig of mint stuck into ice."

Walter Barr, Charlotte, N.C.

SIR WALTER RALEIGH'S SACK POSSET
One and one-half quarts

Heat 1 cup of ale and 1 cup of sherry, and add 1 quart of boiling milk; sugar to taste and sprinkle with grated nutmeg; allow this mixture to stand in a warm place for an hour, and just before serving add the yolks of 2 eggs; beat well, and serve hot.

From The Making of Palatable Table Wines, *by Bernard P. Chamberlain,
Charlottesville, Va.*

E. SMITH'S FINE MILK PUNCH
Four and one-fourth quarts

1 qt. milk	½ pt. lemon juice
2 qts. water	1 qt. brandy
Sugar to taste	

Mix the milk and water together and heat until "a little warm"; add the sugar, lemon juice, and stir well together; then add the brandy; stir it again, and run it through a flannel bag until it is very fine; then bottle it. It will keep a fortnight or so.

Adapted from The Compleat Housewife, *by E. Smith, Williamsburg, Va., 1742.
Special permission, Colonial Williamsburg, Inc.*

SYLLABUB

The "Syllabub Era" is often associated with this old recherché drink, which is made in various ways. A modern syllabub is little more than whipped cream, flavored with wine and sweetened to taste. The early way is to whip the cream and, as the foam rises to the top, skim off, making a foamy, light, and less caloric, drink. To make a "Whipt Syllabubs," E. Smith gives this version which I have copied from her *Compleat Housewife:*

"Take a quart of cream, not too thick, and a pint of sack, and the juice of 2 lemons; sweeten it to your palate, and put it into a broad earthen pan, and with a whisk whip it, and as the froth rises, take it off with a spoon, and lay it on your syllabub glasses; but first you must sweet some claret, or sack, or white-wine and strain it, and put seven or eight spoonfuls of the wine into your glasses, and then gently lay in your froth. Set them by. Do not make them long before you use them." [A whipped cream in France is "Chantilly." The Italian Zabaglione (an eggnog flavored with Marsala wine) may be a prototype for many American egg-custard drinks.—M. B.]

From The Compleat Housewife, *by E. Smith, Williamsburg, Va., 1742.*
Special permission, Colonial Williamsburg, Inc.

JENNIE BENEDICT'S EGGNOG
Almost one gallon

12 egg yolks, beaten until light
12 tablespoons sugar
12 tablespoons whiskey (¾ cup)
12 tablespoons Jamaica rum (¾ cup)

12 egg whites, stiffly beaten
3 cups heavy cream, whipped
Vanilla ice cream

Beat the egg yolks until light, which takes a good deal of beating. Add sugar gradually and beat again until light. Then add whiskey and rum very, very slowly, beating all the time. Fold in the stiffly beaten egg whites, and, lastly, fold in whipped cream. Add a ball of vanilla ice cream to each cup. [With this Miss Benedict served little thin lemon wafers. See "Cakes" for recipe.—M. B.]

Contributed by Mrs. Harris W. Rankin,
Paducah, Ky.

"GRASSHOPPER" DESSERT
Serves one

1½ tablespoons cream
1 oz. crème de cacao
1 oz. crème de menthe
½ cup crushed ice

Fresh strawberry, chunk of pineapple, or fresh mint for garnish

Place all but garnishing in a blender and blend until foamy. Or shake in cocktail shaker. Pour immediately into a dessert glass. Serve garnished if desired. Serve with after dinner coffee spoons or straws.

This makes a light dessert after a heavy meal, or it may be served as a cocktail.

Mrs. Gerard Anderson, Burlington, N.C.

DR. MIDDLETON'S "CUP OF TEA"

The authenticity of "Restored Williamsburg"—as the visitor is quickly aware—is not accidental. It is the result of long and painstaking research, followed by the equally painstaking labor of artisans. Directing the research for the vast project is Dr. Arthur Pierce Middleton, who in a few hours recounts more facts on Colonial living than the uninitiated could ferret out in years.

During my visit to Dr. Middleton's department (to look over Colonial recipes), the conversation turned to my favorite subjects, food and drink. Soon I popped the usual question, "How about *your* recipe for the book?" Delighted I am to give you his recipe for "A Cup of Tea."

"Bring water to a boil. Preheat an earthen teapot. Put 1 heaping teaspoon of black tea in the pot for each cup and 1 extra teaspoon 'for the pot.' Have pot close to the kettle of boiling water. Pour in 1½ cups of boiling water. Let steep 3 minutes—no less, no longer. Fill teapot with boiling water, let stand 3 more minutes, then pour at once."

Dr. Arthur Pierce Middleton, Director of Research,
Colonial Williamsburg, Inc., Williamsburg, Va.

GLENWOOD PLANTATION MINT TEA DRINK
Twelve to fourteen glasses

This is refreshing and altogether heavenly.

2 cups sugar
2 cups water
Juice 4 lemons

2 cups hot strong tea
2 cups crushed mint leaves

Let sugar and water come to a boil. Mix with lemon juice. Pour hot strong tea over mint leaves. Let stand until cool. Strain and pour into syrup and lemon juice mixture. Pour into glasses half-filled with finely crushed ice; decorate with mint, and serve at once.

Mrs. Edward P. Munson, Glenwood Plantation House, Napoleonville, La.

EXECUTIVE MANSION RUSSIAN TEA
Serves fifteen

This Russian tea is served often for state and social parties at the North Carolina Executive Mansion.

3 tablespoons tea (leaves)
6 whole cloves
3 1-inch sticks cinnamon
3 cups boiling water

½ cup orange juice
3 tablespoons lemon juice
1 scant cup sugar
3 extra cups boiling water

Place the tea, cloves, and cinnamon sticks in a teapot; cover with the 3 cups of boiling water. Cover and let steep for 5 minutes. Strain into another vessel; add the orange and lemon juices and sugar; stir to dissolve sugar. Just before serving add 3 cups of boiling water.

Mrs. Walter Pearce, Hostess, The Executive Mansion,
Raleigh, N.C.

NOTE: The base for this tea should be kept warm until serving time; then add the boiling water and serve immediately. It also may be served cold, poured over ice cubes in ice tea glasses.

ANTOINE'S CAFE BRULOT DIABOLIQUE
Serves four

1 1-inch stick cinnamon	3 lumps sugar
8 whole cloves	3 jiggers brandy
Peel of 1 lemon, cut thin	3 cups strong coffee

Place in a silver brûlot bowl (or a chafing dish) the cinnamon, cloves, lemon peel, and sugar. Place brandy in a large ladle; ignite brandy and pour over ingredients in bowl. Keep ladling brandy over ingredients until sugar is dissolved. Gradually add coffee, ladling the mixture until flames fade. Serve immediately.

From Antoine's Restaurant, New Orleans, La.
Special permission, Roy Alciatore, Proprietor

LOVEFEAST COFFEE
Eight and one-fourth gallons

This is an old Moravian coffee.

3 lbs. coffee, any good grade	1 gal. whole milk, or ½ gal. single cream
7 gals. water	
4 lbs. sugar	

Get water boiling hot. Put grounds loosely in a bag and leave in boiling water for 15 minutes. Take out the bag and add sugar and milk just before taking from the stove.

Mr. W. J. Hege, from Pages from Old Salem Cook Books,
Winston-Salem, N.C.

FRENCH CHOCOLATE
Serves four to six

1 cake grated chocolate, French if possible	2 to 3 tablespoons sugar, or to taste
1 qt. rich sweet milk	Whipped cream
	Little brandy, if desired

Melt the chocolate in small amount of hot water. Bring milk to boil, but do not boil. Mix chocolate with milk and return to boiling point. Remove; sweeten to taste or let each person sweeten to taste. Serve hot with whipped cream to which ½ teaspoon brandy has been added, or a drop or two of brandy may be added to chocolate. Cocoa may be made in same manner, using 1 level tablespoon of cocoa to each cup of milk.

Mrs. Edward R. McLlean, New Orleans, La.

THE KING'S ARMS TAVERN FROSTED FRUIT SHRUB
(*Successor to Travis House*)
Serves six to eight

For centuries this fruit drink has been served at Williamsburg's King's Arms Tavern, successor to the Travis House. This original recipe, along with a variant from Mrs. Leta Booth, who presides at the tavern, follows.

The Original Recipe

Juice of 4 lemons
Juice of 6 oranges
1 cup pineapple juice

1 cup of juice from pickled fruit
½ cup spice syrup

Mix; chill. Serve in small glasses topped with orange sherbet.

Spice Syrup

1 cup sugar
1 cup water
1 tablespoon clear corn syrup

1 tablespoon whole cloves
2 1-inch pieces of stick cinnamon

Stir over hot water until sugar dissolves. Simmer for 15 minutes. Strain and cool.

WILLIAMSBURG SHRUB
Serves six to eight

This is Mrs. Booth's recipe. Mix together ½ part grapefruit juice to ¼ part pineapple juice and ¼ part apricot juice. Place scoop of orange sherbet in small fruit juice glass, and pour shrub in over it to fill glass. Serve at once. [To 1 qt. grapefruit juice, use ½ pt. pineapple juice, ½ pt. apricot juice. Yield: 1½ qts.—M. B.]

Mrs. Leta Booth. Both recipes, by special permission, John D. Green, Vice-President, Williamsburg Restoration, Inc., Williamsburg, Va.

3. Soups, Stews, and Chowders

The French, to whom the South is indebted for many original recipes, are noted for their richly flavored soups. The secret of this subtle flavor is the stock-pot, pot-au-feu, *which constantly simmers on the back of the stove, receiving daily injections of strength from leftovers and added seasonings. This stock is served from the stove or is used as the base for many other soups. The modern housewife does not often have the facilities to keep a* pot-au-feu *simmering, but she may prepare good stock and refrigerate it for later use.*

One of the best stocks is a bouillon, made from one meat with basic vegetables and seasoning, or a consommé made of several meats with glutinous qualities. Consommé is richer than bouillon and may be chilled and served in a congealed state. Bouillon may be boiled down to make consommé.

The bouillon and consommé recipes given here are good stocks to be used in the original form, or as bases for other soups. The wise housewife will save the liquid from canned vegetables or from boiled ones, to go into soups.

LOUISIANA BOUILLON
Three quarts

This elaborate bouillon may be boiled down to a consommé.

1 large beef soup bone	2 turnips, sliced
1 knuckle of veal	2 onions, sliced
4 qts. water	6 carrots, sliced
12 cloves	1 stalk celery
1 bay leaf	1 tablespoon sugar
4 peppercorns	½ teaspoon Kitchen Bouquet
1 blade mace	1 tablespoon sugar
1 handful parsley	Whites of 2 eggs
½ lemon, sliced	

Place meat with water in heavy iron pot and simmer—but never boil—for three hours. Add other ingredients except egg whites and cook one hour longer. Strain; cool. Reheat, and stir in whites of 2 eggs, slightly beaten. Salt to taste, and serve in cups with slice of lemon and sprig of parsley.

From The Louisiana Plantation Cook Book, *by Mrs. James E. Smitherman, Shreveport, La.*

MADRILENE

2 carrots
1 small white turnip
2 leeks
2 cloves stuck in a small parsnip
1 stalk celery
Knuckle of veal
5 qts. cold water
2 lbs. chopped round beef

1 No. 2 can tomatoes
1 clove garlic
1 bay leaf
Parsley
Small can beets, beet juice
Pepper
2 teaspoons rock salt

Peel and wash the soup vegetables, and cut up in big pieces. Put the knuckle of veal to soak in the water for a half-hour. Add other ingredients. Heat slowly and let simmer for 5 or 6 hours, being careful to skim when necessary. Strain carefully through fine wet cheesecloth. Cool and remove grease. Color to pale red with beet juice, and season to taste. May be served cold with slice of lemon, or hot with chopped parsley.

Mrs. Eli B. Springs, from Old North State Cook Book, *Charlotte, N.C.*

CONSOMME WITH POACHED EGGS
Serves four

This is an old Southern way of serving eggs with soup or consommé which Louise Holt found popular in France.

4 eggs

4 cups rich consommé, bouillon, or any clear soup

Heat consommé and allow to simmer while eggs are being poached. Place one egg in each soup plate or bouillon cup; pour consommé gently over egg. Serve at once with grated cheese or spoon of unsweetened cream.

Louise Murray Holt, Greensboro, N.C.

"ANNABEL'S" CUCUMBER CONSOMME
Serves four to six

2 cans beef consommé, heated
1 cup cucumber pulp and juice
1 envelope plain gelatin
2 tablespoons minced onion

1 tablespoon garlic wine vinegar
1 tablespoon lemon juice
1 tablespoon Worcestershire sauce

Heat consommé; peel and grate cucumber. Pour the juice over gelatin, and let soak a few minutes. Add gelatin and remaining ingredients to consommé. Bring to boil and remove from heat. When cool, pour into consommé cups. Congeal. Serve with blob of sour cream on each cup.

Annabel Carson, St. Petersburg Beach, Fla.

GREEN TURTLE SOUP OR CONSOMME

Have turtle killed and cut up by fisherman. After meat has been cut from the carcass, take the **carcass, flippers,** and **shell** (cut into squares) and cover with **cold water.** Add small pieces of **celery** and **onion;** simmer for 2 hours. Strain; season with **salt and pepper** to taste. This makes jellied consommé or it may be served hot. A touch of **sherry** adds flavor.

Polly Fisher, from Katch's Kitchen, *West Palm Beach, Fla.*

VIRGINIA OYSTER SOUP
Serves eight

Oyster Soup, often called stew, is universal and is made in many ways, from heating the milk and pouring the scalding liquid over oysters which have been warmed with butter in the serving dish (the Grand Central Station variant), to grinding them into a mixture and serving as a bisque. A creole dish is whole oysters served in a thick sauce. Here is a Virginia recipe:

1 qt. oysters (save liquor)
3 cups milk
2 tablespoons butter

2 tablespoons flour
1 cup extra milk
Salt, pepper

Drain liquor from oysters. Heat the liquor and milk in a saucepan. Blend thoroughly the butter and flour. Mix the butter and flour mixture in 1 cup cold milk, and gradually pour hot milk on the flour-butter-milk. Return to fire in a double boiler and cook 15 minutes. Add salt and pepper to taste. Add oysters and cook until they ruffle at the edges. Serve with a slice of lemon.

Mrs. J. H. Boatwright, from The Guild Cook Book, *Portsmouth, Va.*

OYSTER BISQUE
Serves eight

1 qt. oysters
4 cups milk
3 tablespoons celery, thinly chopped
2 tablespoons bell pepper, thinly chopped

Peel of 1 lemon, thinly cut
Mace or nutmeg to taste
Salt to taste
4 tablespoons flour
5 tablespoons butter
1 tablespoon Worcestershire sauce

Put raw oysters through meat grinder; pour into pot, and set on the side of the stove to get slightly warm, but never cook. Put milk into a double boiler; add celery, peppers, lemon peel, mace or nutmeg, and salt to taste. Make a rich cream sauce of the milk mixture, flour, and butter (blend butter and flour, and stir in milk), stirring until thick. When sauce has thickened, remove lemon peel and mace (if stick mace is used), turn off heat, and slide in the oysters. Add Worcestershire sauce. Serve at once, hot.

Mrs. John Heard Hunter, Savannah, Ga.

CONCH SOUP
Serves eight

The conch is found in waters along the entire Southern coast, but this soup seems to be an indigenous Key West dish.

1 doz. small conchs
Water
½ lb. salt pork, chopped fine
2 medium-sized onions, thinly sliced
½ large can tomatoes
1 large potato, cubed

1 heaping tablespoon raw rice
6 bay leaves
Tabasco, Worcestershire sauce
Salt to taste
1 small can evaporated milk (6 oz.)

Grind the conchs fine; put into pot half-filled with water and bring to boil. Drain off water, and refill with fresh water. Fry out pork with the onions; when golden brown add tomatoes, potatoes, and rice; add this mixture with bay leaves to the conch and boil until vegetables are done. The conch will be done at the same time. Add dash of Tabasco, Worcestershire sauce, and salt to taste. Just before serving, add evaporated milk, but be sure not to boil after milk is added.

From The Key West Cook Book, *Key West, Fla.*

MRS. LAURENS' CRAB SOUP

Mrs. Laurens' recipes have appeared in the *Charleston Junior League Cook Book* and others. Here is one prepared especially for this book.

1 qt. picked crab meat, about 4 cups	1 teaspoon finely chopped parsley
1 cup butter	¼ teaspoon mace
2 tablespoons flour	¼ teaspoon nutmeg
1 teaspoon or more, salt	2 cups milk
¼ teaspoon red pepper	3 cups cream, heated
	4 tablespoons sherry

Melt butter in the top of double boiler. Add flour and seasoning, except wine. Add milk; stir until thick. Add crab meat. When ready to serve, add heated cream and sherry.

Mrs. John Laurens, Charleston, S.C.

FORT SUMTER SHE-CRAB SOUP IN CUP
Serves eight

Fort Sumter Hotel has long been known for serving authentic Charleston dishes in the traditional manner. Through the courtesy of John S. Cator, president, we have a few of the choicer recipes. This Crab Stew, made of the succulent she-crab meat and eggs, has vegetables added to give extra richness and unique flavor.

2 cups she-crab meat with eggs	1 cup small lima beans, cooked
2 small onions, chopped fine	Salt, pepper to taste
2 tablespoons butter	1 teaspoon Worcestershire sauce
2 tablespoons flour	1 cup cream
4 cups hot milk	4 tablespoons sherry
1 cup grated corn, cooked	

Simmer onions in butter, slightly; add crab meat and let heat. Add flour and follow with hot milk; stir slowly and let boil about 10 minutes; add corn, lima beans, and seasoning; let simmer another 10 minutes. Add cream. Before serving, add sherry; reheat.

John S. Cator, President, Fort Sumter Hotel, Charleston, S.C.

SALVATORE'S AVOCADO CREAM CRAB SOUP
Serves about six

Salvatore Frosceno is executive chef of the Columbus Hotel, Miami. He specializes in creating recipes using tropical fruits combined with sea food and other products. This soup is an example.

1 qt. potato soup, strained, homemade or frozen in cans
1½ cups sweet milk
1 large avocado, peeled, mashed

Dash of Tabasco sauce
⅛ teaspoon chili powder
⅓ lb. lump crab meat
Extra slices ripe avocado

Combine all ingredients except extra slices of ripe avocado in top of a double boiler. Heat thoroughly, stirring occasionally to prevent lumps. Serve hot or cold, topped with the slices of avocado as garnish.

Contributed by Bertha Cochran Hahn, Miami News Food Editor

MRS. GROVES'S SHRIMP SOUP
Serves eight

2 lbs. cooked picked shrimp
6 cups milk
3 blades celery
1 medium onion
Peel 1 lemon
½ cup flour
2 tablespoons butter

1 teaspoon salt
2 cups heavy cream
2 tablespoons Worcestershire
sauce
1 teaspoon Tabasco sauce
1 cup sherry

Grind shrimp. Put milk (except 1 cup), celery, onion, and lemon peel into double boiler to simmer ½ hour. Thicken with ½ cup flour blended with 1 cup milk. Add butter, salt, and cream. Fifteen minutes before serving add Worcestershire, Tabasco, sherry, and shrimp. Keep hot, but do not let boil.

Mrs. Robert W. Groves, Savannah, Ga.

INDIAN SEA FOOD SOUP (*Sopa India*)
Serves six to eight

This is a sea food soup with a "split pea soup" base. Make the split pea soup base as follows:

½ lb. split peas
1 qt. water
1 cup whole corn kernels

1 small can okra
2 cups cooked rice
4 Stone Crab claws, steamed

In a large kettle simmer the split peas and water for one hour; add the corn, okra, rice, and stone crab claws. Keep warm.

Meanwhile, prepare the following sea foods:

6 ozs. scallops, cut into small pieces
6 ozs. clams, cut into small pieces
6 ozs. raw crawfish, cut into pieces
6 ozs. Red Snapper, uncut
6 ozs. crab meat
6 ozs. oysters
1 cup olive oil
½ cup sherry

Braise the sea foods in the olive oil until sea food is half done (half tender). Add the mixed sea foods to the split pea soup base; simmer the soup for 15 minutes. Add the wine just before serving. Serve hot.

The Columbia Restaurants, Tampa, Fla.

LA POULE PRINCESS
Serves six to eight

This original recipe is very refreshing for hot weather.

6 cups chicken broth, strained
6 eggs, beaten
4 tablespoons lemon juice
½ teaspoon salt
¼ teaspoon pepper
3 tablespoons sherry wine
1 tablespoon curry powder

When the chicken broth has been brought to a slow boil, gradually pour in the beaten eggs to which the lemon juice has been added; add salt and pepper. Add sherry just before removing from the fire. To give piquancy, stir in curry powder. Place in the icebox for several hours. Serve very cold.

Mrs. John Heard Hunter, Savannah, Ga.

BUTTER BALLS FOR SOUP

½ cup butter
½ teaspoon salt
1 cup flour
Ice water

Cream butter; add salt and flour; moisten with ice water; form into little balls (about size of a walnut). Roll in flour, and add to any desired soup. Cover and let simmer 10 minutes on low heat. Serve with the soup.

Mrs. T. G. Hoddick, from The Alexandria Woman's Club Cook Book, *Alexandria, Va.*

MARION FLEXNER'S SUMMER VEGETABLE SOUP
Serves twelve

This soup, made by Marion Flexner, has a rich broth base which may be used as a stock for any recipe or gravy calling for broth or stock.

Soup Stock

1 large knuckle of veal	1 bunch celery tops
1 lb. lean beef with marrow bone	1 tablespoon salt
3 qts. water	½ teaspoon black pepper
1 onion	1 qt. tomatoes
Dash of Tabasco or cayenne	

Cook the above 3 hours, or until meat is tender. Strain, and add to the broth the following seasoning and vegetables except corn and potatoes:

3 stalks celery, diced	2 cups okra, cut into 1-inch rings
2 carrots, cut in rings	½ cup diced green beans
½ cup shelled peas	½ cup butter beans
½ cup shredded green cabbage	2 onions, diced
1 teaspoon sugar	2 ears corn
1 small turnip, diced	2 small potatoes, diced

Simmer 1½ hours or until vegetables are tender. Add corn and potatoes, and cook 30 minutes longer, until corn and potatoes are done. Serve a piece of soup meat in each plate. This makes a hearty meal if served with a green salad, corn bread, and a piece of fruit pie.

From Dixie Dishes, *by Marion Flexner, Louisville, Ky.*

OLD SALEM TOMATO SOUP, SPICED

1 qt. can tomatoes	2 bay leaves
2 cups hot water	1 tablespoon butter
1 tablespoon sugar	½ onion, chopped
1 teaspoon salt	1 tablespoon chopped parsley
4 peppercorns	1 tablespoon flour
4 cloves	¼ teaspoon soda

Put tomatoes, water, sugar, salt, cloves, peppercorns, and bay leaves on to boil. Put butter into a small saucepan; when it bubbles add onion and parsley. Fry five minutes, being careful not to burn it. Add flour, and when well mixed stir into the tomatoes. Add ¼ teaspoon soda and more seasoning if needed. Cook for 10 minutes.

Miss Grace Siewers, from Pages from Old Salem Cook Books, *Winston-Salem, N.C.*

LEEK SOUP

1 bunch leeks	2 tablespoons butter
1 large onion	2 cups hot water
1 potato	1 cup milk
1 clove garlic	Salt and pepper to taste

Cut leeks, onion, potato, and garlic into small pieces; cook in melted butter, stirring constantly until well coated. Add hot water and simmer slowly 30 minutes. Add milk, part cream for extra richness. Season with salt and pepper. Reheat and serve.

Mrs. Robert L. Meyer, Jr., from The Alexandria Woman's Club Cook Book, *Alexandria, Va.*

QUICK BORSCH
Serves six

2 No. 303 cans beets and juice	Salt and pepper to taste
2 cans beef consommé (Campbell)	Sour cream
	2 tablespoons vinegar

Pour the beet juice into a heavy saucepan. Run the beets through a sieve or blender; add beets to the juice. Add the consommé, salt, and pepper to taste. Put 1 tablespoon of sour cream into the soup tureen; add the vinegar; mix well. Pour the hot soup mixture over this. Stir and serve with generous portions of sour cream.

Mrs. Lambert Davis, from The Chapel Hill Cook Book, *Junior Service League, Chapel Hill, N.C.*

BUCKS COUNTY BEAN SOUP
Serves eight to ten

1 lb. dried navy beans	½ green pepper, chopped
1 ham bone with meat on it	1 cup chopped celery
3 qts. cold water	1 medium carrot, cubed
1 bay leaf	Salt to taste
1 teaspoon ground black pepper	Chopped chives and croutons for
1 1-lb., 12-oz. can tomatoes	garnish
1 large onion, chopped	

Soak the beans in cold water overnight. In a large soup kettle, place ham bone, water, bay leaf, and pepper. Simmer the ham bone for about 2 hours. Add the drained beans and simmer until the beans are tender. Add remaining ingredients, except the garnishings. Simmer for 1 hour. Garnish each soup plate with chopped chives and croutons.

Mrs. Phillip H. Dougherty, Henderson, N.C.

HEARTY BEEF SOUP
Serves six to eight

This is a grand winter soup—a hearty one-dish meal.

6 slices bacon, chopped
½ cup chopped onion
1½ pounds ground chuck beef
1 1-lb., 12-oz. can tomatoes with juice
1 10¼-oz. can frozen potato soup
1 10½-oz. can condensed beef consommé
2 cups water
3 carrots (about 2 cups), sliced ¼-inch thick

1 cup chopped celery stalk with some minced tender celery leaves
1½ teaspoons salt
¼ cup cornstarch, blended with enough cold water to make smooth paste
½ teaspoon ground black pepper
½ cup red wine
Grated Parmesan or grated Cheddar cheese to taste
Saltine crackers

In a large kettle, sauté the bacon until transparent; add the onion and fry until golden brown. Add the beef and stir over medium heat for about 5 minutes, or until beef is browned. Add the next 7 ingredients.

Bring to a boil; reduce heat. Cover kettle and simmer for 40 to 50 minutes, stirring often. Blend cornstarch with water; add to soup. Stir well, and bring to boil again. Add pepper and wine. Sprinkle with the cheese, and serve hot with saltine crackers.

Porter Cowles, Chapel Hill, N.C.

SPANISH BEAN SOUP WITH CHORIZO (*Spanish Sausage*)
Serves eight

1 lb. Garbanzos (Spanish beans)
1 tablespoon salt
Water to cover
1 beef bone
1 ham bone
2 qts. water
4 ozs. white bacon, cut fine

1 onion, peeled, chopped fine
1 lb. potatoes, peeled, diced
1 pinch saffron
1 tablespoon salt
1 Chorizo (Spanish sausage), sliced into thin slices

Soak the Garbanzos overnight with 1 tablespoon of salt and enough cold water to cover beans. When ready to cook, drain the salted water from the beans.

Put the beans, beef bone, and ham bone into a large soup kettle; cover with the 2 quarts of water. Boil slowly for 45 minutes. Fry the bacon and onions together; add to the beans and bones. Also at this time add the potatoes, saffron, and 1 tablespoon of salt. Cook slowly until the potatoes are done. Remove from the fire, and add the sausage which has been cut into thin slices.

The Columbia Restaurants, Tampa, Fla.

BLENDER CURRY SOUP
Serves Four

This is from a former White House chef.

½ cup milk
½ cup heavy cream
1 10½-oz. can cream of chicken
soup, undiluted
1 heaping tablespoon shredded coconut

¼ raw apple, peeled and cored
½ teaspoon salt
½ teaspoon mace
1 teaspoon curry powder
1 cup crushed ice

Place all ingredients except ice in blender container; cover and run on speed 4 (or low) until smooth. Add the ice and run on speed 7 (or high) until ice is liquified. Serve cold.

*René Verdon, Culinary Consultant for
Hamilton Beach, contributed by
Miss Martha S. Bailey, New York, N.Y.*

FRENCH ONION SOUP WITH CHEESE
Serves eight

2 cups sliced onions
2 tablespoons butter
1 tablespoon flour
2 qts. rich beef stock
1 teaspoon salt

Pepper
½ cup freshly grated Parmesan or
Swiss cheese
Toasted French bread

Place onions and butter in saucepan and cook slowly until golden brown. Add flour; mix and cook a few minutes. Add the stock and salt and pepper. Pour into earthenware casserole; sprinkle on it half the cheese; float toasted slices of bread on top, and sprinkle with remainder of the cheese. Place in hot oven until cheese has melted and browned. It is important to use freshly grated cheese because it melts on the soup in great globs instead of clouding the soup like powdered cheese. (Try Gruyère cheese.)

Miss Clara Bond Anderson, Burlington, N.C., and New York, N.Y.

CREAM OF CURRY SOUP
Serves four

This is a warm weather soup.

4 cups milk
2 egg yolks, well beaten
Salt, pepper to taste

2 tablespoons curry powder
Grated coconut

Heat milk in double boiler. Beat well the yolks of eggs, and pour hot milk over them; beat again. Cook in double boiler until slightly thick. Add salt, pepper, and curry powder. Cool; set in refrigerator until very cold. Serve in cups garnished with bit of grated coconut.

Gretchen Van Buren White, from What's Cookin'?, *Corpus Christi, Tex.*

GAZPACHO (*a la Mexicana*)
Serves four

1 clove garlic, chopped
1 medium-size cucumber, chopped
(coarse pieces)
1 medium-size green pepper, chopped (coarse pieces)
4 medium-size tomatoes, chopped (coarse pieces), or 1 cup canned tomatoes
2 tablespoons olive oil
1 scant teaspoon salt

1 teaspoon cumin seeds
1 teaspoon chili powder
1 dash cayenne pepper
½ cup tomato juice
1 cup sour cream
½ cup milk (or tomato juice)
Finely chopped chives, cucumber, green pepper, and celery for garnish

Put all ingredients except the sour cream, milk (or ½ cup tomato juice), and garnishings in the container of an electric blender; blend until smooth. Remove to a bowl and stir in the sour cream which has been thinned by the milk or tomato juice. Serve very cold in soup bowls or glass finger bowls. Garnish with fresh chopped vegetables.

This makes an excellent low calorie soup if, instead of the sour cream, you use yogurt or buttermilk.

Mrs. Thomas F. Torrey, Madison Heights, Va.

SOPA DE FRIJOLES (*Pinto Bean Soup*) WITH TORTILLAS

Bean Soup, made with the frijol or pinto bean, is akin to black bean and split pea soup but is richer and has more body.

Soak 1 lb. beans (enough for average family) overnight; drain. Put on to cook in plenty of fresh **water**. When beans are tender, put them through a sieve to obtain a rich brown purée. Reheat purée (use stock that beans were cooked in to thin it to desired consistency). While it is cooking, make "tortillas" or patties of **dried bread crumbs**, **grated cheese**, and **beaten egg**. Mold into balls, and fry them quickly in very **hot fat**. Drop cheese balls into soup shortly before serving.

Mrs. Mati Stearns A, from La Cocina Mexicana, *by "Sally Ann,"*
Food Editor, El Paso Herald-Post, *El Paso, Tex.*

MRS. SMITH'S MUSHROOM SOUP
Serves six

1 lb. mushrooms	⅛ teaspoon pepper
4 tablespoons butter	Whipped cream
4 cups milk	Paprika
2 teaspoons salt	

Wash mushrooms and put through food chopper. Melt butter in frying pan and add ground mushrooms. Cook 10 minutes. Heat milk; add cooked mushrooms, salt, and pepper. Before serving add 1 tablespoon whipped cream to each plate; sprinkle with paprika.

Mrs. James W. Smith, from Home-Tried Recipes, *Americus, Ga.*

CREME VICHYSSOISE
Serves six

Irish potato soup is highly respected in the South; the most elegant is Vichyssoise, a cream potato soup to be served hot or cold.

4 leeks or 3 peeled medium onions	2 cups milk
2½ cups potatoes, pared, diced	1 cup heavy cream
3 cups boiling water	2 teaspoons salt
2 cups chicken broth, canned may be used	¼ teaspoon pepper
	2 tablespoons minced chives
1 tablespoon butter or margarine	¼ teaspoon paprika

Cut the leeks and about 3 inches of their green tops into fine pieces. Cook with the potatoes in about 3 cups boiling water until very tender. Drain; then press through a fine strainer into saucepan. Add chicken broth, butter, milk, cream, salt, and pepper; mix thoroughly. Reheat to blend. Serve hot or very cold, garnished with chopped chives and paprika.

Douschka B. Wolff, from The Cotton Blossom Cook Book, *Atlanta, Ga.*

CREAM OF CORN SOUP
Serves four

This recipe is from Hardimont, Southern estate of Mr. and Mrs. J. Crawford Biggs. Originated as a luncheon dish, it may be made in large or small quantities (allow 1 cup of strained corn to each cup of cream) and refrigerated for days.

2 cups yellow corn, cream style
2 cups rich fresh cream, thick
1 slice onion

Cayenne, salt, and pepper to taste
1 tablespoon butter

Mash corn through sieve or food press. Add to cream, onion, and seasoning and put into top of double boiler. Simmer until onion is tender, stirring constantly. Just before it is done, add butter and remove onion. If too rich, thin with thin cream.

Condensed from recipe by Mrs. J. Crawford Biggs, Hardimont, Raleigh, N.C.

VIRGINIA PEANUT SOUP
Serves fifteen

Peanut soup is to Virginia what white bean soup is to Boston. Charles Hofer, maître d'hôtel of the Hotel Roanoke, says this soup is a favorite among guests.

½ cup butter
1 small onion, diced
2 stalks celery, diced
3 tablespoons flour
2 qts. chicken broth

2 cups peanut butter
⅓ teaspoon celery salt
1 teaspoon salt
1 tablespoon lemon juice
Ground peanuts

Melt butter in cooking vessel, and add onion and celery. Sauté for 5 minutes, but do not brown. Add flour and mix well. Add hot chicken broth and cook ½ hour. Remove from stove; strain; and add peanut butter, celery salt, salt, and lemon juice. Just before serving, sprinkle with ground peanuts.

Fred R. Brown, Chef, Hotel Roanoke, Roanoke, Va.

CREAM OF CHESTNUT SOUP

1 lb. chestnuts, boiled, shelled	1 crushed clove
Water	1 crushed allspice
½ cup chopped celery	1 teaspoon paprika
1 teaspoon chopped onion	2 tablespoons flour
2 cups chicken stock	2 tablespoons butter
1 sprig thyme	1 cup cream
1 crushed bay leaf	1 cup sweet milk

Boil chestnuts about 1 hour; shell, and pound them to a fine paste. Place in a soup pot and cover with water. Add vegetables, chicken stock, and seasoning. Boil together until celery and onion are tender; thicken with the flour and butter rubbed to a paste. At the last moment add cream and milk. Let boil up once and serve very hot with cheese straws. [Italian chestnuts do need to be boiled only about 30 minutes. Almonds or crushed pecans may be substituted for chestnuts, and seasoned to taste. Almonds and pecans do not need spices or highly seasoned herbs.—M. B.]

From The Louisiana Plantation Cook Book, *by Mrs. James E. Smitherman, Shreveport, La.*

GUMBO

Gumbo, says *The Original Picayune Creole Cook Book,* is not an evolution but an original Creole conception, "something *sui generis* in cookery," peculiar to New Orleans. The basis or secret of New Orleans gumbo is a filé powder introduced by the Choctaw Indians living on the reservation on Bayou Lacombe, near Mandeville, Louisiana. Made of young sassafras leaves (dried and pounded on a stone mortar, then strained through a hair sieve), the powder was "manufactured" by the Indian squaws and first brought to the French Market to be sold along with sassafras roots for medicinal purposes. The early Creoles discovered that the powder had a delicate flavor as well as a glutinous quality and began using it in soups and stews. The result is the delicious gumbo and its numerous offspring. Okra, which has a similar "tacky" quality, is substituted in many sections for filé powder. The uninitiated should use filé powder sparingly and be careful not to let the stew boil after the powder has been added or it will become stringy and unfit to serve.

Gumbo Filé, the basic gumbo, is made of chicken, ham, and oysters. Beef, turkey, squirrel, and varieties of sea food are used, as well as vegetables and combinations. A piece of lean ham is usually used when meat or fowl is the principal meat.

GUMBO FILE
Serves six

5 to 6 lb. chicken
Salt and pepper
1 large slice ham
1 tablespoon lard
Chicken fat
3 tablespoons flour
½ onion, chopped fine
½ tomato, cut in small pieces
1½ qts. boiling water

1 bay leaf
3 sprigs thyme, or 1 teaspoon
    powdered thyme
Salt and pepper to taste
Cayenne to taste
2 doz. oysters and juice
3 sprigs parsley, chopped
2 tablespoons butter
1 tablespoon filé powder

Clean and cut the chicken into small pieces. Sprinkle with salt and pepper. Cut the ham in small pieces. Put the lard and some of the chicken fat into a saucepan or soup kettle; add the ham and fry for about 5 minutes. Remove from the fat, then fry the chicken, browning it on both sides but not cooking it. Take chicken from hot fat as it browns. Add flour to hot fat and make a roux (a thick brown sauce) by stirring constantly to keep from burning. Let brown; add the onion, chopped fine, and let brown to a golden color. Add tomato and let cook for a few minutes; add the boiling water gradually, stirring well. Add the ham, chicken, bay leaf, thyme (tied with a white thread), pepper, salt, and cayenne to taste. Set on a slow fire and cook until the meat is almost tender; then add oysters, which have been washed in cold water to remove all particles of shell, the oyster water, which has been strained, the chopped parsley, and butter. Continue cooking for about 15 minutes longer. Add the filé powder slowly, stirring well. Serve with steamed rice and crackers.

From The Creole Kitchen Cook Book, *by Virginia Cooper, New Orleans, La.*

GLENWOOD PLANTATION OYSTER, SHRIMP, AND CRAB GUMBO
Serves eight to ten

This Gumbo contains the 3 principal sea foods used in Creole Gumbo; okra substitutes for filé.

2 onions
6 fresh tomatoes
1 pod red pepper
1 sprig parsley
1 sprig thyme
2 cups fresh okra
1 slice ham
1 tablespoon lard

2 doz. oysters
1 lb. shrimp (scalded, peeled,
    cleaned)
½ doz. crabs (scalded, cleaned, cut
    in half)
1 bay leaf
3 qts. water
Salt, pepper

Chop onions fine; peel tomatoes; chop and save juice. Chop red pepper, parsley, and thyme. Wash okra; stem and slice thin; cut ham in squares.

Put lard to melt in a soup pot; add chopped onions, ham, and the sliced okra. When well browned, add tomatoes with juice; cook until tender. Then add oysters, shrimp, and crabs (which have been prepared). Add red pepper, bay leaf, parsley, and thyme. When everything is well fried and browned, add 3 quarts of water. Let simmer gently 1 hour or longer. Season to taste with salt and pepper. Serve with cooked rice.

Mrs. Edward P. Munson, Glenwood Plantation House,
Napoleonville, La.

MRS. HUDSON'S LOUISIANA GUMBO
Serves sixteen to eighteen

1 large hen (about 6 lbs.), cut into pieces as for frying
5 lbs. okra, sliced horizontally, about ½-inch thick
Fat for frying chicken and okra (shortening)
3 medium-size onions, sliced
2 No. 2 cans tomatoes
1 large, or 2 small pods of hot red pepper
1 tablespoon Worcestershire sauce
Salt and pepper to taste
4 cups water
Cooked rice to serve with gumbo (½ cup cooked rice for each serving, more if desired)

Fry the chicken in a large heavy skillet in deep fat (350 degrees) long enough to brown all sides. Drain off part of the grease, leaving enough to fry the okra—about ½ inch. Fry the okra until browned. Add more grease if all okra cannot be fried at one time. Drain okra. Combine chicken and okra in a large kettle (preferably an iron pot). Add all other ingredients except the rice. Bring to boil, and reduce heat to low; cover the pot, and simmer slowly until the chicken slips from the bones; remove the bones. Continue to simmer until chicken is mixed in small bits through the gumbo, about 3½ to 4 hours. Stir the gumbo often, adding extra boiling water if mixture becomes too thick. This will make about 4 quarts.

Serve hot with a mound of rice in the middle of each soup bowl.

This gumbo improves in flavor if served the second day. Freeze any left over.

Mrs. Manning Hudson, New Albany, Miss.

GUMBO GOUTER (*Old Creole Recipe*)
Serves six

1 large eggplant, peeled, cut into hunks
3 green bell peppers, seeded, cut into pieces
½ lb. okra, pods cut into halves
2 large onions, peeled, chopped
1 clove garlic, minced

1 rounded tablespoon shortening (lard or vegetable shortening, or butter)
1 1-lb. can tomatoes
½ teaspoon sugar
Salt and cayenne pepper to taste
1 lb. cooked shrimp, optional
Cooked rice

Prepare the vegetables. Put the shortening into a large heavy saucepan; heat until melted. Add the vegetables, tomatoes, sugar, salt, and pepper. Cover tightly and let simmer over low heat for 1½ hours, stirring often to keep it from scorching. Serve over cooked rice, or, 5 minutes before serving, stir in the shrimp. Reheat.

From New Orleans Recipes, *by Mary Moore Bremer*

SHRIMP MULL—BLYTHE ISLAND
Serves eight to ten

2 qts. water
2 No. 2 cans tomatoes
1 whole lemon, sliced
1 can tomato soup
2 cloves garlic, sliced
1 cup diced bacon
1 cup chopped onions
½ cup butter
1 cup chopped celery
1 teaspoon celery seed

15 drops Tabasco
1 14-oz. bottle tomato catchup
2 tablespoons Worcestershire sauce
¼ teaspoon allspice
¼ teaspoon curry powder
5 lbs. raw, peeled shrimp
1 cup sherry
½ cup butter
Cracker crumbs

Put water, tomatoes, lemon, tomato soup, and garlic into a heavy stewing kettle. In a frying pan, brown the bacon and onions in the butter. Add to the mixture in the kettle. Add celery, celery seed, Tabasco, catchup, Worcestershire, allspice, and curry powder. Simmer for 2 hours. Add shrimp; cook gently 1 hour; add sherry and butter, and thicken with cracker crumbs. Serve with flaky cooked rice. [For rice see p. 284.]

Judge E. C. Butts, from Coastal Cookery, *St. Simons Island, Ga.*

JAMBALAYA LAFITTE
Serves six

Jambalaya (often spelled Jambalayah) is a stew with or without sea food in it. This contains sea food as well as the basic ingredients.

1 tablespoon bacon drippings
½ cup chopped onions
1 tablespoon flour
½ lb. ham (raw or cooked), chopped
½ lb. link sausages (little breakfast sausages), skinned
1 lb. raw shrimp, peeled and deveined
½ cup peeled and chopped tomatoes

1 clove garlic, mashed
2 cups chicken broth
1 medium-sized pepper, chopped
1 small pod red pepper, seeded and chopped
1 tablespoon chopped parsley
½ teaspoon chopped thyme
¾ cup raw rice
Salt and pepper to taste
1 doz. raw oysters, drained, patted dry

Heat the bacon drippings in a heavy kettle (with top). Add the onion. When the onion has browned slightly, add the flour; stir until browned slightly. Add the ham, sausages, shrimp, and tomatoes. Let simmer in the covered kettle for ½ hour; add the garlic, broth, green pepper, red pepper, parsley, and thyme. Wash the rice; add the rice, and season to taste with salt and pepper. Cover and cook slowly until rice is done but not gummy. Add the oysters and cook 2 to 3 minutes longer.

This dish, served with a green salad, makes a whole meal.

Mrs. Thomas F. Torrey, Madison Heights, Va.

CAPTAIN RASSMUSSEN'S CLAM CHOWDER, WILLIAMSBURG INN
Serves eight

Captain Rassmussen was the keeper of the St. Augustine Lighthouse during the early part of this century. He became famous in the St. Augustine region for his clam chowder, which he served in a small restaurant at the foot of the lighthouse. This is his chowder as served at Williamsburg Inn.

1 qt. clam meat (around 5 dozen clams)
2 qts. boiling water
¼ lb. white bacon
¾ cup butter
1 stalk celery
1½ lbs. onions
1¼ lbs. potatoes
1 small green pepper
2½ cups tomatoes
¼ teaspoon dry thyme
¼ tablespoon mixed spices, ground fine
Salt to taste
½ small bottle Lea & Perrins Worcestershire sauce
Chopped parsley
1 tablespoon sherry, optional

Allow clams to remain in shells unopened. Place in colander and wash thoroughly. Place in boiler and add the ½ gal. boiling water. Simmer on low fire until the clams are tender. Remove from the fire and strain, but retain strained stock. Remove clams from shells. Grind clams fine and add to stock. Place on a low flame and continue to cook slowly. Dice the white bacon and let it fry until crisp. Strain off the fat from the bacon and do not use the meat parts. Add butter to the bacon fat. To this fat add the celery, onions, potatoes, pepper, and tomatoes which have all been put through the food chopper. Add clams and stock, thyme, ground spices, and salt to taste. Add half of the contents of a small bottle of Lea & Perrins Worcestershire sauce. Let cook on a slow fire, stirring very often for an hour. Remove from fire and finish with chopped parsley. One tablespoon of sherry may be added just before serving if desired.

Special permission, John D. Green, Vice-President, Williamsburg Restoration, Inc.
Williamsburg, Va.

BOUILLABAISSE

After having eaten the Bouillabaisse of Paris, Thackeray was inspired to write his famous "Ballad of Bouillabaisse." Later when introduced to the dish as made in New Orleans he coined the much-quoted tribute: "In New Orleans you can eat a Bouillabaisse, the like of which was never eaten in Marseilles or Paris." *The Picayune Creole Cook Book* offers the following remarks concerning it: "The reason [for Thackeray's praise] is clear, for in those old French cities the Bouillabaisse is made from the fish of the waters of the Mediterranean sea, notably the Sturgeon and Perch combined, while in New Orleans it is made from those matchless fish of the Gulf of Mexico, the Red Snapper and the Redfish. It will be noticed that it takes two kinds of fish to make a Bouillabaisse. The first Bouillabaisse was made in Marseilles, and the old Creole tradition is that it was the discovery of two sailor-fishermen, who were disputing as they sat in a schooner as to the proper way of cooking a Sturgeon and Perch combined. Both essayed; one succeeded in making a delightful dish that would have gladdened the heart of any old French *bon vivant*. The other failed. The successful one enthusiastically offered to teach his friend, and as the latter was following his directions explicitly, and the finishing touches were being given to the dish, the teacher, seeing that the critical moment had come when the fish must be taken from the fire, or it would be spoiled if cooked a moment longer, cried out, bringing down his hand emphatically: 'Et quand ca commence a bouiller—Baisse!' Hence the name 'Bouillabaisse,' which was given to the dish from that moment. . . ."

It is made as follows:

Head of red snapper	3 cloves garlic
1½ qts. water	6 allspice
1 onion, sliced	2 tablespoons olive oil
Herb bouquet (thyme, bay leaf, parsley)	2 onions, chopped fine
	½ bottle white wine
6 slices redfish	6 large fresh tomatoes, or ½ can
6 slices red snapper	tomatoes
Salt, pepper	½ lemon, sliced thin
3 sprigs thyme	Salt, pepper, and cayenne to taste
3 sprigs parsley	1 good pinch saffron
3 bay leaves	Buttered toast

"First cut off the head of the Red Snapper and boil it in about one and a half quarts of water, so as to make a fishstock. Put one sliced onion and an herb bouquet consisting of thyme, bay leaf and parsley, into the water. When reduced to one pint, take out the head of the fish and the bouquet and strain the water and set it aside for use later on.

"Take the six slices of Redfish and the six slices of Red Snapper (of equal sizes) and rub well with salt and pepper. Mince the three sprigs of thyme, three sprigs of parsley, three bay leaves and three cloves of garlic, very, very fine, and take all six allspice and grind them very fine, and mix thoroughly with the minced herbs and garlic. Then take each slice of fish and rub well with this mixture until every portion is permeated by the herbs, spices and garlic. They must be, as it were, soaked into the flesh, if you would achieve the success of this dish. Take two tablespoons of fine olive oil and put into a very large pan, large enough so that each piece of fish will not overlap the other. Chop two onions very fine and add them to the heating oil. Lay the fish slice by slice in the pan and cover, and let them smother for about ten minutes, turning once over so that each slice may cook partly. Then take the fish out of the pan and place slices on a dish. Pour a half bottle of white wine into the pan and stir well. Add a half can of tomatoes (or six large fresh ones sliced fine) and let them boil well. Add a half lemon, cut into very thin slices, and pour over a pint of the liquor in which the head of the snapper was boiled. Season well to taste with salt, pepper and a dash of cayenne. Let it boil until very strong and reduced to almost one-half; then lay the fish, slice by slice, apart one from the other, in the pan, and let boil five minutes. In the meantime have prepared one good pinch of saffron, chopped very fine. Set it in a small deep dish and add a little of the sauce in which the fish is boiling to dissolve well. When well melted, and when the fish has been just five minutes in the pan, spread the saffron over the top of the fish. Take out of the pan, lay each slice on toast, which has been fried in butter; pour the sauce over and serve hot immediately. You will have a dish that Lucullus would have envied."

From The Original Picayune Creole Cook Book, *The Times-Picayune Publishing Company, New Orleans, La.*

PINE BARK STEW

Pine Bark Stew, a fish stew with a dark brown color and pungent flavor, is a South Carolina Pee Dee River dish provoking controversial tales as to the origin of its name and the method of making it. Some sources state that the stew derives its name from the chocolate-like color similar to pine bark; others, from the pine bark used to kindle the open fire over which the stew is cooked. From *The Pee Dee Pepper Pot,* Darlington, South Carolina, is a third explanation:

"Since seasonings were unobtainable during Revolutionary War days, the tender small roots of the Pine tree (found by digging about 20 feet from the trunk of the tree) were used for flavoring (the stew). With homemade ketchup as a base, the only other seasoning was red pepper."

Recipes for the stew call for redbreast, blue bream, bass or trout, or salt water fish such as sheepshead. Fish and onion with tomatoes and high seasonings form the usual base, but Irish potatoes are often added.

DARLINGTON COUNTY'S PINE BARK STEW
Serves eight

1 lb. fatback
2½ lbs. onions
3 cans tomato soup
1 large bottle tomato catchup
3 tomato soup cans of water
1 tablespoon Worcestershire sauce

1 tablespoon salt
1 tablespoon black pepper
½ tablespoon red pepper
6 lbs. fish (before dressed)
2 lbs. rice, cooked separately

Cut the fatback into small pieces and cook in a 10-quart vessel until well done (until fat is cooked out). Remove the meat; add chopped onions to the fat and cook thoroughly. Then add the tomato soup, catchup, water, and seasonings. Bring to a good boil and taste for seasoning. If possible, use small whole pan fish or any firm fish (such as trout) cut into pieces. Drop the fish into mixture and allow to boil on slow fire for 30 minutes. Do not stir after adding fish, but the pot may be lifted and whirled gently to keep stew from sticking to the bottom or scorching. Remove and allow to cool slightly. Serve prepared (dry) rice on each plate, deep dish preferred, with soup poured on. Allow 1 fish (if whole fish are used) with bread for each serving. If extra helpings are desired, water can be added while cooking. Reduce to ½ proportions for 4 people. (2 or 3 extra servings may be added.)

Mrs. B. W. Johnson, from The Pee Dee Pepper Pot, *Darlington, S.C.*

UNCLE JIM LOONEY'S KENTUCKY BURGOO
Serves sixty

Kentucky Burgoo, introduced in Kentucky around 1810 by Colonel Gus Jaubert, is said to be a version of a French stew once made in iron cauldrons and served to the crews of French sailing vessels. Cissy Gregg, home consultant for the *Courier-Journal,* has condensed this recipe from one said to have been Uncle Jim Looney's—the "Burgoo-Master," of Lexington, Kentucky, who inherited the "mantle" from Colonel Jaubert. The original recipe calls for "800 lbs. of lean beef with no bones or fat attached, one dozen squirrels for each 100 gallons—if they are in season—and 240 pounds of fat hens or roosters, besides potatoes, cabbage, tomatoes, carrots and other vegetables." Enlarging on Burgoo, Mrs. Gregg says in part:

"The best historian of Kentucky Burgoo was Sam W. Severance, who wrote for the *Courier-Journal* some years back under the pseudonym of 'The Burgoo-Master.' He says that Burgoo dates back to Biblical times and is actually what Esau sold his birthright for—a mess of pottage."

2 lbs. pork shank
2 lbs. veal shank
2 lbs. beef shank
2 lbs. breast lamb
1 4-lb. hen
8 qts. water
1½ lbs. Irish potatoes
1½ lbs. onions
1 bunch carrots
2 green peppers
2 cups chopped cabbage

1 qt. tomato purée
2 cups whole corn, fresh or canned
2 pods red pepper
2 cups diced okra
2 cups lima beans
1 cup diced celery
Salt and cayenne to taste, Tabasco, A-1 Sauce, Worcestershire sauce to taste, since it should be highly seasoned
Chopped parsley

Put all the meat into cold water and bring slowly to a boil. Simmer until meat is tender enough to fall from the bones. Lift meat out of stock. Cool and chop up meat, removing the bones. Pare potatoes and onions; dice. Return meat to stock; add potatoes, onions, and all other vegetables. Allow to simmer along until thick. (Burgoo should be very thick, but still soupy.) Season along but not too much until it is almost done. As stew simmers down, the seasoning will become more pronounced. Add chopped parsley just before stew is taken up. Stir frequently with a long-handled wooden paddle or spoon during the first part of the cooking and almost constantly after it thickens.

This is made in a 4-gallon water-bath kettle and cooked approximately 10 hours. The cooking time is broken in half by cooking the meat the first day, adding vegetables, and continuing the second day.

[Mrs. Gregg suggests that a butter-flour roux may be added for thickening, but she has not found it necessary.—M. B.]

Cissy Gregg, Home Consultant, Courier-Journal, *Louisville, Ky.*

MRS. DURANT'S BRUNSWICK STEW
Nine quarts

For years Deree Taylor Durant has made this Brunswick Stew for her family and friends. Although the quantity may be cut, Mrs. Durant warns that it is difficult to include all listed ingredients in a small stew.

1 hen	1 qt. can tomatoes, or 3 lbs. fresh
2 lbs. stew beef	tomatoes
(2 squirrels and 2 lbs. veal are	1 cup real butter
excellent additions)	2 tablespoons salt
1 qt. green butter beans (limas)	½ cup tomato catchup
1 lb. tender okra	1 cup vinegar
4 medium size onions	1½ cups sugar (right)
1½ doz. ears corn	1 teaspoon black pepper
½ pk. Irish potatoes	Good pinch cayenne (¼ tea-
1 large bunch celery	spoon)
	1 tablespoon prepared mustard

Put all the meats into a large pot with enough cold water to cover. Cook until tender and the meat falls from the bones. While the meat is cooking, prepare the vegetables.

Remove meat from broth, and set aside to cool. To the broth add vegetables. (Celery, onions, and okra should be well cut.) Add butter and 2 tablespoons salt. Cook until tender; then add the meat which has been taken from the bones and pulled or cut into little pieces. Stir constantly from the bottom of the pot, or the stew will stick and scorch. If there is not enough broth to cover and cook vegetables, water may be added. After mixtures of meat and vegetables have been blended, cook to a thick mush. Add seasoning, cook for 5 minutes, remove from fire.

Mrs. R. F. Durant, Burlington, N.C.

BRUNSWICK STEW FOR SIX
Serves six generously

3 tablespoons bacon drippings
1 4- to 5-lb. stewing hen (a nice plump one), disjointed
Salt and pepper
2 cups water
1 No. 2 can tomatoes
3 onions, sliced
½ teaspoon sugar

½ cup white wine
2 cups fresh small lima beans, or 1 10-oz. package frozen
1 12-oz. can niblet corn, or 2 cups fresh cut off the cob
1 cup toasted bread crumbs
Salt, pepper, and cayenne to taste
1 tablespoon butter, optional

Heat the bacon drippings in a deep heavy skillet. Rub the pieces of chicken well with salt and pepper. Lightly brown the chicken in the fat, turning to brown all sides. Add the water, tomatoes, onions, sugar, and wine. Cover and simmer the chicken over low heat until the chicken is tender (about 1½ to 2 hours). Remove the chicken and pull meat from the bones. Return the chicken meat to the skillet. Add the limas and cook until they are beginning to get tender. Add the corn and cook for 20 minutes, or until corn is tender. Add the bread crumbs; season to taste with the salt and peppers. If the chicken is not fat, add the butter for richer flavor. This tastes best if made the day before and reheated. The secret of this stew is to follow the directions accurately.

Mrs. Viola Neese Johnson, Burlington, N.C.

CHICKEN STEW DUNBAR, WITH DUMPLINGS
Serves six

1 broiling chicken
Water to cover (boiling)
½ tablespoon salt

¼ teaspoon pepper
2 tablespoons butter
1 bay leaf

Dress clean and cut up fowl. Put in stewpan with boiling water and simmer slowly until tender. When nearly done, add remainder of ingredients. Serve with the following dumplings.

Dumplings

3 cups flour
1 teaspoon salt
1 teaspoon sugar

2 eggs
1 tablespoon lard
1 cup milk

Sift dry ingredients; cut in lard. Beat eggs into milk; mix all well. Drop by spoonfuls into stew. Cover and let cook about ½ hour. Serve around chicken.

Mrs. Edwin Fendig, from Coastal Cookery, *St. Simons Island, Ga.*

LAMB STEW WITH MUSHROOM DUMPLINGS
Serves six

3 lbs. forequarter of lamb, cut in
    pieces
Seasoned flour
½ sliced onion

Fat
3 carrots
5 cups boiling water
2 tablespoons chopped parsley

Roll lamb in seasoned flour; brown with onions in hot fat in kettle. Add carrots and boiling water; simmer slowly about 2 hours. Make mushroom dumplings as below. Remove stew to hot platter; surround with dumplings, and sprinkle with parsley.

Mushroom Dumplings

1 cup flour
2 teaspoons Royal baking powder
½ teaspoon salt

½ cup condensed mushroom soup
Water to make soft dough

Sift dry ingredients; add soup and water to make a soft dough. Drop by spoonfuls into boiling stew; cover tightly and cook 10 minutes without raising cover.

From Recipes Tested and Tried, *by Anne Young White
and Nola Nance Oliver, Natchez, Miss.*

GUINEA STEW
Serves eight to ten

1 guinea
1 can whole-grain corn
1 can tomatoes
1 chopped onion

3 small Irish potatoes, diced
1 small red pepper
2 tablespoons butter
Salt to taste

Cook guinea until well done; remove all bones and skin; cut up meat. Add vegetables and seasoning and cook until thick. Serve hot.

From Lady Jo's Southern Recipes, *by Lady Jo Kirby Beals, Texarkana, Ark., Tex.*

MRS. WILLIAMSON'S TURKEY HASH
Serves thirty

The late Mrs. Williamson was widely known for her "Old South" break-fasts. The *pièce de résistance* was turkey hash made from a whole roasted turkey. Along with this, she served broiled grapefruit or fruit juices, hominy grits with butter, eggs à la chafing dish, little sausage cakes, beaten biscuits, and coffee. To prepare the turkey:

1 15-lb. (dressed weight) cold, brown-roasted turkey	1 heaping teaspoon black pepper
Water to cover	1½ tablespoons poultry seasoning
Leaves of a stalk of celery	2 or 3 cups chopped celery stalks
1 onion	1 large onion, chopped
Salt	Salt to taste
1 small loaf bread	2 tablespoons butter

Put all turkey meat into a large bowl. Break up all of the turkey bones; place in a deep pot (economy cooker size); cover with cold or tepid water, and simmer for 2 or 3 hours, or until the stock has strength and flavor. Add celery leaves and onion. Stir occasionally, and add a little salt. While stock is brewing, cut up all the meat (not too small) including the skin, but little fat, discarding all sharp bones and cartilage.

If fowl was roasted without any stuffing, crumble the bread, and toast lightly in a moderate oven with the pepper, poultry seasoning, celery, onion, and salt. Moisten the seasoned crumbs with turkey stock and let stand. (Celery seed may be substituted for celery.)

When the essence of bones has been absorbed in the cooking stock, strain; return to large pot and pour in the cut meat. Stir occasionally for blending, and simmer (do not boil furiously at any time) for about 1 hour or more; then pour in the seasoned crumbs and stir often to prevent sticking or burning. Cook for at least ½ hour longer. If hash is made the night before for breakfast, it is all the better for ripening. In the morning, reheat just to boiling point; then add 2 tablespoons butter. Serve on rounds of toast or with hot waffles or pancakes made of flour or meal.

Mrs. Finley L. Williamson, from Soup to Nuts, *Burlington, N.C.*

4. Salads

Although of doubtful parentage, the Southern salad has a long and distinguished ancestry. In Helen Bullock's The Williamsburg Art of Cookery *(Colonial Williamsburg) are recipes for an oyster salad and several salad dressings. The first green salad bowl in Colonial Virginia appears to be the one described in Mrs. Mary Randolph's recipe in* The Virginia Housewife, 1831. *This is a combination of greens, "dressed" in a modern manner with a tarragon vinegar dressing.*

Today almost all vegetables, fruits, meats, sea foods, game, and poultry are served as salads. The essentials are to have the vegetables crisp and cold (wrapping them in damp towels and refrigerating them makes them crisp), have compatible mixtures, and blend them with a good dressing. The dressing "makes" the salad.

Here are a few suggestions for salad (or other dishes) garnishings:

1. To curl celery and carrots cut down through the scraped celery stalk, or the carrot, dividing it into thin strips to within about a half inch of the small end. The strips should be about 4 inches long. Drop into ice water and let stay until curled. Take out; drain carefully; and store in icebox.

2. To make little carrot flowers groove the whole peeled carrot by scraping down the sides with the tines of a fork or with point of scissors. Cut crosswise into thin rings. Let stay in ice water until each ring curls like a flower petal.

3. For the radish rose select firm, crisp radishes with rose-like form. Begin at the tip of the radish and cut down through the red skin and into the white meat, leaving about ⅛ of an inch of the base uncut. With a sharp knife point, separate the skin from the white inside meat and place radish in ice water. The outer skin will curl back like a rose. Little spring onions are prepared in the same manner. At the base of each rose, cut an incision and slip in rose leaves, sprigs of parsley, or evergreen.

4. For little stuffed beets boil or buy canned, small marble-sized beets, or cut large beets into small balls with melon ball cutter. Marinate beets 12 hours in vinegar seasoned with pickling spices (mixed), salt, pepper, and sugar to taste.

Remove; drain; stick into each beet a whole blanched almond, or scoop out a tiny ball and place pearl onion in beet. These are excellent stuffed with crab meat or any sea food or meat salad.

THELMA HAZARD'S STUFFED TOMATO
Serves eight

Firm ripe tomatoes, peeled, cored
2 3-oz. pkgs. cream cheese
½ cucumber, grated
Few drops onion juice

2 teaspoons minced parsley
Salt, paprika
½ cup heavy cream, whipped
¾ cup mayonnaise

Mix cream cheese, cucumber, onion juice, minced parsley, and seasonings. Toss with 3 tablespoons mayonnaise. Stuff tomatoes with this mixture, and top with dressing made from whipped cream and ½ cup mayonnaise. Serve on lettuce.

Mrs. W. H. Hazard, Haw River, N.C., from Soup to Nuts, *Burlington, N.C.*

VARIATIONS: (1) Stuff tomatoes with chicken salad; garnish with olives and mayonnaise. (2) Combine corn, boiled and cut off the cob, with diced cucumber and chopped hard-boiled egg. Serve with mayonnaise. (3) Combine celery and diced broiled sweetbreads and chopped eggs, mixed with mayonnaise. (4) Stuff tomato with caviar seasoned with lemon juice; garnish with sieved boiled yolk and white of egg.

MOLDED ROQUEFORT CHEESE SALAD
Serves six

2 3-oz. pkgs. cream cheese
1 small pkg. Roquefort cheese (3 to 4 oz.)
¾ cup milk
1 envelope unflavored gelatin
3 tablespoons cold water

½ teaspoon salt
1 tablespoon lemon juice
½ cup chopped pecans
A little green coloring
½ cup heavy cream, whipped

Blend cheeses together until soft. Add milk and mix well. Soften gelatin in cold water and melt over hot water. Add to cheese mixture. Add salt, lemon juice, nuts, and food coloring. Fold in whipped cream. Turn into molds and chill until firm. Serve on crisp lettuce. Garnish with radish roses or cucumber slices, if desired.

Mrs. R. T. Grinalds, Macon, Ga.

MOLDED CUCUMBER-CHEESE SALAD
Serves four to six

1 cup cottage cheese
½ cup cream cheese
1 teaspoon sugar
½ teaspoon salt
1 tablespoon chopped chives or chopped spring onions, or both

1 cup cucumber pulp, juice reserved
1 tablespoon tarragon vinegar
1 envelope plain gelatin
White and cayenne pepper
Paprika

Beat together the cheeses (use all cottage cheese if preferred), add sugar and salt, stir in chives or onion. Peel and grate enough cucumbers to make the pulp. Combine the juice with vinegar and soak the gelatin in mixture. Heat gelatin over hot water until thoroughly dissolved. Add gelatin to cheese mixture and blend well. Season with white pepper and a pinch of cayenne. Pour into a 1½-pint mold or individual molds. Serve on lettuce leaves. Garnish by sprinkling with paprika and mayonnaise or sour cream topping. Sliced stuffed olives and crisp sweet cucumber pickles should accompany this.

MRS. BROUGHTON'S PERFECTION SALAD
Serves eight

2 tablespoons gelatin
½ cup cold water
½ cup mild vinegar
Juice 1 lemon
2 cups boiling water

½ cup sugar
2 teaspoons salt
2 cups celery, cut in small pieces
1 pimiento, finely cut
1 cup finely shredded cabbage

Soak the gelatin in cold water 5 minutes; add vinegar, lemon juice, boiling water, sugar, and salt. Strain, and when beginning to set, add remaining ingredients. Turn into a mold and chill. Serve on lettuce leaves with mayonnaise dressing or cut in dice and serve in cases made of red or green peppers; or the mixture may be served in molds lined with pimientos. A delicious accompaniment to cold sliced chicken or veal. Chopped green peppers and grated carrots may be added.

Mrs. J. Melville Broughton, Raleigh, N.C.

EGGS GELATIN
Serves three

Eggs Gelatin is a special French luncheon dish brought back by Mrs. Holt from Paris. It is simply a "soft-boiled egg" in clear aspic. The secret is to obtain, but not pass, the perfect stage of the boiled egg.

6 boiled eggs
2 cups beef, or any tasty bouillon
   or consommé

1 envelope plain gelatin
Mayonnaise seasoned with herbs
   to taste

Boil the eggs (gently) for 5 minutes, no longer, no less! Plunge them into cold water for few minutes; peel carefully and set aside. Use ¼ cup of the bouillon to soak the gelatin. Heat the remaining bouillon and stir in the gelatin to dissolve. Pour into a 1-quart mold or 3 small ones. Let set until it begins to stiffen; place the eggs in the gelatin, and chill until firm. Serve with mayonnaise.

Hard-cooked eggs may be stuffed and used in the same manner.

Louise Murray Holt, Greensboro, N.C.

"LIBMOR'S" SPANISH BEAN SALAD
Serves four

2 cups cooked green lima beans,
   fresh or canned, or frozen
2 teaspoons chopped parsley
1 clove garlic, minced
Salad oil

1 tablespoon vinegar
Salt and pepper to taste
Tomato wedges
1 Spanish onion, sliced thin
Paprika

If fresh beans are used, rinse them in cold water immediately after cooking; drain canned beans; drain cooked frozen beans and rinse in cold water. Mix the beans, parsley; add garlic with a fork. Gradually add salad oil until beans are coated; add vinegar drop by drop. Chill thoroughly; add the salt and pepper. Serve in a salad bowl with wedges of tomato around edge of bowl. Garnish top with onion rings; sprinkle with paprika.

Mrs. Robert C. Moore, Maple Wood Farm, Graham, N.C.

GUSPACHA SALAD

"Slice **cucumbers** very thin, also **onions** and peel **tomatoes;** fill a glass dish with alternate layers of this mixture with **bread crumbs (stale)** sprinkled over each layer. Cover all with **French dressing** and garnish with **lettuce,** and serve icy cold."

Col. Talbott, from Gay Nineties Cook Book, *by F. Meredith and August Dietz, Jr., Richmond, Va.*

GAZPACHO ASPIC
Serves six to eight

1 12-oz. can V-8 Juice
1 envelope plain gelatin

½ can (10½-oz. can) beef consommé

1 teaspoon sugar
2 tablespoons minced onion
1 teaspoon minced green pepper
1 tablespoon Worcestershire sauce
1 dash Tabasco sauce

½ teaspoon angostura bitters
2 tablespoons garlic wine vinegar
Vegetable oil
Sliced cucumbers

In a saucepan pour 1 cup of V-8 juice. Soften the gelatin in the remaining V-8 juice. Add to the V-8 juice in the saucepan the beef consommé, sugar, onion, green pepper, Worcestershire, Tabasco, and bitters. Bring to a boil; add the softened gelatin and stir until gelatin has melted. Remove from heat; add the vinegar. Coat the insides of individual molds (or 1 1-qt. mold) with vegetable oil, draining off excess oil. Fill molds ¾ full of aspic. Cool. Garnish the tops of each mold with thin slices of peeled cucumber. Chill until set. Unmold and serve on lettuce or watercress. Serve with mayonnaise or salad dressing.

Mrs. Ray Gieger, Leesburg, Fla.

ASPIC WITH VEGETABLES
Serves six to eight

A "built-in" dressing comes with this salad.

4 envelopes unflavored gelatin
5½ cups chicken broth, or 5½ cups hot water mixed with 5 teaspoons instant chicken bouillon
1 tablespoon tomato paste
2 egg whites, slightly beaten

2 eggshells, crushed
¼ cup red wine
2 cups cooked green peas (more if desired)
2 cups cooked carrots, sliced
½ cup mayonnaise or salad dressing

Soften the gelatin in 1 cup of the chicken broth, or broth made by dissolving the instant bouillon in 5½ cups boiling water. Combine the remaining chicken broth, tomato paste, egg whites, eggshells, and softened gelatin in a large saucepan. Bring to boiling, stirring slowly with a wooden spoon or wire whisk. When the egg whites foam to the top (catching all particles so the aspic will be crystal clear), remove pan from the heat and let set undisturbed for 10 minutes. Strain the aspic through a damp clean tea towel which has been placed in a colander or strainer. Let the aspic drip into a large bowl. Do not squeeze the towel. Stir the wine into the aspic. Reserve 1 cup of the liquid aspic. Divide the green peas and carrots equally between 6 to 8 individual molds (according to size of mold), placing the vegetables in layers in the molds. Pour over aspic to fill them ¾ full. Mix the reserved cup of aspic with the mayonnaise. Chill the aspic until it begins to set. Spread the mayonnaise-aspic over the vegetable-aspic, filling the molds. Unmold on lettuce. The mayonnaise will be on the bottom.

NOTE: If desired, pour a thin layer of aspic in flat pan. Chop to garnish base of molds.

Mary Louise Carrigan, Burlington, N.C.

AVOCADO SALAD

The avocado, like shrimp and tomato, appears frequently and in varied dress in Southern salads. One of the simplest ways to serve it is to peel, slice, or halve the fruit and marinate it with tart French dressing. Lime, lemon juice, and onion add to the piquancy of the dressing and bring out the rich, nutty flavor of the meat. Nuts, sea food, and citrus fruits are harmonious with avocado. It is also good in an aspic; or stuffed with shrimp, crab meat, caviar, chicken salad, vegetable, or fruit combinations. Tossed with greens it is superb. See "Avocado Dip (Guacamole)."

AVOCADO MOUSSE
Serves sixteen

2 3-oz. pkgs. lemon jello
2 cups boiling water
1 teaspoon salt
Dash pepper
4 tablespoons lemon juice

1 cup mayonnaise
1 cup heavy cream, whipped
2 cups mashed avocade pulp (3 pears)

Dissolve jello in boiling water. Add salt and pepper. When cool, add lemon juice. When ready to congeal, fold in mayonnaise, cream, and pulp. Turn into wet mold and place in icebox to congeal.

Mrs. Percy Thomas, from Southern Recipes, Montgomery, Ala.

SOUR CREAM POTATO SALAD
Serves eight

4 cups diced, cooked potatoes
½ cup diced cucumbers
1 teaspoon minced onion
¾ teaspoon celery seed

1½ teaspoon salt
½ teaspoon black pepper
3 hard-boiled eggs

Toss potatoes, cucumbers, onion, celery seed, salt, and pepper together. Add the diced whites of the hard-boiled eggs. Mash the 3 yolks of the eggs and combine with:

1½ cups sour cream
½ cup sharp, tart mayonnaise

½ cup vinegar
1 teaspoon prepared mustard

Add dressing to potato mixture and toss lightly. Allow to stand in icebox 15 minutes before serving on crisp lettuce. If there is any left over, it is quite as good the second day.

Mrs. William Oliver Smith, Raleigh, N.C.

DIFFERENT POTATO SALAD

Boil potatoes in jackets (allow one to each person). Peel; cut in cubes; mix with:

Chopped celery
Diced cucumber
Minced onions

Sliced radishes
Salt and pepper to taste

Combine with following boiled dressing:

Boiled Dressing for Salad

3 tablespoons sugar
1 generous tablespoon flour
1 teaspoon salt
Pinch dry mustard

½ cup vinegar
½ cup water
Butter size of walnut
2 eggs, well beaten

Mix dry ingredients; add liquids. Cook until thickened; add butter. Remove from stove; slowly add 2 well beaten eggs. Return to stove; cook until eggs have thickened.

Mrs. H. P. McKay, Onancock, Va.

OLD-FASHIONED CREAMED POTATO SALAD
Serves four to six

This is an early Mississippi recipe.

6 Irish potatoes
Salt, pepper, and spice to taste
1 tablespoon butter

2 hard-boiled eggs
2 tablespoons vinegar

Boil the potatoes until very soft; peel and mash them while hot. Season to taste with salt, pepper, and spice (nutmeg). Add the butter. Boil the eggs hard. Take the yolks and dissolve in the 2 tablespoons of vinegar. Pour vinegar and egg mixture over the potatoes and mix well. Put the potatoes on a plate and slice the whites of the eggs in circles and place on the potatoes to garnish.

Lidie Roberts, Pickens Station, Miss.

ROBERT PORTERFIELD'S WATER CRESS SALAD
Serves two

Robert Porterfield, who grows water cress at the head of a spring for the purpose of making salads, forsakes the theatre when possible, to pursue his hobby—cooking. This is his favorite salad.

One double handful of water cress, ready to be mixed. Just before serving make the following dressing:

3 tablespoons garlic vinegar
6 tablespoons olive oil
1 teaspoon dry mustard
½ teaspoon Worcestershire sauce
Pinch paprika

Pinch black pepper
2 pinches garlic salt
Pinch brown sugar
1-oz. cube Roquefort cheese, broken with a fork

Add Roquefort cheese after mixing other ingredients. Add more oil or vinegar if necessary. Pour dressing over water cress in wooden bowl. Toss a number of times and serve immediately.

Robert Porterfield, Director, The State of Virginia Theatre, Abingdon, Va.

PAT'S SUMMER SALAD
Serves four

You may add to or subtract from the vegetables without seeming to detract from the taste.

½ head lettuce, shredded
1 large tomato, diced rather small
½ green pepper, grated or minced fine
1 small onion, grated
½ teaspoon celery seed
1 small carrot, grated

1 cucumber, diced small
1 tablespoon minced sweet pickle, bread and butter pickle, or minced mixed pickle
½ bunch celery, chopped fine
3 hard-boiled eggs

Mix the above, tossing lightly so as not to crush vegetables. Let stand in icebox an hour or more so that all flavors blend. Be sure to grate the onion because this gives a special seasoning. Just before serving, add one by one the following seasonings, sprinkling or dribbling over the top:

1 scant teaspoon salt
¼ teaspoon black pepper
1 teaspoon sugar
¼ teaspoon dry mustard
1 tablespoon mayonnaise

2 tablespoons garlic vinegar
2 tablespoons olive or salad oil
Lettuce
Hard-boiled eggs to garnish

When all seasonings have been added, toss to mix; serve in individual wooden salad bowls, garnished by lettuce and sliced or halved hard-boiled eggs. If garlic vinegar is not available, rub large mixing bowl with garlic before preparing vegetables. Warning: This is tedious to prepare, but worth it!

Pat Holmes, Graham, N.C.

DRUNKARD'S DREAM

In Nashville there is a society of men, The Society of Amateur Chefs, who take pride in their cookery and have developed a number of original dishes. The following all-inclusive original recipe was given me by the Society with explicit strings attached—THE CUP OF HAM GRAVY SERVED OVER THE SALAD MUST BE POURED OVER THE MOMENT BEFORE SERVING, THE GRAVY MUST BE PIPING HOT! This salad may be made for a large or a small group. This recipe is for "a large platter" of guests.

"Drunkard's dream is composed of, basically, **shredded leaf lettuce,** **chopped radishes, chopped spring onions, diced dill pickles,** and **chopped tomatoes,** built up on a large meat platter in alternate layers and topped off with several slices of **crisp fried bacon,** over all of which is poured, just before serving, **one cup of red ham gravy,** *hot."*

A. C. Gibson, Menu Director, Nashville Chapter, The Society of
Amateur Chefs, Nashville, Tenn.

HOTEL IRVIN COBB CHEF'S SALAD BOWL

This lush combination of green vegetables and meats is tossed either with Thousand Island dressing or a French dressing. Toss together **chopped lettuce,** **celery, green peppers, radishes, tomatoes, parsley,** and top with **shredded** **cheese, turkey meat, anchovies,** and **bacon** (crisp). Garnish the whole bowl with **olives** and **pickles.**

J. T. Theobald, Manager, The Hotel Irvin Cobb, Paducah, Ky.

GREEN GODDESS SALAD

This famous salad is served often by General and Mrs. Courtney H. Hodges.

1 can anchovies	1 cup stiff mayonnaise
2 green onions	Tarragon vinegar
1 clove garlic	Wine vinegar
1 cup parsley	Mixed salad greens of all kinds
Anchovy paste	

Chop anchovies, onions, garlic, and parsley until they are almost a paste; add anchovy paste, then mayonnaise; season with tarragon and wine vinegar until the consistency is that of thin mayonnaise. Put in icebox until ready to serve; then pour over bowl of mixed salad greens. Lightly toss, as dressing must stay on greens and must be served immediately.

Mrs. Courtney H. Hodges, San Antonio, Tex., from
What's Cooking on Governors Island, Governors Island, N.Y.

LIL PHILLIPS' "WESTERN" SALAD BOWL
Serves four to six

Lil Phillips makes no claim to the prototype for this recipe—the (Western) Caesar Bowl—but this version is a compliment to the already famous salad.

Garlic Oil—Make ahead

2 peeled cloves garlic, cut in quar- ¼ cup salad or olive oil
 ters

Let garlic stand in oil—not in refrigerator—for several hours, or overnight. Then remove garlic.

Croutons—Make ahead, too

2 cups bread cubes (about 4
 slices)

Heat oven to 300 degrees (slow). Meanwhile, cut bread into ¼ inch cubes. Place in shallow baking pan, and toast 25 to 35 minutes, or until golden, turning often with a fork. Cool. Or make day before and store, wrapped in waxed paper.

The Salad Greens

2 small heads romaine or lettuce

Wash salad greens; drain and dry thoroughly (about 2 quarts). Chill until salad time.

Tossing the Salad

½ cup grated Parmesan cheese	6 tablespoons salad or olive oil
¼ cup crumbled bleu cheese	1 raw egg
Salt to taste	3½ tablespoons lemon juice
½ teaspoon pepper	1 tablespoon Worcestershire sauce

Sprinkle the cheese over the greens. Then sprinkle on the salt and pepper. Next drizzle the oil over all. With a flourish, drop the raw egg on top. Now pour lemon juice and Worcestershire onto the egg. Give the salad a good gentle tossing. For the finishing touch, pour the garlic-flavored oil over the croutons; add to the salad and toss just a bit. Serve pronto, while croutons are crunchy. If you wish, serve this as a first course—that's the Western way. (The Southern, as a salad course.)

VARIATIONS: omit bleu cheese and use ⅔ cup Parmesan, or add 8 cut-up anchovies with cheese, or omit Worcestershire sauce and use ½ teaspoon dry mustard.

Mrs. Earl Norfleet Phillips, High Point, N.C.

LOUIS PAPPAS FAMOUS GREEK SALAD
Serves four

It has been almost 40 years since the first Louis Pappas restaurant was established at Tarpon Springs, Florida. The founder served with General Pershing as cook and was with the famous Wild Cat Division in France. After his death, his wife, "Mamma," and their sons, Michael, Lucas, and Jack continued the management of the Pappas restaurants at Tarpon Springs and St. Petersburg. They have kept the cuisine traditionally Greek, with, of course, a Southern influence. This salad is one of the many dishes that have made the Pappas name famous.

Make a potato salad as follows, and set aside in refrigerator:

6 boiling potatoes	½ cup thinly sliced green peppers
2 medium-sized onions, or 4 green onions, cut in thin slices	½ cup salad dressing (homemade mayonnaise)
¼ cup fine chopped parsley	Salt

Boil potatoes in jackets about 30 minutes, or until soft but not mushy. Peel and drain, cool. Slice in a bowl and add sliced onions, chopped parsley, and peppers. Fold in the salad dressing, using more if desired. Sprinkle lightly with salt. Makes about 3 cups.

Prepare the following:

1 large head lettuce, washed, drained, leaves pulled apart

12 roka leaves (Greek vegetable) or 12 sprigs water cress

2 tomatoes, cut into 6 wedges each

1 peeled cucumber, cut lengthwise into 8 fingers

1 avocado peeled and cut into wedges

4 portions of Feta (Greek cheese)

1 green bell pepper, cut into 8 rings

4 slices canned cooked beets

4 peeled cooked shrimp

4 anchovy fillets

12 black olives (Greek style preferred)

12 medium hot Salonika peppers (bought in bottles)

4 fancy cut radishes

4 whole green onions

½ cup distilled vinegar

¼ cup each olive and salad oil blended

Oregano

Method of Serving

Line a large platter with the outside leaves of lettuce, and place the 3 cups potatoes in a mound in center of platter. Cover with the remaining lettuce which has been shredded. Arrange roka or watercress on top of this. Place tomato wedges around outer edge of salad with a few on top and place the cucumber wedges between the tomatoes, making a solid base of the salad. Stand the avocado wedges by the cucumber fingers. Place the slices of cheese on top of salad mound and arrange the green pepper slices over all. On the very top of mound place the beet slices with a shrimp on each and an anchovy fillet on top of each shrimp. The olives, small hot peppers, and small green onions may be arranged as desired. The entire salad is then sprinkled with the vinegar, then the blended oils. Sprinkle oregano over all and serve at once. Toasted French garlic bread is served with this. This is what Louis Pappas called a "Salad for 4 persons."

Special permission of Michael (Mike) Pappas, from The Louis Pappas Restaurants, St. Petersburg and Tarpon Springs, Fla.

TABBOULEH (*Cracked Wheat Salad*)
Serves six to eight

This is a fine Lebanese salad.

1 scant cup fine cracked wheat (may be bought in good food stores)

1 lb. ripe tomatoes, chopped

½ bunch green onions and tops, chopped

1½ large bunches parsley, chopped

½ cup chopped fresh mint
1¼ teaspoons salt
½ teaspoon black pepper
⅛ teaspoon ground cinnamon

Juice of 2 lemons
¼ cup olive oil
Lettuce or cabbage leaves

Wash the wheat; place in a small bowl and cover with cold water. Let stand 30 minutes. Chop the tomatoes, green onions, parsley, and mint and mix in a large bowl. Drain the wheat and squeeze it dry with the hands; stir it into the salad. Mix in the salt, pepper, and cinnamon. Toss lightly. Toss with the lemon juice and olive oil. Serve in lettuce or cabbage leaves.

Mrs. Ernest Koury, Shallowford Community,
Alamance County, N.C.

BOILED DRESSING
Two cups

For cole slaw and any recipe calling for a "boiled dressing."

1 egg
$\frac{1}{16}$ teaspoon red pepper
1 teaspoon dry mustard
¾ cup vinegar
½ cup sugar

1 tablespoon butter
¼ cup water
½ cup milk
1 tablespoon flour

Beat the egg in the top of a double boiler; add the red pepper, dry mustard, vinegar, sugar, butter, and water; cook, stirring constantly, over boiling water until heated; make a paste of the milk and flour; stir into the egg mixture. Cook, stirring constantly, until the dressing is as thick as heavy cream.

Mrs. R. F. Anderson, from Soup to Nuts, *Burlington, N.C.*

NOTE: The recipe above will make enough dressing to toss with 4 cups of shredded cabbage for cole slaw.

NU-WRAY SMOTHERED LETTUCE
Serves four

Reminiscent of the early days in North Carolina stands the Nu-Wray Inn at Burnsville. Here for three generations the same family has preserved the true spirit of hospitality. Here it is that home-cured ham, fried chicken, and other delicious dishes await the guest.

This fine old-fashioned salad is known in some regions as "Mountain Salad" or "Wilted Lettuce."

"Select **fresh spring lettuce** before it heads. Chop enough lettuce to fill bowl. Add 3 young onion heads and onion tops chopped fine. Add 1 teaspoon sugar, and salt to taste. Pour over 2 tablespoons of vinegar. Fry 5 slices of cured country bacon crisply, and place strips upon lettuce. Pour hot bacon grease over all. Serve immediately."

From Old-Time Recipes from the Nu-Wray Inn, *by Esther and Rush T. Wray,*
Burnsville, N.C.

POKE SALAD
Serves four

This is a new way to prepare pokeweed greens.

2 lbs. young tender pokeweed leaves, stripped from the stalk
1 teaspoon salt

3 tablespoons bacon drippings
4 spring onions and the tops, chopped
3 eggs

Wash the leaves and break off the stems. Place in a vessel containing about 1 inch of boiling water and the salt. Cover and boil until the leaves are wilted. Drain and chop the leaves.

Melt the bacon drippings in a heavy iron skillet, and fry the onions in the fat for a few minutes. Add the poke and stir it into the onions and fat. Cover and cook slowly for about 10 minutes, or until the onion and the poke are tender. Remove the top from the skillet and break the eggs into the vegetables; stir until the eggs are well scrambled into the greens.

Mrs. Thomas F. Torrey, Madison Heights, Va.

STUFFED LETTUCE SALAD
Serves four to six

1 medium-size head iceberg lettuce
½ lb. Roquefort cheese
1 3-oz. pkg. cream cheese
2 tablespoons cream
1 tablespoon chopped chives

1 pimiento, chopped
8 stuffed olives, sliced
3 dashes Tabasco sauce
1 hard-cooked egg, sieved
Paprika

Wash the lettuce; drain. Remove any wilted outside leaves. Cut out the center leaves, leaving a shell about 1-inch thick. Save the inside leaves for other uses. Mash the cheeses with cream to make a smooth paste. Blend in the chives, pimiento, olives, and Tabasco sauce. Fill the lettuce head with the cheese mixture. Sprinkle over the sieved egg. Sprinkle with paprika. Chill thoroughly.

To serve, slice with a sharp knife into 4 to 6 sections. Lay on salad plates. Serve with French dressing or any desired salad dressing.

Mrs. Kenneth Allyn, Richmond, Va.

GARBANZOS ENSALADA (*Chick-Pea Salad*)
Serves six to eight

1 15-oz. can garbanzos (Old El Paso Brand), drained
1 clove garlic, crushed
½ cup red wine vinegar or tarragon
¼ cup salad oil, or olive oil
½ teaspoon salt
½ teaspoon sugar
Fresh ground black pepper to taste
½ cup stuffed olives, sliced thin

¼ lb. boiled, cooked ham, sliced in thin strips
1 medium onion, minced
1 tablespoon green pepper, minced
1 cup salad greens, broken into pieces
Lettuce leaves to line salad bowl
2 hard-cooked eggs, cut into rings
Wedges of tomatoes

Mix all ingredients together, except the lettuce leaves, hard-cooked eggs and tomatoes. Line a salad serving bowl with lettuce leaves; pile the salad into bowl. Garnish the top with egg rings, and circle the bowl with tomato wedges.

Mrs. Walter Pursley, St. Petersburg, Fla.

CONGEALED BROCCOLI SALAD
Serves twelve to fourteen

1 10-oz. package frozen chopped broccoli, cooked until tender
5 hard-cooked eggs
2 envelopes plain gelatin
1 10½-oz. can beef consommé, minus 2 tablespoons

¾ cup mayonnaise
Juice of 1 lemon
1 tablespoon Worcestershire sauce
1 teaspoon salt
Mayonnaise for garnish, or any dressing

Cook the broccoli until tender and soft. Put the drained broccoli through a ricer or food mill. Sieve the eggs through a ricer or food mill. Soften the gelatin in ¼ cup of the consommé. Heat remaining consommé in a saucepan; stir in the softened gelatin. Cool the gelatin mixture. Mix the gelatin mixture with the broccoli and eggs. Fold in the mayonnaise; add the lemon juice, Worcestershire, and salt. Pour into 12 to 14 individual molds or into a 1-quart ring mold. Chill until firm. Unmold on lettuce, and garnish with a small amount of mayonnaise or dressing. If served in a ring mold, set a small bowl of mayonnaise in the center of ring. This salad should be either served immediately after removing from molds, or unmolded and kept refrigerated until served. It is rich and takes the place of a vegetable.

Mrs. Albert A. Stoddard, Burlington, N.C.

WINE-CRANBERRY SALAD
Serves eight to ten

2 3-oz. pkgs. raspberry jello
1¼ cups hot water
1 can (1 lb.) whole cranberry sauce
1 No. 303 can crushed pineapple
½ cup sweet wine (port)
1 3-oz. pkg. Philadelphia cream cheese
1 cup sour cream
½ cup chopped nuts

Dissolve the jello in the boiling hot water. Stir in the cranberry sauce, pineapple, and wine. Pour into a 1½-quart mold. Cool until mixture begins to set. Mash the cream cheese, and fold in the sour cream. Stir in the nuts. Spread the cheese mixture evenly over the jello mixture. Let chill until firm. Unmold so the cheese will be on the bottom. Slice and serve on lettuce.

Mrs. Josephine Hill Carrigan, Burlington, N.C.

GRAPEFRUIT SALAD
Serves twenty-four

4 envelopes plain gelatin (correct)
1 cup cold water
1 cup boiling water
1 cup sugar
2 No. 2 cans grapefruit sections
1 No. 2 can crushed pineapple

Soak the gelatin in the cold water; dissolve in the boiling water; stir in sugar and fruits. Molded in a fancy (2-qt.) mold, this makes a splendid salad to serve with baked ham, turkey, or sea food.

Mrs. Broadus Wilson, Raleigh, N.C.

CITRUS FRUIT SALAD WITH LEMON-HONEY DRESSING
Serves six

1 pkg. lemon, lime, or orange flavored gelatin
¾ cup boiling water
Dash salt
½ cup grapefruit juice
½ cup orange juice
2 cups diced grapefruit sections, drained
½ cup fresh water cress leaves, extra for garnishing
1 cup sliced strawberries
Extra grapefruit sections

Dissolve gelatin in boiling water; cool. Add salt and fruit juices. Pour a thin layer in an oiled (vegetable oil) pyrex dish (8″ × 10″ × 2″). Chill until firm. Arrange diced grapefruit and cress leaves on the gelatin; cover with another thin layer of gelatin. Chill; arrange the strawberries on the second layer of gelatin, and pour remaining gelatin over. Unmold on a platter; garnish with water cress and grapefruit sections. Serve the dressing over each serving. This makes a three-layer gelatin mold with the fruits in between. Slice.

Lemon-Honey Dressing

1 egg, well beaten
¼ cup lemon juice
½ cup strained honey
3 tablespoons milk

1 cup cottage cheese
Dash salt
⅛ teaspoon mace

Combine egg, lemon juice and honey in top of double boiler; cook over hot water, stirring constantly, until it thickens. Cool. Beat the milk and cottage cheese together; add salt and milk; stir into honey mixture. Cool. Makes 1½ cups.

Mrs. C. Willard Billby, Gainesville, Fla. (a Florida Citrus Recipe
Contest Winner)

LEROY'S HOLIDAY CRANBERRY SALAD
Serves four to six

One cup ground raw cranberries, measured after putting through food chopper.

1 cup sugar
1 3-oz. pkg. lemon-flavored jello
½ cup boiling water
1 cup orange juice

2 teaspoons grated orange rind
1 9-oz. can crushed pineapple
½ cup broken pecan meats
1 cup chopped celery

Mix sugar and cranberries together, and let stand several hours. Add the jello to the boiling water, and stir until dissolved. Add orange juice and stir, then add cranberries and other ingredients and pour into mold. Serve on crisp lettuce and garnish with mayonnaise.

From Old-Time Recipes from the Nu-Wray Inn, by Esther and
Rush T. Wray, Burnsville, N.C.

ORANGE AND DATE SALAD
Serves two

One-half cup sliced dates, soaked for 1 hour in French dressing. Serve in center of lettuce leaf, and surround with sections of orange. Add French dressing over all, and 1 teaspoon of mayonnaise in center of each serving.

From New Orleans Recipes, *by Mary Moore Bremer, New Orleans, La.*

WARM SPRINGS HARVESTER SALAD
Serves six

This is the salad served by Chef C. M. Stephens for President Franklin D. Roosevelt at Warm Springs to accompany the traditional Thanksgiving turkey (described on p. 193).

1½ cups red apples, peeled, cored, diced
3 tablespoons lemon juice
1½ cups bleached celery, diced

1½ cups dates, chopped
Dash salt
¾ cup mayonnaise

Combine the apples with the lemon juice. Blend the apples, celery, dates, and salt with the mayonnaise. Serve on crisp lettuce.

Special permission, C. W. Bussey, Business Manager,
Warm Springs Foundation, Warm Springs, Ga.

VIOLA IRELAND'S BRIDE'S SALAD
Serves twenty

Mrs. Ireland created this salad for a bride's party. The cooked custard dressing base gives a different taste.

2 No. 2 cans white cherries
2 No. 2 cans sliced pineapple
2 No. 2 cans Bartlett pears

1 lb. marshmallows
1 pt. heavy cream, whipped

Pit cherries; drain and cut up fruit and marshmallows. Make the following custard:

Custard Dressing

4 egg yolks
1 tablespoon cornstarch

1 tablespoon dry mustard
1 cup sweet milk

In the top of a double boiler, put the egg yolks, cornstarch, and mustard; stir well; then add milk and let cook until custard thickens. Remove from heat; let cool. When custard is cold, add fruit; mix. Last, whip 1 pint of heavy cream and fold into fruit and custard mixture.

Place in a large shallow mold and chill overnight. Turn out on a flat silver platter and garnish with crisp lettuce cups. Serve the salad in the lettuce cups. (This salad does not hold a firm mold, but rather gives the suggestion of one. To make a firm salad add gelatin to hot custard.)

Mrs. John Rich Ireland, Burlington, N.C.

MARY'S SALAD FOR A LUNCHEON
Serves six to eight

Cooked breast of 1 large hen, diced
2 standard-size cans fillet of anchovies
6 strips of bacon, cooked crisp
3 hard-cooked eggs, sliced
2 tablespoons crumbled Roquefort cheese
1 head of lettuce, endive, or romaine (or a combination of the greens)
1 cup celery diced
Ripe olives (as many as desired)
3 medium-size tomatoes, quartered
Radish roses, carrot curls, thin cucumber slices for garnish
Salad oil
Plain vinegar French dressing
Salt and pepper to taste

In a large salad bowl toss together the first 9 ingredients. Prepare and set aside the garnishings. Keep all refrigerated until time to serve. Just before serving, toss the salad together with salad oil and French dressing, using only enough to well coat the salad. Season to taste with salt and pepper. Garnish the bowl with radish roses, carrot curls, and cucumber slices.

This makes a hearty luncheon. Serves 6 bountifully and can be stretched to serve 8.

Mrs. Blackwell Robinson, Greensboro, N.C.

SCOTLAND NECK FROZEN FRUIT SALAD
Serves six to eight

Apricots, nuts, and grapes with other fruits give this salad an exotic flavor.

1 3-oz. pkg. cream cheese
2 tablespoons cream
1/3 cup mayonnaise
2 tablespoons lemon juice
1/4 teaspoon salt
2 tablespoons sugar

1 No. 2 can Royal Anne cherries, pitted
1 can (1 cup) sweetened apricots, cut
1 can (1 cup) chopped pineapple
1 cup seeded grapes, cut
½ cup pecan meats, cut
1 cup marshmallows, cut
1 cup heavy cream, whipped

Mix cheese with cream. Add mayonnaise, lemon juice, salt, and sugar. Combine with cut fruits, nuts, and marshmallows. Fold in whipped cream, and mix together. Pour into refrigerator tray and freeze. Serve on lettuce.

Mrs. James Pittman, from "Idle Chatter," by Carolyn H. Satterfield, The Scotland Neck Commonwealth, Scotland Neck, N.C.

DAURICE'S FRUIT SALAD IN SOUR CREAM
Serves six to eight

1 cup canned fruit cocktail, drained
1 cup crushed pineapple, or pineapple cut into small chunks; drained
1½ cups mandarin orange sections
½ cup grated coconut
½ cup maraschino cherries, halved
1 cup miniature marshmallows, or large marshmallows, cut in chunks
2 cups sour cream

Mix all together in a deep salad bowl. Place in refrigerator for around 12 hours, or until marshmallows are soft. Stir several times. Serve on lettuce.

Mrs. R. D. Lea, Chesterfield County, Va.

MILLION-DOLLAR SALAD
Serves fourteen to sixteen

This rich salad (similar to "Heavenly Hash," or "Angel Hash"), has at last been properly named.

3 lbs. white grapes, or white canned cherries
2 cans pineapple
1 lb. marshmallows
½ lb. blanched almonds
Juice of 2 lemons
4 eggs
1 cup milk
2 cups heavy cream, whipped

Cut and stone grapes or cherries. Cut pineapple, marshmallows, and almonds into cubes. Put these ingredients into large porcelain bowl, and pour lemon juice over.

Make a custard of eggs and milk. When cold, add cream, beaten stiff. Add to the fruit, etc. Let mixture stand 24 hours. Serve cold.

Mrs. Thomas E. Strange, from St. Anne's Parish Recipe Book, *Annapolis*, Md.

FROSTED MELON MOLD
Serves six to eight

This unusual salad is surprisingly easy to prepare.

1 fairly large cantaloupe (yellow meat is prettier)
1 3-oz. pkg. lemon jello
1 envelope Knox gelatin
3½ cups water

White seedless grapes or other fruit
Cream cheese
Heavy cream

Make a fruit jello using lemon jello and 1 package of unflavored Knox gelatin according to package directions. Use a total of 3½ cups water. Add small white seedless grapes or any other desired fruit.

Peel the melon; cut slice from end, and remove seeds; fill center with jello and fruit mixture. Prop melon up in refrigerator until center congeals. Replace slice cut from end. Frost the entire melon with cream cheese thinned by heavy cream. Return to refrigerator and chill 24 hours. Serve on an aspic tray garnished with grape leaves and white grapes. Slice all the way through, and serve with a good French dressing.

Mrs. James P. Smith, Paducah, Ky.

MRS. PATTERSON'S CHEESE BALLS
About forty

This little cheese ball is made to accompany salads, or it may be served on crackers as an hors d'oeuvre.

1½ lbs. cheese
1 small can pimientos
Worcestershire sauce

Red pepper
Mayonnaise
Ground peanuts

Grind cheese and pimientos together in meat grinder; add a little Worcestershire sauce and red pepper. Soften with enough mayonnaise to hold mixture together. Form into small balls. Roll each in ground peanuts, and put in icebox to harden.

Mrs. Stuart Patterson, Vicksburg, Miss.

OYSTER SALAD

Oyster Salad seems to be one of the first listed in the Southern salad category. This is an "Old Recipe, Lynchburg, Virginia."

"Drain the Liquor from **one-half Gallon fresh Oysters** and throw them into some hot **Vinegar** on the Fire; let them remain until they are plump, not cooked. Then put them at once into **clear, cold Water**. Drain the Water from them and set them away in a cool Place, and prepare your DRESSING: Mash the **Yolks of four hard-boiled Eggs** as fine as you can and rub into it **two Teaspoonfuls Salt, two Teaspoonfuls black Pepper** and two Teaspoonfuls **made mustard**, then rub two large Spoonfuls Salad Oil or melted Butter in, a few Drops at a Time. When it is all smooth, add **one raw Egg**, well beaten, and then **one Teacup good Vinegar**, a Spoonful at a time. Set aside. Mix Oysters, Celery (nearly as much Celery as Oysters) cut up into small Dice, and two good sized **pickled Cucumbers**, cut up fine, tossing up well with a Silver Fork. Sprinkle Salt to your Taste. Then pour Dressing over all."

From The Williamsburg Art of Cookery, *by Helen Bullock*

CUCUMBER BELLEVUE WITH CRAB MEAT OR SHRIMP
Serves six

1 cup crab meat, cooked, or 1½ cups shrimp, cooked, whole
⅛ teaspoon cayenne pepper
1 cup chopped celery, fine
2 medium cucumbers, diced finely
1¼ cups hot water
2 slices onion, or 1 teaspoon onion juice
1 teaspoon salt
1 teaspoon sugar
1 teaspoon lemon juice
2 tablespoons tarragon vinegar, a sprig of tarragon from bottle if possible
2 tablespoons unflavored gelatin, soaked in little cold water
1 drop green coloring

Flake the crab meat, or prepare shrimp; mix with the cayenne pepper and chopped celery. Peel cucumbers and dice, fine. Add cucumbers to crab-celery mixture; let drain in refrigerator. Heat the 1¼ cups of water along with the onion and other seasonings, allowing to simmer for 5 minutes, but not reduce in quantity. Soak gelatin in cold water. Strain water and seasonings; add gelatin and thoroughly dissolve. Tint with coloring, if desired, or leave it clear, giving it a "bellevue" (clear view). Grease a mold (a fish or lobster mold is pretty for this); add ¼ inch of gelatin mixture and allow to congeal; pour in crab meat mixed with 3 tablespoons of gelatin and allow to set; then add another layer of gelatin, etc., until mold is filled, ending with gelatin on top. If desired, mix crab mixture with gelatin and pour all in together, instead. Serve garnished with sprigs of parsley on top, and lettuce or water cress around. Curled celery, carrots, and olives are nestled in among the garnishing, or hard-boiled egg slices. Serve with home-made mayonnaise. [Try 1½ cups pink salmon, adding 1 drop red coloring.—M. B.]

Mrs. Angus Craft, St. Petersburg, Fla.

SHRIMP REMOULADE
Serves eight to ten

This recipe is served as an hors d'oeuvre; on shredded lettuce it becomes a salad, or a first course. [2 pounds shrimp will serve 8 to 10.—M. B.]

4 tablespoons olive oil
2 tablespoons vinegar
1 teaspoon salt
2 teaspoons Creole mustard

6 green onions (small, minced)
2 stalks celery, minced
Few drops Tabasco sauce
¼ teaspoon paprika

Make French dressing of oil, vinegar, salt; add remaining ingredients. Pour over boiled shrimp. Let stand in icebox 4 or 5 hours before serving.

John D. Jastremski, from De Bonnes Choses à Manger, *Houma, La.*

GRAPEFRUIT OR ORANGE-CRAB SALAD
Serves four to six

1 lb. crab meat
Fresh grapefruit sections from 1
    large grapefruit, or 3 oranges
1 cup chopped celery

¼ cup chopped blanched almonds
French dressing or mayonnaise
Lettuce

Mix the crab meat, grapefruit or orange sections with the celery and almonds. Toss with French dressing or mayonnaise. Serve on lettuce.

Mrs. G. E. Thurber, Lake Worth, Fla.

SHRIMP-CABBAGE SALAD
Serves six to eight

1 lb. cooked, cleaned shrimp, bro-
    ken into large pieces
2 cups finely shredded cabbage
1 small onion, finely chopped
½ cup chopped celery
1 tablespoon chopped green pep-
    per

1 tablespoon chopped pimiento
½ teaspoon black pepper
¼ teaspoon salt
Cole slaw dressing, or boiled
    dressing (see "Sauces")
Whole tomatoes

Mix all ingredients except the dressing and tomatoes. Toss with dressing. Cut the tops off tomatoes; scoop out centers. Fill tomatoes with salad.

VARIATIONS: Add the sections from 1 peeled whole orange to the salad. Substitute 2 cups canned green beans for the cabbage for a shrimp-bean salad.

Mrs. Catherine Rhea, Rock Hill, S.C.

SHRIMP-POTATO SALAD
Serves eight to ten

6 medium potatoes, boiled, peeled while still warm
3 tablespoons salad oil
2 tablespoons garlic wine vinegar
½ teaspoon salt
½ teaspoon cayenne pepper
¾ cup mayonnaise
½ cup prepared mustard

1 lb. boiled shrimp, peeled, broken into halves
3 hard-cooked eggs, chopped
1 cup chopped celery
Sliced stuffed olives for garnish
¼ cup capers for garnish
Lettuce

Boil the potatoes until tender but not mushy; peel and cube while still warm. Place in a large mixing bowl; sprinkle over the salad oil and vinegar; toss lightly. Add remaining ingredients, except the garnishings, in order given. Arrange in a salad bowl, and garnish with sliced olives and capers. Serve on lettuce.

Mrs. M. M. McCann, Charlotte, N.C.

BASIC SHRIMP OR LOBSTER SALAD
Serves six

1 lb. boiled, cleaned shrimp, broken into halves, or 2½ cups cooked, cubed lobster meat
½ cup French dressing
3 hard-cooked eggs, chopped
¾ cup chopped celery
Salt and pepper to taste
6 sweet pickled gherkins, sliced, optional

2 tablespoons tiny cocktail pickled onions, optional
Mayonnaise
Lettuce, whole ripe tomatoes, or whole green peppers
Capers

Prepare the shrimp or lobster meat. Pour over the French dressing. Marinate in refrigerator several hours. Pour off the dressing; discard dressing. Mix the shrimp, eggs and celery; season to taste. If desired add the pickles and onions. Toss with mayonnaise to bind the salad. Serve on lettuce or in scooped out tomatoes or in green peppers which have been seeded. Sprinkle capers over each serving.

Mrs. David L. Rawls, from The Suffolk Cook Book, *Suffolk, Va.*

CRAB LOUIS
Serves four

1 lb. cooked backfin crab meat, or canned or frozen king crab meat
1 small head lettuce, shredded
5 hard-cooked eggs, 2 chopped, 3 quartered
½ cup chopped celery
¼ cup drained capers
Crab Louis dressing
2 tomatoes, cut into wedges
1 avocado, sliced lengthwise, optional
Ripe or stuffed olives

Shred the crab meat into a mixing bowl, and pick out shell particles. (If canned meat is used, drain. Thaw frozen meat and squeeze out water.) Toss the crab meat with the lettuce, the 2 chopped eggs, celery, and capers. Toss with Crab Louis dressing (see "Sauces"). Divide among 4 salad bowls. Garnish each bowl with the quartered eggs, tomato wedges, avocado, and olives.

CRAB RAVIGOTE
Serves four

2 cups cooled flaked crab meat
Home-made mayonnaise
Juice ½ lemon
Cayenne pepper to taste
Salt, optional
4 large shells
Paprika
2 hard-boiled eggs, sieved

Pick over crab meat, removing all shell. Mix lightly with mayonnaise and lemon juice. Season to taste with pepper and salt if desired. Fill crab shells. Dust with paprika, and sprinkle with sieved eggs.

Mrs. W. H. Wootton, Baltimore, Md.

FRUITS OF THE SEA MAYONNAISE RING
Serves six to eight

This piquant congealed ring is filled with shrimp, crab flakes, or lobster.

1 3-oz. pkg. lemon jello
2 cups boiling water
1 cup mayonnaise
1 cup heavy cream, whipped

2 tablespoons chopped chives
2 tablespoons chopped pimientos
2 tablespoons capers

Sea food to fill center of ring
Dressing to marinate sea food
(use favorite red dressing)

Dissolve jello in a scant pint of boiling water. When cool, add mayonnaise, whipped cream, chives, pimiento, and capers. Marinate the shrimp, crab, lobster in a red dressing ½ hour before serving. In the meanwhile, pour jello mixture into a wet ring mold. Just before serving time, unmold ring and fill center with sea food. Garnish with tomato cubes, hard-boiled egg, asparagus tips, or any desired garnishing.

Mrs. W. H. Stratford, Haw River, N.C., from Soup to Nuts,
Burlington, N.C.

BEET RING WITH CRAB IN AVOCADO
Serves six

1 3-oz. pkg. lemon jello
2 cups boiling water, or beet stock
Juice 1 lemon
2 cups fresh beets, riced, or 1 can beets, riced
4 tablespoons prepared horseradish

Salt to taste
Crab meat
Avocados
Roquefort cheese dressing

Dissolve jello in water and lemon juice. Chill until it begins to congeal. Add beets, horseradish, and salt. Pour into an oiled ring mold and chill until firm. Turn out on lettuce. Fill with Roquefort cheese dressing (see p. 436), and surround with halved avocados filled with crab meat.

Mrs. A. Glenn Holt, from Soup to Nuts, *Burlington, N.C.*

TOMATO FRAPPE (*With Shrimp*)
Serves eight

1 cup tomato juice
1 tablespoon grated onion, or ½ teaspoon onion juice
1 teaspoon minced green pepper
¼ teaspoon celery seed
½ teaspoon salt
¼ teaspoon sugar

Dash red pepper
⅛ teaspoon black pepper
1 cup heavy cream, whipped
½ cup mayonnaise
2 lbs. cooked, peeled shrimp
Lettuce

Place tomato juice, onion, green pepper, and seasonings in saucepan and simmer for 5 minutes. Strain; chill. Combine with the whipped cream and mayonnaise. Taste and reseason. Pour into individual molds or shallow square mold. Freeze. Unmold on lettuce and serve with 4 or 5 shrimp around each serving, and mayonnaise. If in square tray, cut tomato ice into squares.

Mrs. E. H. Morris, Jr., Raleigh, N.C.

MOLDED EGG AND CAVIAR SALAD
Serves eight

6 hard-cooked eggs	Pinch mustard
1 2-oz. jar caviar	8 slices tomato
2 tablespoons melted butter	Shredded lettuce
Juice ½ lemon	Mayonnaise
1 teaspoon Worcestershire sauce	Anchovies

Put eggs through a food grinder. Mix in caviar, butter, lemon juice, Worcestershire, and mustard. Pack tightly into very small individual molds, or demi-tasse cups. Cover and chill in refrigerator overnight. Unmold egg mixture on peeled tomato slices and place on lettuce. Top each serving with mayonnaise and a rolled anchovy.

Mrs. Ethel Townsend Coke, from The Junior League of Dallas Cook Book, *Dallas, Tex.*

BASIC CHICKEN OR TURKEY SALAD
Serves ten to twelve

1 hen (about 6 lbs.) or 1 small "butterball" turkey	1 medium onion, quartered
½ teaspoon powdered ginger	½ teaspoon garlic powder (optional)
1 teaspoon ground sage, or poultry seasoning	2 teaspoons salt
2 stalks celery, broken	Water to cover

Put hen and all ingredients in a large kettle with cover. Bring to boil and reduce heat to simmer. Simmer until chicken or turkey is ready to fall from bones. Cool; skin; bone chicken. Cut the meat crosswise to make bite-size cubes (meat may be ground if for sandwiches or canapés). Mix with the following:

Juice of 1 lemon	Boiled dressing or mayonnaise to coat the salad well
4 hard-cooked eggs, chopped	
3 cups finely diced celery	2 tablespoons Durkee's dressing

Mix in a large bowl with the chicken or turkey in order given. Allow the chicken to soak in the lemon juice a few minutes before adding other ingredients.

VARIATIONS: Other ingredients may be added: green grapes, chopped nuts, chopped apple, chunks of pineapple, etc.

MRS. DURANT'S OLD FASHIONED CHICKEN SALAD
Serves eight

This old-fashioned salad contains no mayonnaise. It is made with egg dressing.

2 broiler-size chickens (2½ to 3 lbs. each)
Salted water (about 1 tablespoon salt)
1 doz. hard-cooked eggs
1 cup butter, softened
⅓ cup sugar
1 cup vinegar
3 cups celery, finely diced
Salt and pepper to taste
Lettuce and mayonnaise for garnish

Boil the chickens in salted water until chicken meat is tender enough to slip from bones. Cool the chicken and pull meat from bones; cut into bite-size cubes. Peel the eggs, and, while still warm, remove the yolks (reserve the whites). In a large mixing bowl, cream the yolks with the softened butter to a smooth paste. Stir in the sugar and vinegar. Toss the chicken with the celery. Mash the egg whites fine (or sieve them) and mix them with the egg-yolk mixture. Place the chicken and celery in a bowl and pour the egg sauce over; stir well; add salt and pepper to taste. Pack the salad in a mold or bowl, and mash it down with the palms of the hand. Cover and let stand at least 12 hours in the refrigerator. Before serving, if the salad looks too dry, stir together a little sugar and vinegar and pour over. Serve the salad either from the bowl, or invert bowl and turn out on a platter ringed with lettuce leaves. Have a bowl of mayonnaise on the table for those who desire it.

This salad will keep fresh for at least 6 days. Cover the bowl with plastic wrap.

Mrs. R. F. Durant, Burlington, N.C.

CHICKEN SALAD SUPREME
Serves eight

2½ cups cold chicken, diced
1 cup celery, chopped fine
1 cup white grapes
½ cup shredded almonds
2 tablespoons minced parsley
1 teaspoon salt
1/16 teaspoon pepper
1¼ tablespoons gelatin
4 tablespoons water
½ cup cream, whipped
½ cup chicken stock
1 cup mayonnaise

Mix chicken, celery, grapes, almonds, parsley, and season with salt and pepper. Soak gelatin in cold water 5 minutes; then dissolve over boiling water. Add gelatin, cream, and chicken stock to mayonnaise and stir until mixture begins to thicken. Fold in chicken mixture. Pack in molds. If desired, place in the bottom of the molds sliced hard-boiled eggs and sliced, stuffed olives. When mold is turned out, it is very decorative.

Alice B. Haig, Washington, D.C. from DAR Cook Book, by Aileen Lewers Langston

HOT CHICKEN OR TURKEY SALAD
Serves six to eight

3 cups cooked chicken or turkey, diced into small cubes
2½ cups celery, diced fine
½ cup salted, slivered almonds
2 tablespoons lemon juice
1½ tablespoons grated onion
½ teaspoon Worcestershire sauce
1 tablespoon Durkee's dressing
Mayonnaise (about 1 cup) to hold mixture well together
1 cup buttered bread crumbs or crushed potato chips
1 cup grated Cheddar or Parmesan cheese

Mix all ingredients except the bread crumbs and cheese into a bowl. Butter a 1½-quart casserole or baking dish. Pour in mixture; top with the crumbs and grated cheese. Bake uncovered for about 20 minutes in a preheated 400-degree oven, or until mixture is hot and topping browned.

NOTE: Serve with buttered toast points and a fresh fruit salad.

TURKEY-RICE SALAD
Serves six to eight

1 pkg. wild white rice (Uncle Ben's), cooked
2 cups cooked turkey (or chicken), cubed
1 cup canned green grapes, drained
½ cup chopped, salted pecans
Salt and pepper to taste
French dressing and mayonnaise
Lettuce and spiced apples to garnish

Cook the rice according to package directions. Let rice cool. Mix the rice with the turkey, grapes, and pecans. Season to taste. Use equal parts of French dressing and mayonnaise to toss the salad. Use just enough to blend the ingredients well.

Mound the salad on a large silver platter; garnish with lettuce and spiced crab apples.

Mrs. Charles H. Pitts, Leesburg, Fla.

CHICKEN AND ORANGE MOLD WITH RICE SAUCE
Serves eight

4 tablespoons gelatin, soaked in ¼ cup cold water
2½ cups chicken stock, well seasoned
⅓ cup orange juice

Salt, pepper to taste
Dash cayenne
1 egg white
Whole orange sections
Breast of chicken

Dissolve soaked gelatin in hot chicken stock. Add orange juice and seasonings. Clear with egg white. Brush 1-quart Charlotte Russe mold with salad oil, and pour in a thin coating of jelly [gelatin mixture] on the bottom. Let stand until set. Place orange sections, free of all membrane, on outer edge of the mold; in center lay strips of cold chicken breast. Cover with jelly and repeat until mold is filled. Chill. Unmold on glass platter; garnish with lettuce leaves and water cress tips. Serve with Cream Rice Mayonnaise, served separately.

Cream Rice Mayonnaise

1 cup home-made mayonnaise
½ cup cold rice, cooked

¼ cup heavy cream, whipped

Combine mayonnaise and rice; fold in whipped cream, beaten until stiff.

Mrs. Richard Ruffner, from The Alexandria Woman's Club Cook Book, *Alexandria, Va.*

CHICKEN ALMOND MOUSSE
Serves six to eight

This is a "party" dish which may be served plain with mayonnaise, or congealed in a ring mold to be filled with boiled shrimp, crab, or lobster meat.

6 egg yolks
3 cups milk
3 tablespoons plain gelatin, soaked in ½ cup water
1 cup chicken broth, heated
2½ cups white chicken meat, minced
1 teaspoon salt
¼ teaspoon white pepper

$\frac{1}{16}$ teaspoon cayenne pepper
¼ teaspoon onion juice
1 teaspoon lemon juice
½ cup chopped, blanched almonds
2 cups heavy cream, whipped
Garnishings of lettuce, parsley, spiced red apples, etc.

In large bowl of electric mixer, beat the egg yolks until thick; slowly pour in the milk, beating constantly; pour into top of large double boiler over warm water. As heat increases, stir constantly, until mixture coats the spoon. Add the softened gelatin to the boiling hot chicken broth; stir until dissolved. Add the broth-gelatin mixture alternately with the chicken to the custard, stirring up from the bottom while mixing. Do not let boil. Add the seasonings and almonds; stir. Cool the mixture; chill until it just begins to set. Watch it; do not let it get *too* set. Fold in the whipped cream. Pour into a 1½-quart ring or any type mold. Chill 12 hours. Unmold on platter; fill center if desired; garnish platter with lettuce or any garnishings desired.

ASPARAGUS MOUSSE
Serves twelve

Mrs. Morrow has for years catered for special parties in Burlington. This mousse is served by her to complement sliced ham or fried chicken.

1 can all green asparagus, cut into small lengths, save liquid
4 tablespoons unflavored gelatin dissolved in cold water
½ cup mayonnaise
½ cup heavy cream, whipped
1 teaspoon salt
Juice 2 lemons
Shelled, blanched almonds (quantity desired)

Heat the liquid from the can of asparagus and pour over the dissolved gelatin. Let cool. Fold in the mayonnaise and cream, salt, lemon juice, and almonds. Add asparagus. When mixture begins to thicken, pour into individual molds. Congeal. Unmold on lettuce cups; serve with mayonnaise.

Mrs. Paul E. Morrow, Burlington, N.C.

5. Eggs and Cheese

TO MAKE AN EGG AS BIG AS TWENTY

When eggs were a dime a dozen and several dozen went into the Sunday cake, this "egg" was used in "grand Sallads," as in *The Lady's Companion*, London, 1753.

"Part the yolks from the whites of 20 eggs, strain the yolks by themselves, and the whites by themselves, boil the yolks in a bladder in the form either of an egg or ball; when they are boiled hard, put the ball of yolks into another bladder, and the whites round about it, and bind it up oval or round, and boil it. These eggs are used in grand sallads.

"If you prefer you may add to the yolks of the eggs, ambergreese, musk, grated biscuits, candy'd pistachoes and sugar; and to the whites, musk, almond-paste, beaten ginger, and the juice of oranges, and serve them up with butter, almond-milk, sugar, and juice of orange."

From The Williamsburg Art of Cookery, *by Helen Bullock*

TO BOIL EGGS

One of the most delicate tasks involved in cooking is to hard-boil or "hard-cook" an egg so that the white will be tender and the yolk of a creamy consistency. While browsing through the early American cook books in the library of Colonial Williamsburg, Inc., I found in Mrs. Mary Randolph's *Virginia Housewife* a little yellowed sheet of paper on which was written in a stylized handwriting this recipe for "How To Cook Eggs": "Place eggs in a tin vessel and pour over them boiling water in the proportions of one quart of water to one dozen eggs. Let them stand closely covered for 15 minutes." This method makes the eggs tender and creamy, just right to stuff, slice, or serve in any dish calling for hard-boiled eggs. Either a tin coffee can with tightly fitting lid or a saucepan makes a perfect cooking vessel.

STUFFED EGGS IN NEST

Cut hard-boiled eggs in halves lengthwise; remove yolks; and put whites aside in pairs. Mash yolks, and add half as much deviled ham and enough melted butter to make a mixture of the consistency to shape. Make into balls the original size of egg yolks and refill centers of whites. Turn the rest of mixture into a nest around eggs. Arrange nest (in baking dish on toast, if desired); pour white sauce over; sprinkle with buttered bread crumbs; and bake until crumbs are browned.

Mrs. T. W. Russell, from Pride of the Kitchen, *Scotland Neck, N.C.*

CREOLE EGGS GRINALDS
Serves six

1 medium-sized onion
2 tablespoons bacon fat
1 No. 2 can tomatoes (2½ cups)
Salt, pepper to taste
½ cup butter

3 tablespoons flour (heaping)
1 cup milk
8 large hard-boiled eggs
1 cup toasted bread crumbs

Chop the onion fine and brown in hot bacon fat. Add tomatoes and simmer until onions are well done. Add salt and pepper to taste. The mixture should be highly seasoned. Make a white sauce of ½ the butter, all of the flour and milk—the sauce should be very thick. When done, add the tomato mixture to the sauce and stir well. Into a buttered casserole, put a layer of tomato mixture, a layer of sliced eggs, and a layer of bread crumbs. Fill the dish so. Cut the rest of butter into slices and put on top. Bake in hot oven (400 degrees) about 25 minutes.

Mrs. R. T. Grinalds, Macon, Ga.

BEPPIE'S EGG PIE
Serves four

"Beppie" was cook and nurse for three generations in the family of the contributor of this cherished old recipe.

5 hard-boiled eggs
½ teaspoon salt
Pepper

¾ cup milk
½ stick butter
Pastry for double pie crust

Line a shallow baking dish (pyrex) with pie crust; place in it a layer of sliced egg; sprinkle with salt and pepper to taste. Dot with butter. Pour over the milk. Cover with crust as for any other pie. Bake in a moderate (350-degree) oven until crust is golden brown, about 40 to 45 minutes. Serve hot.

Mrs. Walter Monroe Brown, Burlington, N.C.

VARIATION: For Cheese-Egg Pie, use the same ingredients as above, except to substitute medium cream sauce for the ¾ cup milk, sprinkle ¾ cup grated cheese over the eggs, and proceed as in "Beppie's" pie.

DEVILED EGGS
Serves six

6 hard-cooked eggs, peeled
1 tablespoon prepared mustard
1 tablespoon Durkee's dressing
⅛ teaspoon cayenne pepper
Mayonnaise to blend mixture
Salt to taste

Garnishings:
Minced parsley
Crumbled crisp bacon
Sliced stuffed olives
Paprika

Peel the eggs while still warm; cut into halves. Mash the yolks with the mustard, dressing, and cayenne; blend in enough mayonnaise to make a thick, creamy mixture. Stuff back into the egg whites. Garnish the tops with parsley, bacon, olives, paprika, or any desired garnishings. Flaked tuna fish, minced shrimp or lobster meat (cooked), minced ham, chopped pickles, etc., may be combined with the egg yolk mixture to stuff the egg whites.

EGGS BENEDICTINE
Serves six

1 cup cream sauce
½ cup grated cheese
2 egg yolks, beaten
4 tablespoons sherry
Salt, pepper

Toasted and buttered bread or bun, English muffin
6 slices tomato
6 slices ham
6 eggs, poached

To the cream sauce add grated cheese, beaten egg yolks, sherry, pepper, and salt. Split English buns (or slice of bread); toast; and butter. Fry tomatoes, and broil ham. On each bun place a layer of ham, then a slice of tomato. Top with a poached egg and pour the sauce over. Eggs Benedictine are often served without the fried tomato. Raw tomato may substitute for the fried tomato.

SHIRRED SWISS EGGS
Serves six

2 tablespoons butter
6 very thin slices Swiss cheese
6 eggs
¼ teaspoon salt

2 tablespoons cream, or top milk
3 tablespoons grated Swiss cheese
Dash paprika

Melt butter in individual baking dishes; lay slice of cheese on bottom of dish. Break egg onto cheese; sprinkle with salt; pour cream over; and sprinkle with grated cheese and paprika. Bake in moderate oven (350 degrees) until whites are set (about 8–10 minutes) and cheese is melted. Serve in dish in which cooking is done.

Mrs. Harry Bush, from Victuals and Vitamins, *Greensboro, N.C.*

ANTOINE'S OMELETTE ESPAGNOLE
Serves four

1 No. 2 can tomatoes
3 tablespoons butter
1 teaspoon salt
Few grains pepper
Few grains cayenne
1 tablespoon parsley, minced
1 sprig thyme
2 cloves garlic, minced
1 bay leaf
1 tablespoon flour

5 tablespoons chopped green pepper
6 chopped shallots, or ½ cup minced onion
½ cup white wine
½ cup canned button mushrooms
½ cup cooked peas
4 eggs
1 tablespoon olive oil

Combine tomatoes with 1 tablespoon butter; simmer 10 minutes, stirring constantly. Add salt, pepper, and cayenne; cook ten minutes. Add parsley, thyme, garlic, and bay leaf. Cook until sauce is thick—about 15 minutes. Melt 1 tablespoon butter; blend in the flour; and cook until a brown roux is formed. Add green pepper and shallots; brown slightly. Add wine, and stir constantly until slightly thickened. Add mushrooms and peas. Beat eggs until well blended, and to them add the tomato mixture. Heat remaining butter and olive oil in a skillet; pour in egg mixture. Shake the skillet until mixture begins to set, lifting edges of omelet to allow uncooked mixture to flow under. When cooked, fold over. Garnish with parsley.

From Antoine's Restaurant, New Orleans, La. Special permission, Roy Alciatore, Proprietor

RUM OMELET

Cook any plain 4-egg omelet; serve on a plated silver dish; pour over ½ cup good rum. Touch lighted match to rum and serve flaming to the table. Be sure the rum is of good quality or it will not burn. (**Powdered sugar and nutmeg** sprinkled over Rum Omelet give extra flavor.)

From New Orleans Recipes, *Peerless Printing Company, New Orleans, La.*

LOST BREAD (*Pain Perdu*), FRENCH TOAST
Serves four

Lost bread or French Toast is an old Creole dish, made in New Orleans, sprinkled with sugar and cinnamon, or served as hot toast to be garnished with bacon, chicken livers, etc. This recipe is not so sweet, but sugar to taste may be added to the egg-milk custard. Tart jelly usually accompanies it.

4 or 5 slices day-old bread, thick
2 well-beaten eggs
1 cup rich milk

1 tablespoon sugar (optional)
Butter
Cinnamon and sugar

Beat egg and milk together to form custard; add 1 tablespoon sugar if desired. Dip each piece of toast into egg mixture until thoroughly coated. Fry in hot butter, browning on both sides. While it is hot, sprinkle lightly with granulated sugar and cinnamon; serve hot.

Mrs. Angus Craft, St. Petersburg, Fla.

EGG CROQUETTES
Serves four

¾ cup chopped mushrooms, fresh
  or canned
3 tablespoons butter
3 tablespoons flour
Milk to make thick sauce (about
  1 cup)
Salt, pepper, cayenne to taste

½ teaspoon Worcestershire sauce
1 teaspoon minced chives, or
  onion
4 eggs, hard-boiled, minced
Bread crumbs
1 egg yolk, beaten

Cook the mushrooms in butter until tender but not browned. Save butter; blend in flour, milk, and seasoning to make a thick sauce. Add mushrooms, chives, minced egg. Chill and form into desired croquettes. Roll in bread crumbs, then in the beaten egg yolk, and back in crumbs. Fry in deep fat (375 degrees) and serve either plain or with a hot sauce.

Mrs. Kate Friedheim, Rock Hill, S.C.

E. Z.'S KIPPER OMELETS
Serves two

These individual omelets were originated by our contributor as a Sunday night "special" for two.

1 small can Kipper herrings with the oil
1½ tablespoons olive oil
1 cup finely chopped onions
4 eggs, well beaten
¼ cup milk

Pinch of garlic powder
Black pepper to taste
⅛ teaspoon salt (or to taste, since herrings have some salt)
Parmesan cheese
Paprika

Mash the herrings in a small bowl. In a 5- to 6-inch teflon skillet, heat the oil and sauté the onions until they are transparent. Add the mashed herring and stir to blend. Take half the onion-herring mixture out of pan and reserve for second omelet. Beat the eggs; beat in the milk, garlic powder, pepper, and salt. Have the skillet hot; pour in half of the egg mixture, and sprinkle with cheese. Cook, tilting the pan once or twice, until the bottom has browned and eggs begin to set. With a spatula, fold over the omelet. Sprinkle the top with cheese and paprika. Remove omelet to warm plate, and add the reserved onion-herring mixture to the skillet. Proceed to make a second omelet as above.

E. Z. Jones, WBBB Radio, Burlington, N.C.

HUEVOS RANCHEROS (*Ranch Eggs*)
Serves eight to ten

16 to 20 eggs (2 per serving)
Butter (about 4 tablespoons)
Milk

Tabasco
8 to 10 slices toast

Bake eggs in buttered muffin tins with a dot of butter, a little milk (about 1 teaspoon per egg), and a drop of Tabasco. Bake at 350 degrees for 8 to 10 minutes, or until whites are set. Serve on toast with the following sauce:

Sauce

3 large onions, chopped
3 large green peppers, chopped
½ cup butter
2 2-lb. cans tomatoes
1 cup canned mushrooms

Salt, pepper to taste
Tabasco sauce to taste
Worcestershire sauce to taste
Chili powder to taste
6 crushed chilipitines

Cook onions and peppers slowly in butter until onions are clear. Add tomatoes, mushrooms, salt, pepper, Tabasco, Worcestershire, chili powder, and chilipitines. Cook slowly for 1 to 2 hours, until thick.

Una Chapman Dowd, from What's Cookin'? *Corpus Christi, Tex.*

TO MAKE AN ENGLISH RABBIT

One of the earliest rabbits, or rarebits, is from Mrs. Hannah Glass's *Art of Cookery*, 1774, in which she says: "Toast a slice of bread brown on both sides, then lay it in a plate before the fire, pour a glass of red wine over it, and let it soak the wine up; then cut some cheese very thin, and lay it very thick over the bread, and put it in a tin oven before the fire, and it will be toasted and browned presently. Serve it away hot."

From The Williamsburg Art of Cookery, *by Helen Bullock*

TEXAS WELSH RAREBIT
Serves three to four

2 tablespoons butter, melted
2 tablespoons flour
1 cup milk
½ lb. box processed cheese
1 (1⅓-oz.) section of Camembert cheese, sliced

2 tablespoons Worcestershire sauce
3 tablespoons sherry or ale
Melba toast

Blend shortening and flour to smooth paste. Add milk and cook, stirring constantly, until thickened. Add cheese; cook until melted. Just before serving, add Worcestershire and wine. Pour over Melba toast.

Mrs. M. W. Lupton, from The Junior League of Dallas Cook Book, *Dallas, Tex.*

RINCTUM-DIDDY OR RED DEVIL
Serves four to six

This is a form of Welsh Rarebit often known as Russian Rarebit. The base is cheese with tomato flavoring and high seasoning.

1 tablespoon butter
1 tablespoon flour
1 egg
1 cup sweet milk
½ lb. cheese, grated

1 can tomato soup (Campbell's)
1 teaspoon soda
1 teaspoon salt
Dash red pepper
Toast or crackers

Melt butter and mix in flour. Beat egg and milk and stir. Let cook 1 minute; then add cheese. After cheese melts, add tomato soup with soda stirred in. Let come to a boil; add salt and pepper, and cook until it thickens. Serve hot on toast or crackers.

Mrs. Raymond Ball, from The Episcopal Pantry, *Danville, Va.*

CATHERINE'S QUICHE LORRAINE
Serves four to five

8 to 10 slices bacon, fried crisp, drained, crumbled
1 9-inch unbaked pie shell
½ pound Swiss cheese, diced (or sharp Cheddar cheese)
1 tablespoon minced onion (optional)
4 eggs, well beaten
1 cup milk
Salt and pepper to taste

Fry the bacon; drain and crumble it. Sprinkle bacon in the bottom of pie shell. Sprinkle the diced cheese over the bacon. Beat the eggs; add the milk, salt, and pepper. Let the mixture set for a short time until bubbles rise to the top. Skim off the bubbles. Pour the egg mixture into the pie shell. Bake in a preheated 350-degree oven for about 30 minutes, or until set. A knife inserted in the middle of pie should come out clean when custard is done. Slice as a pie and serve hot. This is a good luncheon dish.

Mrs. William S. Chandler, Burlington, N.C.

BASIC CHEESE SOUFFLE
Serves six to eight

The secret of a successful soufflé depends largely upon the proper beating of the egg whites. A wire whisk (or balloon whip) is best for beating. The eggs should be as voluminous as possible, beaten stiff and moist-looking, not dry, and *folded* in gently, never stirred in. Flour or potato starch should be used in the sauce, and some cooks add cream of tartar to support the egg whites. The soufflé may be baked in a hot (425 degree) oven, or it may be placed in a pan of hot water and baked at about 325 degrees. A buttered soufflé dish should be used to bake the mixture, with a buttered brown paper collar tied around the outside rim of the dish to allow for extra rising. The number of eggs used is an individual choice; the more eggs, the larger the soufflé. Cheddar cheese, Swiss cheese, Gruyère, Parmesan, or a combination of cheeses go into a cheese soufflé.

With a good basic sauce a variety of soufflés can be turned out: vegetable, sea food, meats, poultry, and dessert soufflés are but a few. Serve the soufflé directly from the oven to the table!

4 tablespoons butter
4 tablespoons flour, or potato starch
¼ teaspoon salt
1 cup milk
4 egg yolks, beaten thick
¼ lb. grated Cheddar cheese, extra cheese for topping, optional

⅛ teaspoon cayenne
4 egg whites, beaten stiff but not dry
¼ teaspoon cream of tartar
Buttered soufflé dish with paper collar

In a large saucepan, melt the butter. Remove from the heat and blend in the flour and salt. Return to the heat; cook, stirring constantly, until mixture bubbles. Slowly stir in the milk. Cook over medium heat, stirring constantly, until the sauce is medium thick. Beat the egg yolks until they are thick. Add a few tablespoons of the hot sauce to the egg yolks and stir; then stir the egg yolks slowly into the sauce. Add the grated cheese and pepper and blend thoroughly. Beat the egg whites until they are foamy; add the cream of tartar and continue beating until the whites are stiff yet moist, and stand in soft peaks. Gently fold the egg whites into the sauce. Pour the soufflé into a buttered 1½-quart soufflé dish. Sprinkle the top with grated cheese, if desired. Tie a band of buttered brown paper (about 2 inches above the rim) around the outside rim of the dish. Bake in a preheated 425-degree oven for 25 to 30 minutes, or until the soufflé is puffed and browned. Serve at once.

CHEESE SOUFFLE WITH GRUYERE CHEESE
Serves four to six

2 tablespoons butter
3 tablespoons flour
½ teaspoon salt
Pepper
¾ cup milk
5 tablespoons grated Gruyére or Swiss cheese

1 tablespoon grated Parmesan cheese
1 teaspoon dry mustard
4 egg yolks
4 egg whites, stiffly beaten

Melt the butter (or margarine) in a pan. Stir in the flour, salt, and pepper. Pour on the milk and stir over heat until it thickens (it must not boil). Add the cheese and mustard; add the egg yolks, one at a time, beating after each addition. Lastly add the egg whites, stiffly beaten. Grease a casserole and tie a band of greased paper around the outside top to support the soufflé as it rises. Fill the casserole with the mixture and bake in a moderate oven (350 degrees) for ½ hour. Remove from oven, take off the paper collar, and serve at once.

Mrs. Vernon F. Hutchens, from 100 Favorite Recipes, *Huntsville, Ala.*

BEAUMONT INN SOUFFLE
Serves four

On the Boone Highway, in the Blue Grass section of Kentucky, is Beaumont Inn, a white-pillared colonial mansion which was once the "Daughter's College" and later "Beaumont College." It is now one of Kentucky's most inviting inns, presided over by Mrs. T. Curry Dedman, Sr., and managed by Charles M. Dedman and T. C. Dedman, Jr. Here the guest finds old country ham, yellow-legged chickens, and beaten biscuit served in a way that suggests an earlier day. This soufflé, or fondue (often called "strata"), is a more modern dish, easy and time-saving.

4 slices of buttered bread, cut in cubes
3 whole eggs, beaten light

2 cups of whole milk
2 cups of grated or ground cheese
Season with salt and white pepper

Place bread in a baking dish; pour over the eggs, milk, and cheese. Season to taste. Let stand 20 minutes or longer. Bake ½ hour in moderate oven (350 degrees).

Special permission, Mrs. T. Curry Dedman, Sr., Beaumont Inn, Harrodsburg, Ky.

MACARONI-CHEESE LOAF
Serves eight

1 16-oz. pkg. macaroni
3 pimientos
1 green pepper
1 onion

3 eggs, well beaten
1 cup grated cheese
Tomato catchup

Cook macaroni in salt water, and drain well. Grind pimientos, peppers, and onion and add with well-beaten eggs and grated cheese to the macaroni. Mix thoroughly, and press firmly into a mold greased and lined with cheesecloth. Steam 1½ hours. Mold onto a platter and serve covered with *hot* tomato catchup and garnished with parsley.

Mrs. L. B. Allen, Jr., Macon, Ga.

CHEESE AND RICE FONDUE
Serves four

1 cup cooked rice, hot
1 cup tomato purée
3 tablespoons butter
2 eggs, beaten very light

½ teaspoon salt
½ teaspoon pepper
1½ cups grated cheese

Mix together and bake in moderate oven in a buttered casserole or mold. If tomatoes are not fancied, substitute 1½ cups white sauce.

From The Louisiana Plantation Cook Book,
by Mrs. James E. Smitherman, Shreveport, La.

PICKLED EGGS

Pickled eggs are a survival of the free-lunch-with-a-stein-of-beer days. Here is an old recipe.

36 hard-boiled eggs
2 cups vinegar
10 allspice
1 teaspoon powdered ginger or a
    ginger root

2 cloves garlic
1 bay leaf
1 pod red pepper
2 extra cups vinegar

Carefully peel eggs, and arrange in large-mouthed jars. Boil 2 cups vinegar with spices, garlic, and red pepper. When vinegar has steeped until flavor of spices has been extracted, add 2 cups more vinegar, bring to a boil, and pour over the eggs. When cold, seal the jars and let stand 1 month. (They may be eaten within 24 hours.)

PICKLED EGGS
One quart

These make an excellent addition to a picnic basket.

2 cups small whole beets, cooked
    and peeled; or canned,
    drained beets
½ cup brown sugar
½ cup white vinegar
½ cup water

Pinch salt
Small piece stick cinnamon or ⅛
    teaspoon ground cinnamon
2 or 3 whole cloves or dash of
    powdered cloves
6 hard-boiled eggs, peeled

Prepare the beets. Combine the sugar, vinegar, water, salt, and spices in a saucepan and bring to a boil. Reduce heat and simmer for 10 minutes. Pour mixture over the beets; let beets stand in this mixture for 3 days. Add the peeled, hard-boiled eggs. Refrigerate; let eggs stand in this mixture three days before serving. Serve cold. The beets give the eggs a lovely pink-red color. For those who are not enamored of beets, the amount may be reduced to two beets, which will be sufficient to color the eggs.

Mrs. Leslie E. Phillabaum, Chapel Hill, N.C.

6. Sea Food

BAKED RED SNAPPER A LA LIDA
Serves six to eight

This recipe applies to any baked fish. Clean a 3½ to 4-lb. red snapper or any other lean fish with head and tail on (do not cut any deeper into fish than necessary). Rub the outside of fish with a combination of **butter, flour, salt, and pepper.**

Stuff fish as follows:

7 slices of toasted bread, crumbed
1 can tomatoes, drained, save juice
2 onions, chopped fine
½ green pepper, chopped fine
½ cup celery, chopped fine
1 chopped clove garlic

1 lump softened butter (about 1 tablespoon)
1 beaten egg
Salt, red pepper
½ lb. chopped raw shrimp
½ pt. chopped raw oysters

Mix the bread crumbs with the drained tomatoes. Add onions, green pepper, celery, garlic, and mix all very well. Add butter, egg, salt, and red pepper to taste. Now add the raw shrimp and oysters and mix thoroughly. Stuff fish and sew up with needle and coarse thread. If any dressing is left, put it on one end of baking dish. *Pour over the fish a gravy made of* the **tomato juice from canned tomatoes, ¼ glass water, juice of 1 lemon, 1 crushed bay leaf, ½ clove garlic, salt, pepper, and 1 tablespoon of flour** sifted over mixture and mixed with a spoon. Bake 1 hour at 350 degrees, and baste often. Strain sauce over fish before serving. A few whole shrimp may be added for garnishing. This is most delicious—I serve it without the sauce sometime.

Mrs. Frank H. Anderson, from What's Cookin'?, *Corpus Christi, Tex.*

BROILED RED SNAPPER

½ lb. red snapper fillet per person
Butter, melted

Salt and pepper to taste
Lemon or lime slices for garnish
Extra melted butter

Line a shallow baking dish with aluminum foil. Lay the fish, skin side down, on the foil. Melt 1 tablespoon of butter for each half-pound fillet. Salt and pepper fish to taste. Garnish the fish with thin lemon or lime slices. Bake in a 350-degree oven until the fish flakes when picked with a fork (about 30 minutes). Baste with extra butter if fish becomes dry. Serve with small cups of melted butter, or serve with Red Snapper Sauce (see "Sauces," p. 443) poured over the fish.

Mrs. Angus Craft, St. Petersburg, Fla.

ANTOINE'S POMPANO EN PAPILLOTE
Serves six

Pompano, which according to Mark Twain, "is as delicious as the less criminal forms of sin," is a tropical fish deriving its name from a greenish plant of the same color. Although not often found farther north than Florida or Georgia, it has been caught off the North Carolina coast.

Pompano en Papillote, meaning "in a paper bag," is the brain child of Jules Alciatore, who baked pompano fillets in paper hearts to celebrate the visit to New Orleans of Alberto Santos-Dumont, the Brazilian balloonist, in the early 1900's. It was an idea stemming from a recipe originated by Antoine Alciatore to honor the Montgolfier brothers who invented the first balloon in 1783. Rich sauce was sealed in the paper hearts with the fish and all flavored with white wine. (For President Franklin D. Roosevelt, champagne was substituted for the other wine.)

Antoine's pompano-in-a-bag is one of the most widely used methods of baking fish (meat or fowl), especially the tender pompano. The procedure may be a simple one. (The fish is prepared as for ordinary baking, slipped into a heavy brown paper bag, tied tightly, and whisked into the oven to stew in its own rich juices. I bake mackerel, speckled trout, bass, or any other baking fish in this manner.) Instead, one may become ensnared—like Jules Alciatore—in paper hearts.

3 medium-sized pompano	½ clove garlic, minced
3 cups water	1½ cups chopped onions (extra)
1 chopped shallot, or 2 tablespoons chopped onion	Pinch thyme
	1 bay leaf
6 tablespoons butter	2 cups fish stock
2¼ cups white wine	2 tablespoons flour
1 cup crab meat	Salt, pepper
1 cup diced cooked shrimp	2 egg yolks

Clean pompano; cut into 6 fillets, removing head and backbone. Simmer head, bones, and water (to cover) until there are 2 cups stock. Sauté shallots and fillets in 2 tablespoons butter; add 2 cups wine. Cover and simmer gently 5 to 8 minutes—until fillets are tender. Sauté crab meat, shrimp, and ¼ garlic clove in 1 tablespoon butter. Add onion, remaining ¼ garlic clove; cook 10 minutes. Add thyme, bay leaf, and add 1¾ cups fish stock; simmer 10 minutes. Blend the flour and butter; gradually add remaining ¼ cup fish stock. Add to crab meat mixture with wine stock drained from fillets; add salt and pepper to taste. Cook, stirring constantly, until thickened. Beat egg yolks; add hot sauce and ¼ cup wine. Mix thoroughly. Place in refrigerator to chill until firm.

Paper Hearts

Cut 6 parchment-paper hearts 8 inches long and 12 inches wide. Oil well, and place spoonfuls of sauce on one side of the hearts; lay poached fillets on sauce and fold over (like old-fashioned fruit pies). Hand seal the edges. Lay hearts on oiled baking sheet. Bake in hot oven (450 degrees) 15 minutes, or until paper hearts are browned. Serve immediately in hearts. Fresh salmon, sea trout, or striped bass may be used.

From Antoine's Restaurant, New Orleans, La. Special permission,
Roy Alciatore, Proprietor

BAKED STUFFED POMPANO A LA GHERADI

From Henry's of Charleston comes a poetic recipe for stuffed pompano. The experienced cook will fill in the details.

"Take a carefully selected **Florida pompano** stuffed and delicately seasoned with a delicious mixture of superior **shrimp**, Carolina's finest **crab meat** and garden-fresh **green onions** in exactly the right proportions and moistened with fine **sherry. Country bacon** and chopped **Spanish olives** are then placed on the fish and this wonderful result of a true artist's skill is allowed to bake in a covered vessel for 15 minutes to create a never-to-be-forgotten sea food taste thrill. Served in a nest of Julienne potatoes." [Mr. Shaffer adds that he uses 100 per cent frozen pre-cut fillets and steaks in sea food dishes.—M. B.]

From Henry's, Charleston, S.C. Special permission,
Walter L. Shaffer, Proprietor

EASY TROUT MARGUERY
Serves four

2 lbs. trout, skinned, cut into fillets
3 tablespoons olive oil
½ cup water

Salt and pepper to taste
¼ cup white wine
Hollandaise Sauce (see Sauces)

Roll the fillets and skewer with toothpicks. Pour the oil into a baking dish; roll the fish in the oil. Add the water; sprinkle with salt, pepper, and wine. Bake in a 375-degree oven until fish flakes (about 45 minutes). Serve with Hollandaise Sauce over the fish.

TROUT IN WHITE WINE SAUCE
Serves six

3 pounds trout fillets
3 tablespoons melted butter or salad oil

2 small chopped onions
Salt and pepper to taste

Have the fillets skinned and boned. Fold each fillet over; skewer with toothpicks. Place in a baking dish over the melted butter and chopped onions. Sprinkle with salt and pepper. Bake in a 350-degree oven, turning the fillets once, until the fish is tender (about 35 to 40 minutes according to the thickness of fish). Make a sauce as follows:

Sauce

6 tablespoons butter
2½ tablespoons flour
Juice of 1 lemon
1 doz. cooked shrimp, broken into small pieces
1 truffle, sliced thin, or 6 black olives, sliced

½ cup sliced, canned mushrooms
12 oysters, drained
½ cup white wine
1 cup well buttered bread crumbs
Grated cheese

In a skillet melt the butter; stir in the flour, and make a roux (paste). Add the lemon juice, stir; add remaining ingredients except bread crumbs and cheese. Pour this sauce over the fish. Sprinkle with bread crumbs and cheese. Run into oven until it is heated thoroughly, and the topping is melted and browned.

From the files of the late William T. Polk, Greensboro, N.C.

FILLET OF TROUT SARAPICO
Serves two

1½ lbs. sea trout
¾ cup cream cheese
¾ cup Roquefort cheese

½ cup Spanish olive oil
1 truffle, brushed
2 Spanish pimientos, chopped

¼ cup champagne
Pinch of salt
Juice of 1 lemon
4 slices American cheese

4 steamed shrimps
2 lemon slices
Few sprigs of chopped parsley

Have the trout skinned and boned and cut into two fillets. Combine cream cheese, Roquefort cheese, oil, truffle, and pimientos. Blend well to a smooth paste. Spread this paste between the fillets (sandwich style). Sprinkle with the lemon juice and salt.

Place the fillets in the center of a large piece of heavy-duty aluminum foil. Pour the champagne over. Seal the fish in the foil, and bake for 30 minutes in a 350-degree oven. Turn back the foil; arrange cheese slices attractively on top of fish, overlapping slices. Place a shrimp on each cheese slice. Return fish to oven and heat until cheese melts. Garnish with parsley and lemon slices. Serve very hot.

The Columbia Restaurants, Tampa, Fla.

FRIED SHAD

R. D. Lea is an avid sportsman, dividing his time between hunting and fishing—then cooking his catch with professional skill. A member of the Chesterfield Sportsman Hunt Club, his hunting is mostly on a 2000-acre club tract in Chesterfield County, Virginia, where deer, rabbit, and other game are plentiful. He fishes, largely for shad, in the Appomattox River between Petersburg and Hopewell, Virginia.

Shad, a salt-water fish, in the spring leaves the ocean and comes to fresh water to spawn. The shad-fishing season opens in Virginia around the first week in April and ends June 1. The fisherman puts out drift seines about 1 hour before the slack of the tide and drifts them until the tide slacks, then pulls in the nets. A good catch is from 15 to 20 shad on a tide.

Mr. Lea prepares what fresh shad is needed for immediate cooking, and freezes the remainder in a deep freeze locker. These he keeps for as long as six months. When thawed, they may be baked or prepared in any way, but his favorite dish is fried.

Clean the shad, and split down the backbone; then cut into 6-inch pieces and gash each piece in several places. Put fish in salt water and soak for 1 hour. Drain and roll in corn meal with salt and pepper added. Put enough shortening into iron pan to almost cover fish. When it is hot, put in fish and fry to a golden brown.

R. D. Lea, Petersburg, Va.

BAKED ROE SHAD
Serves six to eight

In selecting a shad it is best to follow Mrs. Randolph's advice (*The Virginia Housewife,* 1831) and choose one weighing from 3½ to 4 pounds. If cooked in a very slow oven (250 degrees) for 4 to 5 hours, in either sweet milk or water, the bones will almost, if not entirely, disintegrate. A more modern method is to incase the fish in paper (see p. 120) or aluminum foil. Some prefer to struggle along with the bones, rather than to use the longer-cooking method. To illustrate both methods, I have chosen several variants. This is an old recipe using the long period.

Take a **four-pound shad**—preferably a roe shad, **with roe removed.** Grease the bottom of a covered roaster to prevent sticking. Place shad in roaster; lard inside and on top with **thin slices of breakfast bacon.** Pour into pan **cold water** sufficient to come well over sides of fish, but not on top. Season with **salt** and **pepper.** Heat on top of stove. Place roaster in oven and bake at 250 degrees for 5 hours. All water will be cooked out and the bones will be absorbed. Excellent.

J.Q.E., from The Episcopal Pantry, *Danville, Va.*

PLANKED SHAD
Serves six

Use 3½-lb. shad, or any white-fleshed fish. Clean and split fish down back. Heat plank very hot; lay fish upon it, skin-side down. Brush fish over with **Wesson oil;** sprinkle with **salt** and **pepper.** Bake 35 minutes in very hot oven. When cooked, pour over **4 tablespoons of melted butter** and the **juice of 1 lemon.**

Mrs. W. S. Beamon, from The Suffolk Cook Book, *Suffolk, Va.*

BAKED SHAD WITH EGG SAUCE
Serves six to eight

Clean one large roe shad (3½ to 4 pounds). Save roe. Stuff with the following:

2 cups bread crumbs	1 teaspoon salt
1 onion, chopped fine	½ teaspoon pepper
Butter, size of an egg	1 cup sherry
Extra butter, salt, pepper	

Mix the bread crumbs, onion, melted butter, and season with salt and pepper. Stuff shad. Place in a baking pan; sprinkle with dots of butter, pepper, and salt. Bake 1 hour, basting often with the sherry. Garnish with slices of lemon and serve with egg sauce.

Sauce

Butter, size of an egg (1 large tablespoon)	3 gills milk (1½ cups)
	Salt, pepper to taste
1 tablespoon flour	2 hard-boiled eggs

Melt the butter; stir in the flour and blend; add milk, salt, and pepper to taste. Cook until thick. Chop the eggs into small pieces and stir them into the sauce boat and serve with the baked shad.

Take the shad roe and save for cooking with eggs.

Mrs. S. S. Cadot, from A Book for Ye Cook, *Fredericksburg, Va.*

CHARLESTON BONELESS SHAD
Serves three to four

This is a method used all through "the low country, from the Santee to Port Royal." If prepared right the bones really dissolve. This is an old "receipt."

1¾ pound shad, cleaned	Chopped onion, fennel seed, mace
Cheese cloth	(if desired)
1 qt. water	Salt and pepper
1 tablespoon vinegar	Bacon strips

Place the cleaned shad in a large piece of cheese cloth for easy handling. Boil it very gently in the water to which the vinegar has been added. Add chopped onion and spices to water if desired. Boil 20 minutes; remove the shad and drain off water. Salt shad inside and out and sprinkle with pepper. Place one or two strips of bacon in fish; fold fish halves together, and place in a heavy roaster, the heavier the better. Place one or two strips of bacon on top of fish. Cover and bake in a 200 degree oven for five to six hours. Add the shad roe about 30 minutes before fish is done.

Uncover and place under broiler just long enough for fish to brown on top. Add more bacon if necessary to give a nice brown.

Kellinger Cotton, Goldsboro, N.C. (From the Henry Belk column, **News-Argus,** *Goldsboro, N.C.)*

STUFFING VARIANT
Serves six

This is a Virginia stuffing often used in Shad—3½ to 4-pound fish which has been salted, peppered, and rubbed well with soft butter:

½ cup melted butter
1 medium onion, minced
½ cup minced celery
1½ cups loaf bread crumbs
½ cup cracker crumbs
½ teaspoon salt
½ teaspoon pepper
¼ teaspoon poultry seasoning

⅛ teaspoon powdered marjoram
⅛ teaspoon rosemary
1 tablespoon Worcestershire sauce
½ cup chicken broth or sweet milk
Bacon strips
2 cups milk

Melt butter in deep skillet; stir in onion, celery, and simmer until soft; add crumbs and seasonings. Moisten with enough broth or milk to form light, moist mixture. Stuff fish and truss with cord. Gash back in four places and lay bacon strips on each gash. Pour 2 cups of milk into large roaster; place fish on rack in milk and bake 2 hours at 325 degrees. Garnish with lemon quarters and fresh parsley.

BAKED SHAD WITH ROE STUFFING
Serves six

1 large roe shad
2 cups water
2 tablespoons vinegar
½ cup chopped onions
½ cup butter
3 eggs, beaten

1 cup bread crumbs
Salt, pepper
2 extra cups water
½ cup lemon juice
2 tablespoons Worcestershire sauce

Boil roe in 2 cups water to which 2 tablespoons vinegar have been added. Remove skin and mash roe. Cook the onion and butter slowly, and add to the roe; add beaten eggs and bread crumbs. Salt and pepper to taste. Put the stuffing into the shad and truss. Bake thirty or forty minutes in 2 cups of water to which has been added the lemon juice and Worcestershire sauce. Baste.

Mrs. Harvey Moore, from Old North State Cook Book,
Charlotte, N.C.

LUZETTE'S SHAD WITHOUT BONES (*Baked in a Bag*)
Serves six

3 to 4 lb. shad
Large square cheese cloth
1 small chopped onion
2 qts. water
2 tablespoons vinegar
8 tablespoons melted butter

Salt and pepper to taste
1 large brown paper bag, greased
    well with vegetable shorten-
    ing
4 strips of bacon, optional

Place the shad in a large square of cheese cloth, sprinkle it with the chopped onion. Lower the fish into a large vessel with the water and vinegar. Gently boil the shad for 20 minutes. Lift the ends of the cloth gently, and remove shad. Generously coat the inside and outside of fish with the melted butter; sprinkle inside and out with salt and pepper. If desired, drape the bacon across the shad. Place in the greased paper bag. Place in a large covered roaster, cover, and bake at 250 degrees for 6 hours. This causes the bones to disintegrate.

Mrs. W. W. Brown, 2nd, Burlington, N.C.

BAKED ROCK FISH

This is an old Edenton recipe with modern temperature added. "Dress a Rock Fish and make gashes on both sides 2 inches apart. Sprinkle salt, black pepper, and flour on both sides of fish. Lay half-length strips of bacon 2 inches apart in bottom of baking pan. Sprinkle lightly with flour. Place fish in the pan on top of bacon, and then put bacon strips on each gash on top of the fish. Cut one medium onion over fish and into the pan. Pour 1 cup of water into pan. Put cover on pan and cook at 350 degrees for 20 minutes. Remove cover and cook until fish is brown. Add water as necessary to make gravy. Have Worcestershire sauce handy at the table as it adds greatly to the flavor." A 3-pound fish will serve four.

Mrs. W. B. Rosevear, Pembroke Hall, Edenton, N.C.

FILET DE SOLE A L'ORLY (*Flounder*)
Serves six

The sole, esteemed by the French as one of the finest fish (it comes from Mediterranean waters) is so similar in taste and texture to the flounder found in the Mexican Gulf, that long ago the Creoles of New Orleans gave the flounder the French name, and adapted the French ways of cooking it. The most famous of the original dishes adapted is Sole à l'Orly. The sole, or flounder, can also be fried in the same manner as any other fish fillet and served with a tartar or other sauce.

Buy 6 fillets of flounder with bones removed. Dip the fillets in milk into which an egg has been beaten (about 2 tablespoons of milk or more if desired). Roll generously in bread crumbs and fry in butter until tender and golden brown. Garnish with parsley and serve with tomato sauce as follows:

1 small can tomatoes (1 cup)	1 sprig thyme, minced
1 teaspoon butter	1 tablespoon butter
2 cups water	1 tablespoon flour
2 cloves garlic, minced	Salt, pepper
1 bay leaf, minced	

Put on the tomatoes to boil; add 1 teaspoon butter and water. Let boil 10 minutes; then add finely minced garlic, bay leaf and thyme. Boil until reduced slightly; then mash through sieve. Heat 1 tablespoon butter in saucepan; add 1 tablespoon flour. Stir until slightly browned; add tomato purée, and season highly with salt, pepper, etc. Stir until thickened. Always garnish with parsley when using this sauce.

From New Orleans Recipes, *by Mary Moore Bremer, New Orleans, La.*

ISLAND FISH DINNER
Serves six to eight

This Island dinner is an old original Roanoke Island (N.C.) recipe which is said to have been created before the Civil War. It is still a favorite meal of that section of North Carolina.

1 5-lb. (or larger) fish (Rock, tuna, or marlin)	Salt and pepper
8 medium boiled potatoes	1 cup hot bacon drippings
2 onions, peeled, chopped	
1 cup crisp bacon crumbs, or fried streak-of-fat, streak-of-lean meat	

Place the fish in a large vessel and cover with water. Boil gently until fish falls apart; drain off liquid. Boil the potatoes; peel while hot. Chop the onions. Fry out enough bacon to make 1 cup of crisp crumbled bits, or fry the streaked meat and chop it. Keep the bacon drippings hot.

To serve: Allow each person to mash a potato (or 2 potatoes) on his serving plate. Mash a chunk of fish over the mashed potatoes. Sprinkle chopped onions and bacon over the fish. Salt and pepper each serving to taste. Pour some of the hot bacon drippings over top of all.

NOTE: The secret of the success of this dish is to keep everything as hot as possible. It may be arranged on one large heated platter.

Mrs. R. O. Stoutenburg, Manteo, N.C.

TO FRY PAN FISH

Pan fish are fish small enough to be fried or cooked whole. These are usually dressed, rubbed with salt and pepper, and rolled in corn meal or flour and fried in either lard or butter. Perch, stream trout, etc., are fried whole. In many Southern sections, particularly along the coast, pan fish are rolled in corn meal and fried in fat deep enough for the fish to turn itself. In others the fish is dipped in flour, then in egg mixture, rolled in bread crumbs, and fried in deep fat. Still a third method is to roll the fish in seasoned flour and fry in shallow butter or lard. Fish fillets are fried in various ways like pan fish.

GRADY CRISCO'S PEPPER FISH

Dress any frying fish in fillets, whole, or steaks. Lay fish on waxed paper; take a pepper shaker and shake on the pepper until the entire surface is black with pepper. Turn fish and pepper other side. Lay fish in hot shallow grease and fry brown. Fish is salted after putting in pan. The pepper gives a distinctive flavor.

Grady Crisco, Charlotte, N.C.

NOTE: Mr. Crisco doesn't say, but the fish could be rolled in corn meal before peppering.—M. B.

SALMON SCRAMBLE
Serves four

Grady Crisco is a skilled fisherman and a pro-amateur chef on fishing trips. Just in case, he always carries along canned salmon. This is his favorite breakfast dish before fishing begins.

6 to 8 slices bacon
1 tall can pink salmon, drained

6 to 8 eggs
Salt, pepper

Fry out the bacon in heavy skillet. Remove bacon; pour off all but 1 or 2 tablespoons grease. Dump in can of salmon; stir until heated. Break in the eggs and scramble all until eggs are cooked. Season with salt and pepper. Serve with the bacon and plenty of hot coffee.

Grady Crisco, Charlotte, N.C.

MOLDED SALMON
Serves six

This tempting dish doubles as a luncheon entrée or a salad.

2 cups salmon
½ tablespoon salt
1½ tablespoons sugar
½ tablespoon flour
1 teaspoon mustard
Cayenne pepper

2 egg yolks
¾ cup water
¼ cup vinegar
2 tablespoons butter, scant
¾ tablespoon gelatin, soaked in 2
    tablespoons cold water

Rinse salmon and separate into flakes. Combine dry ingredients, egg yolks, water, and vinegar. Cook in double boiler, stirring constantly until mixture thickens. Add butter and soaked gelatin. Mix with salmon. Pour into a greased mold and chill. Serve with lettuce and mayonnaise. Chopped cucumbers and cream may be added to the mayonnaise. [The same proportions of any fish flakes, crab meat or lobster may be used in this to replace salmon.—M. B.]

Mrs. Luther Evans, from The Alexandria Woman's Club Cook Book,
Alexandria, Va.

CLAMS FORESTIERE *(Stuffed Clams)*
Serves four

According to the eminent contributor of this recipe, "Whether littlenecks or cherrystones (clams), they are marvelously versatile. They are delicious when accented with a simple squeeze of lemon, a blend of lemon and soy sauce, or a traditional tomato cocktail sauce. But, to some tastes, they are best of all when stuffed."

24 fresh cherrystone or littleneck
    clams (see note)
¼ cup water
3 slices bacon, cut into small
    squares
½ lb. mushrooms, caps and stems,
    finely minced
1½ tablespoons finely chopped
    shallots
⅛ lb. cheese, Gruyère or Swiss
2 tablespoons finely chopped pars-
    ley

1 small clove garlic, finely minced
¾ cup fine, fresh bread crumbs
½ cup finely minced heart of cel-
    ery
3 tablespoons dry white wine
1 egg yolk
Salt and freshly ground black
    pepper
½ cup grated Parmesan cheese
Lemon wedges

Preheat oven to 400 degrees.

1. Wash the clams well and place them in a kettle. Add the water, cover, and steam until clams open. Remove the clams and let them cool. Take the clams from the shells and chop them on a flat surface. There should be about ⅔ cup chopped clams. Set aside. Reserve the 24 clam shells.

2. Cook the bacon in a large saucepan until bits are crisp. Remove the bacon bits and reserve. Pour off all but 2 tablespoons of fat from the saucepan. Add the mushrooms to the fat in the saucepan. Add the shallots and cook, stirring, until mushrooms are wilted. Let cool.

3. Chop the cheese into tiny cubes. Add the cheese, parsley, garlic, bread crumbs, celery, wine, and egg yolk to the mushroom mixture. Add salt and pepper (to taste). Combine the chopped bacon and chopped clams with the other ingredients.

4. Fill the reserved clam shells with the mixture and sprinkle with Parmesan cheese. Bake 10 minutes or longer until filling is bubbly and golden brown. Serve hot with lemon wedges.

NOTE: Canned clams may also be used in this recipe. Drain the clams and measure out approximately ⅔ cup. Proceed with the recipe, starting with step 2. In lieu of the reserved clam shells, spoon the mixture into scallop shells or small ramekins and bake.

Craig Claiborne, Food News Editor, The New York Times, N.Y.

MRS. BARKLEY'S BAKED CRAB MEAT
Serves four

This baked crab meat recipe was given to Mrs. Harris W. Rankin, Paducah, Kentucky, by the daughter-in-law of Vice-President Barkley. The recipe is "from the table" of the first Mrs. Alben W. Barkley, a native of Paducah.

1 lb. crab meat, well-picked to remove bits of shell	Juice ½ lemon
4 tablespoons butter	1 teaspoon Worcestershire sauce
2 tablespoons flour	1 teaspoon chopped parsley
1½ cups milk	Dash cayenne pepper
¼ teaspoon salt	¼ teaspoon celery salt
Juice 1 small onion	2 eggs, well-beaten
	Bread crumbs

Make a thick cream sauce as follows:

Melt butter in heavy saucepan; blend in flour; add milk and stir constantly until thickened. Season with salt, onion, lemon juice, Worcestershire sauce, parsley, cayenne, and celery salt. Add the unbeaten eggs and stir, but do not let boil. Mix well with the crab meat. Place in a glass baking dish. Cover with buttered bread crumbs and bake for 30 to 40 minutes in a medium (350-degree) oven.

Mrs. David M. Barkley, Washington, D.C.

COMMONWEALTH DEVILED CLAMS WITH SHRIMP AND CRAB MEAT
Serves four to six

The historic Commonwealth Club of Virginia has added many honors to the tradition of Southern cuisine. W. W. Lamond, Jr., in giving me several of the Club's memorable dishes, says that he has chosen the recipes which the members think are the outstanding ones associated with the Club. This is one from the group.

1 pt. fresh cherrystone clams, chopped fine
½ cup chopped shrimp
½ cup chopped crab meat
2 tablespoons Lea and Perrins sauce

1 dash Tabasco sauce
1 tablespoon prepared mustard
Roux consisting of 2 tablespoons butter with flour (about 2 tablespoons) to thicken
Cracker crumbs

Combine all ingredients, except roux, in a heavy frying pan over a hot flame; bring to cooking heat and add roux; stir until mixture is smooth and thick (about the consistency of a heavy oatmeal; add clam juice if the mixture is too dry); cook approximately 15 minutes. Heap mixture into clean clam shells; pat cracker crumbs on lightly and bake in a 350-degree oven until brown.

W. W. Lamond, Jr., Manager, The Commonwealth Club, Richmond, Va.

SAVANNAH DEVILED CRABS
Serves four

1 lb. crab meat
2 boiled eggs, mashed
1 cup bread crumbs
2 tablespoons Worcestershire sauce

1 teaspoon Tabasco sauce
½ teaspoon salt
2 tablespoons Durkee's dressing
2 tablespoons mayonnaise
Melted butter

Mix crab meat with mashed boiled eggs; add ½ cup of bread crumbs, Worcestershire sauce, Tabasco sauce, salt, dressing, and mayonnaise. Put into shells; cover crabs with ½ cup crumbs and melted butter. Bake 15 minutes in a moderate oven (350 degrees).

Mrs. Robert W. Groves, Savannah, Ga.

HOT CRAB MEAT SALAD (*Baked*)
Serves six

1 lb. crab meat
4 eggs, hard-cooked, mashed
4 slices bread, crusts trimmed off
1 cup milk
1 small onion, chopped

1 cup mayonnaise
1 teaspoon Worcestershire sauce
Dash Tabasco
Salt and pepper to taste
1 cup buttered bread crumbs

Mix the crab meat and mashed eggs together. Soak the bread in the milk; then squeeze out; crumble the bread. Stir in remaining ingredients except buttered bread crumbs. Pour into a buttered 1½-quart casserole. Sprinkle with the bread crumbs. Bake, uncovered, in a 350-degree oven for 30 minutes.

Mrs. C. L. Haney, Raleigh, N.C.

CRAB MEAT MORNAY
Serves eight to ten

½ cup butter
1 small bunch green onions, chopped
½ cup finely chopped parsley
2 tablespoons flour
1 pt. light cream (half-and-half)

½ lb. Swiss cheese, grated
1 lb. lump crab meat
2 tablespoons sherry
Salt to taste
Cayenne pepper to taste

Heat the butter in a heavy skillet, and sauté the onions and parsley until onions are a golden color. Blend in the flour; stir in the cream. Add the cheese and simmer slowly until the cheese is melted. Gently fold in the crab meat; reheat. Add the sherry, and season to taste with salt and pepper. Serve this in a chafing dish as an hors d'oeuvre, with Melba toast rounds, or in patty shells for a main course luncheon dish.

This recipe may be doubled.

Mrs. Charles Ivey Williamson, Mobile, Ala.

SAUTEED SOFT-SHELL CRABS
Serves four

12 soft-shell crabs, cleaned
Flour
Butter
Salt and pepper

Parsley, chopped
Lemon wedges
Tartar sauce

Clean the crabs; pat them dry. Dredge them lightly all over in flour (shake in a paper bag with the flour). In a skillet heat enough butter to about ½ inch in pan. When butter is bubbling hot, put in enough crabs so pan will not be crowded. Fry until golden brown on one side; turn and brown other side. Season lightly with salt and pepper to taste as they cook. Remove crabs to a hot platter and serve with some of the pan juices over them. Sprinkle with chopped parsley and serve with lemon wedges and tartar sauce.

Dr. R. O. Stoutenburg, Manteo, N.C.

YBOR CITY DEVILED CRABS
Thirty-six large croquettes

This is the original recipe for Ybor City Deviled Crabs as sold by vendors on the streets of Tampa's Latin Quarter.

Croquette dough:

3 1-lb. loaves of stale (dry) American bread

1 loaf (1-lb.) Cuban bread (dry), ground fine and sifted

1 level tablespoon paprika

1 teaspoon salt

Remove the crust from the three American loaves of bread; discard crust. Soak the bread 15 minutes in water to cover. Drain off the water, and squeeze bread until almost dry. Add the sifted bread gradually to the soaked bread until mixture is the consistency of dough. Add paprika and salt; mix thoroughly. Form dough into a ball and refrigerate for approximately two hours.

Crab Meat Filling

5 tablespoons vegetable oil
3 small onions, finely chopped
½ red or green bell pepper, finely chopped
4 cloves garlic, mashed or minced
1 level teaspoon crushed red hot peppers (Italian style)

2 bay leaves
½ teaspoon sugar
1 teaspoon salt
1 6-oz. can tomato paste
1 lb. fresh crab meat (claws) picked over, shredded

Heat oil. In the oil slowly fry the onions, bell pepper, garlic, and crushed hot pepper for 15 minutes. Add bay leaves, sugar, salt, and tomato paste. Stir; then cover and simmer 15 minutes on low heat. Add the crab meat and simmer 10 minutes. Uncover; pour into a bowl, and refrigerate for two hours.

To make the crab croquettes:

Take about 3 tablespoons of the chilled croquette dough and make a small ball. Press the ball out in the palm of the hand, and place in the center 1 tablespoon of the chilled crab meat mixture. Seal the dough around the crab meat and form it into a boat shaped croquette with two pointed ends. Dip each croquette into the following mixtures:

Egg Mixture

2 eggs, well beaten
½ cup milk
¼ teaspoon salt
Black pepper to taste

Coating

1 cup cracker crumbs
½ cup flour

Mix the above. After croquettes have been dipped into the egg mixture, roll them in coating mixture. Dip the croquettes back into the egg mixture and again roll them in the cracker crumb mixture. Lay them on a platter and chill for 2 hours. Fry them in deep fat heated to 375 degrees (in a basket) until golden brown. Fry only a few at a time. Drain on absorbent paper. Serve hot.

As a party hors d'oeuvre, these may be made in miniature size, using about 1 tablespoon of dough for each croquette to ⅓ tablespoon of crab meat. The number of croquettes depends on size.

The Columbia Restaurants, Tampa, Fla.

DEVILED IMPERIAL CRAB IN SHELLS OR AVOCADOS
Serves four

1 lb. backfin lump crab meat
1 tablespoon Durkee's dressing
3 tablespoons mayonnaise
1 tablespoon Worcestershire sauce
1 cup coarsely rolled cracker crumbs

1 tablespoon paprika
3 tablespoons melted butter
4 crab shells or crab shell baking ramekins, or 2 large avocados, halved

Combine the crab meat, dressing, mayonnaise, and Worcestershire sauce lightly, so as not to break the crab meat lumps; mound them into the crab shells or avocado halves. Combine the cracker crumbs with the paprika; pat the crumbs on top of the crab meat. Pour the melted butter over. In a shallow pan pour ¼-inch water. Place the shells or avocados in the pan. Bake at 350 to 375 degrees for 15 minutes. If crumbs are not browned, turn heat to broiling for a few seconds to brown the tops. The crab meat should be hot for serving.

W. W. Lamond, Jr., Manager, The Commonwealth Club,
Richmond, Va.

CRAB CAKES—EASTERN SHORE, VIRGINIA
Eight medium cakes

1 lb. crab meat
½ cup bread crumbs
½ cup melted butter
1 teaspoon prepared mustard

2 eggs
Salt and pepper
Carnation milk

Mix crab meat and other ingredients. Add enough whole Carnation milk to form soft patties. Fry in deep fat.

Mrs. H. P. McKay, Onancock, Va.

LOBSTER SOUFFLE
Serves six

3 tablespoons butter
3 tablespoons flour
1 cup light cream
4 egg yolks, well beaten
½ teaspoon salt
⅛ teaspoon cayenne pepper
¾ teaspoon dry mustard

2 cups finely diced cooked lobster meat
2 teaspoons lime juice, or lemon juice
4 egg whites, beaten stiff
¼ teaspoon cream of tartar
Buttered soufflé dish

Melt the butter in a saucepan; stir in the flour and cook, stirring, until a smooth roux is made; slowly add the cream and cook, stirring constantly, until a medium thick sauce is made. Beat the egg yolks until thick and lemon colored. Add a little of the hot sauce to the egg yolks, and then turn the egg yolks into the sauce. Stir in salt, pepper, and mustard. Mix the lobster meat with the lime juice, and add it to the sauce. Beat the egg whites until foamy; then add the cream of tartar and beat until egg whites are stiff but not dry. Fold the egg whites into the crab mixture. Butter the bottom of a 1½-quart soufflé dish; pour the mixture in dish and set the dish in a large pan of hot water (about 2½ inches of water). Bake in a 325-degree oven for 1½ hours, or until the top is browned and the soufflé puffy. Serve at once.

VARIATION: To make a shrimp or crab meat soufflé, substitute 2 cups of finely diced cooked shrimp or 2 cups flaked crab meat for the lobster.

Mrs. Eula Wilson, Greenwich, Conn.

LOBSTER THERMIDOR, ARNAUD'S
Serves one

Lobster Thermidor is said to have been named in honor of Napoleon when a member of the illustrious family was visiting in the United States. This recipe was originated by the late Count Arnaud Cazenave, founder of Arnaud's Restaurant.

1 lobster, boiled and split	½ cup mushrooms, chopped
½ lb. butter	¼ cup green onions, chopped
1 cup flour	Butter
2 cups milk	Grated cheese
3 egg yolks, beaten	

Boil and split lobster. Make a cream sauce by melting butter and mixing in flour. Blend; add milk and mix well over a slow fire. Cool; add beaten egg yolks. Chop mushrooms and onions together, and sauté in butter with the lobster meat (picked from the shell). Add lobster mixture to the cream sauce. Refill shell; sprinkle with grated cheese. Place in the oven to brown.

From Mrs. Germaine Wells, Arnaud's Restaurant, New Orleans, La.

GRAY FOX LOBSTER A LA NEWBURG
Serves four

1 lb. Maine lobster meat	1 cup cream
Sherry	Season to taste with salt, cayenne, etc.
½ cup butter	
¼ cup flour	2 egg yolks
1 cup milk	

Soak the flaked lobster meat in good sherry for 1 hour. Then add to sauce made as follows: Melt butter in saucepan, stir in flour and blend. Add milk and cream and stir until it thickens. Just before serving blend with the two egg yolks (beaten). After eggs have been added do not boil, but keep mixture hot. Serve in any manner desired. [This is often served in casserole, or may be served on toast points.—M. B.]

Charles F. Herman, Proprietor, The Gray Fox Restaurant, Pinehurst, N.C.

WILLIAMSBURG INN SEA FOOD NEWBURG
Serves six

1 tablespoon butter	2 cups milk
2 tablespoons flour	

Place butter in top of double boiler; heat until melted. Stir in the flour; gradually add the milk and cook, stirring, until sauce is thick; set aside.

½ pound butter	½ pound cooked, shelled shrimp
1 pint fresh shelled oysters	½ cup sherry wine
½ pound crab meat	½ teaspoon paprika

Place the butter in a saucepan over medium heat; when melted, stir in the sea foods and sauté, stirring gently, for 5 minutes. Blend the white sauce, wine, and paprika into the sea food. Heat thoroughly. Serve as desired, over toast, on crackers, over rice, etc.

By special permission, John D. Green, Vice-President, Williamsburg Restoration, Williamsburg, Va.

STUFFED CRAWFISH
Serves two

2 1-lb. crawfish
½ cup butter
1 tablespoon olive oil
1 cup flour
1 teaspoon salt (or to taste)
1½ cups milk

5 dashes Tabasco sauce (more if desired)
1 egg, beaten
¾ cup white wine
Tomato catchup
Parmesan cheese

Remove the meat from the crawfish and dice; reserve shells. Make a cream sauce: in a skillet heat the butter and olive oil; stir in the flour and salt to make a smooth roux (paste). Stir in the milk and Tabasco; simmer, stirring constantly, until the sauce has thickened; stir in the beaten egg and wine; simmer until sauce thickens again to a thick consistency. Add the diced crawfish, and then place mixture into the crawfish shells. Garnish the top of each with a light coating of tomato catchup and sprinkle tops with grated Parmesan cheese. Bake in a 400-degree oven for 20 minutes.

The Columbia Restaurants, Tampa, Fla.

CURRIED CRAWFISH
Serves four

4 crawfish tails
1½ cups white sauce
½ teaspoon curry powder
1 teaspoon onion juice
Few grains cayenne
2 teaspoons Key lime juice

Salt, pepper to taste
1 cup shredded fresh coconut
1 cup chopped cashew nuts
½ cup mashed, crisp chicharrone
2 hard-boiled eggs, chopped
½ cup any good chutney

Boil crawfish; then remove meat from tails and cut into cubes. Heat white sauce and add curry powder, onion juice, cayenne, lime, salt, pepper, and crawfish. Serve on rice. Surround with small dishes containing other ingredients so that each person may make his own mixture. (Chicharrone is made of pork skin fried until free of grease and very crisp. They can be purchased in most grocery stores.)

From The Key West Cook Book, Key West, Fla.

ABOUT OYSTERS A LA ROCKEFELLER

Perhaps we should explain why we have not given a recipe for Oysters à la Rockefeller. This is one secret Antoine's Restaurant has never divulged. When the request was made for the recipe, Roy Alciatore gave the same reply that the Alciatore family has been giving for years, "We have a policy—." He did give us permission to use the only 10 recipes ever given (at that time) for publication, and a general list of the ingredients in the Oysters Rockefeller.

Oysters à la Rockefeller is a dish originated by Jules Alciatore (father of Roy Alciatore, the present owner) patterned after Snails Bourguignon which Antoine Alciatore, the founder, served at the first Antoine's in the 1850's. The snails for this dish were imported into New Orleans from Burgundy. As the years passed New Orleans became aware of the fine Gulf oysters and Antoine began serving them in place of the snails. A variation for the sauce was created to suit the succulent oyster. The new dish (oysters resting on a pan of heated salt rock) instantly became a success. Simultaneously, John D. Rockefeller became known as the richest man in the United States, and in his honor the rich dish was named "in the manner" of Rockefeller.

The mystery of the dish's ingredients (there are 18 in the sauce) and the ceremony accompanying its serving have added much to its prestige. Each order goes to the table tagged with a card bearing the number of times it has been served—an idea borrowed from the Tour d'Argent in Paris, where a serving number card is attached to each order of the famous Pressed Duck. Among the known ingredients in the sauce for Oysters à la Rockefeller are: chopped celery, minced shallots, minced fresh chervil, minced fresh tarragon leaves, crumbs of dry bread, Tabasco, and herbsaint—instead of absinthe. (Herbsaint is a cordial made of Southern herbs, mostly anise.) These ingredients are pounded in a mortar; then forced through a sieve. One tablespoon of the mixture is placed on each pair of oysters, resting twin-fashion on a half shell in their own juices. The shells are embedded in rock salt in a pan, six shells to each serving. The whole is whisked into the oven to heat—piping hot. No, spinach is not mentioned.

OYSTERS A LA CASINO
Serves four to six

2 doz. oysters on half-shell	1½ teaspoons butter
¼ seeded green pepper	1½ teaspoons Roquefort cheese
½ medium onion	1 teaspoon Worcestershire sauce
4 slices bacon	

Chop green pepper and onion very fine and combine. Cut the bacon slices with scissors into thirds crosswise and in halves lengthwise. Melt butter with

Roquefort cheese and add Worcestershire sauce. Place piece of bacon on each oyster; then spread each with a little of the green pepper and onion mixture; top all with a little of the butter and cheese mixture dropped from the point of a spoon. Arrange oysters on shells on the broiler rack. Place under a medium broiler heat and broil from 10 to 15 minutes, or until oysters are tender.

From Recipes Tested and Tried, *by Anne Young White and
Nola Nance Oliver, Natchez, Miss.*

THE OYSTER LOAF ("*La Mediatrice*")

In New Orleans there is an oyster loaf known as the "Peace-Maker," said to have been so named because the late-homing husband often brought a hot loaf to soothe his irate wife. The New Orleans loaf is filled with fried oysters, served with wedges of lemon or lemon juice. E. Smith, in her *Compleat Housewife* (London, 1739), describes this loaf as "Penny Loaves" filled with stewed oysters, garnished with lemon, or "you may fry the oysters in batter to garnish the loaves." Miss Smith's loaves were toasted in a pound of butter, the oysters seasoned with "a blade of mace, a little white pepper, a little horseradish and a piece of lean bacon, and half a lemon." Mary Moore Bremer gives this version of "La Mediatrice": "Nothing in New Orleans is better known than the 'Peace-Maker' and it is a foolish husband who does not rely on it in case of need. In the old days when a man told his wife he was detained on business, the peace-maker was a good thing; and even now, when Santa Claus and these excuses have been laid on the shelf, at one o'clock in the morning 'La Mediatrice' remains a good thing.

"The top crust of a loaf of French bread is cut off and the inside taken out, leaving a long, boat-like affair; this is buttered and slipped into the oven to toast. It is then filled with about 2 dozen fried oysters and the top, which has been buttered and toasted, replaced. It keeps hot for a long time and is fine."

From New Orleans Recipes, *by Mary Moore Bremer, New Orleans, La.*

COMMONWEALTH BROILED OYSTERS, HAM, AND CORN CAKES UNDER GLASS BELL
Serves about five

This recherché combination of pan-broiled oysters, broiled ham, and corn cakes served under a glass bell (*sous cloche*) is Southern food supreme. To serve this, a stack of six corn cakes (4 inches in diameter) is topped with a slice of Smithfield ham large enough to cover the corn cakes; then the oysters are heaped on. The oysters and ham on the cakes are covered *immediately* with a glass bell and served *immediately* with a generous portion of melted butter on the side. Sometimes extra corn cakes are served with syrup or molasses.

The Pan-Broiled Oysters

1 qt. oysters
2 teaspoons butter
1 tablespoon Worcestershire sauce

½ teaspoon celery salt
Paprika to color

Drain the liquor from oysters, place in heavy iron skillet with 2 teaspoons butter; add Lea and Perrins sauce and celery salt. Sauté oysters until done, turning them often. Just before finishing, color with paprika. Drain before serving.

To Broil the Ham

Use best grade of cooked Smithfield ham; cut thin slices with most of the fat removed. Broil or grill until hot. A portion consists of enough ham to cover a 4-inch corn cake.

Serve on Commonwealth Club Corn Cakes (see p. 306).

W. W. Lamond, Jr., Manager, The Commonwealth Club, Richmond, Va.

GLENWOOD OYSTERS FARCIS
Serves six

Glenwood Plantation House, on Louisiana Highway 29 at Napoleonville, Louisiana, is the ancestral estate of Edward P. Munson's family, and dates back to the early 1800's. In recent years Mr. and Mrs. Munson opened the house to guests. Here, with servants whose ancestors served for generations, the Munsons extend hospitality and set before their guests a lavish Southern table. This is one of a group of original Glenwood recipes.

3 doz. oysters
½ cup butter
1 cup shallots, chopped very fine
1 cup parsley, chopped very fine
½ cup celery, chopped very fine

1 tablespoon flour
½ cup dried bread crumbs
Salt, cayenne to taste
1 egg, beaten
6 large oyster shells

Heat the oysters until plump; drain and cut them into small pieces. Melt the butter, and in it cook the shallots, parsley, and celery. Blend in the flour, oysters, and bread crumbs. Remove from fire; season to taste. Mix in the beaten egg. When mixture has cooled, fill the shells; cover with bread crumbs, and dot with butter. Just before serving, run shells into oven to brown and serve immediately while very hot.

Mrs. Edward P. Munson, Glenwood Plantation House, Napoleonville, La.

OYSTERS A LA DRISCOLL
Serves six

This recipe is named for Charles Driscoll, former columnist for the *New York Tribune*. Since the proportions in the original recipe were not measured, this recipe has been worked out for 6. The seasonings may be changed "according to taste."

About 3 doz. Bull Bay oysters (select oysters)	1 tablespoon Worcestershire sauce
3 tablespoons fresh butter	1 tablespoon tomato catchup
1 cup minced tender, green onions	Salt and pepper to taste
½ cup crisp, minced celery	1 cup bread crumbs, extra crumbs
¼ cup chow-chow pickle	1 egg, beaten
½ cup fresh, minced parsley	6 cleaned, heated oyster shells
	Extra butter

Mince the oysters. Heat the butter in a skillet; stir in the oysters along with the minced onions, celery, pickle, and parsley. Add the Worcestershire, catchup, salt, and pepper. Cook for a few minutes over medium-low heat. Gradually stir in the bread crumbs until the mixture is thickened, stirring constantly. The mixture should be reasonably moist. Remove from the fire; stir in the beaten egg. Stuff into the shells. Sprinkle with bread crumbs and dot with butter. Brown in a 375-degree oven just long enough to brown the crumbs.

Walter L. Shaffer, Proprietor, Henry's,
Charleston, S.C.

OYSTERS "JOHNNY REB"
Serves six

In The Old Southern Tea Room in Vicksburg, Mississippi, Mrs. McKay carries on the tradition of delicious Southern cooking and cordial hospitality, serving distinctive Southern dishes in an atmosphere of unusual charm. The following is an original recipe served in the Tea Room:

1 qt. select oysters	1 teaspoon lemon juice
1 tablespoon finely minced parsley	1¼ cups cracker crumbs (not cracker meal)
2 tablespoons shallots, finely chopped	3 cups top milk
¼ teaspoon salt	6 tablespoons butter
Red pepper to taste	

Butter shallow casserole. Put layer of oysters in bottom of dish. Sprinkle parsley, shallots, salt, pepper, and a little lemon juice. Sprinkle cracker crumbs, then another layer of oysters, parsley, shallots, and crumbs. Just before baking, pour milk over contents of casserole, letting milk mix with oysters. Dot with thin slices of butter. Bake ½ hour in a slow oven (325 degrees).

Mrs. W. I. McKay, Owner, The Old Southern Tea Room, Vicksburg, Miss.

SOUTHERN FRIED OYSTERS
Serves four to six

1 qt. large oysters, drained
Cracker meal
3 eggs mixed with ½ cup water

1 teaspoon salt
2 tablespoons baking powder

Drain oysters; coat them with cracker meal. Dip each oyster in egg and water mixture. Have another dish of cracker meal mixed with the salt and baking powder. Dip oysters in this and fry in deep fat about 5 minutes. (These are light and wonderful.)

Mrs. Robert W. Groves, Savannah, Ga.

CURRIED OYSTERS
Serves six to eight

Curried oysters is an elegant buffet dish. Serve from a chafing dish on toast points or over rice.

2 tablespoons butter
½ teaspoon onion juice
1 tablespoon flour
2 teaspoons curry powder
½ cup oyster liquor drained from
    oysters to be used in dish

½ cup milk
1 small teaspoon salt
1 qt. oysters

Heat the butter and onion juice in a skillet. Stir in the flour and curry powder. When the mixture bubbles, stir in the oyster liquor, milk, and salt. When the sauce is smooth and begins to boil, add the oysters and cook until they are plump and curled around the edges, about 4 minutes. Keep hot until serving time.

NOTE: This recipe may be doubled.

Mrs. Nathaniel L. Ball, Jr., from
Charleston Receipts, *The Junior League of Charleston, Inc., S.C.*

MRS. HARDEE'S ESCALLOPED OYSTERS
Serves six

This is the recipe we have used many years for escalloped oysters. For 1 qt. of oysters, toast about 14 slices of bread, slowly in the oven, then let bread get cold and hard. Roll with rolling pin until finely crumbed. Use 1 stick of butter or a little more, and add 1 tablespoon sherry, sprinkled over top layer of oysters. Mrs. Hardee's recipe (below) calls for no liquid.

"1 qt. oysters, drain and pat dry. In a baking dish arrange a layer of oysters alternating with a layer of **browned bread crumbs.** Sprinkle each layer of oysters with **salt** and **pepper** and **pieces of butter.** Continue this process until all are used. The top layer should be crumbs dotted generously with butter. The secret of this good dish is to be sure that the oysters are dry and to use plenty of butter as no other liquid is used. Bake in moderate oven (350 degrees) until oysters are tender." [About 25 minutes.—M. B.]

Mrs. A. K. Hardee, Graham, N.C., from Soup to Nuts, *Burlington, N.C.*

SHRIMP-DEVILED EGG CASSEROLE
Serves six

6 deviled eggs, stuffed halves
1½ lbs. boiled, prepared shrimp
1 small can mushrooms

2 cups cheese sauce
Salt, pepper to taste

Line a baking dish with a layer of deviled egg halves, then a layer of shrimp, then one of sliced mushrooms. Over all pour a cheese sauce seasoned to taste with salt and pepper. Bake in 400-degree oven until brown. [To make cheese sauce, add cheese to any standard white sauce.—M. B.]

Mrs. Lewis F. Schenck, Christ Church, Macon, Ga.

SHRIMP CREOLE FRICASSEE, HOMESTEAD
Serves eight

2 lbs. fresh Jumbo shrimp
4 teaspoons shortening (right)
4 tablespoons flour
2 tablespoons chopped onion
2 tablespoons chopped green peppers
1 tablespoon chopped celery
1 cup chopped, peeled tomatoes

¾ cup sauterne
2 cups clam broth
Salt, pepper to taste
½ teaspoon chopped garlic
1 sprig thyme
2 sprigs parsley, chopped
2 bay leaves
Rice baked in ring mold

Peel shrimp; remove black vein, and wash well. Make a roux with shortening and flour. Add onions, green peppers, celery, which have been fried to a golden brown. Add tomatoes, shrimp, wine, and clam broth and all seasonings. Simmer 20 minutes. Season again to taste. Serve in a ring mold of baked rice. [See p. 286.]

Frank H. Briggs, General Manager, The Homestead, Hot Springs, Va.

ANTOINE'S SHRIMP MARINIERE
Serves six

This luncheon dish has remained a general favorite at Antoine's for almost a century. It is a rich "à la king" type of a dish, highly seasoned and cooked with "oyster water" or the broth from shrimp. Chicken or fish stock may be substituted.

1½ lbs. raw shrimp
2 cups white wine
2 minced shallots or ¼ cup minced onion
1 cup oyster water, fish stock or chicken broth
2 tablespoons butter

2 tablespoons flour
¾ cup shrimp stock
Juice ¼ lemon
2 egg yolks, beaten
½ cup light cream
Toast points
1 tablespoon chopped parsley

Shell shrimp and remove the black vein. Combine wine, shallots (or onion), and oyster water; bring to the boiling point and add shrimp. Simmer 15 minutes. Melt the butter and blend in the flour making a thick roux. Add ¾ cup of stock the shrimp have been cooked in. Cook, stirring constantly until mixture thickens. Add shrimp; cook 10 minutes. Add lemon juice. Beat egg yolks; add cream. Add hot shrimp mixture, stirring constantly. Serve in ramekins or on toast. Garnish with parsley.

From Antoine's Restaurant, New Orleans, La. Special permission,
Roy Alciatore, Proprietor

WRIGHTSVILLE BEACH STEAMED SHRIMP

This tender steamed shrimp with lobster-like succulence is an Eastern Coast delicacy which is easy to prepare and fun to serve. Mrs. Foley goes each day (when at her Wrightsville cottage) to the Sound to get the shrimp fresh from the shrimp boats.

Select 1 pound of fresh shrimp for each person. Don't worry, this is not too much! Rinse shrimp and place them in the top section of a shrimp-steamer (a vessel with double-boiler sections, the top having holes to allow steam to escape upward) in alternate layers with salt, pepper, Tabasco sauce, or any other preferred seasoning sprinkled over each layer. In the bottom section, pour 1 pint of vinegar to each 4 pounds of shrimp. Let vinegar boil and steam until shrimp are pink—about 15 to 20 minutes. Take out shrimp and put into a large covered dish like a tureen. In the center of each person's plate place a hot bowl of melted butter. Give each person a "bib" and let him peel his own shrimp at the table, and dunk them in the butter. With this Mrs. Foley serves a green salad and hard French bread.

Mrs. E. H. Foley, Burlington and Wrightsville Beach, N.C.

SHRIMP CASSEROLE
Serves four to six

Katharine Mundy, owner of The Columns, divides her time between her guest house and her gift shop. This is one of The Columns' favorite dishes.

1 lb. cooked, cleaned shrimp
1 cup mushrooms
1 cup blanched almonds
Grated Parmesan cheese
3 cups medium-thick cream sauce
    to which

½ cup sherry wine has been
    added
Cracker crumbs

Grease a casserole or baking dish. Fill in layers by putting shrimp first, then mushrooms, almonds, and last, the cream sauce. Repeat until ingredients have all been used. Cover top with cracker crumbs and grated cheese. Bake in a 350-degree oven for 30 minutes. Serve hot.

Katharine A. Mundy, The Columns, Lynchburg, Va.

SHRIMP WITH ARTICHOKE HEARTS IN CHEESE SAUCE
Serves six

Line a baking dish with alternate layers of 1 lb. cooked shrimp and 6 sliced artichoke hearts, and over it pour sauce as follows:

Cheese Sauce

2 tablespoons butter
½ teaspoon paprika
½ pt. cream

½ pt. milk
3 tablespoons flour
¼ teaspoon cayenne pepper

Melt butter and mix in the flour and seasonings to a smooth paste. Then add ½ pint of cream and ½ pint sweet milk. Cook slowly until well blended and thickened; then add:

1 tablespoon tomato catchup
1 tablespoon lemon juice
1 cup New York cheese, grated

1 tablespoon Worcestershire sauce
3 tablespoons real sherry wine

Blend all together and pour over shrimp and artichoke hearts. Add grated cheese to the top and heat thoroughly in oven. Serve with French bread and green salad.

Miss Nonie Morgan, Woman's Editor, The Macon News, Macon, Ga.

SHRIMP CURRY
Serves eight to ten

The coconut milk makes this curry extra special. This is a recipe worked out by various experiments.

1½ pts. coconut milk, (2 cups fresh or frozen fresh coconut in 1 qt. boiling water)
4 tablespoons butter
1 cup chopped onion
1 medium-sized apple, peeled, chopped
1 stalk tender celery, chopped
1½ cups beef consommé, or stock
4 tablespoons flour mixed with cold water to make thin paste

1 tablespoon curry powder (more or less to suit taste)
Dash or two of Tabasco
3 to 4 tablespoons catchup to give rich color
Salt and pepper to taste
½ cup sherry wine
2½ to 3 lbs. cooked, deveined shrimp
Fluffy cooked rice

Bowls of chutney, chopped peanuts, almonds, grated coconut, pickles, etc.

Prepare the coconut milk several hours before making curry. Place grated coconut in deep vessel and pour the boiling water over it. Let stand until water cools. Pour all into a cheese cloth, saving every drop of liquid and let drain thoroughly. Then press all liquid out of coconut. Discard coconut and save the milk for the curry. Place butter in large heavy skillet and heat, add chopped vegetables and consommé. Simmer until vegetables are tender, and almost dry. Now stir in the coconut milk and heat to boiling. Add the flour mixture slowly and when it begins to thicken add seasonings, catchup, and the wine. Simmer until a velvety consistency and add the shrimp. If coconut milk is not available, milk may be used. Serve over rice with bowls of nuts and relishes to accompany.

EMPIRE SHRIMP CREOLE
Serves six to eight

9 to 12 cooked, deveined shrimp per person
4 strips bacon
2 cups chopped onion
1 clove garlic, minced
⅔ cup chopped green pepper
1½ cups chopped celery
2 tablespoons flour
4 cups canned tomatoes

1 tablespoon Worcestershire sauce
1 teaspoon soy sauce
3 to 4 dashes of Tabasco
1 bay leaf
4 tablespoons tomato catchup
1 tablespoon brown sugar
Salt and pepper to taste
1 cup fluffy cooked rice per serving

Cook and prepare the shrimp and refrigerate. Fry out bacon in a large heavy skillet until crisp. Remove bacon and drain on absorbent paper. In the bacon drippings, sauté the chopped vegetables until the onions are soft. Push vegetables aside and stir in the flour to make a roux (paste). Add all ingredients except the rice and bacon. Bring to boil, reduce heat, and simmer until sauce thickens. Reseason with salt and pepper and remove the bay leaf. Ten to 15 minutes before serving add shrimp and allow to heat (do not boil) more than one or two minutes. Serve at once over hot rice. Crumble bacon over sauce.

Taylor Carr, Manager of The Gulf Works, St. Petersburg Beach, Fla.

QUICK SHRIMP AND CRAB MEAT CREOLE
Serves eight to ten

1 lb. cooked shrimp
1 lb. crab meat
2 tablespoons butter
Buttered and toasted bread crumbs (2 to 3 cups)
1 can condensed cream of mushroom soup

2 teaspoons tomato catchup
1 tablespoon Worcestershire sauce
$\frac{1}{16}$ teaspoon cayenne pepper
$\frac{1}{2}$ teaspoon salt

In a large casserole (1½- to 2-quart size) or glass baking dish, alternate layers of shrimp, butter, bread crumbs, and crab meat until all has been used. Mix the soup with remaining ingredients; pour over the sea food and crumbs. Top with a layer of buttered crumbs. Bake in a 350-degree oven for 20 to 30 minutes, or until hot and crumbs have browned.

Miss Caroline L. Porcher, from Charleston Receipts, *The Junior League of Charleston, Inc., S.C.*

SHRIMP PIE
Serves four

Shrimp Pie is one of Charleston's most cherished dishes. Mrs. Laurens' is an original recipe.

2 cups prepared shrimp, cooked
2 large slices bread soaked in 2 cups of very hot sweet milk
½ teaspoon salt

1 tablespoon butter
1 wine glass sherry
⅛ teaspoon nutmeg
Dash red pepper

Mix the bread and milk with seasonings. Add the shrimp and bake in a buttered baking dish 1 hour at 400 degrees.

Mrs. John Laurens, Charleston, S.C.

SCALLOPS IN SHELLS
Serves four

1 lb. fresh scallops
1 cup water
¾ teaspoon salt
1½ tablespoons onions, minced

¾ cup (3 oz.) mushrooms, sliced thin
⅛ cup butter
4 large scallop shells or baking dish

Soak scallops for 1 hour in cold, salted water. Wash and dry. Parboil, covered, in water 6 minutes. Remove, cut in desired pieces, sprinkle with salt, cover again and let stand. Fry the minced onion and mushrooms in butter for 4 or 5 minutes. Cover and set aside. In a separate pan make the following sauce:

⅛ cup butter
2 tablespoons flour
¾ cup hot milk
1 cup scallop juice (or substitute milk)
½ teaspoon salt
Dash pepper
Grated lemon rind to taste

⅛ cup grated Parmesan cheese, optional
⅛ cup sherry
¼ teaspoon lemon juice
1 tablespoon melted butter
Bread crumbs
Parsley
Lemon wedges

Melt butter; add flour; stir in carefully the hot milk and scallop juice. Add salt, pepper, lemon rind, and cheese. Allow to simmer gently, stirring to prevent burning. When mixture has consistency of cream sauce, add sherry, allow to come to boil again; add lemon juice. Take ½ of the sauce and mix into the scallops and mushrooms. Put into scallop shells. Cover each shell with some of the remaining sauce. Sprinkle buttered crumbs on top. Bake in 375-degree oven for 15 to 20 minutes or until crumbs are browned. Garnish with parsley and lemon wedges.

VARIATION: To make a scallop curry, use the recipe as above, but marinate the scallops in 1 cup of sherry for 1 hour before parboiling. Add ¼ teaspoon of curry powder instead of the ⅛ cup of sherry to the sauce. Put into shells and continue as for the first recipe.

Mrs. Stockton Terry, from Favorite Foods of Virginians, *Lynchburg, Va.*

FROGS' LEGS POULETTE
Serves eight

8 prs. frogs' legs
3 tablespoons fat
3 tablespoons flour

1 cup chicken stock
½ teaspoon salt
Pepper

2 egg yolks
½ cup cream
½ teaspoon lemon juice

½ teaspoon chopped parsley
Toast

Clean and separate the frogs' legs; cook slowly 10 minutes in fat, being careful not to brown. Remove legs; add flour to fat. When fat and flour have been blended, add chicken stock. Stir until sauce boils; add salt, pepper, and frogs' legs. Simmer until tender. Add egg yolks lightly beaten with the cream; stir until hot, but do not let boil. Add lemon juice and parsley and serve on toast.

Mrs. D. C. Plemmons, from Soup to Nuts, *Burlington, N.C.*

FROG LEGS SUPREME
Serves two

These are deep-fried.

1 lb. fresh frog legs (4 sets)
Juice of ½ lemon
Pinch each of salt, white pepper, and garlic powder
4 strips of bacon

2 eggs, beaten
1 cup flour
Cole slaw, minced fruit, and cocktail sauce for garnish

Season the frog legs with the lemon juice, salt, pepper, and garlic powder. Wrap each set of legs in a strip of bacon and secure tightly with a toothpick.

Dip the legs into the beaten eggs, then roll them in flour.

In a deep fryer, heat the shortening to 300 degrees. Fry the frog legs for 15 minutes. Serve them hot on warm plates. Garnish the plates with cole slaw, minced fruit, and cocktail sauce.

Columbia Restaurants, Tampa, Fla.

FROGS' LEGS SAUTE

Use fresh frogs' legs if possible (otherwise fresh-frozen); clean thoroughly and marinate in **milk** or **cream** seasoned with salt before the frogs' legs are submerged. Leave in cream 30 minutes. Remove legs from cream, and roll thoroughly in flour and sauté in heavy frying pan until done and golden brown. Serve immediately with Tartar Sauce. [See p. 441.]

H. L. Thomas, General Manager, Grove Park Inn, Asheville, N.C.

TORTUGA RUBIA (*Pink Turtle*)
Serves four

This is a famous Key West dish.

4 medium-thin slices turtle steak
Salt and pepper to taste
Flour to roll turtle in
Cooking fat

1 clove garlic
2 tablespoons sherry mixed with
2 cups sour cream
Paprika to color sauce

Roll the turtle in flour seasoned with salt and pepper. Brown in heavy iron skillet in any good cooking fat in which a finely chopped clove of garlic has been sautéed. Pour over the turtle the sour cream and sherry and add enough paprika to make the sauce a rosy pink. Bake in a 300-degree oven until very tender. Button mushrooms may be added to sauce if desired. Serve with fluffy rice—to applause. [For rice, see p. 286.]

From The Key West Cook Book, *Key West, Fla.*

YELLOW TURTLE EGGS (*Omelet*)
Serves four

1 lb. turtle eggs
Salt, pepper to taste

3 tablespoons butter

Remove membrane from eggs very carefully. Place in colander and wash. Salt and pepper eggs; allow them to stand 10 minutes. Melt butter in frying pan until it bubbles. Reduce heat to a simmer and wait. (If eggs are put into fat which is too hot, they will burst.) Handle the eggs carefully; slide them into the frying pan, and cook slowly for 20 minutes. Remove from skillet and serve as you would an omelet, but do not fold over. Serve with grits and American cheese. These eggs can be obtained only when the turtle kraals are stocked; and then rarely. [There are land turtles, "cooters" and "gophers," hard-shell inland turtles, and soft-shell turtles in Florida. The recipes here are for sea turtle.—M. B.]

From The Key West Cook Book, *Key West, Fla.*

7. Meats

GROVE PARK BEEF A LA MODE OR POT ROAST

Beef à la Mode, cooked by a method handed down from French ancestors to the Creoles of the Deep South, is one of the most famous of the traditional Southern dishes. This recipe from Grove Park Inn is for 12 pounds, but it may easily be scaled down to suit individual needs.

Use 2 pieces (2 roasts) of round beef weighing about 6 pounds each. Season with salt and pepper; place in a vessel with a spoonful (tablespoon) of fat or butter and roast until nice and brown all over. Then sprinkle with 2 tablespoons of flour and cook until flour is brown. Add 1 quart of boiling water and a pint of claret; add small onions, small carrots, celery, and tomatoes. Cover and boil in the oven. Remove the carrots when soft and continue cooking the beef until well done. Slice beef thin and serve carrots and onions around for garnish. Carrots and onions must be thoroughly done, sliced crosswise when served. Serve with hot gravy.

H. L. Thomas, General Manager, Grove Park Inn, Asheville, N.C.

YORKSHIRE PUDDING FOR ROAST BEEF DINNERS
Serves four

1 egg
5 tablespoons sifted flour
½ teaspoon salt

1 cup milk
6 tablespoons hot beef drippings

Thoroughly beat egg and add 2 tablespoons of sifted flour; mix. Add 3 tablespoons sifted flour and the salt, mixing well. Add milk and thoroughly combine with an egg beater. Into a deep pie dish pour 6 tablespoons of hot beef drippings. Now place the dish in the oven under the roast and let the beef drippings become sizzling hot. Beat the pudding mixture again and pour it into the sizzling fat. Place on shelf in oven under roast and cook about 50 minutes in hot oven (425–450 degrees). Will come out with a brown crispy outside and soft center.

From Cooking Round the World and at Home, *Eureka Springs, Ark.*

PRIME RIB ROAST OF BEEF
Serves six

This recipe is for the thermometer-timed roast, but may be roasted by ordinary timing. The standard chart is 15 minutes per pound for rare roast; 20 to 25 minutes for medium-rare; 27 to 30 minutes for well-done.

3-rib beef roast, with ribs left in	Salt, pepper
2 cloves garlic, split lengthwise	Flour

Cut gashes in fat part of roast and insert garlic cloves. Season with salt and pepper rubbed into meat. Sear quickly in hot pan on top of stove to seal in juices. Make a small incision through the skin of the meat and insert thermometer so that the bulb reaches the center of the roast. Put into uncovered roasting pan and roast in 300 to 325-degree oven until thermometer reaches 140 degrees. Serve at once with pan drippings, or make a brown gravy by adding 1 tablespoon of flour to each tablespoon of fat. Stir until flour browns; add salt and pepper to taste and 1 cup of hot water to each tablespoon of fat and flour. Simmer until it thickens; serve in separate gravy boat.

Mrs. Bryan Grubb, Columbia, S.C.

BEEF TENDERLOIN WITH BEARNAISE SAUCE (*Filet de Boeuf a la Bearnaise*)
Serves eight

1 whole beef tenderloin, about 6 lbs.	1 bay leaf
2 tablespoons butter	1 wine glass sherry, or Madeira if possible
1 large onion	1 clove garlic

Have butcher lard the meat, or if possible thread at 1-inch intervals with needle and shoestring larding, or cut slits in meat and stuff lard into incisions. Spread with the butter.

Chop onion and garlic and strew in bottom of open roasting pan. Place roast on mixture and pour over it wine in which bay leaf has been steeping. Remove bay leaf. Set oven at 400 degrees; preheat. When temperature reaches 350 degrees put in meat and bake for 35 minutes for rare, or from 45 to 50 for medium done. Slice fillet and serve with the following:

Bearnaise Sauce

1 cup tarragon vinegar	¼ teaspoon dry mustard
2 tablespoons chopped shallots or young onions	3 egg yolks
	Salt, pepper

1 teaspoon Worcestershire sauce
3 tablespoons melted butter
Chopped parsley if desired

6 tablespoons tomato purée, optional

Combine vinegar, shallots or onions, and mustard in a saucepan. Simmer until vinegar has reduced to less than half. Cool, beat in 3 egg yolks, and season with salt, pepper, and Worcestershire sauce. Return to heat and pour butter in slowly, beating constantly. Strain and whip until it has a creamy consistency like mayonnaise. Chopped parsley and/or tomato purée may be added to the hot sauce if desired.

Mrs. Harper Barnes, Arlington, Va.

FILLET OF BEEF WELLINGTON

This elegant roast is simple in preparation, since the meat may be partially prepared the day before serving.

4 to 5 lb. whole fillet of beef
½ cup butter, softened
Salt and black pepper
½ cup each of diced celery, onion, and carrots
1½ teaspoons fresh or dried rosemary
⅓ cup chopped parsley
½ cup dry red wine
Pâté de fois gras, homemade or canned (see recipe)
Plain pie pastry (double a recipe for a 9-inch shell)

1 egg yolk, beaten with 1 teaspoon water
1 cup veal or chicken stock (canned or made with bouillon cubes or instant bouillon)
3 tablespoons extra pâté de fois gras
1 truffle, sliced, or ½ cup sliced mushrooms

Wipe the meat dry; spread the butter over the entire surface. Sprinkle lightly with salt and pepper. In a shallow roasting pan, spread the vegetables and seasonings; sprinkle the wine over. Preheat the oven to 450 degrees. Lay the meat over the vegetables and roast for around 50 minutes, turning the meat several times. Remove the roast from oven and cool completely. It may be stored in refrigerator overnight. Reserve the pan drippings in the pan. When the meat is cold, cover the entire surface with a coating of pâté de fois gras (coating should be about ¼-inch thick). Roll out the pastry about ⅛-inch thick; wrap the pastry around the beef; trim the dough and seal it with moistened fingertips. Brush the pastry crust with the beaten egg mixture. Preheat oven to 425 degrees. Prick the pastry in a few places to vent the steam. Lay the beef on a baking sheet and bake about 20 to 30 minutes, or until the crust is well browned and done through. Transfer the fillet to a heated platter and keep warm.

In the roasting pan in which fillet was roasted, add the veal or chicken stock, the extra pâté de fois gras, truffles or mushrooms. Simmer on top of stove for about 15 minutes. Keep hot.

Slice the meat with a very sharp knife into desired thickness. Serve with the hot sauce.

NOTE: The fillet crust may be decorated with cutouts of pastry (leaves, flowers, fruits, etc.) or extra strips may be crisscrossed to make a lattice effect.

Always serve the meat on heated plates.

STEAKS

Southern steaks are cooked in many ways; broiled, steamed "country style" in brown gravy; planked, grilled, made into Hamburgers, "Cheeseburgers," etc. In fact, steak—in the South—now means what it does in other regions; it is cooked according to individual taste. The set rules are few, for much depends upon the grade and cut of the beef.

PORTERHOUSE STEAK WITH SPECIAL SAUCE
Serves six

2¼ lbs. porterhouse steak, 1½ inches thick
1 clove garlic, chopped
3 tablespoons butter
1 tablespoon tomato sauce
1 tablespoon prepared mustard

1 tablespoon drained, fresh horse-radish
Few drops Worcestershire sauce
Salt, pepper to taste
Paprika to taste

Broil steak 4 inches below flame or on charcoal grill. While it cooks, heat a serving platter and rub with garlic. Spread evenly with the remaining ingredients, letting them melt and blend. When steak is done, place on platter, turning once to cover with sauce.

Mrs. Sawnie Aldredge, Jr., from The Junior League of Dallas Cook Book, *Dallas, Tex.*

MARINADE FOR FILET MIGNON

The fillet, noisette, or any cut of tenderloin is often marinated before cooking. This marinade gives extra flavor. It is enough for 6 fillets.

¼ cup salad oil
Juice 1 lemon
¾ cup tarragon vinegar
1 bay leaf

1 onion, chopped
1 clove garlic, chopped
1 tablespoon parsley, minced
Pinch thyme

Prepare steaks for cooking. Marinate for 1 hour, turning often. Drain; wipe dry, and sauté in hot butter 6 minutes, allowing 3 minutes to each side. Serve with Espagnole (brown gravy) sauce with mushrooms or truffles; or with any desired sauce (see "Sauces").

FILLET STEAK SALTEADO
Serves two

1 lb. beef tenderloin fillet, diced into bite-size cubes
½ cup olive oil
2 garlic cloves, chopped
1 Spanish onion, chopped
2 raw potatoes, peeled, diced
Deep fat

2 Spanish sausages (Chorizos)
15 mushroom buttons
1 teaspoon salt (or salt to taste)
White pepper to taste
½ cup red wine
Green peas and parsley for garnish

In a baking dish or large skillet sauté garlic, onion, and green pepper in olive oil until tender. Add tenderloin and cook until meat has almost reached desired state of doneness.

In a small skillet, sauté mushrooms in butter until tender.

In a separate deep fryer, fry the potato in deep fat for 10 minutes at 350 degrees, or until brown.

Add the Spanish sausages, mushrooms, salt, pepper, and potatoes to the meat. Add the wine, stir well, and cook until thoroughly heated. Serve hot. Garnish the dish with green peas and a sprig of parsley.

The Columbia Restaurants, Tampa, Fla.

BEEF STEAK WITH PEPPERCORN SAUCE (*Filet de Boeuf a la Poivrade*)
Serves two

This is a French steak with butter and peppercorn sauce that is now widely served. The recipe was obtained by Mr. Switzer from New Orleans. Any size steak may be used, allowing approximately one pound of steak per serving.

1 2-lb. steak, cut 1¼ to 1½ inches thick (broiled as desired)
¼ cup peppercorns (more if desired)

4 to 6 tablespoons of butter (according to size and thickness of steak)

"Prepare the steak for broiling (in oven or on outside grill). In the meantime, break the peppercorns with a mortar and pestle, not grinding them to a powder, but leaving the pieces large enough so that each bit will be a distinct 'bite.' Melt the butter (you have to judge by quantities of the steak and persons to be served). Just before serving, pour the hot butter over the peppercorns. Serve the sauce over the hot steak. The sauce is better with a rare steak."

Joseph Switzer, Cleveland, Ohio

MARYLAND PLANKED STEAK WITH STUFFED TOMATOES

Pan-broil steak a few minutes, time depending on thickness and how well done it is wanted. Preheat [oak] plank. Place steak on plank. Prepare mashed potatoes with a great deal of butter; milk, seasoning, and the yolk of 1 egg. Stuff tomato for each person [see Vegetables for variants], and have ready cooked carrots or peas, or any vegetable which may be cut into small pieces. Pipe potatoes with a large pastry tube, outlining plank. Place tomatoes on the plank wherever they fit in best. Pipe tomatoes with potato mixture and make "nests" of other vegetables. Run into oven until all is hot and potatoes are just golden brown. Decorate with parsley; put plank on tray or platter and serve.

Mrs. N. C. Powell, Baltimore, Md., from The Monticello Cook Book,
Charlottesville, Va.

PLAIN CHARCOAL LONDON BROIL (*Flank Steak*)
Serves four

2 lbs. flank steak, cut about 1-inch thick
1 teaspoon salt
1 tablespoon ground black pepper

4 tablespoons softened butter
Sprigs of parsley

Sprinkle the meat with salt and pepper. Place on a grill over hot coals, 2 inches from the firebed. Broil 3½ minutes on each side, turning meat only once. Remove to slicing board; spread top of meat with the butter. Cut with a sharp knife in deeply diagonal thin slices. If the meat is not cut at a deep diagonal angle, the meat will not be tender.

VARIATION: Meat may be marinated in any beef marinade for an hour before broiling. Proceed as above, but, if an oily marinade is used, the butter is not necessary.

FLANK STEAK WITH MARINADE (*Charcoal*)
Serves four

2 lbs. flank steak, cut in diagonal
   1-inch strips
½ cup red or white wine
⅓ cup soy sauce
1 clove garlic, chopped

½ cup chopped onions
1 tablespoon lime juice
2 tablespoons brown sugar
1½ teaspoons salt
Pepper to taste

Cut the meat as directed. Make a marinade of the remaining ingredients. Pour over the meat and refrigerate 24 hours. Drain; reserve the marinade. Grill quickly over hot coals, turning once. Allow 2 minutes for each side. Baste often with the marinade.

Mrs. James H. Anderson, San Bernardino, Calif.

MATAMBRE (*Stuffed Flank Steak*)
Serves six to eight

This is a one-dish meal, and well worth the preparation.

2 flank steaks (about 1½ to 2
   lbs.), butterflied
1 cup frozen mixed vegetables,
   defrosted
½ cup finely chopped onion
¼ cup each of chopped green
   pepper and pimiento
2 teaspoons finely minced chili
   pepper

1 garlic clove, crushed
1 teaspoon salt
1 cup beef broth
1 stalk celery, sliced crosswise
1 carrot, peeled, sliced crosswise
1 medium onion, peeled, sliced
1 clove garlic, chopped

Preheat oven to 350 degrees. Pound the butterflied steaks as thin as possible. Trim off any excess fat, and cut the edges straight so that the finished steaks will be roughly square, about 12 × 12 inches. Lay the steaks side by side, overlapping the edges an inch or two, so that when they are rolled they will hold together as one steak.

Combine the mixed vegetables, chopped onion, green pepper, pimiento, chili pepper, crushed garlic, and salt; mix thoroughly. Spread the mixture evenly over the steaks, covering the entire surface. Roll the two steaks up, jelly-roll fashion, as tight as possible. Tie the roll securely every two inches. Use five lengths of string and cut off the extra string after tying each knot. Put the roll in a shallow casserole with a cover; add the beef broth, sliced celery, carrot, onion, and chopped garlic. Cover the casserole and braise for two hours, basting several times with the broth. Remove the Matambre from the casserole and place it on a platter about fifteen minutes before serving time to let it "rest." This will make the meat firmer and the carving easier.

It is important that the meat be sliced with a very sharp knife, and carved neatly so that the vegetables will remain intact. Do not remove the strings before carving. Furnish the server with the usual fork and a flat serving piece, like a pie knife, to transfer the meat slices to plates.

This may be served plain or with a chili sauce. (See "Sauces" for Mrs. McKenzie's Chili Sauce, p. 450.)

Mrs. O. Ray McKenzie, Burlington, N.C.

BROILED STEAK WITH STOCKADE SPECIAL DIP
Serves four to six

This steak sauce is said to have been originated by a private in the army who upon the submission of the following recipe was released from a term in the stockade to a kitchen detail. The officer who released the "chef" was then a colonel in the U.S. Army. He is the contributor of the recipe. The sauce is good for any steak strips, rare preferred.

The Sauce

1 lb. butter
Juice of 3 lemons
½ cup Worcestershire sauce
1 teaspoon Kitchen Bouquet
1 clove garlic, minced

1 tablespoon freshly ground pepper
1½ teaspoons dry mustard
¼ teaspoon Tabasco sauce

Mix all ingredients in the top of a double boiler. Heat over boiling water, but do not boil the sauce. Serve as soon as thoroughly heated as a dip for steak. Makes 2 cups of sauce.

The Steak

Prepare a 3-inch thick sirloin steak. Broil to desired state (rare, medium, or well done) over charcoal. Slice in ½-inch strips. Dip strips in the hot sauce.

Harry W. Thompson, Memphis, Tennessee, from A Taste of Texas, compiled for Neiman-Marcus, Dallas, Tex. (Random House)

BARBECUE BEEF RIBS (*Long Ribs*)
Serves four to six

3 lbs. long ribs of beef, cut into 3 to 4-rib sections
1 teaspoon salt
2 cups barbecue sauce (see Sauces), more if necessary

½ green pepper, sliced lengthwise into strips (optional)

Rub the salt into the ribs. Heat a heavy roasting pan (with cover) on top of the stove. Preheat oven to 350 degrees. Quickly sear the ribs on top of the stove. With rib side up, pour ½ the barbecue sauce over. Cover the pan and place it in the oven. Allow ribs to bake covered for 35 minutes. Remove cover and turn ribs. Bake for around 2 hours, basting every 15 minutes with remaining sauce and the pan drippings. When meat has baked 1 hour, stir in the pepper strips. If meat becomes too dry, add more than the 2 cups of sauce, or water. Meat is done when it is fork tender and well browned.

NOTE: The ribs may be barbecued over charcoal. Rub ribs with the salt and place them on a grill about 3 inches from coals to sear. Raise the grill (or remove them from direct heat) to 5 inches above coals. Baste ribs with small amounts of sauce every 10 minutes, turning ribs often. When ribs are fork tender, remove and serve.

Alfred G. Lea, St. Petersburg, Fla.

BEEF BURGUNDY
Serves four to six

2 lbs. beef chuck, cut into 1 to 1½-inch cubes
2 cups Burgundy
2 tablespoons salad oil
1 large onion, sliced thin
1 bay leaf
½ teaspoon each of dried thyme and oregano

1 tablespoon Worcestershire sauce
1 cup beef bouillon
2 tablespoons tomato catchup
1 teaspoon salt
Pepper to taste

Place the cubed meat in a bowl; pour the wine over and marinate for 3 to 4 hours in refrigerator. Drain off marinade and reserve. Heat the salad oil and brown the meat on all sides in the oil. Pour meat into a casserole with cover; add remaining ingredients and wine marinade. Cover and bake at 325 degrees for about 3 hours, or until meat is tender. If dish becomes too dry, add warmed bouillon.

VARIATION: Small peeled potatoes, little onions, and quartered carrots may be added 1 hour before meat is done. Add extra bouillon to cook the vegetables. The sauce may be thickened with 1 tablespoon flour mixed with a little water.

Mrs. H. H. Lea, Spray, N.C.

BEEF FONDUE BOURGUIGNON
Serves four to six

The South owes the Swiss credit for this simple yet delicious dish.

Chafing dish or heatproof dish over alcohol lamp (or an electric fry pan)
2 lbs. sirloin steak, 1½ inches thick
1½ cups cooking oil
Salt and ground black pepper

Wooden skewers (bamboo)—Do not use metal skewers or forks
Any desired meat sauces, or mustards, dressings, etc., in bowls

Heat the oil in a heatproof dish, such as chafing dish, etc. The oil should be bubbling hot. Cut the meat into 1½-inch cubes. Skewer the cubes, and let each guest cook his own meat to desired doneness. Have salt and pepper mill along with meat sauces on the table, having each sauce in a separate bowl. Let guests season meat and dip into desired sauce or sauces. Have forks on hand for dipping meat into sauces.

NOTE: Serve with baked potato, tossed green salad, and French bread.

Alfred G. Lea, St. Petersburg, Fla.

BEEF STROGANOFF
Serves two to four

This is a surprisingly easy, quick to prepare, company dish.

1 lb. sirloin steak, sliced paper thin
4 tablespoons butter
1 medium onion, chopped
1 cup sliced mushrooms, fresh or canned

Butter
Nutmeg to taste, use generously
Salt, pepper to taste
1 cup sour cream, warmed
Kitchen Bouquet, optional

Slowly sauté the onion in the butter until tender in a large skillet. Increase heat and quickly sauté the beef. It should be rare on the inside.

In a separate saucepan, sauté the mushrooms in butter. Season to taste with a generous amount of nutmeg, and salt and pepper.

Add the mushrooms to the beef and onions. Stir in the heated sour cream. Taste for seasoning; correct. If desired, add a few drops of Kitchen Bouquet for color and flavor. Heat, but do not boil. Serve over buttered noodles or rice.

Mrs. Leslie E. Phillabaum, Chapel Hill, N.C.

SKILLET MEDLEY
Serves six

Other vegetables or seasonings may be added to this "quickie" one-dish meal.

1 lb. ground chuck
3 tablespoons soy sauce
2 large onions, peeled, cut in lengthwise sections
2 cups green cabbage, cut into strips
1 cup celery cut on bias, Chinese fashion

3 medium-size potatoes
2 medium-size green peppers
1 No. 2½ can tomatoes
1 teaspoon sugar
1 tablespoon Worcestershire sauce
2 tablespoons cognac
1 can beef consommé

In a heavy skillet sear the meat over high heat until meat is grey. Stir in the soy sauce. Add all ingredients except consommé. Stir mixture; add enough consommé to cover the vegetables. Cover the pan and allow to simmer around 30 minutes, or until vegetables are tender. Serve over cooked rice, noodles, or on toasted buns.

Mrs. William G. Vetterlein, Tucson, Ariz.

GENGHIS KHAN
Serves six

Named for the famous warrior Ghengis Khan, this Mongolian dish is a mixture of three meats and vegetables. It may be cooked on flat bars in the oriental style, or on a griddle or grill. This is the charcoal method on a grill.

Garlic flavored oil, or salad oil
6 serving pieces of chicken
1 lb. lean pork, cut into strips 2 inches long and ½-inch thick
1½ lbs. sirloin beef steak, cut ½-inch thick; cut into strips 2 inches long

3 large green peppers, cut into strips ½-inch wide
2 large onions, peeled, cut into rings ⅙-inch thick
Mushroom caps, as many as desired

Have fire coals burned to the grey stage. With a pastry brush paint the grill with garlic oil. The grill should be close to the coals, not more than 3 inches. Lay on the pieces of chicken first and cook until they lack about 10 minutes of being done. Turn the chicken often. Then place the pork strips on; cook in same manner for around 10 minutes or until well done. Last, about 3 minutes before serving, lay on the steak strips; cook them 3 minutes for rare, longer if desired for well done.

In the meantime, paint another section of the grill with oil, and spread out the vegetables on it. Cook them for around 10 minutes, or until tender.

Serve each person a piece of chicken and portions of the pork, beef, and vegetables. As the meat is taken from the grill, dip each piece in Genghis Khan Sauce. (See "Sauces," p. 445.)

Alfred J. Brown, Lincolnton, N.C.

SOUTHERN SUKIYAKI
Serves six to eight

¼ cup salad oil
1 lb. sirloin steak, cut into very thin strips
2 medium-size onions, sliced thin
2 bunches of green onions (with the tops), cut into 3-inch length pieces
3 stalks celery, cut into thin strips, then into 3-inch sections
1 can bamboo shoots, drained
4 small carrots, scraped, cut into thin strips

1½ cups beef consommé or bouillon
½ cup soy sauce
½ small green cabbage head, chopped
½ lb. fresh mushrooms, sliced (or canned mushrooms, drained)
3 tablespoons sugar
Hot steamed rice

Heat the oil in a large skillet; quickly brown the beef in the oil. Remove meat to a warm platter and keep warm. Add the onions, green onions, celery, bamboo shoots, and carrots to the skillet; add ¾ cup of the consommé, the soy sauce, and the sugar. Cook for about 8 minutes over medium-high heat; reduce heat; add the remaining consommé and the cabbage. Simmer for about 7 minutes, add the mushrooms and cook 3 minutes longer. Do not overcook, because the vegetables should be a little crisp and the meat rare to medium rare. Return the meat to skillet; stir until heated. Serve over hot rice.

Betty J. Albertson, from Treasured Recipes, *by The Helen Freeman Guild, Miles Methodist Church, Norfolk, Va.*

ORIENTAL HASH
Serves six to eight

This is a wonderful dish for church suppers, "teen-agers," buffets, a one-dish family meal.

1 lb. ground round steak
1 No. 2 can tomatoes
2 onions, minced
2 green peppers, minced
1 can kernel corn (2 cups)
Salt, pepper to taste
1 8-oz. pkg. fine noodles

1 6-oz. can Spanish sauce
1 can pitted ripe olives and juice
  (1 cup)
1 cup of grated cheese
Cracker crumbs
Dots of butter

Sear steak in a hot pan. Add tomatoes, onions, corn, peppers, salt, and pepper. Cook 10 minutes, stirring frequently. Cook noodles in boiling salted water; drain. Put noodles in flat baking dish and pour meat mixture over them. Cover with Spanish sauce and juice from ripe olives. Dot top with olives. Sprinkle with grated cheese, cracker crumbs (not cracker meal), and a few dots of butter. Bake 1 hour in moderate oven covering at first and then remove top and allow to brown. Serve hot.

Mrs. H. P. McKay, Onancock, Va.

HAMBURGERS WALTER TROHAN
Serves four to six

This recipe is by Walter Trohan, chief of the Washington Bureau of the *Chicago Tribune*, and, to quote Morrison Wood, "one of the Capitol's best-known correspondents as well as gourmets." This hamburger has since been listed on the Bismarck Hotel, Chicago, menu. It has been widely copied throughout the South as well as in other regions.

1 lb. ground round steak
1 small can Smithfield Ham
  Spread, or deviled ham
Salt

Pepper
Roquefort or bleu cheese
Dry red wine
Butter

Blend 1 small can of Smithfield Ham Spread or deviled ham with 1 pound of fresh-ground steak. Add very little salt, and freshly ground pepper to taste.

Cut pieces of Roquefort or bleu cheese into 1¼ inch squares about ½ inch thick. Mold hamburgers around these squares, and put them in a crock. Cover the hamburgers with dry American red wine, and let them stand, covered, in the refrigerator for about 3 hours. At the end of marinating time, put a little butter into the skillet, with a little of the marinade, and pan broil the hamburgers to taste (rare, medium, or well done). Remove to a hot plate; add a little more butter and marinade to the pan; let boil up, and pour the sauce over the hamburgers.

From With a Jug of Wine, *by Morrison Wood* (Farrar, Straus, and Company, N.Y.)

MUSCATROLLI
Serves eight

Each year in Nashville, The Society of Amateur Chefs has access to and full use of a modern packing house, where they annually prepare one of Nashville's exclusive old favorites—around Christmas time—Beef Round, the preliminary preparations of which entail several weeks of pickling before it is cooked.

Another dish which has been a consistent favorite of the club is Muscatrolli, developed by A. C. Gibson from an old Italian dish of the same name but much more highly seasoned. Mr. Gibson has given us his recipe. [Similar to "Johnny Marzetti" or "Johnny Morzette."]

1 lb. shell macaroni
1 lb. ground lean beef
1 lb. onions chopped fine
2 tablespoons butter
Salt, pepper, garlic salt

1 lb. mild cheese (Velveeta), cut small
1 No. 1 can tomato purée
1 No. 1 can mushrooms

Sauté beef and onions in butter. Cook macaroni in usual way; add cheese to sauté and stir until melted. Add tomato purée; add mushrooms; include liquor from mushrooms; and add salt, pepper, and garlic salt to taste. Mix with macaroni; stir constantly until well mixed. Serve with hot sliced and buttered Vienna or rye bread. Better if allowed to cool and then reheated before serving. Cold Burgundy adds finishing touch.

A. C. Gibson, Menu Director, Society of Amateur Chefs, Nashville, Tenn.

LASAGNE MARY LOUISE
Serves ten to twelve

2 cups chopped onions
¼ teaspoon garlic powder, or 2 garlic cloves, minced
1½ tablespoons olive oil
1½ lbs. ground beef (lean beef)
2 tablespoons oregano
1 teaspoon Italian seasoning

½ oz. pickling spice, tied in double thickness cheese cloth
2 No. 2 cans tomatoes
2 small cans tomato sauce
1 6-oz. can tomato paste
1 cup undrained mushrooms
Salt and pepper to taste

Pepperoni sausage (about 30 thin slices from roll size of twenty-five cent piece in diameter)

1 standard size package lasagne noodles

12 slices Provolone cheese

12 slices Mozzarella cheese

1 3-oz. can grated Parmesan cheese

1 3-oz. can Romano cheese

2 2-qt. casseroles or 1 4-qt. casserole

In a large skillet, sauté the onions and garlic powder (or cloves) in the olive oil until golden brown. Add the ground beef and stir until meat turns grey. Sprinkle 1 tablespoon of oregano over beef and stir until meat browns well. Transfer meat mixture to a large saucepan; add remaining ingredients except the noodles and cheeses. Cover the saucepan and simmer for 1 hour or more depending on how much time you have.

In the meantime, boil the noodles according to package directions. In each of the 2-qt. casseroles (or 1 large one), pour enough beef sauce to cover the bottom. Then alternate layers of noodles and cheeses (like noodles, Provolone, Mozzarella, grated cheeses), making two layers of noodles and cheeses. Pour the remaining sauce over the noodles and cheeses. Bake in a 375- to 400-degree oven until the mixture is bubbling hot. Just before taking from oven, sprinkle with grated cheeses. Serve hot.

NOTE: Lasagne may be frozen after the sauce is poured over. Allow casserole to cool. Freeze in casserole securely covered with plastic wrap and aluminum foil. Take from freezer and bake at once. It does not have to be thawed. Be sure to bake long enough for lasagne to be hot and bubbling in the middle.

Mrs. J. Parks Garrison, Jr., Burlington, N.C.

BETTY ELLIS' ITALIAN SPAGHETTI
Serves four

This recipe was inherited by our contributor from the Rosasco family, of Pensacola, Florida, and through Admiral and Mrs. Ellis has become a favorite in Navy circles.

3 cloves garlic, chopped fine

2-oz. bottle olive oil

1 large or 2 small onions, sliced

1 lb. ground round steak (not hamburger)

1 6-oz. can tomato sauce (paste)

1 1-lb., 12-oz. can tomatoes

1 teaspoon sugar

Chili powder to taste

Salt and pepper to taste

½ cup canned tiny mushroom buttons

1 1-lb. pkg. spaghetti (long, thin)

Chop the garlic cloves and fry them in the heated olive oil; add onions and fry until slightly brown. Add the ground steak (be sure to use ground round steak as regular hamburger is too fat) and stir until no red meat appears. Add tomato sauce, tomatoes, and seasoning. Cook several hours over very low heat, covered. Add water if sauce thickens too much. Just before serving, add drained mushrooms. Cook spaghetti according to directions on box. Serve on a large platter with the sauce heaped over. Serve with grated Parmesan cheese. Tossed green salad and French bread slashed and heated with garlic butter are grand accompaniments.

Mrs. William E. Ellis, Washington, D.C.

HAMBURGER CASSEROLE
Serves six

This casserole is quick and easy!

1 lb. ground beef
1 large onion or 2 medium onions, chopped
4 medium-size potatoes, peeled, sliced
1 tablespoon each of Worcestershire sauce and tomato catch-up

¼ teaspoon salt
Ground black pepper to taste
1 can beef consommé
¾ consommé can water
Grated cheese (optional)

In a heavy skillet, cook the ground beef, onions, and potatoes until the meat is slightly brown. Pour into a 2-qt. baking dish; stir in the consommé, seasonings, and water. Bake in a 350-degree oven until potatoes are fork tender. Cover the hamburger mixture until 5 minutes before serving. Sprinkle top with cheese and bake uncovered until cheese melts.

Serve with a tossed salad, green vegetable, and Garlic French Bread. (See bread recipes.)

Mrs. Darrell Springer, Seminole, Florida

BAKED JAMBALAYAH
Serves six

2 cups, cold cooked chicken, veal, lamb, etc.
½ cup cold diced ham
1 cup raw rice
2 cups canned, stewed tomatoes
1 cup chopped celery

1 cup chopped onion
½ green pepper, minced
Salt and pepper to taste
Bread crumbs
Melted butter

Mix the meat with the rice and tomatoes and simmer on top of stove for 15 minutes. Add chopped vegetables and season to taste. Pour into a greased casserole and cover with bread crumbs. Drizzle melted butter generously over top. Bake in a 350-degree oven for 45 minutes or until thoroughly set and brown on top. Serve hot with tossed green salad.

Mrs. Joseph E. DuBois, Metaire, La.

CORNED BEEF HASH
Serves six to eight

Kosher Corned Beef (see below)
8 medium potatoes, peeled, diced
3 medium onions, chopped

Bacon drippings
Poached eggs

Prepare the corned beef as directed in recipe. Slice beef very thin, allowing several slices for each person. In a large frying pan, fry the potatoes and onions in bacon fat until vegetables are tender. Place the slices of corned beef on top of vegetables. Simmer on low heat until thoroughly heated. Stir meat and vegetables together. Serve hot; top each serving with a soft poached egg (or an easy-over fried egg).

Mrs. R. O. Stoutenburg, Manteo, N.C.

KOSHER CORNED BEEF

This beef may be served as a "boiled dinner," for sandwiches, hash, etc.

1 5-lb. kosher brisket of corned beef
¼ cup vinegar
Cold water
1 teaspoon each of thyme, rosemary, caraway seeds, salt, and pepper

1 tablespoon dill seeds
6 cloves garlic, sliced (less if desired)
Vegetables for the dinner: whole potatoes, peeled; cabbage, quartered; carrots, scraped; whole onions, peeled

In a large kettle place the beef, vinegar, and enough cold water to well cover the brisket. Bring to a boil and scoop off the foam. Add all the seasonings; reduce heat to simmer. Simmer beef for 3½ hours. Remove beef from liquid.

If beef is to be served as a boiled dinner dish, place the beef in a baking dish and pour over it 1 cup of the liquid it was boiled in. Set aside. Meanwhile prepare the vegetables. Allow 1 potato, 1 carrot, 1 onion, and ⅛ head cabbage per person. Boil in the liquid until potatoes, onions, and carrots are tender. Boil the cabbage only 20 minutes. One-half hour before serving time, put the beef in a 350-degree oven and bake for ½ hour. Serve it hot, sliced, with the hot vegetables. Serves 10 to 12 for dinner.

If beef is to be served for sandwiches, remove it from liquid and chill thoroughly. With a sharp knife, slice across the grain into paper thin slices.

See separate recipe for Corned Beef Hash.

Mrs. R. O. Stoutenburg, Manteo, N.C.

VIRGINIA SPICED BEEF ROUND

This famous recipe is a favorite in Tidewater, Virginia. It is served, sliced paper thin, with beaten biscuits, for eggnog parties around the Christmas season. The recipe was given to Mrs. MacNair by a resident of Norfolk, Virginia, during World War II.

Rub thoroughly a round of beef—12½ lbs.—with a little salt and 2 ounces of saltpeter. Place in a tub or keg and pour over it the following mixture:

2 cups salt
2 cups black molasses
1 oz. ground allspice

1 oz. ground cloves
½ oz. ground nutmeg

Let the beef stand in the mixture twenty-one days, turning each day. Remove; tie closely with cloth and put into pot of cold water and boil several hours until meat is tender. Let stand in the water to cool. Cool; slice very thin.

Mrs. Van MacNair, Berkeley Plantation, Westover, Va.

CHILI CON CARNE

Chili Con Carne, according to "Sally Ann" (*La Cocina Mexicana*), "is no such basic staple of diet in Mexico as it is supposed to be—but is an Americanized dish."

Cut pieces of pork, beef, veal, or mutton into chunks about ½ inch square, and fry until crisp in very hot fat with a chopped clove of garlic. When meat is browned, pour in enough sauce of chili colorado (which you have already prepared and have in the refrigerator) to cover the meat and let it boil. Add cooked frijoles (pinto beans) if you like, and never hesitate to put in a few pieces of onion and green chili. Chili con carne is best served on hot steamed rice along with a green salad and plenty of good strong hot coffee. It is an excellent way to utilize leftover meats. [For Chili Colorado, see p. 451.]

From La Cocina Mexicana, *by "Sally Ann," Food Editor,* El Paso Herald-Post, *El Paso, Tex.*

TAMALE PIE
Serves four to six

2 cups yellow corn meal
6 cups boiling water

1 teaspoon salt

Stir meal in boiling water (salted) until it begins to thicken. Cook slowly 30 minutes.

1 lb. ground meat (beef or any)
2 onions, chopped fine
1 clove garlic
Chicken fat or oil

1 teaspoon salt
2 tablespoons chili powder
Pinch red pepper
2 cups, mashed canned tomatoes

Fry the meat, onions, and garlic until golden brown in chicken fat or oil. Add dry ingredients, tomatoes, and juice. Cook slowly 1 hour.

Line greased pan with half the corn meal mush; pour meat sauce on mush, then cover with mush. Bake in oven 1 hour at 350 degrees.

Rose Tunkle, from What's Cookin' in Birmingham?, *Birmingham, Ala.*

LARRAPIN TONGUE WITH BLACKBERRY SAUCE
Serves four to six

1 fresh beef tongue
Salt water
1 tablespoon mixed pickle spice
1 or 2 (fresh) bay leaves
Dried celery tips
Cloves

Salt
1 glass blackberry jelly or jam
1 cup raisins, cooked until tender
    in 1 cup water
Juice of 1 lemon

Cook tongue till very tender in salted water containing a tablespoon of mixed pickle spice, one or two extra bay leaves, and a few dried celery tips. When very tender, remove the skin, trim off the root-end and stick the solid meat full of clove. Place in a greased baking pan, dust with salt, pour over the jelly, beaten with a fork, and the raisins. Add the lemon juice and bake 20 minutes, at 350–375 degrees basting often. Serve hot or cold.

Janice Schmid, from Katch's Kitchen, *West Palm Beach, Fla.*

WALNUT MEAT LOAF (*Beef*)
Serves eight

1 egg
⅓ cup milk
2 lbs. ground beef

2 tablespoons finely minced onion
⅛ teaspoon pepper
1½ teaspoons salt

1½ teaspoons Worcestershire sauce

½ cup tomato catchup

¼ cup water

Beat egg. Add milk and combine with meat, onion, and seasonings except catchup. Flatten out on waxed paper in rectangular shape ¾ inch thick. Combine ingredients for stuffing (given below). Shape stuffing into a roll on top of the meat, close to the lengthwise side. Roll so that the meat completely covers the stuffing. Remove waxed paper and place meat roll in a shallow baking pan. Mix catchup with water and pour over meat roll. Bake at 375 degrees for 1 hour. Garnish with orange slices and toasted walnuts.

Stuffing

3 cups soft bread crumbs
2 tablespoons minced onion
1 teaspoon salt
⅛ teaspoon pepper
1½ cups chopped celery

¼ teaspoon poultry seasoning
½ cup milk, water or stock
1 cup coarsely chopped walnuts (black)

Mrs. Thomas Tyson, Burlington, N.C.

DAUBE GLACE (*Beef or Veal*)

1 6-lb. yearling veal roast, or beef round 4 inches thick
1 cup peppered vinegar
Salt
Garlic
1 kitchen spoon lard (large tablespoon)
6 onions, cut fine
6 carrots, cut in large pieces
½ bunch parsley, chopped
1 stalk celery, chopped
Thyme

4 bay leaves
Red pepper (pod or cayenne)
Black pepper
1 teaspoon ground allspice
1 doz. cloves
6 green peppers (optional)
6 or 8 raw (fresh) pig's feet, or 2 calf's feet and 2 to 4 pig's feet
2 egg whites
4 hard-boiled eggs
2 lemons, sliced

Have daubé larded by butcher. Put into pan or bowl and pour over it peppered vinegar with salt to taste. Allow to soak 24 hours, turning once. Rub pot with garlic. Brown with lard like ordinary daubé (sear in pot with lard). After browning well, fill pot with water; put in onions, carrots, parsley, and celery. Add thyme, bay leaves, red pepper (pod or cayenne), black pepper, ground allspice, and cloves (green peppers optional). Wash pig's feet thoroughly and add. Boil slowly several hours until the meat of the feet comes readily apart. The liquid should cook down to about ½. Strain the liquid while hot. Clarify the juice by returning it to stove, and as it boils add 2 egg whites and crushed shells. Boil 10 minutes. Season liquid to taste by adding salt and cayenne pepper (if needed). Take out the pig's feet and pull the meat apart, removing all bones very carefully. Put the daubé and the boned pig's feet on a platter or in a deep bowl and pour the strained liquor over same. Set to jell. Garnish with 4 hard-boiled eggs and 2 lemons, sliced, or put them in bottom of mold or platter.

Mrs. H. Payne Breazeale, from Bon Appétit!, *Baton Rouge, La.*

STUFFED BABY VEAL BREAST OR SHOULDER
Serves six

Any desired dressing may be substituted in this excellent way to roast veal.

4 lb. breast of veal, with bone removed to make pocket
Salt
1 garlic clove, grated
Pepper
½ teaspoon ground ginger
Dressing (see below)
2 tablespoons diced celery
2 tablespoons diced carrots
2 tablespoons diced green pepper
2 tablespoons diced tomato
2 tablespoons diced onion
1 teaspoon lemon juice
1 bay leaf
6 tablespoons chicken fat

Rub the meat well with salt mixed with garlic clove, pepper, and ginger. Fill the pocket with dressing, and close with skewers. Place in a roasting pan with remaining ingredients except chicken fat. Lard roast with the chicken fat; cover and roast for 2 to 3 hours, basting every half hour. Serve with brown gravy.

Dressing

2 to 3 slices bread, cold water to soak
3 tablespoons chicken fat
1 small onion, grated
2 eggs, beaten
Salt, pepper
2 crackers, rolled
Milk or cream
1 tablespoon minced parsley
½ cup minced celery
Few grains ginger

Soak bread in cold water; press dry. Melt fat and add onion and bread. Cook until fat is absorbed. Add cracker crumbs, egg, and seasonings. Moisten with milk or cream.

Brown Gravy

3 tablespoons fat
3 tablespoons flour
2½ cups soup stock

¼ teaspoon Kitchen Bouquet
½ tablespoon Escoffier Sauce
Salt, pepper

Use fat from drippings in baking pan; add flour and brown. Add liquid and seasonings. Cook for a few minutes, strain. Serve with roast.

Mrs. Robert C. Moore, Maple Wood Farm, Graham, N.C.

KRAUT ZORINA WITH VEAL AND PORK
Serves six

¾ lb. raw lean veal, diced
¾ lb. raw pork, diced
2 tablespoons butter

1 can kraut
1 cup sour cream

Sauté the mixed veal and pork cubes until slightly brown in about 2 tablespoons of butter. Add the can of kraut with juice. Cover and allow to simmer 1 hour. Just before serving, add the sour cream.

Mrs. W. L. Shoffner, from Soup to Nuts, *Burlington, N.C.*

BAKED CALF'S LIVER

Take whole liver and make small holes all through; fill with bits of bacon and onion. Place in a roasting pan with flour, salt, and pepper on top. Put strips of bacon across the top. Baste frequently. Serve with gravy. Slice very thin on a slant.

Mrs. Florence Fay Valiant, from St. Anne's Parish Recipe Book,
Annapolis, Md.

CALVES LIVER A LA JOHNNIE MAY
Serves two

5 tablespoons butter
1 lb. calves liver, thinly sliced

6 tablespoons garlic vinegar

Melt one tablespoon of the butter in a heavy skillet; sauté quickly, turning to brown both sides. The liver should be slightly pink inside. Keep warm on heated platter. In the pan drippings add remaining butter and the vinegar. Heat to boiling, stirring constantly. Pour over liver and serve at once.

Dr. and Mrs. Ernest Reid, St. Petersburg Beach, Fla.

BRAINS TERRAPIN
Serves four to six

2 sets calf's brains
1 tablespoon butter
1 tablespoon flour
¼ teaspoon salt
Cayenne pepper
1 cup thin cream

1 egg, well beaten
1 tablespoon sherry
½ cup fresh mushrooms, sliced
    (optional)
Toast points

Parboil brains for about 20 minutes, or until firm and tender. Remove membrane and blanch in cold water. Cut into desired cubes or squares. Melt butter in saucepan and stir in flour and seasoning. Add cream and let simmer until it thickens. Stir in the well-beaten egg, and remove after about 1 minute from fire. Add 1 tablespoon sherry wine and the brains. Reheat for a few seconds. Mushrooms may be added to this dish. If mushrooms are used, sauté ½ cup fresh, cut mushrooms in butter until tender and add along with brains to sauce. Slightly more sauce should be made. Serve over toast points and garnish with parsley.

Mrs. Charles Cardozo, Winston-Salem, N.C.

SWEETBREADS

Sweetbread is a glandulous substance from the calf's throat and is a most delicate and delicious food. In past eras (as well as today) the sweetbread was the dish supreme, prepared in fabulous ways: with truffles and foies gras, cock's-combs and kidneys, with croutons and tongue, in croustades of puff-paste—dressed in the rich sauces of the day and given the French names in vogue. The basic dish for these fancibles is the blanched cold sweetbread from which the two secondary basic dishes have evolved—pan-broiled sweetbreads (glazed), or creamed sweetbreads. From these two recipes a variety of dishes may be made, using the tender "morsels" to blend with mushrooms, cream sauces, eggs, green peas and other ingredients in the same manner as tender white chicken meat is served.

First, blanch the sweetbreads in cold water for several hours, changing the water each hour until they become white. Then boil them (put on in cold water) with a little **vinegar or white wine**, for 15 to 20 minutes, until they are poached firm. Take out, rinse carefully, and pick off skin and membrane. Lay them out flat and set a plate firmly on them to press slightly. When drained, lard them with **melted butter or salad oil**. If desired, roll them in **bread crumbs or flour seasoned with salt and pepper** and fry until golden brown in **butter**. or, lard them and broil in oven or in skillet to a rich brown glaze. Serve with sauce made of pan drippings or any cream sauce.

To cream, proceed from blanching stage, in same manner as for creamed chicken.

SWEETBREADS AND MUSHROOMS SHERRY
Serves four to six

1 pr. sweetbreads, broken in de-
    sired pieces
1 lb. fresh mushrooms
2 tablespoons butter
2 tablespoons flour

2 cups coffee cream
Salt, pepper to taste
¼ teaspoon nutmeg
¼ cup sherry

Parboil sweetbreads. Wash, peel, and slice mushrooms. In one saucepan, make a cream sauce by melting butter; blend in ½ of the flour. Add 1 cup of the cream and stir until it thickens. In a separate pan, melt the remaining butter and sauté the mushrooms until tender; stir in the remaining flour; add the other cup of cream and simmer until it thickens. Add cream sauce to mushroom sauce; season to taste; add nutmeg and sherry. Reheat but do not let boil. Serve on toast points, in pastry shells, or bake in casserole (375-degree oven) with cheese topping until cheese browns.

One-half cup blanched, chopped almonds may be added to above recipe. To make a nice Creole dish, the sweetbreads may be added to 2 cups of any good Creole sauce containing onion, garlic, tomatoes, and green pepper to taste.

Mrs. Frank Hall, Reidsville, N.C.

"BLIND HARE"

"Blind Hare" is an old recipe calling for ground meat baked in an oval mold.

3 lbs. veal
2 lbs. beef
1 lb. ham
1 teaspoon salt
½ teaspoon pepper

4 beaten eggs
2 cups bread crumbs
2 grated nutmegs
1 tablespoon cinnamon

Mince the meat all fine. Mix all ingredients together. Place in oval-shaped loaf, and sprinkle with bread crumbs. Bake 3 hours (moderate low, 325-degree oven).

Mrs. H. A. Landes, from The Galveston Souvenir Cook Book,
Galveston, Tex.

BAKED CHOPS WITH SOUR CHERRIES
Serves four

4 thick loin pork chops
Salt
Pepper
1 cup raw rice

1 No. 2 can sour red cherries
1 tablespoon sugar
Grated peel ½ lemon
Dash cinnamon

Salt and pepper chops and brown on both sides. Place uncooked rice in bottom of casserole. Pour cherries and juice over rice. Sprinkle sugar, lemon peel, and cinnamon over this and arrange chops on top. Cover and bake 1¼ hours at 350 degrees.

Mrs. F. P. Farrell, from The Columbia Woman's Club Cook Book,
Columbia, S.C.

CURRIED STUFFED PORK CHOPS
Serves four

4 thick double pork chops
½ cup raisins, chopped
2 teaspoons brown sugar
4 tablespoons finely minced onion
2 tablespoons finely ground dry bread crumbs

½ teaspoon curry powder
1 scant teaspoon salt
½ cup Danish cherry kijafa wine (or kirsch)
1 tablespoon Angostura bitters
½ cup beef consommé or water

Cut a pocket in the center of each pork chop. Combine the raisins, sugar, onion, bread crumbs, and curry powder in a bowl. Rub the salt over outside of pork chops. Divide the stuffing mixture into 4 parts; insert a portion in the pocket of each chop.

Preheat oven to 425 degrees. Arrange chops in a shallow baking dish or roasting pan. Bake until chops begin to brown (about 20 minutes). Mix the wine and Angostura. Remove the chops from oven and pour off excess fat. Spoon ½ of the wine mixture over the chops. Reduce heat to 400 degrees and bake 15 minutes longer. Spoon remaining wine mixture over chops and bake an additional 15 minutes. Remove chops to warm platter. Add ½ cup beef consommé or hot water to the roasting pan. Stir brown bits from bottom of pan. Bring liquid to a boil and let boil for several minutes. Serve the pan sauce over the chops.

R. W. Messer, Burlington, N.C.

ITALIAN RICE WITH PORK CHOPS
Serves fourteen to sixteen

This party dish is a "Southernized" Italian classic.

3 tablespoons bacon fat or cooking oil
2½ lbs. pork chops, cut into pieces
2 cups chopped onions
2 green peppers, chopped
1 bunch celery, chopped
2 lbs. ground beef
1 small can tomatoes (1 lb.)
4 6-oz. cans Italian tomato paste
2 cans mushrooms (2 cups)
4 tablespoons chopped parsley
1 tablespoon salt
1 teaspoon thyme
1 teaspoon pepper
½ teaspoon marjoram
½ cup butter (1 stick)
1½ lbs. rice (uncooked)
3½-oz. box grated cheeese
Hard-boiled eggs for garnishing
Paprika

Melt fat in large saucepan. In this fry pork chops which have been cut into small pieces. Remove when brown and set aside. In the combined fats sauté the onions, green peppers, and celery. Stir in the beef and cook until grey in color. Add tomatoes and tomato paste, mushrooms, parsley, and all other seasoning. Add pork and simmer over low heat for about 1 hour; then add butter.

Boil rice in salted water; rinse and drain. Mix with the above sauce. Place in a large, shallow baking pan; top with grated cheese. Decorate with hard-boiled eggs, halved and dusted with paprika. Bake in hot oven (425 degrees) 30 minutes before serving.

Mrs. Neida Pratt, from 100 Favorite Recipes, *Huntsville, Ala.*

GRIFFIN'S BARBECUE
Serves about eighty

Henry Belk, editor of the Goldsboro *News-Argus*, gives the pertinent facts about the recipe and originator. "Mr. Griffin caters for special University of North Carolina events, flies barbecue upon call by chartered plane as far away as Virginia. He was called on by Kenneth Royall, when Royall was in the cabinet, to serve his barbecue at the Pentagon at an affair honoring General Marshall. Ann Jeffries, Hollywood star and Goldsboro native, long had Griffin send barbecue air express (in dry ice) for her parties."

Dig a pit 18 inches deep and 36 inches wide. Sprinkle pit lightly with sand. (Fresh sand should be applied after every cooking to avoid rancid odors.) Place iron rods across top of pit. Place a 70–75 pound pig, which has been dressed and split open, on the rods and cook slowly for 12 hours over oak coals. At the end of 10 hours turn the pig so the skin side is down.

When pig is done remove from the pit. Remove all bone, gristle and skin; chop meat with a cleaver. (Advantage of chopping with cleavers rather than using meat grinder is that this method conserves flavor and juices in the meat.)

For home consumption or small parties, hot sauces may be added to meat while cooking to improve the barbecue. Allow ½-lb. cooked barbecue per person.

Lloyd Griffin, Griffin's Barbecue, Goldsboro, N.C.

BARBECUE PIG, SCOTLAND NECK STYLE
Serves forty to fifty

Scotland Neck in Halifax County, North Carolina, is famous for superior Southern Barbecue. This authentic recipe is for "pit cooked" barbecue, cooked over oak coals.

Preparation

Dig a hole or pit sufficiently large so that when the pig is placed over it there will be a 4-or-5-inch margin at both ends and at one side; the other side should have a margin of at least 20 inches so that coals can be easily placed under the pig when cooking. The depth of the spit should be such that the pig will be 8 to 10 inches from the coals when cooking. Put 3 or 4 iron rods across the pit to put pig on.

Since coals (only) are used in cooking, a fire will have to be built in a separate location. This should be on an elevated wire grating with a 2-or-3-inch mesh so that the coals cannot drop through. Hardwoods, preferably oak, make the best coals.

Select a pig which will weigh approximately 65 pounds when dressed. Cut off head and slit down entire length of belly. Open up so that pig will lie flat.

Sauce

A sauce for mopping (basting), while cooking, is made by using 1½ quart of vinegar seasoned to taste with red pepper pods. A simple mop can be made by tying a rag around the end of a stick.

Cooking

Place the pig on the iron rods across pit with the skin up, and it stays in this position until it is nearly finished cooking. Put a thin layer of live coals in the pit under the entire surface of the pig, and replenish coals from time to time. Cook slowly—it should take from 6 to 7 hours. Mop the skin side with the sauce 3 or 4 times while cooking. In this position the pig should cook practically done and to a beautiful brown on the under side. However, be careful not to put the coals under it too fast or too freely as it will burn. When it is determined that it is done, rub the skin side with a thin coating of lard and turn the pig over so that the skin side will be over the coals. Let stay long enough for the skin to become brown and crisp. While skin is browning, add some salt to the vinegar sauce and mop freely the cooked side. This is for the purpose of seasoning.

When the cooking process is completed take the pig off and allow to cool only long enough to be handled. Cut up into small pieces with a knife; DO NOT run it through meat chopper. When it is cut up, put it into a large container and season it to taste using the same sauce as for the cooking, but with salt added. The seasoning should be worked into meat thoroughly.

This should be served with cole slaw and real corn bread.

Mr. and Mrs. Henry T. Clark, Sr., Scotland Neck, N.C.

HOSKINS' BARBECUE GREEN SHOULDER
Serves eighteen to twenty

This is by W. Cramey Hoskins, Louisville, Kentucky, who according to Cissy Gregg is a "barbecuer from way back."

Mr. Hoskins selects an 8-to-10-pound shoulder. The sauce is as follows:

Sauce

1 medium onion, minced
1 clove garlic, minced
¼ lb. butter
Juice ½ lemon
Peel of the lemon, cut in slivers
1 cup brown sugar
1 cup vinegar and water, mixed
    (½ cup each, but depends on
    taste)

1 cup tomato catchup
2 tablespoons Worcestershire
    sauce
1 teaspoon Tabasco sauce
½ teaspoon chili powder

Put the minced onion and garlic into skillet with the butter and allow to cook rather slowly until onion and garlic brown slightly. Mix all other ingredients together and add to the butter sauce. Use only the yellow part of the lemon rind. Put over heat and let get hot but not boil.

Either lay the meat on grill or place it on a spit. Cook for approximately 30 minutes before starting to baste with sauce. Then turn and swab the meat with the sauce at 20-minute intervals. The timing will vary according to the type of grill used. Mr. Hoskins made his grill. The firebed is 42 inches from the grill which provides very slow cooking. He uses wood for fuel—oak, ash, and beech. The fire is started 1 hour ahead so that there will be a bed of hot coals before the meat is put on. For the 8-to-10-pound shoulder he allows 5½ hours. Ribs, which he cooks by the same method, are cooked 1 hour and 50 minutes. As a rule, by the time the meat is basted and roasted for this length of time it has become so well seasoned it needs no additional sauce. Mr. Hoskins says that barbecuing is slow work and cannot be hurried; so he warns the barbecuer to start in time. [We have used the Hoskins Sauce to barbecue oven-cooked shoulder, ribs, and ham.—M. B.]

Recipe from Cissy Gregg, Home Consultant,
Courier-Journal, Louisville, Ky.

ELIOT ELISOFON'S SPARERIBS HAVOC
Serves four to six

Until he wrote *Food Is a Four Letter Word*, Eliot Elisofon had been more widely known for his photography than for his cooking. After a perusal of his book on food and intrigue (around the world), one is likely to wonder which is his greater talent.

His Spareribs Havoc, named for June Havoc, he describes as follows: "I have had two kinds of spareribs, the Chinese sweet and sour style, then the hot barbecued ribs served in Dixie. I decided to try to combine the two styles into one. I used honey instead of sugar, which the Chinese prefer, because of its more exciting texture and flavor. The Pickapeppa Sauce is a hot sauce from Jamaica which I discovered there on a recent trip. It is not only a hot sauce but it also contains the flavors of tropical fruits. Since this is not easily available a substitute could be a dash of 'Hot Sauce' and several slices of lemon. A piece of candied ginger cut into tiny bits would be a fine addition to the sauce. The 'Hot Sauce' should be used sparingly as there is no intention of making a really hot barbecued rib, but only a suggestion of it. Go easy on the cayenne as it can steal the show from all other flavors. Norma Millman christened the dish Spareribs Havoc and here it is:

2–3 lbs. spareribs, separated
Bacon fat or Crisco
2 tablespoons soy sauce
2 tablespoons white vinegar (try pear vinegar)
2 tablespoons honey

1 teaspoon salt
1 pinch both black pepper and cayenne
Dash of Pickapeppa Sauce
1 cup diced pineapple
1 jigger cointreau

"Brown ribs in hot skillet using a tiny bit of bacon fat or Crisco. Add sauce when ribs are well seared; then add vinegar and honey and spices. If no

Pickapeppa Sauce is available, add 2 slices lemon and 2 pieces of crystallized or candied ginger cut into small pieces. When ribs are well cooked through, add pineapple, mix thoroughly, and serve. Sauce should be thick to coat ribs. It is not necessary to add flour or cornstarch to the sauce if it is made correctly." ("But add a jigger of cointreau at very end of making ribs."—E. E.)

From Food Is a Four Letter Word, *by Eliot Elisofon*

BACKBONE WITH DUMPLINGS
One-half pound per serving

The backbone of the pig is one of the most succulent parts of the meat, and may be boiled plain, stewed with dumplings, or baked as spareribs. For dumplings, wash and cut the backbone into serving pieces, place in covered vessel with water to little more than cover, and boil for 2 hours, or until tender. Season when half done with **salt, pepper, and red pepper.**

Make a regular dumpling dough as for chicken [see p. 321] roll out and cut into squares or strips. While broth is simmering, drop in dumplings, one at a time and do not stir. If they seem to cling together, take a long-tined fork and gently separate them. When dumplings are all in, cover and simmer for 15 minutes. If meat is very lean, add **1 tablespoon of butter** just before serving. Serve with the meat.

To bake backbone, prepare as above. Lay out in flat baking pan; sprinkle with **salt, pepper,** and lightly with **flour.** Add **several tiny pods of red pepper** to meat. Pour in about 1 to 1½ cups **hot water**; bake in 450-degree oven for 15 minutes. Reduce heat to 325 degrees and bake until tender and browned, about 2 hours. Spareribs are baked in same way.

Mrs. Robert J. Powell, Fayetteville, N.C.

ROAST SUCKLING PIG WITH RED APPLE BALL SAUCE

One of the earliest Southern pork dishes was a suckling pig with a red apple in its mouth. This recipe, "from Old Virginia," is modernized for oven roasting.

For roast suckling pig, use only the very young pig not over six weeks old. Scald by immersing in very hot water (not boiling) for 1 minute. Remove from the water and use a very dull knife to scrape off hair in order that skin will not be broken. Then cut slit from the bottom of the throat to the hind legs and remove the entrails and organs, being careful not to break the brains. Wash thoroughly in cold water and chill. Fill with any desired poultry stuffing and sew opening. Roast in a moderate oven (350 degrees) from 3 to 4 hours.

Apple Ball Sauce for Suckling (for Goose, too)

1 cup sugar
1 cup water
Grated rind ½ lemon

Red vegetable coloring
4 whole cloves
1½ cups apple balls

Make a syrup of sugar and water, adding lemon rind, red coloring, and cloves. Cook for several minutes; strain out rind and cloves, and drop in the apples which have been cut with a potato ball cutter. Cook until apples are clear and tender.

ROAST PORK BROWNLEA
Serves six

4 to 5 lb. pork rib roast (or other cuts)
1½ cups rosé wine
1 tablespoon each of Worcestershire sauce, soy sauce, and Angostura bitters
2 dashes Tabasco sauce
2 small onions, sliced thin

2 tablespoons tomato catchup
½ teaspoon salt
1 teaspoon black pepper
1 cup chicken bouillon (make with 1 teaspoon instant bouillon and water)
Apricot preserves, heated slightly

Marinate the pork in the wine for 12 hours, turning it often. Remove the roast to a heavy roaster with top (a heavy aluminum one is best). To the wine marinade add the sauces. Pour over the roast. Begin roasting with the fat side down; arrange the onion slices on top of the roast; dribble over them the catchup. Sprinkle with salt and pepper. Cover and roast at 325 degrees for 35 minutes per pound. After 1 hour, turn the roast fat side up, and roast uncovered for remaining time, basting often with the pan drippings. When meat is done, glaze the top with a thick coating of apricot preserves. Increase heat to 400 degrees and roast until the glaze bubbles. If the pan becomes too dry during cooking time, add chicken bouillon as needed. Serve with pan sauce.

KELLY'S STUFFED PORK ROAST
Serves six

3 lbs. loin of pork
⅓ cup green pepper, minced
⅓ cup onion, minced
1 clove garlic, minced
¼ cup salad oil

2 8-oz. cans tomato sauce
1 cup hot water
1 tablespoon chili powder
1 cup seedless raisins
2 cups cooked rice

¼ cup brown sugar, firmly packed

½ teaspoon salt

¼ cup water

½ cup sliced ripe olives

Make a stuffing mixture of the following: Sauté green pepper, onion, and garlic in oil until tender. Add tomato sauce and hot water; bring to boil. Combine with chili powder, sugar, salt, and ¼ cup water; add with olives and raisins to sauce. Boil 4 minutes. Add ¼ cup of this sauce to cooked rice. Have the butcher loosen pork from bones just enough to form a pocket; stuff pocket with rice mixture. Cook, covered, in Dutch oven (moderate, 350 degrees) for 1 hour. Pour rest of sauce over roast; continue cooking for 1 to 1½ hours, basting frequently.

Mrs. Joseph P. Kelly, from Soup to Nuts, *Burlington, N.C.*

VIRGINIA HAM

"A good Virginia Ham ought to be 'spicey as a woman's tongue, sweet as huh kiss, an' tender as huh love.'" So says "De Ol' Virginia Hamcook" in *De Virginia Hambook,* edited by F. Meredith Dietz.

The Virginia, or Tidewater Ham, dates back to 1652, when the English cavaliers brought with them some little pigs, bred for food and later turned out to roam the country. When they became plentiful they were hunted as wild boar. The largest concentration of these pigs was on a small island, now known as Hog Island. The pigs raised in the tidewater section have a delicious flavor, the result of the diet of peanuts which the planters grow. Smithfield, Virginia, early became one of the largest shipping centers for the Tidewater Ham, and today the Smithfield Ham is known in this country and abroad as one of the finest of cured hams.

MRS. SYKES'S OWN SMITHFIELD HAM

In Smithfield, Virginia, is a comfortable inn, which to the traveler has the appearance of a charming home. That in fact is what Mrs. Sykes's inn means to hundreds of thousands who have visited there within the past 200 years. (The main part of the building was used as an inn as early as 1752.) Here Southern cuisine is at its best, and heading the lengthy bill of fare is the Smithfield Ham. Mrs. Sykes has had so many requests for her recipe that she had had one printed for her guests and friends:

"Wash a Smithfield Ham in hot water with a stiff brush. Put in boiler of water large enough for ham to float. When it gets to boiling point, turn flame low, so it won't even bubble. Cook until bone on large end leaves ham (about 1 inch). Then take it out of boiler. Don't leave it in the water to cool. When cool, skin and trim off some of fat. Put in hot oven so it will brown in 10 minutes." [No, Mrs. Sykes uses no decorating or garnishing unless for special parties.— M. B.]

Mrs. D. W. Sykes, Sykes' Inn, Smithfield, Va.

TENNESSEE COUNTRY HAM BAKED WITH PICKLED PEACHES

"Nancy Nash," an expert at ham cooking, says, "This is the most delicious recipe for boiling and baking ham that I have ever seen."

15- to 20-lb. country ham
Water to cover
2 cups vinegar
2 cups sugar
6 whole peppercorns

6 whole allspice berries
1 pod red pepper
6 whole cloves
Crushed peach pickle
Syrup from peaches

Put ham in large container and cover with water. Into the water put 1 of the cups of sugar, 1 cup of vinegar and the spices tied in a bag. Boil rapidly for 1 hour; then add 1 additional cup of sugar and 1 cup of vinegar. Boil until ham is tender when pierced with the tines of a fork. Remove ham from water and skin. Place ham in a large broiling pan; score the fat side and cover with crushed peach pickle. Bake ham 45 minutes (moderate 350-degree oven), basting 3 to 4 times with the syrup from can of peach pickle.

"Nancy Nash" (Mrs. B. Frank Womack), Foods Editor,
The Nashville Tennesseean Magazine, Nashville, Tenn.

A TEXAS WAY TO BAKE HAM (*with Corn Meal Coating*)

Ham cooked by this method is very tender and juicy. The coating of meal is removed after ham is cooked. The ham may be garnished in any desired way.

Wash a ham carefully and lay it in a pan with the skin side down; make a dough of corn meal and water soft enough to handle; cover with this dough all parts of the ham that have no skin, making it about ¾ inch thick; slip ham into moderate oven (350 degrees) and bake 20 minutes for each pound.

Mrs. C. E. Kelly, from How We Cook in El Paso, El Paso, Tex.

VARIATION: Season flour highly with ground spices, make a paste by adding water, and coat ham with paste. Bake as above.

HAM IN BING CHERRY-COGNAC SAUCE

This is for a precooked, or raw, cured ham.

1 pre-cooked (or raw), cured
    ham—10 to 12 lbs.
White wine
1 large can bing cherries, drained,
    reserve juice and cherries

Brown sugar
Cognac

In a roasting pan—with cover—place the ham fat side up. Add enough white wine to the juice of the cherries to make 1½ inches of liquid in the pan. Bake the ham according to instructions on the ham wrappings, keeping it covered until half the cooking time has elapsed. Baste often with pan juices. Remove the roaster cover; score the ham, and sprinkle it generously with brown sugar. Sprinkle the sugar generously with cognac. Continue baking until ham is done. Remove ham to a platter and garnish the ham with the cherries. Slice and serve hot or cold, serving the heated sauce with the slices. Allow ¼ lb. (uncooked) ham per person.

Bill Cox, Mineral Wells, Tex.

BEA'S COUNTRY HAM, BAKED

Country ham baked this way is juicy and retains its natural color.

1 country ham (any size)
Glaze (see recipe)

Crumbs

Wash and scrub a country ham until all accumulated crust has been removed; pat the ham dry. Place it skin side down in a large uncovered roasting pan. Insert a meat thermometer deep into the middle of the large end on ham, but do not let it touch the bone. Bake in a slow (275 degrees) oven until the thermometer temperature reaches 160 degrees. When ham can be handled, cut off the skin; score the fat into diamond shapes. Make the glaze and with a spoon place the glaze into the scored lines in the fat. Sprinkle the ham with fine bread crumbs, cracker crumbs, corn flake crumbs, or any type of crumbs. Increase heat to no more than 300 degrees; bake until the crumbs are nicely browned and the glaze is melted. Cool; slice paper thin.

Glaze

6 tablespoons brown sugar
6 tablespoons dry mustard

Vinegar

Blend the sugar and mustard; gradually add *just* enough vinegar to make a stiff paste. Be careful not to get the sauce too thin. Use as directed above. If more glaze is needed, make extra paste.

Mrs. W. CLary Holt, Burlington, N.C.

HAM GLACE

This ham argues that ham should cool in its own liquid.

"Carefully wash a 10 to 12 lb. ham and plunge into a big kettle of water, ham completely under. Then toss in 1 tablespoon of whole cloves, a stick of cinnamon, 3 cloves of garlic, 1 cup vinegar, and 1 cup of sugar. Let it remain in the kettle over a very low heat for 3¼ hours. Stifle every boiling bubble that appears. After turning the heat off, let the ham remain in hot liquor 4 hours. Take from water. Remove the top skin; trim, and pat in the following mixture: 1 cup brown sugar and 1 tablespoon dry mustard. Dot whole cloves on fat. Put in a baking pan. Add ¼ cup vinegar, ¾ cup water, and bake in a 350-degree oven for 1 hour. Do not baste until ham is browned. Fifteen minutes before ham is taken from oven make this sauce:

In a saucepan mix 1 teaspoon dry mustard, ¼ teaspoon powdered cloves, ¼ teaspoon cinnamon, 2 tablesponns vinegar, and a small glass of apple jelly. Heat all this over slow fire until jelly is melted. Then put ham on platter, and pour this hot syrup over ham. Carve ham to bone like lamb, and over each slice put spoonful of sauce.

Jack S. Willson, from Katch's Kitchen, *West Palm Beach, Fla.*

GERTRUDE CARRAWAY'S CAROLINA COUNTRY HAM

This recipe for sugar-and-pineapple-coated ham, given me by Gertrude Carraway, has appeared in the *DAR Cook Book.*

"Soak a smoked ham overnight. Clean thoroughly. Put ham in a large container and cover with cold water. Put in an apple and an onion—big if the ham is big, small if small. Pour in a cup of molasses and a teaspoonful of mixed pickling spices. Cook very, very slowly. Allow 20 minutes to the pound. Cut off heat just before the meat leaves the bone. Let the ham remain in the water until it has cooled. Remove it later; skin, and cut off the fat.

"Spread with brown sugar mixed with Worcestershire sauce. Cut slices of canned pineapple in halves (to look like crescents) and place in rows on the ham, sticking each half slice with cloves. Bake it for a short time, or until the sugar turns brown."

Gertrude Carraway. New Bern, N.C.

GLAZED SUGAR-CURED HAM WITH CHAMPAGNE SAUCE

Put a 12-pound sugar-cured ham in a kettle. Cover with cold water; bring to a boil and let simmer at boiling point for about 3 hours. Skin the ham and sprinkle heavily with **brown sugar and honey**. Place in a roasting pan, add 1 pint of champagne in the bottom of the pan, set in oven and roast (moderate oven) until brown. Slice ham and serve separately with the following sauce:

2 tablespoons sugar	4 tablespoons butter
2 cups champagne	Salt, pepper to taste
4 cups brown gravy	

Put the sugar in a casserole and cook to a brown caramel (or caramelize in heavy skillet on top of stove). Add the champagne; boil for 5 minutes. Add 2 pints of brown gravy; boil for 10 minutes. Season with salt and pepper and add butter. Serve hot.

From Recipes Tested and Tried, *by Anne Young White*
and Nola Nance Oliver, Natchez, Miss.

HAM BAKED IN MILK
Serves two to four

1 thick slice smoked ham	2 tablespoons brown sugar
1 tablespoon dry mustard	1½ cups hot milk

Combine sugar and mustard and rub well into both sides of the ham. Place in casserole; cover with hot sweet milk, and bake in moderate (350-degree) oven until ham is tender, about 30 minutes. When ham is done, the milk will be mostly absorbed. If too dry before ham has cooked, more milk may be added.

Mrs. W. B. Rosevear, Pembroke Hall, Edenton, N.C.

TEXAS STUFFED HAM

This is for a cured ham which may be baked. Bone the whole ham; stuff with the following:

4 cups bread crumbs	1 lb. ground pecans
2 cups honey	

Mix bread, honey, and pecans; stuff into ham; bake, and slice.

Mrs. Edwin Taegel, from What's Cookin'?, *Corpus Christi, Tex.*

BROWN SUGAR STUFFED HAM

Prepare ham by boiling and skinning—any ham under 2 years old or Western ham. Drain overnight. Cut deep gashes, 1 inch apart, to bone lengthwise from hock to end. Make a dressing of 1½ cups chopped pickle and 1 cup brown sugar. Add equal amount of bread crumbs (cold corn bread). Moisten with liquor drained from the ham. Stuff into gashes and put in thick dressing over the ham. Bake slowly in moderate oven, basting constantly. Add brown sugar and vinegar (preferably from spiced pickles) to basting liquid. Serve cold.

Mrs. P. B. Barringer, from The Monticello Cook Book, *Charlottesville, Va.*

HAM MOUSSE
Serves four to six

2 tablespoons gelatin
½ cup cold water
Boiling water
1 cup heavy cream, whipped

4 teaspoons mayonnaise
2 cups ground, cooked ham
2 teaspoons mustard
1 teaspoon horseradish

Soften the gelatin in cold water and add enough boiling water to dissolve. Whip cream and add mayonnaise. As soon as gelatin is cold, strain it into cream mixture. Mix ham with seasoning and add to cream. Pour into a wet mold; place on ice. When ready to serve, turn out on platter and garnish with lettuce and sliced crystallized pickles.

Mrs. Lee Herzberg, from Bon Appétit!, *Baton Rouge, La.*

HAM LOAF WITH MUSTARD SAUCE
Serves eight

2 lbs. lean pork shoulder
1 lb. lean raw ham
1½ cups milk

1 cup bread crumbs
Pepper to taste
1 can tomato soup

Grind pork and ham together twice; mix with milk, crumbs, and pepper to taste. Make into loaf and bake in moderate 350-degree oven for 1½ hours. After 30 minutes pour over it 1 can tomato soup. Serve with following sauce:

Sauce

¼ cup butter
1 teaspoon flour
½ cup sugar

½ cup vinegar
½ cup prepared mustard
½ cup Campbell's bouillon

Melt butter; stir in flour until smooth. Add other ingredients and cook in double boiler until thick. Serve hot over browned loaf.

Mrs. Robert M. Holder, Atlanta, Ga.

CASSEROLE OF HAM AND SWEET POTATOES
Serves six to eight

2 cups milk
1 tablespoon chopped onion
Bit of bay leaf
3 cloves
1 tablespoon diced celery and leaves
4 tablespoons butter or margarine

6 tablespoons flour
2 cups diced cooked ham
Salt to taste
2 cups mashed, cooked sweet potatoes
3 tablespoons chopped nuts

Heat milk slowly with onion, bay leaf, cloves, and celery; strain. Melt butter; stir in flour, and gradually add hot milk. Cook over low heat, stirring constantly, until thick and smooth. Add ham and salt to taste. Pour into casserole; top with sweet potatoes, and sprinkle with nut meats. Bake at 375 degrees for 30 minutes.

Mrs. James A. Dowie, from The Alexandria Woman's Club Cook Book, *Alexandria, Va.*

FRIED HAM WITH RAISIN-CHAMPAGNE SAUCE
Serves four

1 slice ham, weighing 1½ lbs., cut 1-inch thick
1 tablespoon butter
Salt, pepper to taste

1 tablespoon flour
1 cup hot water
½ cup seedless raisins
1 cup sherry or champagne

Melt butter in heavy frying pan. Put in ham and fry over low flame, allowing around 15 minutes' cooking time. Turn ham often so that it will not get too brown. Remove from pan and set in warmer. In the pan drippings, blend the flour with grease; add 1 cup hot water and raisins. Allow to reduce to about one-half; add wine or champagne and let boil until sauce thickens. Cut ham in serving pieces and pour the sauce over them.

A variety of sauces may be served over this: mushroom, mustard, tomato, Espagnole, or any of the ham sauces.

Mrs. Kilmer Myers, San Francisco, Calif.

FRIED KENTUCKY COUNTRY HAM (*with Red Gravy*)

To fry good country ham is not so simple. From experts in the art, I have selected the following recipe.

"Slice ham medium thick; place in frying pan without shortening; do not cook too fast; turn several times to avoid burning. When evenly browned on both sides, remove from the frying pan; add ½ cup of *cold* water to ham gravy and let it cook until gravy turns red."

J. T. Theobald, Manager, The Hotel Irvin Cobb, Paducah, Ky.

VARIATION: There have been many heated discussions about the right way to make Red Ham Gravy—with water or coffee. I make mine by adding a cup of strong black coffee to pan drippings. Let boil down and there will be a layer of reddish brown sauce on bottom with layer of clear ham grease on top. When blended this makes a wonderful gravy.

DEVILED BACON
Serves two

1 egg, beaten slightly
½ teaspoon dry mustard
½ teaspoon sugar
2 dashes Tabasco sauce
1 teaspoon wine vinegar

4 slices bacon
½ cup finely crushed cracker crumbs, or prepared cracker crumbs

Beat the egg; add the mustard, sugar, Tabasco, and vinegar; stir to blend. Dip each slice of bacon in the egg mixture; then roll it in cracker crumbs. Preheat oven to 400 degrees. Lay bacon strips on a rack in a broiler pan. Bake until bacon is crisp and browned. Serve with hot cakes and syrup, or with spoon bread.

Mrs. Colin Dunn, Mineral Wells, Tex.

PORK SAUSAGE

John Farley, in his *London Art of Cookery*, 1787, gives a recipe for "Apples With Sausages" and says also "Sausages, fried and with stewed cabbage, make a good dish." "Cold peaspudding, reheated, with sausages all round up edge-ways" he considered worthy. In the Deep South sausages with rice—"Sausage Pilaff"—is an ancient dish still served; in other sections sausage cakes baked in a casserole with Irish potatoes make a respected dish. [For Sausage Pilaff, see p. 184.]

The fried sausage cake is perhaps the most favored breakfast sausage, although cased meat is often served. To fry sausage cakes, mold the meat into little patties, fry in scant grease very slowly until well done yet not too brown and hard. To give a crunch crust and dressed-up appearance, roll the sausage cake in bread crumbs and fry in butter.

Apples fried with sausage are cooked in very much the same manner as John Farley suggested. Fry out the cakes in heavy iron frying pan (as above), pour off all but about 1 tablespoon of the fat. Core unpeeled apples (or pared), slice in rings about ⅛ inch thick or thicker. Remove sausage from pan, keep warmed. Place apple rings in the fat and cover. Cook very slowly for 5 minutes, turning once. Sprinkle apples with brown sugar and continue slow cooking until apples are tender. Remove cover and let apples take on a nice glaze in the sugar-fat mixture. Place apples in center of platter and arrange sausage cakes around; sprinkle with ground cinnamon or cloves. Serve hot.

The apples may be cut in slices and poured into fat. Add ½ cup water. Cover, and let apples simmer until liquid has been absorbed. Remove cover; sprinkle on brown sugar and stir all together. Flavor with powdered spices. Serve in same manner as apple rings.

SAUSAGES IN ALE
Serves six to eight

2 lbs. "pig" pork sausages (in cases)	2 tablespoons butter or bacon fat 1½ cups ale

Melt butter or fat in frying pan. Prick sausages in several places with fork, and brown rapidly all over in the heated fat. Pour off fat; add ale and bring to boil. Cover and simmer (do not let boil) for 30 minutes. Serve with waffles or scrambled eggs.

Mrs. Allen Cucullu, from Favorite Foods of Virginians,
Lynchburg, Va.

SAUSAGE PILAFF (*Pilau*)
Serves four

1 lb. cased sausage Water	1 cup raw rice 2 cups broth from sausage

Boil cased pork sausage in enough water so that at the end of 1½ hours' boiling time, there will be 2 cups of liquid. Add 2 cups of rice to sausage and liquid; put in steamer and steam for about 1½ hours. Serve hot.

Condensed from recipe by Mrs. E. S. Pegues, from
Mt. Pleasant's Famous Recipes, *Mt. Pleasant, S.C.*

TRIPE

Tripe, "the large stomach of ruminating animals," is considered a delicacy by many Southerners. The meat is first pickled, but today one may buy the already pickled or prepared tripe at all large markets. The prepared meat may be fried or stewed with any meat sauce. It is creamed like chicken or highly flavored with wine. Most often it is fried. The prepared tripe is boiled until tender, then cut into desired strips, dipped into beaten egg, rolled into bread crumbs, and fried in hot lard until golden brown. It is served with lemon wedges.

PIG'S FEET

Until a few years ago, I had no idea that pig's feet were ever cooked any way but "pickled," or spiced. Then once in New Orleans I was persuaded to try a beautifully browned delicacy which resembled a chicken leg, yet was served with a hot wine sauce. Further perusal of the subject has led to other equally surprising secrets about pig's-feet cookery. Here is an example:

Boil pig's feet (always thoroughly cleaned, of course) in salted water to cover well. When meat is tender, remove, split, and drain. Salt and pepper to taste. Sprinkle over a few drops of lemon juice and then brush lightly with melted butter. Beat up 1 egg for each 2 feet, with 2 tablespoons of cream. Dip the feet in egg mixture, then in flour, or roll in bread crumbs. Fry in deep fat for about 3 minutes, or in a heavy pan with shallow butter. Serve with any sauce—Sauce Robert, tartar, raisin-wine, tomato sauce, or just pass bottles of commercial condiments. Allow 1 foot for each serving.

CHITTERLINGS (*Chit'lin's*)

For months I was undecided about the status of chitterlings among the best recipes. Then one evening, Pat placed only two steaks out to be broiled. When I asked him why he had not counted himself in on the steaks, he replied disdainfully, "I'm eating at home tonight, we got something *special,* 'Chit'lin's' and turnip greens." For those who think like Pat, here is a recipe.

Wash chitterlings thoroughly and cover with boiling salted water. Add 1 tablespoon of whole cloves and 1 red pepper pod cut into pieces. Cook until tender. Drain. Cut in pieces about the size of an oyster. Dip each piece in beaten egg and then in cracker crumbs. Fry in deep fat until golden brown. (Chitterlings are the small intestines of swine. They may be found at Southern butcher shops.)

LAMB AND MUTTON

Lamb is the flesh of young sheep; after one year of age the flesh is considered to be mutton. Mutton is rarely sold in the United States as lamb is more tender and juicy and has a milder flavor.

There are many schools of thought on the proper way to cook lamb, especially the leg which is the most popular cut in this country. The English advise roasting the leg for about 15 minutes per pound in a 400-degree oven, or until a thermometer reaches 145 degrees; this is a medium-rare stage which is preferred by many. For well-done lamb, roast 18 to 20 minutes per pound.

The French prefer a two temperature method. Cook meat in a very hot (450 degrees) oven for 15 minutes, then reduce heat to 350 degrees. For medium rare, cook 10 to 12 minutes per pound; for well done, 13 to 15 minutes per pound.

Americans use a low temperature method. Cook meat in a preheated slow oven (325 degrees). For medium rare, cook 30 minutes per pound, or to 175 degrees on meat thermometer; for well done, cook 35 minutes per pound or to 180 degrees on the thermometer.

For the saddle of lamb, breast, lamb stew (baked), and other cuts of meat, a slow (325 degrees) cooking seems universally the preferred method. Lamb chops are best when broiled medium rare.

In this section we are dealing only with lamb. The individual recipe suggests a cooking temperature. The cook may use his own choice as to the method preferred.

Note: *Compiled largely from* Modern French Culinary Art *by Henri-Paul Pellaprat.—M. B.*

BARBECUE LEG-O'-LAMB

Brown leg of lamb well under broiler on all sides in roaster. Turn oven on to 350 degrees and continue cooking. Baste often with the following sauce and bake in open roaster until well done: 3–5 lb. leg—cook 45 minutes per pound; 6–8 lb. leg—cook 30 minutes per pound.

Sauce for Basting

1 medium onion, chopped	½ tablespoon prepared mustard
2 tablespoons butter	2 cans tomato sauce
¼ cup catsup	2 tablespoons vinegar
½ lemon, sliced	2 tablespoons brown sugar

3 tablespoons Worcestershire sauce	Salt, cayenne, and black pepper to taste
1 tablespoon horseradish	

Brown onion in butter; add rest of ingredients and simmer 30 minutes.

Miriam Cohn, from What's Cookin' in Birmingham?, *Birmingham, Ala.*

LEG OF LAMB WITH CURRY STUFFING
Serves eight to ten

5 lb. boned leg of lamb	2 to 3 teaspoons curry powder
3 tablespoons lemon juice	1 teaspoon salt
1 clove garlic, minced	½ teaspoon pepper
1 onion, chopped	½ cup chopped peanuts
2 tablespoons butter or margarine	¼ cup each, chopped olives and
3 fresh pears or 3 canned pears, drained	shredded coconut
	1 cup toasted bread crumbs

Rub lamb inside and out with lemon juice; let stand for 5 minutes. Sauté garlic and onion in butter. Core pears and chop into coarse pieces. Add to onion mixture with rest of ingredients. Cook slowly for 5 minutes. Stuff meat lightly and secure with skewers; sprinkle over more salt, pepper, and curry powder. Bake the extra stuffing separately. Roast meat at 450 degrees for 15 minutes; reduce heat to 325 degrees and continue cooking 2½ hours, or until meat is tender. Baste often with pan juices.

Westen Ermatinger, Food Editor, Times, St. Petersburg, Fla.

MINTED LEG OF LAMB (*with Creme de Menthe*)
Serves six to eight

5 to 6 lb. leg of lamb	⅓ cup salad oil or French salad dressing
8 to 10 slivers of garlic cloves	½ cup white crème de menthe
2 teaspoons salt	1 large onion sliced
1½ teaspoons fresh ground black pepper	Sprigs of fresh mint if available, or sprigs of fresh parsley for garnish.
½ teaspoon ground ginger	
2 teaspoons oregano	
1 cup white wine vinegar	

Rub the leg of lamb dry (never lard lamb). Make incisions in the flesh and insert into each a sliver of garlic. Mix the seasonings and rub well into the flesh of the leg. Place in a large bowl and pour over the wine and oil mixed together. Place in refrigerator and marinate for at least 6 hours, turning often.

Remove lamb to a roasting pan. Reserve marinade. Preheat oven to 325 degrees (or use the two-temperature French method). Insert a meat thermometer into flesh of lamb but do not let it touch the bone. Arrange onion slices on top of lamb. Roast for 30 minutes per pound for medium rare, or until thermometer reaches 175 degrees. After the first 30 minutes begin basting the lamb with the marinade, and dribble on at the same time a portion of the crème de menthe. Baste the leg every 20 minutes with small amounts of marinade and crème de menthe. When meat is done, remove to a warm platter and let rest 15 minutes before slicing. Stir remaining marinade and crème de menthe into pan drippings. Serve with the sliced meat. Garnish with mint sprigs or parsley.

Frank Hall, Reidsville, N.C.

ROLLED SHOULDER OF LAMB WITH PINEAPPLE-MINT SAUCE
Serves four to six

3½ to 4 lb. lamb shoulder	½ cup hot water
Salt, pepper to taste	¼ cup chopped fresh mint leaves
½ teaspoon ground ginger	½ cup pineapple syrup
½ teaspoon garlic salt	1 tablespoon vinegar
1 tablespoon butter	Salt

Have shoulder of lamb boned and rolled. Rub the salt, pepper, ginger, and garlic well into meat. Place on a trivet in roasting pan. Roast in 325-degree oven, allowing from 25 to 30 minutes per pound. When roast has cooked about 30 minutes, baste with 1 tablespoon of butter stirred into ½ cut hot water. Baste with juice in pan often. Serve with the following sauce, slightly heated:

Several hours before serving combine mint leaves, pineapple juice, and vinegar. Add salt to taste. Let set in warm place to steep. Just before serving heat slightly.

Mr. and Mrs. Kent Belmore, Hickory, N.C.

LAMB TERRAPIN
Serves eight

Mrs. Devers passed us this recipe with the quip, "I gives it to you as 'twas guv to me."

Yolks of 3 hard-boiled eggs	1 teaspoon Worcestershire sauce
1 tablespoon flour	Dash salt
2 tablespoons butter, softened	2 cups cold lamb, diced
1 cup milk	2 tablespoons sherry
¼ cup cream	Whites of 3 hard-boiled eggs

Put yolks through ricer. Beat yolks, flour, butter, milk, cream, and seasonings until smooth with a wire whisk. Add the lamb and let all boil up for a second or two to heat through. Add sherry. Serve on thin slices of buttered toast or with mounds of fluffy, dry rice. Sprinkle finely cut egg whites over top. Excellent for Sunday night supper.

Mrs. Jacob L. Devers, Fort Monroe, Va.

13 BOY CURRY (*Lamb*)
Serves four

Roast a lamb one day before preparing this dish. Dice as much of this lamb as necessary.

¼ cup butter or oil	1 cup raisins
¼ cup minced onion	2 cups diced cooked lamb
¼ cup flour	1 cup diced pared apple
2 teaspoons curry powder	1 cup water
2 cups leftover thin gravy (canned consommé or beef broth)	1 teaspoon salt
	4 cups cooked rice

Melt butter in kettle. Add onion and sauté until tender. Stir in flour and curry. Gradually pour in gravy, while stirring. Add next 5 ingredients and cook until curry is smooth and thickened. Serve over hot cooked rice. Have several dishes around table with following:

Grated coconut	Chopped crisp bacon
Chopped onions	Chopped pickles
Chopped peanuts	Raisins or currants
Chopped whites of hard-cooked eggs	Hot chutney (Major Grey's or Calcutta Club)
Chopped yellows of hard-cooked eggs	French-fried onion rings

Sprinkle these one at a time over the curry and rice—put chutney and onion rings on side of plate and dish is ready to serve.

Pete Freeman, from The Cotton Blossom Cook Book, *Atlanta, Ga.*

SADDLE OF LAMB
Serves six to eight

1 saddle of lamb roast	1½ teaspoons ground black pepper
1 teaspoon salt	

1 teaspoon oregano
¼ teaspoon garlic powder
¼ cup Italian French dressing

¼ cup tarragon vinegar
Mint sprigs or parsley for garnish

Have the butcher saw across the ribs close to the backbone to make carving the meat easier. Sprinkle the meat with dry ingredients and rub into the meat. Stand the saddle on the ribs in a roasting pan. Roast uncovered in a preheated slow (325 degrees) oven for 35 minutes to the pound, or until meat thermometer reaches 180 degrees. Baste the lamb every 15 to 20 minutes with the French dressing mixed with the vinegar. Remove to a warm platter. Serve Potato Croquettes (see "Vegetables"), small broiled potatoes, or turnips (boiled) around the meat. Garnish with fresh mint or parsley sprigs.

If desired serve a mint sauce ("see Sauces") with the meat.

Dr. James Hinson, Summerfield, N.C.

LAMB CHOPS OR CUTLETS CYRANO
Serves four

The lamb chop (*côtelette* as it is called in France), or the English "cutlet," is the rib chop. This is a version of the French *côtelette* served with a Chateaubriand sauce. (See "Sauces.")

8 rib lamb chops, about ¾ to 1 inch thick
½ teaspoon salt
1 teaspoon ground black pepper
2 tablespoons of butter
8 cooked artichoke bottoms (fresh, canned, or frozen), heated in butter

8 small chicken livers, fried in butter
Chateaubriand sauce
Mushrooms, sautéed, optional

Sprinkle the chops on both sides with the salt and pepper. In a heavy skillet or electric frying pan, heat the butter. Brown the chops well on both sides over 350-degree heat. Remove to a warm platter and keep warm. In a separate saucepan heat the artichokes in a small amount of butter. Sauté the chicken livers in the same pan the chops were cooked in, browning them on all sides. Cook about 5 to 7 minutes according to size. Place an artichoke heart under each lamb chop. Top each chop with a fried chicken liver. Pour over each chop a light coating of the sauce. Garnish tops with sautéed mushrooms, if desired.

Mrs. W. H. May, Jr., Burlington, N.C.

LAMB CHOPS CHESTNUT STUFFING
Serves six

Have 6 lamb chops cut English style—that is from the double loin—about 1½ to 2 inches thick. Have them boned. Split chops making 2 pockets. Stuff pockets with chestnut dressing. Sew up with a coarse thread or fasten with short skewers. Sprinkle with salt and pepper, brush with melted butter. Place in broiling pan at least 3 inches from flame. Brown on both sides, turning carefully once. Cook to desired state (about 25 minutes). Remove from pan; cut string, and remove. Serve on hot toast. Garnish with stewed prunes, stoned and stuffed with whole roasted chestnut, or mint jelly. Pour over pan drippings or melted butter blended with any standard mint sauce.

Stuffing

1 cup chestnuts, boiled or roasted, peeled and mashed
1 cup bread crumbs
1 tablespoon butter
1 teaspoon salt
1 teaspoon pepper
½ teaspoon lemon juice

Melt butter; stir in chestnuts, bread crumbs, lemon juice, and seasoning. Stir around in pan to blend into fluffy mixture. Stuff each side chop with 1 large tablespoon of dressing.

Mrs. Kilmer Myers, San Francisco, Calif.

LAMB SHISH KEBAB (*with Vegetables*)
Serves six

2 lbs. lean lamb—leg or shoulder
1 tablespoon salt
2 tablespoons minced onion
2 garlic cloves, crushed
2 teaspoons ground coriander
1 teaspoon ground ginger
1½ teaspoons curry powder
1½ teaspoons fresh ground pepper
3 tablespoons lemon juice
3 tablespoons red wine vinegar
⅓ cup olive oil, or vegetable oil
Mushroom caps
Green pepper squares
Small onions, optional (canned parboiled type)
Tomato wedges
Pitted olives (optional)

Trim as much fat as possible from lamb. Cut into 1½-inch cubes. Combine all seasonings, lemon juice, vinegar, and oil to make a marinade. Marinate the meat in marinade for at least 6 hours, turning often. String the meat on skewers, alternating the meat, mushroom caps, green pepper, and onions if used. Broil 3 inches from a charcoal firebed, turning frequently and basting with the marinade. Broil around 20 minutes. Thread tomato wedges on last and broil about 5 minutes. Remove skewers to warming area to keep warm until serving time. If olives are used, thread them with tomatoes.

W. W. Brown, 2nd, Burlington, N.C.

8. Poultry

PRESIDENT ROOSEVELT'S THANKSGIVING TURKEY WITH SAGE DRESSING
Serves six to eight

This typical Southern turkey was always served at the Georgia Warm Springs Foundation as the Thanksgiving *pièce de résistance* for the late President Franklin D. Roosevelt and Mrs. Roosevelt. The dinner was prepared by Chef C. M. Stephens. The complete menu is as follows:

Crisp Hearts of Celery
Assorted Olives
Fruit Cocktail
Roasted, Sliced Turkey   Sage Dressing
Cranberry Sauce
Gravy   Hot Rolls
Creamed Parsley Potato Balls
English Peas in Patty Shells
Julienne Carrots   Harvester Salad
Plum Pudding   Hard Sauce
Pumpkin Pie
Demi-Tasse

The Turkey

Rub 10-pound turkey inside and out with 1 tablespoon of salt. Stuff with the following:

The Stuffing

6 medium-sized onions, chopped   5 cups bread crumbs
Turkey liver, cut in small cubes   Cold water

Salt, pepper to taste
3 tablespoons butter
Powdered sage

Chopped parsley
Garlic, chopped if desired

Chop the onions, and cut up the turkey liver. Soak bread crumbs in water and squeeze dry; season to taste with salt and pepper. Melt butter in a frying pan, and cook onions and liver until tender. Add the bread crumbs and seasonings. Let it all cook, constantly stirring until almost dry. Then the stuffing is ready.

To stuff and truss the bird, begin by placing spoonfuls of stuffing in the neck end, using enough to fill the skin. Fold the wings close to the body and hold them by inserting 2 skewers through the wing, body, and wing on the other side. Fasten the thighs in the same manner with one skewer. Draw the skin over the neck and fasten to back with skewer. Rub the outside of the bird with 1½ tablespoons of salt, 5 tablespoons of fat, and 2 tablespoons of flour mixed together.

Lay the turkey, breast down, in an open roasting pan and place in a moderate (375-degree) oven. When brown, turn the fowl on its back, basting every 15 or 20 minutes with ¾ cup hot water and ½ cup melted butter. Cook for 20 to 25 minutes to the pound, depending on the age of the bird. [See also Harvester Salad, p. 87.]

Special permission, C. W. Bussey, Business Manager,
Warm Springs Foundation, Warm Springs, Ga.

CHART FOR ROASTING TURKEY OR CHICKEN

Young Chicken

Lbs.	Temp.	Min. per lb.	Time
4–5	300°	30	2 to 2½ hrs.

Turkey

Lbs.	Temp.	Min. per lb.	Time
10–16	300°	18–20	3½ to 4½ hrs.
18–23	300°	16–18	4½ to 6 hrs.
24–30	300°	15–18	6 to 7½ hrs.

This chart is the one used by Miss Laura Reilley, hostess at the Governor's Mansion at Raleigh, North Carolina. We do not cook our turkeys quite so long. A 20-pound young turkey should be roasted in three hours. It is best to know one's bird before setting a definite time limit on it. Buy ½ lb. dressed turkey per person; buy ¾ to 1 lb. chicken per person.

ALBERT'S SMOKED TURKEY

For those who do not have a smoker to smoke poultry, game, or meats, the contributor of this recipe has given us a description of a homemade type which may be easily duplicated.

Buy a No. 2 size galvanized washtub. On the outer side of the bottom of the tub, near the rim, make a circle about 5 inches in diameter. Punch the circle full of large nail holes (or a few even larger holes), filling the circle as full as possible with holes. Have a circle of metal bradded so that the vent holes may be closed if necessary. Brad a metal handle in the middle of the outside of the bottom so the tub may be handled easily. This tub will fit over a large outside grill.

When smoking anything, place the tub ¼ of an inch above the bed of charcoals in the grill to allow the fire breathing air. Build the fire to one side of the grill as the meat should not be directly over the fire. Leave plenty of room on the grill for the food to be smoked.

To give extra flavor, add a handful of hickory chips, which have been soaked at least 12 hours in water, to the well-burning coals. Then proceed to smoke. Add charcoal and chips as cooking progresses. There should be smoke coming continuously from the vents in the tub.

The Turkey

Split the turkey in half. Place the turkey on the opposite side of the fire on the grill rack. Put the tub over the turkey with the vented side above the turkey. Smoke the turkey, allowing 35 minutes per pound. Baste often with the following sauce, which has been simmered 10 minutes.

6 tablespoons salad oil	1 clove garlic
2 tablespoons vinegar	1 crushed, dried red pepper
Juice of 1 lemon	

Baste turkey with sauce. Do not let the turkey stay in smoker too long or it will dry out. Allow ½ pound of uncooked turkey per person.

Albert A. Stoddard, Burlington, N.C.

TURKEY-IN-THE-BAG

This simple modern way to roast an unstuffed turkey is in the same manner as the famous *Pompano en Papillote*.

Rub carefully dressed bird all over with good cooking oil or butter. Sprinkle very lightly with salt and flour. Inside of turkey rub 1 teaspoon of salt for every 5 pounds of dressed meat. Put in a large paper bag (any type which will fit); roll the ends tightly and place on roasting pan. Set the oven at 300 degrees. Do not open the bag to baste. Just follow the chart below and go to a football game, to the hair-dresser, or anywhere!

Cooking Chart

7 to 10 pounds—30 minutes per pound
10 to 15 pounds—20 minutes per pound
15 to 18 pounds—18 minutes per pound
18 to 20 pounds—15 minutes per pound
20 to 23 pounds—13 minutes per pound

When turkey is done, remove from oven and allow to stand 5 or 10 minutes. Then cut top out of bag and lift out the golden-brown bird. In the bottom of the bag, there will be plenty of rich stock which can be diluted for gravy or dressing. (An apple or ¼ cup of wine may be placed inside turkey before it is put in bag.) The giblets should be boiled separately, and if slowly simmered, will be done the same time as the turkey. Dressing should be made and baked separately.

Mrs. Don S. Holt, Concord, N.C., from Soup to Nuts, *Burlington, N.C.*

GALANTINE OF TURKEY (or *Chicken*)

This recipe, which appeared originally in the Danville, Virginia, *Episcopal Pantry,* calls for chicken. Mrs. Rushworth says that the recipe came from an English cook book given her by her husband's sisters in England, and that she thinks when one puts forth such an effort, a turkey should be substituted for chicken. But the same recipe may be used for either.

1 turkey or chicken	3 yolks hard-boiled eggs
1 lb. veal	A few pistachio nuts
½ lb. ham	Some strips of tongue
Salt and pepper	Stock
4 or 5 truffles	Chaudfroid sauce

Bone the bird entirely, cutting it open down the center of the back. Pass the veal and ham twice through a mincing machine and season well. Wet a board and spread the bird (open) on it; sprinkle with salt and pepper. Lay the veal and ham over it with the truffles, egg yolks, and pistachios in center and strips of tongue at each side. Make into a roll and fasten in a buttered cloth. Boil gently in well-flavored stock about 1½ hours; then roll in a clean cloth and press a little until cold. Then cover with white chaudfroid sauce (cold Cream Sauce, variety seasoning), and garnish with truffles or beetroot and lettuce. The galantine may be glazed instead of covered with white sauce and garnished with aspic.

Mrs. L. J. Rushworth, Danville, Va.

WILLIAMSBURG INN BREAST OF TURKEY SUPREME
Serves twelve

This prize recipe won for Chef Fred Crawford of Williamsburg Inn first prize at the Chef's Tournament at Virginia Beach in 1947 for the preparation of his dinner in which Breast of Turkey Supreme was the entrée. The sponsors were the Virginia State Chamber of Commerce and the jury consisted of some of the oustanding food editors and epicures in the country.

Sliced breast of turkey
1½ cups butter
1 cup flour
1 tablespoon salt
¼ teaspoon white pepper

4 cups chicken stock
2 cups milk
2 cups cream
¼ lb. toasted almonds

Melt butter; add flour; and stir until smooth. Add salt and pepper. Heat chicken stock, milk, and cream separately. Pour heated stock into above mixture and stir until smooth. Add milk and cream. Allow to cook over slow flame for 10 minutes. Serve sauce very hot over sliced breast of turkey and steamed noodles or rice. Sprinkle with toasted almonds over turkey and sauce.

By special permission, John D. Green, Vice-President,
Williamsburg Restoration, Inc., Williamsburg, Va.

TURKEY PATES
Serves six

12 English muffins (bakery)
2 cups cold white and dark meat
   turkey, chopped

2 cups thick gravy, left over
1 small onion
1 bunch parsley

Hollow out muffins by cutting out a large hole in bottom. Set in oven to crisp and brown, watching carefully to keep from burning. Heat cold turkey, gravy, onion, and a little parsley chopped fine, until boiling hot. Fill hot pâté shells with turkey and gravy. Decorate with sprigs of parsley and serve at once. Chicken or duck is delicious in the same way. Serve with cranberry jelly, etc.

Mrs. E. L. Pfohl, from What's Cookin'?, *Winston-Salem, N.C.*

TURKEY MOLE (*Pavo Mole*)

The second most important sauce in Mexico (served often in the United States) is mole, and a dish prepared with mole is to Mexico what turkey with chestnut dressing is to the United States.

This recipe is for turkey with the rich native mole or sauce.

1 young turkey
12 toasted almonds
1 slice stale bread
12 raisins
1 tablespoon ground chocolate
Ground cloves
1 teaspoon ground cinnamon
¼ teaspoon anise seed
1 tablespoon toasted sesame seed

3 to 6 tablespoons powdered chili pulp
6 tablespoons fat
1 minced onion
1 clove garlic
2 tablespoons flour
3 cups tomato sauce
3 cups turkey stock
Salt

"Cut the turkey as for fricassee and boil until tender. Pass through the fine blade of a food chopper the almonds, toasted bread, raisins, and chocolate. Mix well with the ground spices and dried chili pulp. Melt the fat and add onion and garlic. When transparent, add the flour and when flour browns, add remaining ingredients. Cook until well mixed and smooth; then add the tomato sauce. Cook for 5 minutes and add 3 cups of stock in which turkey was boiled. Salt. Cook a few minutes longer; add pieces of turkey (picked from bones). Cook gently until thick and serve with a sprinkling of sesame seed."

Mrs. Peter De Wetter, Fort Bliss, Tex., from La Cocina Mexicana, *by "Sally Ann," Food Editor,* El Paso Herald-Post, *El Paso, Tex.*

TO FRY CHICKEN

There are two ways to fry chicken "Southern style." It may be fried crisp with the gravy served separately, or fried and steamed in the gravy. The important things are to have the chicken well browned and thoroughly cooked.

Crisp Fried Chicken

1 frying size chicken, 2 to 2½ lbs., disjointed
1 cup flour
½ teaspoon each of salt and black pepper

¼ teaspoon each ground ginger and garlic powder (optional)
Fat for frying (⅔ Crisco, ⅓ butter; or salad oil and Crisco)

Rinse and pat the chicken dry. Mix the dry ingredients in a brown paper bag. Shake a few pieces at a time in the bag; shake off excess flour. Heat about 1 inch of fat in a heavy iron frying pan or an electric frying pan. When fat is smoking hot, lay in the chicken (do not crowd the pan). Cover the chicken and cook until it is just gold brown on one side. Turn chicken; cover pan and cook until under side is browned. Remove the top. Cook until the chicken is now a deep rich brown on one side; turn and fry until the other side is brown. Reduce the heat and let chicken fry slowly until it is fork tender, turning it once or twice. When done, drain on absorbent toweling. Place in a large paper-lined pan and keep warm in oven until serving time, or serve at once.

Gravy, Cream Style

Pour off all but about 2 tablespoons of fat. Stir in 2 tablespoons flour, stirring and scraping from the bottom of the pan to get all crisp bits. Slowly stir in 2 cups milk (or water). Cook until thickened; season to taste with salt and pepper. If more gravy is desired add extra flour and milk. Serve hot in gravy boat.

Country Style Chicken

To fry chicken Country Style: Remove the well-browned chicken from the pan. Make the gravy as for Crisp Fried Chicken, using either milk or water for liquid. Cook until the gravy begins to thicken. Place chicken back in the gravy; cover the vessel and steam slowly, turning chicken once or twice, until the gravy has thickened. If necessary, add a little additional milk or hot water to thin gravy.

1 chicken serves 4 to 6.

GIBLET GRAVY

Giblets from any fowl (neck, gizzard, liver, heart)
Cold water
1 stalk celery with tops, cut in long lengths
1 large onion, peeled, halved
1½ tablespoons poultry seasoning, or mixture of thyme, rosemary, sage
Salt and pepper to taste
1 teaspoon dry mustard
4 tablespoons flour or cornstarch
1 teaspoon Kitchen Bouquet, optional
1 tablespoon catchup
1 tablespoon Worcestershire sauce
Dash Tabasco sauce
1 teaspoon soy sauce, optional
2 to 3 hard-cooked eggs, peeled, sliced

Wash and remove all skin from giblets. Place in heavy pot with celery, onion, salt, pepper, and poultry seasonings. Cover with at least 1½ quarts cold water. Bring to boil and simmer until meat is done (about 1 hour). Remove liver after 10 minutes boiling, reserve. When meat is tender, remove to a bowl and cool. Strain the broth and skim. Return 1 quart broth (add water to make 1 quart if liquid boiled down) to pot. Mix dry mustard with flour or cornstarch, and mix with enough cool broth or water to make a thin paste. Stir into broth and bring to boil. Add the Kitchen Bouquet if a brown color is desired; add catchup and sauces. Boil slowly until gravy is smooth and thickened. Meanwhile, chop up meat fine and return it to the gravy. Heat thoroughly, and just before serving stir in gently the slices of egg, or float them on top of gravy. Serve over poultry dressing or rice.

FRIED CHICKEN, OLD DOMINION
Serves two to four

This is an exciting dish of fried chicken served on a waffle with Virginia ham, candied sweet potatoes and bananas.

Have a 2-pound chicken split and opened through the back; dress nicely and season. Sprinkle the chicken with cream and rub with a small amount of flour.

Have some clarified butter in a sauté pan. Fry the chicken in it until it is cooked and has attained a fine color (golden brown); then finish cooking in a slow oven (325 degrees) for 30 minutes. Remove the chicken from the pan and pour 1 cup of cream and 1 soupspoon of Virginia maple syrup in the pan; stir and let boil for a few minutes; then strain sauce. Serve chicken and sauce separately.

Arrange the chicken on a platter on a crisp waffle with sliced Virginia ham and garnish with rings of candied sweet potato and bananas.

Frank H. Briggs, General Manager, The Homestead, Hot Springs, Va.

COASTAL FRIED CHICKEN WITH BROWN CRUMB GRAVY
Serves four

1 1½-lb. spring chicken (frying chicken)	Flour for dredging chicken
	Fat for frying
Salt and pepper	

Sprinkle the chicken with salt and pepper to taste. Dredge it well with flour (see basic Fried Chicken recipe). Have ready in a heavy skillet hot fat (350 to 375 degrees), deep enough almost to cover the chicken. Lay in the large pieces first; cover with close-fitting lid. Cook to a golden brown, turning once. Drain on absorbent paper, and serve with rice and brown gravy. To achieve tender and juicy chicken, the fat must be hot, the chicken turned but once, and a lid on the pan.

Brown Crumb Gravy

Pour off all but 2 to 3 tablespoons grease (1 tablespoon grease for each cup of gravy); stir in 1 tablespoon of flour for each tablespoon of grease; heat and stir until the flour browns. Stir in 1 cup of water for each tablespoon of grease and flour. Stir from bottom of pan and around sides to get all brown crumbs in pan. Cook and stir until gravy thickens. Season to taste with salt and pepper.

Mrs. Edwin Fendig, from Coastal Cookery, *St. Simons Island, Ga.*

"OLD SOUTHERN" SMOTHERED CHICKEN
Serves two

This recipe is a specialty of the Old Southern Tea Room.

2 halves broiling chicken
½ cup milk
2 tablespoons flour
Salt and pepper

Fat for frying
Butter
Juice of 1 lemon
1 cup water

Dip chicken in milk; sprinkle with flour seasoned with salt and pepper; fry in deep fat until brown, take out, place in roasting pan, dot with butter, sprinkle with lemon juice, and add 1 cup water. Put in a 325- to 350-degree oven and cook until tender (about one hour), basting every now and then.

Mrs. W. I. McKay, Owner, Old Southern Tea Room, Vicksburg, Miss.

CHICKEN LIVERS IN WINE SAUCE WITH SAFFRON RICE
Serves four to six

4 to 6 slices bacon (1 slice per person)
2 tablespoons bacon drippings
1 tablespoon butter
2 tablespoons minced onion
2 tablespoons chopped celery
1 cup fresh mushrooms, sliced, or 1 cup canned mushrooms, drained

1 lb. chicken livers, cut into quarters
1½ tablespoons cornstarch mixed with 2 tablespoons water
1 cup dry white wine
¼ teaspoon salt
1 tablespoon each Worcestershire and soy sauce
1 dash Tabasco sauce

½ cup slivered toasted almonds or pistachios

Cooked saffron rice, cooked according to package directions, ½ cup or more per serving

In a heavy skillet or electric frying pan, fry the bacon until crisping stage. Remove from pan and curl each strip around a rod or handle. Drain on absorbent paper; reserve. Pour off bacon drippings, leaving 2 tablespoons in pan; add butter to bacon fat. Fry the onion and celery in hot fat until transparent; add the mushroom and livers; sauté for around 4 minutes, turning liver to brown lightly on all sides; remove from heat.

In a small saucepan, mix the cornstarch mixture, wine, and seasonings. Bring to boil and simmer until sauce begins to thicken.

Pour the sauce into the liver and vegetables; return pan to heat and bring back to boiling point; reduce heat and serve hot over hot saffron rice. Sprinkle each serving with the nuts and garnish with a curl of bacon.

Mrs. Charles B. Cardozo, Richmond, Virginia

ISABELLA'S CHICKEN MARENGO
Serves four to six

1 broiler size chicken, 2½ to 3 lbs.
3 tablespoons salad oil
1 medium-size onion, chopped
1 clove fresh white garlic, minced
2 tablespoons minced fresh parsley
1 1-lb., 12-oz. can good Italian tomatoes

2 12-oz. cans tomato paste
Salt and pepper to taste
12 small white onions, pickling size
12 mushroom caps
2½ tablespoons butter
Vermouth
1 cup green stuffed olives

Prepare the chicken for broiling or frying. Make a basic sauce as follows:

Basic Sauce

In a skillet heat the oil and sauté the onion and garlic until golden brown. Add the parsley, tomatoes, and tomato paste. Season with salt and pepper. Stir and simmer the sauce on low heat for 2 hours, stirring it often. This is a good basic sauce for the chicken and numerous other dishes.

Broil or fry the chicken until tender, using any favorite method of broiling or frying. Arrange the chicken in a casserole and pour over it a generous supply of the basic sauce.

Sauté the little white onions and mushroom in the butter until browned. Arrange these over the chicken and sauce. Add vermouth to taste. Cover and bake at 350 degrees for 1 hour. Five minutes before serving garnish the top with the olives.

If not to be served at once, reduce heat to 200 degrees and the chicken will keep well.

Mrs. Lambert Davis, Chapel Hill, N.C.

CHICKEN BARBARA (*Trademark*)
Serves six

On the Great Falls Road, near Rockville, Maryland, is Normandy Farm, one of the South's most famous eating establishments. Marjory Hendricks, owner-manager, has created many wonderful dishes bearing the Farm trademark, "The Goose-Girl." This recipe is an original trademark creation.

3 whole chicken breasts	1 large onion, sliced
2 cloves garlic	Salt and pepper
6 celery top stalks and leaves	Dash rosemary

Cut the breasts from (broiler) chickens (or the whole chicken may be steamed and breast removed). Surround chicken breasts with 1 cut clove of garlic, the celery stalks and leaves, and the sliced onion, and *steam* until tender. When half done, season with salt, pepper, and dash of rosemary. When completely done and tender, allow to cool. Remove the skin from the breasts and cut each in half, making six pieces in all. Rub each portion with the second cut clove of garlic. Dip in waffle batter and fry in deep fat at 375 degrees until golden brown.

Serve each portion of Chicken Barbara with ½ cup of lemon-flavored sauce *under* (not over) the chicken breast in its golden-brown coat. Garnish with water cress.

Waffle Batter for Chicken Barbara

3½ cups sifted flour	3 egg yolks, beaten
1 teaspoon salt	2½ cups buttermilk
2½ teaspoons baking powder	3 egg whites, stiffly beaten
1 teaspoon soda	

Sift the flour, salt, baking powder, and soda together. Put this flour mixture aside. Beat up egg yolks until frothy; then add buttermilk to the egg yolks and beat again. Whip egg whites until stiff but not dry. Add flour mixture to the egg-yolk mixture, beating until smooth. Lastly, fold in the beaten egg whites.

Lemon Sauce for Chicken Barbara

To 3 cups of seasoned white sauce made with rich milk, add the juice of 3 lemons and blend in smoothly. Add a little yellow vegetable food coloring or add 2 to 3 well-beaten egg yolks and blend in smoothly.

Special permission, Marjory Hendricks, Owner, Normandy Farm, Rt. 189, Rockville, Md.

BREAST OF CHICKEN WITH WILD RICE
Serves one

Breast of a young roasting chicken
Salt and pepper to taste
Butter
1 small onion, chopped
Small amount garlic, to taste

1 carrot and celery stalk, minced
1 large mushroom, chopped
1 small glass each of sherry and cognac
1 cup cream
1 cup wild rice, uncooked

Bone and skin the breast of a young roasting chicken. Season the breast with salt and black pepper; place in buttered heavy frying pan; add 1 small onion (chopped), garlic, carrot, celery, and fry slowly; add mushroom, sherry, cognac, and cream; cover and simmer slowly until breast is tender (done). Take 1 cup of wild rice, which has been washed in cold water, boil about 20 minutes, rinse in cold water, and put in rice steamer to heat. Dress rice in a timbale on platter and pour sauce over chicken. (The chicken is placed on rice if desired, or rice may be seasoned with butter, salt and pepper.)

John S. Cator, President, Fort Sumter Hotel, Charleston, S.C.

ADALYN LINDLEY'S CHICKEN A LA BARBARA
Serves six to eight

1 roasting chicken
1 cup flour
Salt, celery salt, pepper, paprika to taste
Chicken giblets
Tops of wings and neck

1 stalk celery
Carrots, parsnips, parsley
1 qt. water
1 tablespoon flour seasoned with salt and pepper
½ cup cream

Mix flour and seasonings and rub chicken inside and out with mixture. Melt ¼ pound of butter and rub over seasoned fowl. Take the chicken giblets, tops of wings and neck, a celery stalk, carrots, parsnips, and parsley (desired amount of each vegetable) and put into about 1 quart of water. Cook like soup for 1 hour. Strain. Mix 1 tablespoon of flour seasoned with salt and pepper with ½ cup cream. Thicken stock with this.

Put the chicken in a hot oven until slightly browned. Every 15 minutes pour ¼ cup stock over. When it is used up put cover on chicken and let simmer in oven until done.

Special permission, Adalyn Lindley, Manager, Neiman-Marcus Tea Room, Dallas, Tex.

COQ AU VIN
Serves four

This is most unusual and a different "chicken in wine."

1 large broiling size chicken, 5 lbs., quartered or cut as desired
Flour
4 tablespoons butter
1 wine glass brandy, heated slightly
1 fresh white clove garlic
1 bay leaf
¹⁄₁₆ teaspoon thyme

2 tablespoons chopped parsley
6 to 8 small white onions, peeled
12 mushrooms, unpeeled
Salt and pepper to taste
1 thick slice good country ham, diced (about 1 lb.)
1 cup good red wine (a little extra wine if desired)
Cooked wild rice

Quarter or cut the chicken as desired. Sprinkle it lightly with flour. Heat the butter in a skillet and sauté the chicken pieces. Arrange the chicken in a large casserole. Pour over the chicken the warmed brandy and ignite it. (If the brandy and chicken are not warm enough, the brandy will not flame). Allow chicken to blaze for a few seconds. Add the clove of garlic, bay leaf, thyme, parsley, onions, mushrooms, and salt and pepper to taste. Dice the ham and add it. Pour over the wine. Cover and bake in a slow oven (325 degrees) until chicken is tender. This dish may be made the day before; as is the case with all casserole dishes, it improves if allowed to set for a day.

Serve with cooked wild rice.

Mrs. Lambert Davis, Chapel Hill, N.C.

NOTE: Never use yellow garlic. Garlic should always be white and preferably have a little streak of green at the core. To maintain freshness, keep garlic in the refrigerator—I. D.

BAKED HEN IN SCUPPERNONG WINE
Serves six

Select 1 nice plump baking hen, weighing 5 to 6 pounds. Prepare for roasting, using stuffing, or roast plain. Cook in moderate oven (350 degrees) until chicken begins to get tender. About one-half hour before serving, pour over 1 cup of scuppernong wine and sprinkle the entire chicken with freshly ground nutmeg. Baste with pan dripping until serving time. Make gravy with the drippings and chopped giblets. [This chicken has a wonderful flavor, the leftover meat makes piquant creamed chicken.—M. B.]

Mrs. J. J. Henderson, Graham, N.C.

CHICKEN IN WINE, GRINALDS
Serves four to six

1 frying chicken, cut in pieces	Olive oil
Flour	1 clove garlic
Salt, pepper	1 cup domestic white wine
Powdered thyme	1 cup domestic sherry
Mace	1 cup chicken broth

Roll chicken pieces in flour and season with salt, pepper, thyme, and mace. Brown in ½ inch of good olive oil. Remove browned pieces and add garlic, wines, and broth to olive oil. Allow mixture to simmer 1 minute; remove garlic. Put chicken in a casserole; pour sauce over, and bake at 350 degrees for about 1 hour, depending on size of bird. While baking, ladle gravy over chicken every 15 minutes or so. Serve piping hot with sauce as gravy.

Mrs. R. T. Grinalds, Macon, Ga.

MOTHER'S CHICKEN AND DUMPLINGS
Serves six

The contributor of this, and several other recipes in this book, traces her ancestry to Tazewell, Virginia, where her grandparents were domestic slaves to a plantation owner. There they learned the art of British, French, and Southern cooking which they passed down to the present generation. With freedom papers granted them, Miss Bailey's grandparents went to Ohio to help with the Abolition movement. The grandfather helped "Eliza" (Harriet Beecher Stowe's *Uncle Tom's Cabin*) cross the Ohio river. According to her grandfather's records, "Eliza" swam the Ohio, and did not cross on ice floes.

1 large stewing chicken (5 to 6 lbs.)	Salt and pepper to taste
Cold water	Dumplings
Seasoning to taste	Gravy

Put the chicken in a large pot and cover with cold water and season to taste. Cover the pot; bring to a boil and then simmer until chicken is tender. Pour off 2 to 3 cups broth to make a separate gravy.

Make the dumplings and drape them across the chicken (do not drop in the broth). Cover the kettle and steam the dumplings 12 to 15 minutes, or until tender. Lift out the dumplings into a bowl, and pour the gravy over them. Serve with the carved chicken.

Dumplings

1 cup flour
1½ teaspoons baking powder
½ teaspoon salt

2 tablespoons shortening (Miss Bailey uses lard)
½ cup milk

Mix dry ingredients and shortening; stir in the milk. Roll the dough out on floured board to about ⅛ inch thick. Cut into strips about 1-inch wide. Drape the dumpling over the chicken as directed.

Gravy

3 cups chicken broth, fat not skimmed
1 tablespoon butter if broth not rich enough with chicken fat

3 tablespoons flour
Water
Salt and pepper

Heat the broth in a skillet. Add butter if necessary. Mix the flour with enough water to make a thin paste. Stir flour mixture into broth; season to taste with salt and pepper. Cook the gravy until it is as thick as heavy cream. Pour over the dumplings.

Miss Martha S. Bailey, New York, N.Y.

GREEN PEPPER CHICKEN (*Hawaiian Style*)
Serves two to four

1 2- to 2½-lb. frying chicken
2 medium-size green peppers, quartered, seeded
¼ cup tarragon vinegar
½ cup pineapple juice
1 tablespoon Worcestershire sauce
1 tablespoon soy sauce
½ cup tomato catchup or chili sauce

1 cup boiling water mixed with 1½ teaspoons instant chicken bouillon, or 2 cubes
3 dashes Tabasco sauce
½ teaspoon salt
1 teaspoon freshly ground black pepper
1 cup pineapple chunks, optional

Have chicken prepared; rinse and pat dry. Lay chicken, skin side down, in a baking dish or casserole with top. Stick the green pepper quarters in between or under pieces of chicken. In a deep bowl mix remaining ingredients except the pineapple chunks. Pour ½ of sauce over the chicken; cover the dish and bake in a 350-degree oven for 20 minutes. Remove top from baking dish and turn the chicken skin side up. Pour over enough sauce to coat chicken. Continue baking in uncovered dish for around 40 minutes, or until chicken is fork tender and browned. Baste often and add sauce as needed to keep chicken slightly moist. If pineapple is to be served in chicken, add it to the dish and stir sauce over it about 10 minutes before serving. Serve with hot cooked rice and the hot pan sauce.

Mrs. Don E. Scott, Jr., Burlington, N.C.

TARRAGON CHICKEN
Serves six

6 half chicken breasts, boned
Reese roll-on garlic oil
Salt and pepper
Flour
4 tablespoons minced onion
2 tablespoons butter

2 tablespoons oil
1 teaspoon dried tarragon
1 cup chicken broth
½ cup dry white wine
1 tablespoon lemon juice
6 slices Mozzarella cheese

Rub both sides of chicken with garlic oil. Salt and pepper chicken; dip in flour; sprinkle with onion. Brown lightly in butter and oil in a frying pan. Remove chicken to a shallow baking dish and sprinkle with tarragon.

Add broth, wine, and lemon juice to drippings and bring to boil. Pour over the chicken. Bake covered in a 350-degree oven for 45 minutes. Remove cover. Place a slice of cheese on each breast and bake uncovered until cheese is melted.

This may be frozen before baking, thawed at room temperature, and baked for 1¼ hours at 325.

Porter Cowles, Chapel Hill, N.C.

CHICKEN BREASTS IN ORANGE-WINE SAUCE WITH WATER CHESTNUTS
Serves four

4 whole chicken breasts, skinned
    or with skin left on
½ cup sherry
1 teaspoon each of salt, black pep-

per, dry mustard, ground
ginger, onion salt, and parsley flakes (mix together)
¼ teaspoon garlic powder

4 tablespoons butter

1 cup fresh orange juice

1 cup chicken bouillon (make with instant bouillon), or chicken stock

2 tablespoons cornstarch, dissolved in 3 tablespoons of the bouillon

1 tablespoon grated orange rind

4 tablespoons orange marmalade, apricot marmalade, or guava jelly

½ cup very thinly sliced water chestnuts

Hot cooked rice

Fresh parsley or orange sections

Open the chicken breasts and lay them in a bowl; pour over the sherry and let marinate for several hours at room temperature; turn often. Remove the breasts and drain them well. Reserve the wine marinade. Pat the chicken dry with absorbent towel and sprinkle inside and out with the dry seasonings which have been mixed together. Place a slice of butter (about 1 teaspoon) in the inside of each breast. Pull the breasts together and skewer them with wooden toothpicks, or tie them with string.

In a heavy skillet with top, or electric fry pan set at 350 degrees, heat the remaining butter to golden brown; fry the breasts in the butter, turning them on all sides so they will be uniformly browned. Add the orange juice and wine marinade. Place top on pan and simmer for 25 minutes, basting often. Add ½ the bouillon, the cornstarch mixture, and grated orange rind. Stir the pan sauce well. Replace top on pan and bring mixture to boiling point. Reduce heat to simmer (250 degrees), and continue cooking until chicken breasts are fork tender. Baste frequently as they cook. If the sauce becomes too thick or reduces itself too much, gradually add the remaining part of the chicken bouillon. 10 minutes before serving time, place a tablespoon of the marmalade or jelly on top of each breast; stir the water chestnuts into the sauce.

Serve 1 breast per person on a mound of rice; spoon the hot sauce over all. Garnish with tips of fresh parsley or mandarin orange sections.

Mrs. John F. Schoonmaker, Freeport, Grand Bahama

BAKED STUFFED CHICKEN LEGS
Serves six

6 large chicken legs, boned

2 cups poultry dressing (see recipe below)

1 teaspoon salt

½ teaspoon each of ground ginger, black pepper and garlic powder

3 tablespoons butter

Chicken broth

1 tablespoon flour mixed with ¼ cup water

2 tablespoons sherry

Salt and pepper to taste

Have the butcher bone the chicken legs. Stuff with the poultry dressing; sew up the legs or tie them securely. Combine the dry seasonings and sprinkle the legs generously. Heat the butter in a skillet; sauté the legs, turning them to brown on all sides until golden brown. Arrange the legs in a baking dish with cover. Pour in enough chicken broth to come up ½ the depth of the chicken. Add more as chicken bakes if pan becomes too dry. Cover and bake in a 350-degree oven for 1 hour. Remove the legs to a warm platter; keep warm; remove the strings. Mix the flour with water and stir into the pan sauce. Cook until it thickens; add the sherry; season to taste with salt and pepper. Pour over the chicken. Serve with hot rice.

To bake as a "quickie." Shake the stuffed legs in "Shake and Bake." Bake according to package directions.

Dressing

Sauté 2 tablespoons of minced onion in 2 tablespoons heated butter until onions are tender. Combine in the pan 2 cups soft bread crumbs, ¼ teaspoon each of dried savory, thyme, marjoram; ⅛ teaspoon curry powder, ½ teaspoon black pepper; 1 tablespoon minced parsley, 2 tablespoons chicken stock or warm water. Toss together. Stuff the chicken legs with mixture.

NOTE: Boned chicken breasts may be used in place of the legs. Use 1 whole breast to stuff. It may be sliced in half, crosswise, to serve. 1 whole breast serves 2.

CHICKEN DIVAN
Serves four

1 bunch fresh broccoli, or 12 ozs. frozen	8 buttered toast points
2 tablespoons butter, melted	Sliced chicken, turkey, or capon breast
3 to 3½ cups creamed potatoes	Paprika
Hollandaise sauce (about 1½ cups)	

Wash fresh broccoli (or prepare frozen as directed on package), and cut off any tough stalk or leaves. Place in open vessel in enough boiling water (slightly salted) and let cook 20 minutes, or until tender. Drain; pour melted butter over; roll broccoli around in butter and keep heated.

Have potatoes prepared (see recipes) and keep hot over boiling water (in double boiler). Have Hollandaise sauce ready, made to be served immediately. Toast and butter bread.

In the center of individual serving places place the toast points. Lay on these several thin slices of chicken, turkey, or capon. Over this place the broccoli spikes. Flute the hot potatoes around edge of plate. Serve the hot Hollandaise sauce over broccoli. Sprinkle entire serving with paprika.

Paul Willard, Fresno, Calif.

MRS. S. G. STONEY'S BAKED CHICKEN AND CORN
Serves four

1 frying-size chicken, cut into serving pieces, coated lightly with flour
Shortening for frying
Salt and pepper

1 cup butter
2½ to 3 cups fresh raw green corn, grated from the cob
½ teaspoon grated nutmeg
Extra salt and pepper

Lightly coat the chicken pieces with flour. Sprinkle with salt and pepper. Quickly brown the chicken in hot shortening until only slightly browned. Remove chicken to a 1½-quart baking dish or casserole with cover. Divide the butter and use half to dot the chicken. Pour the green corn over the chicken. Dot the corn with the remaining butter; sprinkle with nutmeg, salt, and pepper. Cover the dish and bake in a slow (300 degrees) oven for about 1 hour, or until chicken is tender. If the dish gets too dry, add additional butter.

Mrs. W. S. Popham (Louisa Stoney), from Charleston Receipts, *Junior League of Charleston, Inc., S.C.*

CHICKEN WITH EGGPLANT
Serves four

1 large eggplant, peeled, cut up
1 frying-size chicken (or desired parts of chicken) cut into serving pieces
Salt and pepper
1 cup sliced onions (more or less)
1 tablespoon butter

1 teaspoon dry mustard
½ teaspoon oregano
Vermouth
1 package frozen artichoke hearts (optional)
Butter
Parmesan cheese

Peel and cut the eggplant into desired size pieces. Arrange the eggplant in a large buttered casserole. Lay the chicken pieces on top of eggplant. Sprinkle with salt and pepper to taste. Sauté the onions in butter, and pour onions and pan drippings over chicken. Sprinkle with the mustard, oregano, and vermouth. Arrange the artichoke hearts over the onions; dot generously with butter. Sprinkle generously with Parmesan cheese. Bake covered in a moderate oven (350 degrees) for 1 hour.

Serve with good Pepperidge Farm French Bread, butter, and Rosé wine. This is a complete meal.

NOTE: If this is to be served for as many as 8 persons, it is advisable to bake it in 2 casseroles. The eggplant takes a great deal of room in the beginning, but it shrinks as it is cooked.

Mrs. Lambert Davis, Chapel Hill, N.C.

BERT'S CHICKEN AND OYSTER CASSEROLE
Serves ten generously

5 to 6 lb. roasting chicken
Water to cover
1 teaspoon each of Accent and sage
2 teaspoons salt
1 teaspoon of black pepper
2 stalks of celery
1 medium onion, quartered
Parsley sprigs

Crushed cracker crumbs (soda crackers)
Salt and pepper
Butter
1½ to 2 lbs. fresh mushrooms, sliced
Fresh oysters, at least 1 qt.
Chicken broth
Milk

The day before making the casserole, boil the chicken in water to cover; season with the Accent, sage, salt, pepper, celery stalks, and onion. Cook until meat is tender. Remove meat from bones; cut into bite-size pieces. Chill the broth, skim off fat, and strain. Reserve broth.

To make the casserole:

In the bottom of a 2- to 2½-quart casserole, arrange a ½-inch layer of crushed cracker crumbs; sprinkle lightly with salt and pepper (if salted crackers are used, no salt is necessary); dot generously with bits of butter. Spread all of the chicken over the crackers. Spread the mushrooms over the chicken. Arrange a second layer of cracker crumbs, salt, pepper, and butter over the mushrooms. Now make a layer of oysters, at least 2 oysters deep, over the crumbs. Sprinkle oysters with a topping of cracker crumbs, salt, and pepper, and dot generously with butter.

Mix equal parts of chicken broth and milk, making up 1 cup at a time. Pour the broth mixture over casserole contents, using enough so the liquid may be seen when dish is tilted. Bake in a 400-degree oven for 45 minutes. Heat may be increased last few minutes to brown top. Garnish each serving with parsley.

Mrs. A. Glenn Holt, Burlington, N.C.

CHICKEN "GO-GO"
Serves six to eight

Chicken "Go-Go" may be broiled over a small hibachi, oriental style, or over an outside charcoal grill.

4 chicken breasts, skinned, boned, cut into 1-inch squares
1½ cups soy sauce
3 tablespoons lime or lemon juice
1 clove garlic, mashed
¼ teaspoon ground ginger
1 teaspoon freshly ground black pepper

3 tablespoons butter
Mushroom caps
Skewers (use bamboo skewers for hibachi, metal skewers for outside grill)

"Go-Go" sauce

Prepare the chicken; place in a shallow dish. Mix the soy sauce, lime juice, garlic, ginger, and black pepper in saucepan. Pour the marinade over the chicken and refrigerate for about 2 hours. Remove the chicken; pour the marinade back into saucepan, and add the butter. Heat the marinade and keep warm. Thread the chicken squares and mushroom caps alternately on skewers. Broil over coals in the hibachi or on outside grill. Turn the skewers often, basting with the warm marinade. Allow each guest to broil his own skewer. This is nice for an informal party. Serve the "Go-Go" sauce in a bowl; spoon over each skewer.

Sauce

1 cup white wine
2 tablespoons butter
1 tablespoon soy sauce
⅓ cup crushed peanuts (crush in blender)

1 tablespoon ground red hot pepper
1 tablespoon minced onion

Mix; heat to boiling. Serve hot.

Mrs. A. F. Soutar, St. Petersburg Beach, Fla.

CHARCOAL CHICKEN CHILI
Serves two

1 large broiler-fryer chicken, halved, skinned (2½ to 3 lbs.)

½ cup crushed red chili peppers (dried chilis)

1 teaspoon ground peppercorns

2 cups sour cream

Prepare the chicken and lay in a flat baking dish. Crush or grind the peppers; grind peppercorns. Mix the peppers with the sour cream. Pour mixture over the chicken. Let chicken stand in the marinade in refrigerator for 3 hours. Turn the chicken often. Remove the chicken and drain. Broil over a very hot firebed, about 4 inches above coals, turning once or twice. Cook for 25 to 35 minutes, according to size of chicken, or until tender. Serve with a chili sauce for chicken (see "Sauces").

A. B. Lea, Jamestown, N.C.

PAELLA "VALENCIANA"
Serves ten to twelve

This is a famous Spanish *Paella* made of meat, poultry, and sea foods.

1 heavy 4-qt. casserole or baking vessel with top

¾ cup Spanish olive oil

3 cloves garlic, minced

1 lb. raw pork, cubed

1 frying-size chicken, cut into serving pieces

1 medium onion, diced

1 green pepper, chopped

½ lb. each of raw, shelled crawfish (or crab meat) and peeled shrimp

4 ozs. each of raw oysters and scallops

½ lb. raw red snapper, cut in bite-size pieces

2 qts. sea food stock (or chicken stock if preferred)

½ cup chopped ripe tomatoes

2½ cups raw rice

2 bay leaves

Pinch saffron and drop of yellow coloring

1 tablespoon salt

Fresh ground black pepper to taste

Petit pois (baby green peas)

Strips of pimientos

White wine

Pour the olive oil in casserole, and heat in 350-degree oven until oil smokes. Add the minced garlic, the pork, and chicken. Braise the pork and chicken in oven, turning often, until browned on all sides. Stir in the onion, green pepper, and the sea foods. Cook the sea foods, stirring once or twice, until the red snapper is almost fork tender (about 10 minutes). Add the sea food stock, tomatoes, and rice. Let mixture come to a boil; add the bay leaves, saffron, coloring, salt, and pepper. Let cook until the rice begins to thicken. Cover the casserole and let bake (350 degrees) for 15 minutes. Garnish the top of the casserole with heated green peas and strips of pimientos. Sprinkle the whole with white wine (about ½ cup). Serve hot from the casserole.

The Columbia Restaurants, Tampa, Fla.

ARROZ CON POLLO (*Rice with Chicken*)
Serves six

Eliza B. K. Dooley says, "This is one of the most typical dishes in Puerto Rico."

1 chicken
½ cup olive oil
Parsley
2 cloves garlic
¾ lb. raw rice

3 cups water
2 teaspoons salt
⅓ cup capers
½ cup olives
Spanish peppers

Disjoint a chicken and cut the larger portions in fairly small pieces. Brown in the olive oil; add chopped parsley and garlic. Now add ¾ of a pound of rice (raw) and, after it has taken on a golden color, add 3 cups of water and cook slowly, keeping covered so as to preserve the aroma. The rice should be cooked through but not broken open. Add the salt, capers, and olives cut up. Garnish with Spanish peppers and serve hot.

From Puerto Rican Cook Book, *by Eliza B. K. Dooley, San Juan, Puerto Rico*

ANTOINE'S CHICKEN CREOLE
Serves four to six

This is a crisply fried chicken in Creole sauce.

1 fryer (2½ to 3 lbs.)
¼ cup olive oil
1 No. 2 can tomatoes
2 tablespoons butter
1 teaspoon salt
⅛ teaspoon pepper
⅛ teaspoon cayenne pepper
1 sprig thyme
1 tablespoon minced parsley

1 bay leaf
3 cloves garlic, minced
1 tablespoon butter
1 tablespoon flour
6 chopped shallots, or ½ cup minced onion
5 tablespoons green pepper, chopped
½ cup white wine

Cut up chicken as for frying; wipe pieces with damp cloth. Sauté in olive oil, turning to brown both sides. Combine tomatoes and butter, and simmer 10 minutes, stirring occasionally. Add salt, pepper, and cayenne. Cook 10 minutes. Add thyme, parsley, bay leaf, and garlic. Cook 15 minutes, or until sauce is thick. Melt 1 tablespoon butter; blend in flour; cook until brown. Add shallots or onion, and green peppers; brown slightly. Add wine, stirring constantly, until slightly thickened. Add chicken; cover and simmer 45 minutes, or until chicken is tender. If desired, place chicken on hot cooked rice, and garnish. For elegance, place chicken (each portion) on halved avocado; pour over the sauce.

From Antoine's Restaurant, New Orleans, La. Special permission,
Roy Alciatore, Proprietor

OLD-FASHIONED CHICKEN PILAFF (*Pilau*)
Serves four

Pilaff or *Pilau* is a French-Creole dish of rice with fowl or meat similar to the Spanish *Paella*.

1 young chicken (fryer about 2½ lbs.)	1 cup diced celery
½ cup butter or chicken fat	2 cups uncooked rice
1 medium onion, chopped	1 qt. chicken broth, about
	Salt, pepper, and nutmeg

Fry disjointed chicken in butter until it begins to brown; add onions and celery, and let simmer until onion is done. Add raw rice; stir thoroughly. Cover with chicken broth; taste with seasoning; let come to a boil. Close saucepan with tight-fitting lid, and let simmer about 18–20 minutes in medium hot (350-degree) oven. *Pilau* should be more moist than dry. Serve in soup bowl with corn sticks on side.

John S. Cator, President, Fort Sumter Hotel, Charleston, S.C.

ALABAMA "COUNTRY CAPTAIN" (*Chicken Curry*)
Serves ten to twelve

Fry 2 chickens weighing 2½ or 3 lbs. each. Make a sauce as follows:

1 tablespoon butter or bacon grease	1 bell pepper, sliced
1 medium onion, sliced thin	1 or 2 cloves garlic
2 No. 2 cans tomatoes	½ cup chopped celery

Cook the onion, pepper, garlic, and celery in the butter until brown, about 10 minutes. Add tomatoes and cook 10 minutes longer. Then add:

1 teaspoon salt
½ teaspoon white pepper (or black)
1 teaspoon thyme

1 teaspoon curry powder
1 teaspoon chopped parsley
Currants
Almonds

Cook all together 5 minutes longer. Put the chicken in pan with sauce. Add 2 tablespoons of the pan lard that chicken was fried in. Cook slowly 45 minutes. Ladle out chicken. Mix the sauce with cooked rice. Sprinkle with currants and almonds. Serve rice and sauce in center of platter with chicken around it. Use only the best pieces of chicken.

Anne Patton, from 100 Favorite Recipes, *Huntsville, Ala.*

INDIAN CURRY
Serves ten to twelve

This is an old original recipe:

1 boiled chicken (about 5 lbs. when dressed and drawn)
2 large onions, chopped
1 stalk celery
1 large can (1 cup) mushrooms, drained
½ teaspoon ginger

1½ tablespoons curry powder
½ cup flour
2 qts. chicken stock
1 6-oz. can tomato paste
Add salt and pepper to taste
Raisins, peanuts

Skim grease from chicken stock; put in iron pot and fry celery, onion, mushrooms, and ginger for five minutes; add curry powder and flour, blending well. Gradually stir in chicken stock; add tomato paste and cook until thickened. Add chicken which has been removed from bone and cut in 1-inch pieces. Serve on rice and garnish with raisins and peanuts.

Mrs. John William McElderry, from Recipes from Southern Kitchens, *Augusta, Ga.*

CHICKEN BLINTZ
Serves eight

Chicken Blintz is an original recipe created by Ernest Coker at his Ye Old College Inn. This is an individual chicken pie made like the old-fashioned "Crab Lantern" fruit pie and fried in deep fat.

Pie Filling

1 tablespoon chopped green onions

4 tablespoons chicken fat or butter

4 tablespoons flour
2 cups chicken stock
Meat from ½ medium-size cooked hen, chopped fine
1 teaspoon chopped pimiento
1 teaspoon Lea and Perrins sauce

1 tablespoon lemon juice
1 teaspoon chopped parsley
Salt, pepper to taste
1 wine glass Burgundy
Pie crust (not too short)

Sauté onion in the butter or fat; blend in the flour and make a brown roux. Add the chicken stock. Add remaining ingredients and stir all together until it thickens.

Roll pie crust thin, and cut in circles 5 inches in diameter (cut by outline of a saucer). Place 1 tablespoon chicken filling in center of pastry circle; fold over and crimp edges as for old-fashioned fruit pies. Fry in deep fat. Serve with a rich brown sauce made with the chicken stock and mushrooms. This may be made like the sauce in the pie filling above. Add mushrooms and wine glass of Burgundy to basic recipe.

Ernest Coker, Proprietor, Ye Old College Inn,
Houston, Tex.

CHICKEN OR TURKEY CHOW MEIN
Serves eight to ten

3½ cups cooked chicken or turkey, cut into bite-size pieces
White turkey meat for garnish (cut chicken breast into thin strips)
2½ cups celery stalks, cut in diagonal strips, ½ inch in length
1 sweet green pepper, seeded, cut into ⅛-inch strips
2 medium size onions, cut down lengthwise into 12 strips each
1 cup mushrooms, sliced thin (or drained canned mushrooms)

4 tablespoons butter
2½ cups chicken or turkey broth
1 teaspoon salt
½ teaspoon black pepper
1 teaspoon Worcestershire sauce
3½ tablespoons cornstarch mixed to paste with 3 tablespoons cold water
3½ tablespoons soy sauce
1 No. 2 can Chinese mixed vegetables (or bean sprouts)
Chow mein noodles
Cooked rice if desired
Extra soy sauce

First, prepare the chicken; set aside.

In a large skillet, sauté the celery, pepper, onion, and mushrooms in the butter for 3 minutes. Add the broth, salt, pepper, and Worcestershire sauce. Bring mixture to a boil; stir in the cornstarch mixture. Cook over medium heat, stirring constantly, until thickened. Add the chicken cubes, soy sauce, and vegetables. Heat thoroughly. Serve over chow mein noodles with rice as side dish. Garnish with strips of white chicken meat.

Mrs. Van MacNair, La Jolla, Calif.

CHICKEN TACOS
Serves twelve

A taco is a rolled tortilla (Mexican pancake) wrapped around or filled with various mixtures such as chili, Mexican beans with grated cheese and avocado slices on top, chicken or beef mixtures, and so on.

1 onion, finely chopped
2 tablespoons butter
1 cup tomato juice
2 peeled green peppers, cooked for short while

1 cup finely chopped chicken or beef, cooked
Dash thyme
Salt to taste
12 tortillas, canned or frozen

Sauté the onions in butter until golden brown; add the tomato juice, green peppers (cooked), chicken or beef, thyme, and salt. Simmer all for a few minutes, or until mixture is not moist.

Place a spoonful of mixture in the center of each tortilla; roll each, and pin with toothpick. Fry in deep hot cooking oil until crisp brown. Stack tacos on hot platter. Remove picks. Pour Guacamole (Avocado) Sauce over all. Serve at once. [For Sauce, see p. 20.]

From Lady Jo's Southern Recipes, *Lady Jo Kirby Beals, Texarkana, Ark., Tex.*

CHICKEN TERRAPIN
Serves twelve

Chicken Terrapin is an old Southern dish similar to creamed chicken.

1 chicken (hen)
1 large can mushrooms
2 cups milk
2 large tablespoons butter
1 large tablespoon flour
3 egg yolks, beaten

Salt, red pepper, nutmeg
Minced onion
Sherry
Minced parsley to taste
Bread crumbs
Butter

Prepare chicken by boiling until tender; cut up as for chicken salad. Simmer mushrooms for ½ hour in covered saucepan (in own juice); drain, and add mushrooms to chicken. Boil milk and add it to the butter and flour creamed together. Drop in quickly the yolks of eggs. Stir constantly over low flame until mixture thickens. Add dry seasonings, minced onion, and sherry wine to taste.

Add minced parsley. Either use baking dish or ramekins. Fill dish or ramekins with chicken mixture; sprinkle with bread crumbs and bits of butter. It can then be set aside until 20 minutes before serving; then run into the oven to heat and brown. Serve steaming hot.

Mrs. Philip Roper, from Christ Church Cook Book, *Petersburg, Va.*

CHICKEN TETRAZZINI
Serves eight

Chicken Tetrazzini is an excellent type of chicken spaghetti. It is sometimes made with a tomato sauce. This is from an old eastern North Carolina recipe originated as a buffet dinner entrée.

1 6-lb. hen, boiled (save stock)	2 tablespoons flour
Butter	1 teaspoon salt, or more
1 large onion, minced	Black pepper to taste
1 small green pepper, minced	1½ cups sweet milk
1½ cups chopped mushrooms, fresh or B & B canned	¼ cup sherry
3 tablespoons minced pimiento	1½ boxes (or more) long thin spaghetti
2 tablespoons butter	½ cup grated Parmesan cheese

Boil chicken until meat falls from bones; save the stock, and skim off fat. When cool, cube chicken (white meat preferred). Sauté in butter the onion, peppers, and mushrooms. Mix with the cubed chicken and pimiento. Make a sauce as follows:

Blend with the 2 tablespoons heated butter, the flour, salt and pepper to taste. Add milk and simmer until medium thick. Add wine last. Blend with the chicken and heat. Boil the spaghetti in the chicken stock, adding water if necessary. When tender, drain spaghetti and mix with the chicken and sauce; stir in the grated cheese. Place in a large greased casserole; sprinkle generously with Parmesan cheese; bake in a 375-degree oven 20 to 30 minutes.

Mrs. Robert J. Powell, Fayetteville, N.C.

CHICKEN PIE WITH COACHWHEEL CRUST
Serves eight

4-lb. chicken cut from bone after stewing in salted water	1½ cups chicken broth
3 tablespoons flour	2 thin slices onion
3 tablespoons butter	1 teaspoon salt
1½ cups milk	1 tablespoon lemon juice

Make a gravy by blending the flour into butter, and adding milk, stock, onion, and seasonings, and combine while hot with the boneless chicken. Pour all into a casserole. Top with coachwheel crusts as follows:

1½ cups flour	½ cup milk
3 teaspoons baking powder	3 pimientos, chopped
½ teaspoon salt	¾ cup grated cheese
3 tablespoons shortening	

Sift dry ingredients together; mix with shortening and milk; then roll out thin. Chop pimientos and grated cheese. Spread cheese and pimientos over crust. Roll up dough like a jelly roll and cut ¾ inches thick into little wheels. Place wheels on top of chicken casserole. Bake at 400 degrees about 30 minutes.

Mrs. Louis E. Kulcinski, from The Columbia Woman's Club Cook Book,
Columbia, S.C.

CHICKEN OR TURKEY A LA KING
Serves six to eight

2 tablespoons butter	½ cup butter, softened
½ green pepper, chopped fine	3 egg yolks
1 cup sliced mushroom caps	1 teaspoon each onion juice and
2 tablespoons flour	lemon juice
½ teaspoon salt	½ teaspoon paprika
2 cups light cream	Toast or patty shells
3 cups cooked chicken or turkey, cubed	

Heat the butter in the top of a large double boiler (or some pan that may be placed over hot water later), heating it on a slow, direct heat. Add the green pepper and mushrooms and cook for about 3 minutes. Stir in flour and salt and cook until mixture is frothy. Gradually stir in the cream; cook, stirring constantly, until sauce thickens. Remove from direct heat and set over hot water. Add the chicken and stir. Cover the pan and let stand until mixture becomes hot, but do not boil.

Cream the butter in a mixing bowl, and beat in the egg yolks, onion juice, lemon juice, and paprika. Stir this mixture into the hot chicken and continue stirring until the sauce thickens a little. Serve hot over toast or in patty shells.

Mrs. William Allison, Statesville, N.C.

HARDIMONT "CREEM CHICKEN"
Serves eighteen

For years a cook for the Biggs family kept a little copy book in which she recorded her own original "receipts." In this faded, yellowed book we found many rich old dishes. Among them is this recipe for Cream Chicken. A variant of this dish is Chicken en Coquilles (see recipe).

"7 cup chicken, 2½ quort creem. Make creem dressing 1 tablespoon to each cup, 3 pound mushroomes, 2½ cup celery, 1 green pepper, 1 tablespoon salt in creem dressing. 1 stick butter in creem dressing, 1 stick in mushroomes."

ABOUT CHICKEN SHORTCAKE

Old-fashioned Chicken Shortcake is made in several ways. A favorite method is to use rich creamed chicken with mushrooms and to place a layer of chicken between flaky pie crusts and pile more chicken on top. This is sliced in wedges and served like cake, or it may be served in little patty shells covered with tiny rounds of crusts to fit the tops of the shells.

A second shortcake, and perhaps the earliest method, is to serve either creamed chicken, or chicken (or turkey) hash, between squares of corn bread which have been cut through like a hot biscuit. The chicken mixture is served between and on top of the corn bread. Leftover chicken and gravy, turkey and gravy, or any meat creamed mixture or hash makes a tempting shortcake.

CREAM CHICKEN SHERRY EN COQUILLES
Serves ten to twelve

10 to 12 large oyster or clam shells
Chopped meat from 5-lb. cooked hen
Sherry
2 tablespoons butter
2 tablespoons flour
1¼ cups light cream
2 tablespoons chopped parsley
⅛ teaspoon red pepper
1 teaspoon onion juice
1 cup fresh sliced mushrooms, or canned; drained; sautéed in 1 tablespoon butter
2 cups buttered bread crumbs

Rinse and dry the shells. Pick the meat from cooked chicken and cut in small dice. Place the chicken in a bowl and cover with sherry. Let set 1 hour, and drain off the wine. Melt the butter in a skillet, and stir in the flour to make a paste. Slowly add the cream, stirring constantly. Add parsley, red pepper, and onion juice. Cook, stirring until the sauce thickens. Add the sautéed mushrooms and diced chicken. Let mixture cool; chill it. Fill the shells with the chilled mixture and sprinkle with bread crumbs. Bake in a 350-degree oven until chicken is hot and crumbs browned.

Mrs. Stuart Papperson, Vicksburg, Miss.

GEORGIA BARBECUE CHICKEN
Serves two to four

Have broiling chicken cut in two (split down back and through breast). Place in a large roasting pan; have barbecue sauce made; pour ½ sauce on now, and bake in a slow oven (300 to 325 degrees) for at least 1 hour—longer will not hurt. Keep basting and turning chicken during cooking period.

Sauce

¼ cup vinegar
½ cup water
2 tablespoons brown sugar
1 tablespoon prepared mustard
1½ teaspoons salt
½ teaspoon black pepper
¼ teaspoon cayenne pepper

Juice 1 lemon
1 large onion, sliced
¼ cup butter
½ cup catchup
2 tablespoons Worcestershire sauce
1½ teaspoons Liquid Smoke

Mix first 10 ingredients; bring to a boil and boil 20 minutes, uncovered. Add catchup, Worcestershire, and Liquid Smoke. Use as directed above. [This is an excellent sauce to baste any fowl or meat; try it on hamburgers.—M. B.]

Mrs. R. T. Grinalds, Macon, Ga.

CHICKEN AND OYSTER CROQUETTES
Sixteen large croquettes

2 large broiler-size chickens, about 3 lbs. each, cooked, chopped fine
1 qt. oysters, cooked in own juice, Chopped fine
2 tablespoons butter
2 tablespoons flour
1 cup chicken broth

1 tablespoon minced parsley
⅛ teaspoon mace
1 teaspoon onion juice
Salt and pepper to taste
1 egg, slightly beaten
Cracker crumbs
Fat for frying

Cube or chop the chicken fine. Boil the oysters over medium heat just until the edges curl; drain; chop oysters fine. Melt the butter in a skillet; stir in the flour; add the broth and seasonings; stir and cook over low heat until the sauce is thick. Combine the oysters and chicken; stir the sauce into the oysters and chicken. Chill the mixture until stiff. Form into cones or any shape croquettes, using about 1 cup to make 2 croquettes (smaller ones may be made for an hors d'oeuvre). Dip into beaten egg and roll in cracker crumbs. Fry in the basket of a deep frying pan in 375-degree fat until golden brown on all sides; drain and serve hot.

If desired, serve with Lemon Sauce for Normandy Farm Chicken Barbara recipe, p. 204. Furnish toothpicks if croquettes are served as an hors d'oeuvre.

By Bridget, a famous Savannah cook, from Coastal Cookery, *St. Simons Island, Ga.*

CHICKEN CROQUETTES
Serves twelve to fourteen

1 hen boiled, meat put through grinder
Dry mustard, salt, and cayenne to taste
1 heaping tablespoon butter
Small piece onion
1 tablespoon flour
1 cup chicken stock
2 egg yolks
Sherry
2 egg whites, unbeaten
Cracker crumbs

Put the tender boiled chicken through meat grinder; season to taste with dry mustard, salt, and cayenne pepper. Put into saucepan the butter, onion, and flour. Mix until smooth. Remove onion; add chicken stock and the chicken. When hot, add yolks of 2 eggs; cook until stiff. Chill. When cold, add sherry to taste. Make into croquettes; roll in unbeaten egg whites and then in cracker crumbs, and fry in deep fat.

Mrs. L. R. Watts, from The Guild Cook Book, *Portsmouth, Va.*

VARIATION: For chicken croquettes, the meat may be chopped fine rather than ground. Try serving with Lemon Sauce from Normandy Farm Chicken Barbara recipe (see p. 204).

LONG ISLAND DUCKLING WITH ORANGE SAUCE
Serves four

4½ to 5 lb. duckling
Salt and pepper
Juice of 1 lemon
2 stalks celery with leaves, broken into sections
1 small onion, cut into quarters
½ small red apple
1½ cups white wine or vermouth
Orange sauce (see recipe)

Chop off the wing tips of duck; wash and dry with towels. Rub inside and out with salt, pepper, and lemon juice. Place celery, onion, and apple in cavity. Place the duck, breast side up, on a rack in a roasting pan. Roast at 325 degrees for 35 minutes. Pour out excess fat and pour the wine over the duck. Continue roasting, allowing 20 minutes per pound (from time duck was placed in oven), or until the legs move easily up and down. Remove duck to a platter and keep in a warm oven. Make the sauce as follows:

Sauce

1 cup chicken stock or bouillon
Juice of 3 large oranges and 1 lemon
Slivered rind of 1 orange

3 tablespoons cognac or curaçao
2 tablespoons brown sugar
1 tablespoon wine vinegar
Orange sections, optional

Skim excess fat from roasting pan set over direct low heat. Stir in chicken stock or bouillon, scraping brown bits from the pan into the sauce. Add the fruit juices and rind and the cognac or curaçao. In a small saucepan, melt the brown sugar and stir in the wine vinegar. Add to the sauce. Stir well and simmer for about 12 minutes. Carve the duck; pour the hot sauce over each serving. Garnish the platter with orange sections if desired.

Mrs. Walter Weese, from Campus Cookery, *Memphis, Tenn.*

BREAST OF GUINEA HEN WITH BING CHERRY SAUCE
Serves two

Separate the breast meat from a guinea hen, and sauté in butter for 10 minutes. Serve with sauce made as follows:

Sauce

1 cup reduced chicken stock
1 heaping tablespoon currant jelly

1½ ozs. port wine
Bing cherries

Pour the first three ingredients into pan in which guinea meat was cooked and let simmer for 5 minutes. Add pitted black bing cherries, and pour over breast of hen before serving. Serve with wild rice.

Charles F. Herman, Proprietor, The Gray Fox Restaurant, Pinehurst, N.C.

BARBECUE GUINEA HEN
Serves eight to ten

2 young guinea hens
3 tablespoons butter

1 cup vinegar
1 teaspoon Worcestershire sauce

1 teaspoon Accent
Salt, pepper, cayenne to taste
¼ teaspoon dry mustard

1 garlic clove, optional
Hot water

Disjoint guinea as for frying chicken; sauté until light brown in butter. Pour off part of fat. Add the vinegar and all seasonings; then pour in enough hot water to just cover guinea; simmer on top of stove in heavy pan until liquid has almost evaporated. Place cover on pan and let guinea steam until liquid is entirely gone. Serve hot with desired barbecue sauce. Wild rice is the usual accompaniment.

Mrs. Charles Mason Crowson, Columbia, S.C.

POULTRY STUFFINGS

PECAN TURKEY STUFFING

This is a famous and fabulous turkey stuffing. "In 1672 a Henry Hughes and some others surrendered land so that the town of Charleston might be built. Perhaps there is some esoteric connection between that and the fact that Mr. Edward Hughes has the most spacious garden and house in the city limits today. Distinguished guests go back to New York and Paris and London boasting to their friends about the pressed turkey and pecan of which they partook in Mr. Hughes' house. For this is more than a mere food: it is a confection. Mr. Hughes allowed us to copy the recipe from his mother's old notebook.

"To the recipe was appended a note which read, 'The most delicious stuffing that has ever been made. A choice old Charleston recipe.' We see no reason to dispute this proclamation. This stuffing is especially good for boned turkey, and is, of course, only for the greatest of state occasions."

1 turkey liver
12 slices toasted bread
3 tablespoons lard
¼ cup butter
1 teaspoon salt
1 teaspoon black pepper
1 teaspoon celery seed, crushed
1 teaspoon dried Nabob thyme
1 tablespoon parsley, chopped fine

½ nutmeg grated
Boiling water
6 hard-cooked eggs
¼ teaspoon ground mace
2 cups salted pecans, chopped
1 can mushrooms, chopped fine
½ cup sherry
1 large onion
1 tablespoon lard

"Boil the liver the day before the stuffing is made. Roll the toasted bread on a biscuit board, then sift through a colander into a large bowl, and add the butter, lard, salt, black pepper, celery seed, thyme, parsley, and grated nutmeg.

Pour in a little boiling water and mix thoroughly by hand. Add the whites of the hard-cooked eggs, riced, and the yolks rubbed smooth with the mace. Then add the salted pecans, mushrooms, and sherry. Mix together thoroughly.

"Put the onion, grated, or finely minced, into a frying pan with the lard. When very hot, add the powdered liver and fry until brown. Allow to cool and then mix thoroughly with the other ingredients. Stuff the turkey, having first rubbed it with salt and pepper both inside and out." Will stuff an 18- to 20-lb. turkey.

Edward H. Hughes, from 200 Years of Charleston Cooking, *by Blanche S. Rhett, Lettie Gay, and Helen Woodward*

OYSTER STUFFING

6 tablespoons butter
4 medium-size onions
1 cup finely chopped celery
5 cups toasted bread crumbs, coarsely crumbled, or small croutons
½ cup turkey broth, consommé or bouillon
½ teaspoon rubbed sage or poultry seasoning

¼ cup chopped parsley
¼ teaspoon thyme
1 tablespoon Worcestershire sauce
½ teaspoon each of salt and pepper
¼ teaspoon dry mustard
1 pt. stewing oysters, cut into quarters

Heat the butter in a large skillet; sauté the onions and celery in the butter until transparent. Stir in the crumbs, broth, and all of the seasonings. Stir in the oysters. Stuff the turkey and truss the bird. Roast as directed.

This oyster stuffing may be baked in a baking dish and served as a side dish. Bake in a 350-degree oven for 25 to 30 minutes. While dressing is cooking pour over it ½ cup of turkey gravy, or an additional ½ cup broth. The dressing should not be too dry if baked. Will stuff a 14- to 16-lb. turkey.

NOTE: If turkey is to be kept several days in refrigerator, the stuffing should be removed. Do not freeze dressing in turkey.

POTATO AND PEANUT STUFFING FOR GOOSE
Three and one-half cups

2 cups hot mashed potatoes
1 cup bread crumbs
½ teaspoon pepper
½ teaspoon salt

1 teaspoon sage
4 tablespoons melted butter
2 tablespoons onion juice
1 cup ground peanuts

Mix in order given. Stuff bird.

SOUTHERN ONION DRESSING
About three cups

This is dry and light.

3 tablespoons melted butter, or part butter part bacon drippings
1 large onion, peeled, minced
1 cup minced celery
2 cups crumbled, dry corn bread
5 slices light bread, toasted, grated

1 pinch thyme
1 pinch powdered poultry seasoning
2 hard-boiled eggs, chopped (optional)
1 teaspoon Worcestershire sauce
½ cup chicken or other stock

Melt butter in heavy pan; add minced onion and celery; sauté until tender. Add all dry ingredients and Worcestershire sauce and stir until thoroughly blended. Add stock. Mix lightly and stuff bird.

If a more highly seasoned dressing is desired, add sage. If dressing is to be made into cakes, add 1 beaten egg to mixture. Form into little patties, and bake like bread until golden brown.

Mrs. Cramer R. Barksdale, Memphis, Tenn.

RAISIN STUFFING FOR TURKEY

Take one pound of freshly minced beef, a small onion, a little parsley and thyme, one pound of seeded raisins, and a tablespoonful of butter. Mix these and cook for about ten minutes. Grate and add some stale bread, or preferably crackers, and with a beaten egg bind the mixture. To keep it moist, add two tablespoonfuls of any good table sauce; salt and pepper to taste. Will stuff a 16- to 18-lb. turkey.

From The Galveston Souvenir Cook Book, *Galveston, Tex.*

9. Game

ROAST MALLARD
Serves six

1 mallard duck about 3 lbs.
½ teaspoon salt
¼ teaspoon pepper
2 tablespoons poultry seasoning
1 small peeled apple, quartered
1 small onion, peeled, quartered

1 stalk celery
1 tablespoon butter
½ cup hot water
1 tablespoon vinegar
Mushrooms, optional
Sherry, optional

Prepare duck as any fowl. Rub inside and out with salt, pepper, and poultry seasoning. Place apple, onion, and celery inside of duck. Put into heavy roaster, breast down. Melt butter in hot water; add vinegar and pour over duck. Cover and place in a 425-degree oven for 20 minutes. Reduce heat to 300 degrees and cook until tender, about 2 hours. Season gravy highly. Mushrooms and sherry may be added.

Mrs. Tad A. Bowdoin, from The Columbia Woman's Club Cook Book,
Columbia, S.C.

REMINGTON FARMS ROASTED WILD DUCK

On the Eastern Shore of Maryland (Chestertown), the Remington Arms Company operates a wildlife center. Here the chef, Kelsor Smith, "may cook as many wild ducks a year as anyone in the country," says Clark Webster, manager of the center. Below is Chef Smith's recipe for wild duck.

Mr. Smith says: "The ducks should be properly and rapidly dressed in the field. Delayed or improper dressing can definitely spoil a potential feast." The ducks may be frozen and thawed just before serving. Allow 1 duck per serving. For each duck:

1 tablespoon sherry
½ teaspoon each celery salt, curry
　　powder, and black pepper
1 teaspoon salt

1 small onion
1 celery stalk
Water
Stuffing (optional)

Place ducks breast up in roasting pan. Sprinkle with sherry and season with celery salt, curry powder, black pepper, and salt. Let ducks sit in pan to marinate for 30 minutes to 1 hour. Chop onion and celery stalk and place in pan. Add ¼ to ½ inch water. Bake about 20 minutes in a 500-degree oven until breast is brown. Turn and bake until back is brown. Cover the pan and cook 1 hour longer at 300 degrees. Total cooking time is about 2 hours. If ducks are to be stuffed, use any favorite poultry stuffing recipe.

Contributed by Charlie Harville, WGHP-TV,
High Point, N.C.

ROASTED WILD DUCKS IN WINE MARINADE
Serves three

3 large wild ducks (1½ lbs. each)	8 whole cloves
Salt and black pepper	1 medium onion, chopped
½ cup lemon juice	1 carrot, diced
Red port wine	1 stalk celery, cut into sections
1 bay leaf	Bacon slices

Wash and dry the ducks. Sprinkle them inside and out with salt, pepper, and lemon juice. Put the ducks in a deep bowl. Pour over wine to cover. Add the remaining ingredients except the bacon. Place bowl in refrigerator and marinate the ducks 24 hours.

Remove ducks from the marinade, reserving the marinade. Truss the birds and place them, breast up, on a rack in a roasting pan. Cover the breasts with slices of bacon. Preheat oven to 450 degrees. Roast the ducks for about 40 minutes for medium-done, and 60 minutes for well-done, basting them often with the marinade. Split the ducks and serve them with a sauce made from the marinade, or any duck sauce.

Marinade Sauce

1½ cups of strained marinade	1 tablespoon lemon juice
1 tablespoon minced onion	1½ tablespoons flour
3 tablespoons minced celery	1 cup chicken bouillon
⅔ cup orange juice	Salt and pepper to taste

In a skillet simmer the first 5 ingredients until reduced to about half original volume. Drain. Blend the flour with the bouillon. Stir the flour mixture into the sauce; add salt and pepper to taste. Simmer until sauce thickens. Makes about 1½ cups. Serve sauce over the ducks.

R. D. Lea, Chesterfield Count, Va.

SEVEN-MINUTE CANVASBACK DUCK
Serves one

E. K. Jaquith, a pioneer air-mail pilot, often flew the Southern coastal route, hunting off the North Carolina coast, when possible, for duck and other wild game. He is an epicure and a staunch believer in the rare-cooked duck. His "stove" was often a bed of hot coals, a beach fire, or a can of Sterno. Here is his simple recipe for "7-Minute Duck."

Pick duck dry; split down back; clean and rinse. Rub inside and out with dry cloth. Season with salt and pepper; rub in butter, bacon grease, or salad oil. Place over hot flame and broil 7 minutes, dividing cooking time for each side. When done, the bird should be rare and tender. Serve at once, piping hot.

E. K. Jaquith, Greenville, Conn.

WILD DUCK IN ORANGE WINE
Serves two

Cut the breast off and cut up remainder of duck as you would a chicken for frying. Salt, pepper, and then roll in flour. Fry in part Crisco and part butter until brown. Pour off grease. Put duck in a covered saucepan and cover with orange wine. Cook over a very slow fire until tender. More wine must be added from time to time as it evaporates quickly.

Mrs. Nolan S. Dougherty, from Bon Appétit!, *Baton Rouge, La.*

MARSH HEN

Marsh hens are a choice and delectable game bird, about the size of a broiling chicken. They are found in the marshes along the coast and are hunted in the fall. These birds are not picked but are skinned. Cut the legs off at the first joint where the feathers begin. With fingers carefully pull the skin back to the body. Split between the legs, just cutting through the outside skin. Then peel all the skin off, cutting off at wing joints and head. Split down the back and clean, saving giblets. Wash very thoroughly and place in refrigerator.

Opinion varies about soaking these birds before cooking. It is generally believed that they are better simply kept in icebox a day or two, seasoned and cooked in your favorite manner. They have a delicate game flavor which soaking in salt water destroys. Allow 1 bird per person.

From Coastal Cookery, *St. Simons Island, Ga.*

MRS. DINGLE'S MARSH HEN

The fried marsh hen at Tip Top Inn has a distinctive flavor and is frequently demanded by Mrs. Dingle's guests. Red wine added to the marinade is part of the secret.

Wash the marsh hen, and cut in half (or serve whole if you prefer). Soak in a little salt water to which ½ cup of red wine has been added. Dip the hen in flour and fry in medium-hot fat until golden brown. Serve hot.

Mrs. R. S. Dingle, Tip Top Inn, Pawleys Island, S.C.

"CASH'S" MARSH HENS

"Cash" is Dr. A. J. Kilpatrick's cook.

First skin the marsh hens. Soak in salt water with red pepper for about 1 or 2 hours. Drain and wash off. Salt and pepper and flour like chicken, and fry until two-thirds done. Make a big pan of gravy and let simmer with butter for 1 hour or until tender.

"Cash" Kilpatrick, from Recipes from Southern Kitchens, *Augusta, Ga.*

GOOSE WITH APPLE AND RAISIN STUFFING

Prepare a 10-pound goose for cooking. Stuff and arrange on rack without any added water. Roast without basting, at 500 degrees for 15 minutes, then at 350 degrees for remainder of time, allowing 20 minutes per pound based on weight before stuffing.

Stuffing

1 cup finely minced onion	¼ teaspoon pepper
3 cups diced apples	¼ cup granulated sugar
7 cups soft bread crumbs	¾ cup melted butter or margarine
1 cup seeded raisins	
1½ teaspoons salt	

Combine the above ingredients; stuff goose, and roast.

From Order of the Eastern Star Cook Book, *Tallulah Chapter No. 16, Spartanburg, S.C.*

STUFFINGS FOR QUAIL OR GAME BIRDS

Wild Rice Stuffing

½ cup raw wild rice
1 qt. boiling water, salt and pepper
½ lb. fresh mushrooms, sautéed in butter or margarine

½ teaspoon sage, pinch of thyme
1 egg yolk, beaten
1 tablespoon melted fat

Boil rice in boiling water until tender, about 25 minutes; drain and rinse; season and add remaining ingredients. Stuff birds and roast as for chicken. Will fill six to eight quail.

Brown Rice Stuffing for Quail

Quail giblets
1 cup brown rice
1 teaspoon salt
4 cups boiling water
3 tablespoons cooking oil

2 tablespoons chopped onion
1 tablespoon chopped green pepper
Salt and pepper to taste

Wash giblets; rinse rice. Cook giblets in salted boiling water for about 25 minutes. Remove giblets; save the broth they were cooked in. Chop giblets into small pieces. Cook rice until tender in the broth; drain. Fry onion and pepper in the oil. Add rice and cooked giblets. Taste for seasoning; add salt and pepper to taste. Stuff birds and bake until tender (about 2 hours in 350 degrees oven). Will fill 6 to 8 quail.

S. G. Kimbrough, Miami, Fla.

ROASTED ROCK CORNISH HENS WITH GIBLET SAUCE
Serves two generously

Rock Cornish hens usually come frozen with package directions for plain roasting. They may be stuffed as preferred.

2 Rock Cornish hens, with giblets
1½ cup rosé wine
2 cups cooked, seasoned wild rice, or poultry stuffing (optional) or celery and onion
1 teaspoon salt

½ teaspoon poultry seasoning
Black pepper
½ teaspoon ground ginger
5 tablespoons melted butter
¼ cup chicken stock
Giblet sauce (see recipe)

Thaw the hens in cold water; drain; remove the giblets. Place all in a bowl and pour the wine over. Marinate for 2 hours, turning the hens often. Drain. Reserve the wine marinade. Cook the wild rice according to package directions and season, or make poultry dressing (see recipe). If rice or dressing is not used, place inside each hen 1 stalk of celery, broken into sections, and ½ of a medium-size onion. Mix the seasonings and rub the hens inside and out (before stuffing them). Place the hens in a heavy roaster with cover; pour over them ⅓ of the butter; add ¼ cup chicken stock or water. Cover the vessel and roast at 350 degrees for 1 hour. After hens have cooked for 30 minutes, remove the cover; baste the hens often with the remaining butter. Continue cooking uncovered for remaining time. Meanwhile, make the giblet sauce:

Giblet Sauce

Giblets from hens
Water
1 small onion, chopped
1 stalk celery cut into sections
1 tablespoon Worcestershire sauce

½ teaspoon dried rosemary
Wine marinade, extra wine to make 2 cups
3 tablespoons pan drippings
3 tablespoons flour
Salt and pepper to taste

Place the giblets in a small saucepan; add 3 cups of cold water, the onion, celery, and seasonings. Cover and boil slowly until the meat is tender. Remove the livers after 10 minutes and reserve. If pan gets too dry, add a little more water. When giblets are tender, chop the livers and gizzards, and shred meat from neck bones; return to saucepan.

Remove roasted hens from roasting pan and keep them warm on a heated platter. Reserve 3 tablespoons of the pan drippings in the roasting pan. Place the roasting pan on top of the stove and stir in 3 tablespoons flour. Cook over medium heat until flour mixture bubbles. Pour in the giblets and broth (if any). Add enough wine to the marinade to make 2 cups. Stir into the roasting pan. Cook slowly, stirring constantly until the sauce is medium thick. Season with salt and pepper. Serve in a sauce boat with the hens.

DOVES ITALIENNE
Serves four

4 doves (1 per person), dressed
Garlic salt, black pepper, flour
¼ cup salad oil, or butter
1 8-oz. can tomato sauce

½ cup beer
4 medium onions, sliced
¼ teaspoon crushed oregano
3 tablespoons chopped parsley

Sprinkle the doves inside and out with garlic salt, pepper, and flour. Heat the salad oil in a skillet; brown the doves on all sides in the oil. Add all ingredients except parsley. Bring to a boil. Cover the pan and reduce heat to simmer. Simmer for about 45 minutes, or until birds are tender. Just before serving, stir in the parsley. Serve with spaghetti tossed with Parmesan cheese, Italian bread, ale, or beer.

Charlie Harville, WGHP-TV, High Point, N.C.

ROAST PHEASANT WITH MADEIRA SAUCE
Serves two

2½ to 3 lb. pheasant, dressed
Salt
Black pepper
3 thin slices lemon
1 stalk celery, cut into thirds
4 to 5 thin slices fat salt pork meat

4 tablespoons melted butter, extra butter if necessary for basting
Thin clean cloth
Madeira Sauce, or Currant Jelly Sauce (see "Sauces," p. 447)

Rinse and dry the pheasant; rub it inside and out with salt and pepper. Place the lemon slices and celery in cavity of the bird. Truss the bird by tying it with heavy string. Cover the breast with the pork meat slices. Cut a piece of thin cloth (cheese cloth or something similar) large enough to completely cover the bird. Dip the cloth in the melted butter and spread it over the pheasant. Place on a rack in a shallow baking pan. Preheat oven to 350 degrees and bake the pheasant for around 30 minutes per pound, or until the legs of bird are tender and soft to the touch. Baste every 20 minutes with melted butter. Remove the pheasant to a warm platter and make the sauce in the roasting pan. Serve the sauce hot with the carved bird.

Serve wild rice as a side dish.

PHEASANT SOUVAROFF (*with Wild Rice Stuffing*)
Serves two

If I have strayed across the Mason-Dixon line to bring you this famous (much-copied) recipe, it is because Pheasant Souvaroff is such a wonderful treat, and because Louis Ploneis, the chef at Jack and Charlie's "Twenty-One" club, believes that any housewife can make it. His advice for cooking any game bird is "plenty of fat, plenty of heat."

1 pheasant
1 slice thin bacon

Butter to fry pheasant in
Stuffing

Make a stuffing of 1 cup cooked wild rice, goose livers, and 2 heads of diced truffles, well seasoned. Insert this stuffing in the bird.

Put some butter or fat in a pan and cook the bird over a hot fire until it is golden brown. When browned, place bird in a casserole (with cover); add to bird:

1 oz. good port   ¼ clove juniper
½ cup finely chopped truffles

Put cover on casserole and seal it with a band of dough. Put into a 350-to-375-degree oven and cook for 40 minutes. Cover should not be removed until ready to serve. Peel off like dough.

Jack and Charlie's "Twenty-One," New York City.
Special permission by H. J. Berns

PHEASANT WITH WILD RICE OR YELLOW HOMINY
Serves eight

Dress 2 pheasants. Split down back and quarter. In a heavy pan on top of stove, melt 2 tablespoons of butter. Sauté quartered pheasants in butter until golden brown. Season to taste with salt and pepper; add 1 cup of sauterne wine, cover pan and let pheasant slowly simmer in wine until tender, turning often. Serve each quarter on buttered toast with buttered wild rice as accompaniment, or serve for breakfast with yellow hominy grits.

Mrs. W. H. May, Jr., Willeli, Burlington, N.C.

MRS. STONEWALL JACKSON'S STUFFED PARTRIDGES

After the Civil War, Mrs. Thomas J. (Stonewall) Jackson came to live in Charlotte, N.C. This recipe is contributed by Mrs. Jackson's granddaughter.

Partridges   A pinch of pepper
Bacon in strips   Butter
A pinch of salt

Select firm, plump birds, allowing 1 partridge per person. Do not split and draw them down the back, but draw them, stuff them, and bake them in a moderate oven as you would a hen. Lay a strip of bacon across the breast of each. Season with salt, pepper, and lumps of butter. Baste frequently. Serve with small triangles of toast which have been buttered on each side. [Use any stuffing as for quail.—M. B.]

Mrs. Randolph Preston, Washington, D.C., from
Old North State Cook Book, Charlotte, N.C.

ROAST QUAIL WITH BRAZIL NUT STUFFING
Serves four to six

4 to 6 quail (1 per person)
Softened butter and salt
2 cups bread cubes or crumbs
1 small onion, cut fine
½ cup celery, thinly sliced
½ cup Brazil nuts, chopped or
  ground

2 tablespooons butter or other
  shortening
½ teaspoon double-action baking
  powder
Boiling water to moisten
Salt and pepper to taste

Rub inside and out of quail with butter; sprinkle with salt. Mix remaining ingredients, using just enough water to moisten. Fill birds with stuffing and bake for 2 hours in 350-degree oven, or until tender. (Cover pan until birds are almost done, then remove cover to brown. A little water should be added to pan when birds are placed in oven, and additional water added if too dry. Serve pan drippings over birds.)

S. G. Kimbrough, Miami, Fla.

QUAILS WITH GREEN GRAPES
Serves four

4 quails, dressed
Salt, pepper, flour
⅓ cup butter
½ cup water
6 small mushrooms, sliced

½ cup seedless green grapes
2 tablespoons chopped hazelnuts,
  or pecans
1 tablespoon lemon juice
4 slices buttered toast

Sprinkle the quails inside and out with salt and pepper. Heat the butter in a skillet, and brown the birds on all sides in the butter. Add the water and mushrooms. Cover and cook over low heat until the birds are fork tender—15 minutes or longer. If necessary, add extra hot water to keep pan from becoming dry. Add the grapes and cook 3 minutes longer. Stir in the nuts and lemon juice. Serve the birds on the toast with the pan sauce poured over them.

Serve with wild rice, whole baked tomatoes, etc.

Charlie Harville, WGHP-TV, High Point, N.C.

BARBEQUE QUAIL
Serves six to eight

6 to 8 quail
Deep fat

2 cups tomato juice
1 cup vinegar

½ lb. butter
1 clove garlic or 1 onion
Red pepper
Black pepper

Salt
½ teaspoon dry mustard
Worcestershire sauce

Split birds down back, and brown in deep fat. Pour off all fat and pour the following sauce over them. Cook slowly for about 2 hours, basting frequently with the sauce:

Heat tomato juice slowly, adding vinegar as it heats. Then add butter. Chop a clove of garlic into this and stir. Add liberal amounts of red pepper, black pepper, salt, and Worcestershire sauce to taste. Add dry mustard. [Pheasant may be barbecued by this recipe.—M. B.]

Mrs. Charles Hollis, Bennettsville, S.C., from The Pee Dee Pepper Pot,
Darlington, S.C.

POTTED SQUAB CHICKEN ON WILD RICE, PLANTATION STYLE
Serves four

4 freshly-killed squab chickens,
    weighing ¾ to 1 lb. each
1 cup red wine
1 cup sherry
2 bay leaves
1 small bunch soup greens, cut in
    small pieces
Few black peppercorns

Salt
Flour
1 cup hot stock or water
½ lb. wild rice
Butter
Salt
1 tablespoon cranberry jelly

Split squab chickens in back and remove breastbone; marinate overnight in the next six ingredients. Strain off the marinade (save), and let chicken dry.

Dip dried squab chicken in flour, and sauté until well browned. Add soup greens (celery tops, parsley, etc.) from strained marinade; let brown. Add 1 tablespoon flour and blend to make roux. Scald with hot stock or water and let simmer slowly under fitting light (over slow heat). When chicken is almost done, add wine marinade to it and finish chicken.

Waterboil rice; season with fresh butter and salt, and place in casserole with chicken on top. Before straining gravy, add cranberry jelly and let melt; then strain over chicken and rice, and serve piping hot.

John S. Cator, President, Fort Sumter Hotel, Charleston, S.C.

ROYALE SQUAB
Serves twelve

12 plump squabs
½ teaspoon salt per squab
⅛ teaspoon pepper per squab
Mushroom stuffing
Softened butter

¾ cup hot bouillon
1 cup vermouth
½ cup butter, melted
Parsley and carrot curls for garnish

Season squabs, inside and out, with salt and pepper; fill with mushroom stuffing. Truss and rub well with softened butter. Place in a shallow pan and roast for 15 minutes in a 400-degree oven. Reduce heat to 300 degrees. Combine hot bouillon, vermouth, and butter. Baste every 20 minutes with this mixture. Roast one hour or until tender. Garnish with parsley and carrot curls.

Mushroom Stuffing

1 medium onion, chopped
½ cup butter
½ lb. mushrooms, ground
10 slices toasted bread, cubed
1 cup chopped celery

2 tablespoons chopped parsley
½ teaspoon poultry seasoning
1 teaspoon salt
¼ teaspoon pepper

Sauté onion in the butter until just golden; add mushrooms and cook (over medium heat) 5 minutes. Toss remaining ingredients with the onions and mushrooms. Use as stuffing. Do not pack this dressing in the squabs tightly because it swells.

NOTE: This recipe may be cut to fewer squabs if desired.

*Mr. and Mrs. Talmage Scroggs, Managers, Alamance Country Club,
Burlington, N.C.*

STUFFED SQUAB WITH CURRANT JELLY
Serves four

Select 4 young tender squabs, dress for baking. Fill with the following stuffing and serve with currant jelly sauce.

Stuffing

3 cups wild rice, cooked (see rice recipe)
Boiled mashed livers of squabs
1 teaspoon finely minced onion or chives
1 tablespoon minced celery
1 teaspoon minced parsley
1 tablespoon minced cooked bacon
½ cup finely chopped sautéed mushrooms
Chicken stock or broth to moisten
Melted butter and hot water
3 tablespoons currant jelly

Mix all dry ingredients; moisten with just enough stock to form light fluffy mixture. Stuff birds and sew or truss. Place in heavy baking dish and bake at 450 degrees until birds are browned. Then reduce heat to 325 degrees. Baste frequently with melted butter and hot water to thin butter slightly. Then add 3 tablespoons of currant jelly to the pan gravy and continue basting until squabs are tender. Serve with the currant sauce pan-gravy. If desired use any poultry stuffing in birds. (Cooking time—35 to 45 minutes.)

Mrs. Frederick S. Dixon, Fayetteville, N.C.

VARIANT: Dressing for 4 squabs:

1 cup chopped almonds or pecans
1 cup bread crumbs
3 tablespoons butter, melted
¼ cup finely minced celery
¼ cup milk
Salt, pepper to taste
1 tablespoon chopped chives

Moisten bread crumbs in milk; blend in other ingredients; stuff squab.

ROAST 'POSSUM WITH SWEET 'TATERS

"To roast a 'possum, first catch the 'possum. Dress it and soak in salt water for 12 hours, then wash and parboil it in salt water until tender. Have ready some sliced sweet potatoes which have been boiled, until done, in clear water. Lay 'possum out flat in roasting pan; put slices of sweet potatoes all around it; add pepper and sufficient stock. Bake in a quick oven until a nice brown. Serve on a platter, using potatoes and parsley for garnishing."

Mrs. W. H. Carroll, from Choice Recipes, *Burlington, N.C.*

NOTE: To dress opossum: to 1 gallon of boiling water add about ½ cup of lime and scald opossum quickly. Pull off hair at once, scrape well; cut off feet, tail, and remove entrails. If head is left on, remove eyes and ears. Cleanse thoroughly with hot water. Cover opossum with cold water, add ½ cup salt or less. Let stand 12 hours. Remove from salted water and pour over hot water almost to cover. Boil until skin is tender. Let stand in broth until time to bake. Bake as above.

TO FRY VENISON STEAK
Serves four to six

Hunting deer in Chesterfield County, Virginia, is one of the earliest and most thrilling forms of the hunt. R. D. Lea, who generally bags his limit at the beginning of the season, gives several of his choice recipes for cooking venison. Only the young venison should be steaked. The age of the deer can be told by the fine grain of the meat and by the hoof. The hoof of an old deer will stand widely apart; the young deer hoof is only slightly parted. The young venison has a coating of fat, and the meat cooks rapidly. Here is his method of frying venison steaks:

Cut steak in 2-pound piece about ¾ inch to 1 inch thick. Soak in salted water for at least 1 hour. Drain thoroughly and dry. In a heavy iron frying pan, put 2 tablespoons of shortening and let heat until hot. Roll the steak in flour seasoned with salt and pepper. Then fry in the hot grease until browned on both sides. Reduce heat and cook slowly, covered, until the meat is thoroughly done. Slice onions on top of steak and smother for about 5 minutes; then remove meat from pan and make brown gravy by adding 2 tablespoons of flour to the drippings. When flour has browned, add 2 cups boiling water and cook until mixture thickens. Season and serve over steak. Serve with currant jelly.

ROAST HAUNCH OR SADDLE OF VENISON
Serves eight to ten

Take a haunch or saddle of venison weighing about 5 pounds. Soak several hours in salted cold water. Remove; dry. Lard the meat with shortening or salad oil as it is rather dry. Put in a roaster in the oven and pour in several cups of water. Onion or garlic may be added if desired, or several tablespoons of red wine or wine vinegar gives a good flavor. Bake in oven, allowing about 15 minutes to each pound, at around 400 degrees. Baste often with melted butter or pan drippings with butter added. Turn the roast several times so that it will brown on all sides. Serve with currant jelly as for venison steaks.

R. D. Lea, Petersburg, Va.

REMINGTON FARMS MIXED GAME PIE

This pie is made from a mixed "bag of birds." It is from the Farm's chef, Kelsor Smith.

1 doz. small birds (if larger ones are included, cut into pieces of similar size)	2 qts. water Salt and pepper to taste 1 small onion, chopped fine

1 small bunch parsley, minced
3 whole cloves
½ lb. salt pork, diced and browned
Water to keep birds covered
2 tablespoons browned flour

3 tablespoons butter
1 recipe for double pie crust
2 cups cooked, diced potatoes
Gravy from the birds

Split 1 doz. small birds; if larger birds are included, cut into pieces of similar size. Place in a saucepan with 2 qts. of water and bring to boil, skimming residue that comes to the top. Add salt and pepper, onion, parsley, cloves, salt pork, water to cover birds, and flour. Allow mixture to boil up. Stir in butter. Remove the pan from the fire and allow to cool.

Line the sides of a buttered baking dish with pie crust. Fill the dish with the birds; add potatoes. Pour in enough of the gravy from the birds to cover. Cover with top crust. Bake in a 375-degree oven until pie crust is done, about 40 minutes.

Contributed by Charlie Harville, WGHP-TV, High Point, N.C.

10. Vegetables

APPLES STUFFED WITH HAM
Serves four

4 large red apples, unpeeled
1 cup baked ham, diced (or any cooked ham)
2 tablespoons butter

¼ cup raisins
¼ cup chopped pecans
2 tablespoons brown sugar

Scoop out the apples, leaving thick enough shell to hold stuffing. Mix 1 cup of the chopped apple removed from shell with the remaining ingredients. Fill the apple cavities with the stuffing. Place apples in a baking dish, and bake in a preheated 350-degree oven for 45 minutes. While apples are baking, baste them often with the following glaze:

4 tablespoons water
4 tablespoons brown sugar

1 teaspoon dry mustard
2 tablespoons vinegar

In a saucepan mix all ingredients. Bring to boiling. Spoon the glaze over the baking apples. Serve the baked apple with an egg omelet or Quiche Lorraine—you have an ample lunch.

Miss Shirley Miller, Norfolk, Va.

ARTICHOKES

There are two kinds of artichokes served in the South: the French, or "Burr," which is utilized in more elegant dishes, and the Jerusalem tuber, generally made into pickle or relish. The latter belongs to the sunflower family and in late summer has a small sunflower bloom which makes a gay house flower. The Burr artichoke is delicious boiled and served hot with drawn butter or cold with French dressing (as a salad), or in other ways.

To boil, first soak in salt water for about 1 hour to draw out insects. Have water boiling and drop in the artichokes. Cook until tender, about 30 minutes. Remove, drain. Accompany each serving with a small container of sauce to dip the leaves in, for within the root of the leaves is the succulent part. The leaves are pulled from the tough stalk, and stalk discarded. The bottom, or "choke" should be tender and is also eaten.

The Jerusalem artichoke, if cooked, is scraped like a potato and blanched in cold water, then sliced and cooked until it can be pierced with a fork. Be careful, or it will cook too long and become tough and hard. Serve with any sauce.

ARTICHOKE HEARTS WITH CRAB MEAT RAVIGOTE
Serves six

Trim 6 artichokes by removing a few outer leaves, the stem, and prickly end. To avoid discoloration, place them in a bowl of cold water to which has been added the juice of 1 lemon or 2 ounces of vinegar. Cook in the same water until heart is tender. Drain by placing upside down. Carefully remove center leaves and the "choke" with your fingers. Fill centers with 1 lb. crab meat, fresh or canned, mixed with Sauce Ravigote.

Sauce Ravigote

1 cup mayonnaise, prepared or homemade
Capers
Chopped parsley
Green onions, chopped
A bit of garlic
Tarragon, fresh or dried
Dry mustard
Salt, paprika
Lemon juice
Artichokes (1 to each person)

Into the mayonnaise mix other ingredients to taste; blend with crab meat. (Serve as salad or luncheon dish.)

From Recipes Tested and Tried, *by Anne Young White
and Nola Nance Oliver, Natchez, Miss.*

VARIATIONS: (1) Serve the hearts hot with Hollandaise or lemon sauce. (2) Fill cooked hearts with cheese sauce; chopped creamed meats such as cream chicken; Crab Newburg or Shrimp; with green peas and mushrooms; Chicken à la King, etc.

ARTICHOKES AU VIN BLANC
Serves six

6 small artichokes
1 tablespoon olive oil
1 clove garlic
1 small onion, minced
⅛ teaspoon powdered savory
2 teaspoons salt
1 cup dry white wine (American)

Trim the tops from the artichokes; cut off the stems and remove the tough outer leaves. Wash and drain.

Place the olive oil, garlic, onion, savory, and salt in a deep pot or casserole with top. Stand the artichokes upright in the casserole, and pour over them 1 cup of American white wine. Cover tightly and simmer slowly (on top of stove) for 45 minutes, adding a little more oil and wine if necessary to keep the vessel from becoming dry. Cook until the hearts are tender. (Remove; spread leaves, and take out the center spongy choke). Serve with the pan sauce poured over them.

From With a Jug of Wine, *by Morrison Wood (Farrar, Straus and Company, N.Y.)*

ASPARAGUS

Asparagus is one of the South's oldest vegetables, elegant yet simple to serve. It is equally good hot or cold and doubles for a salad (see Salads). Boiled, it is served with a variety of sauces, Butter, Bread Sauce, Vinegar sauces, and the famous Hollandaise. With a cream cheese sauce it becomes a delightful casserole, or it may be served on toast.

MRS. BROUGHTON'S ASPARAGUS SUPREME
Serves six

This asparagus dish was often served by Mrs. Broughton in the Governor's Mansion at Raleigh.

1 large can white asparagus, use green, if more tender
2 hard-boiled eggs

½ cup grated cheese
1½ cups cream sauce
½ cup blanched almonds

Slice eggs; add grated cheese to cream sauce. Place alternate layers of asparagus, sauce, eggs, and almonds in casserole and bake 20 minutes at 350–375 degrees or until golden brown.

Sauce

1½ tablespoons butter
1½ tablespoons flour
Few grains pepper

Salt to taste
1½ cup hot milk

Melt butter; add flour mixed with seasoning and stir until well blended. Add hot milk gradually while stirring constantly. Bring to boiling point; boil 2 minutes. (Add cheese just before pouring over asparagus.)

Mrs. J. Melville Broughton, Raleigh, N.C.

TO BOIL FRESH ASPARAGUS
Serves six to eight

1 bunch asparagus, about 2 lbs.
Salted boiling water, 1 teaspoon
 salt to each qt. water

Deep saucepan (or large tin
 coffee pot with drainer removed)

Untie the asparagus; wash it well; cut off the tough ends. As a rule, if the bottom end is bent the stalk will snap where the tender part of the stalk begins. Be careful not to break off the tips. Retie the asparagus into 1 or 2 bunches. Have the cooking vessel half filled with boiling water. Stand the asparagus upright in the vessel. Allow it to cook and steam for about 15 minutes. Drain; carefully remove asparagus and serve as desired.

ASPARAGUS PARMESAN
Serves four

1 lb. fresh asparagus, cooked (or
 frozen, cooked)
3 tablespoon butter, melted

¼ cup white wine
¼ teaspoon black pepper
Grated Parmesan cheese

Place the asparagus in a shallow baking dish. Pour over the melted butter and wine. Sprinkle with pepper. Heavily coat the top with grated Parmesan cheese. Bake in a preheated 400-degree oven for 10 to 15 minutes, or until cheese melts. Serve hot.

FRENCH FRIED ASPARAGUS
Serves four

1 can asparagus
2 eggs
½ teaspoon salt

⅛ teaspoon pepper
Cracker (or bread) crumbs
Fat

Drain asparagus. Beat together the eggs, salt, and pepper. Dip each asparagus stalk into egg mixture; then roll into cracker crumbs. Fry in hot fat, not too deep. Serve at once.

Mrs. Robert J. Powell, Fayetteville, N.C.

LOUISIANA ASPARAGUS SHORTCAKE
Serves four to six

1 bundle fresh, or 1 can asparagus, drained; save 1½ cups
 liquor

Parsley and paprika to garnish

Boil fresh asparagus until tender, cutting off tough ends. Save 1½ cups liquor. If canned is used, drain; save liquor.

The "Cake"

2½ cups sifted flour
1 teaspoon salt
2½ teaspoons baking powder

½ cup lard
Sweet milk, ice cold
Butter

Sift flour with salt and baking powder; cut in shortening (lard) and mix with enough ice cold milk to make a soft dough that you can just handle. Roll out to fit 2 layer cake pans, or one, if it is deep. If thick layer is made, split the baked layer and spread well with butter, having already made the following sauce.

Sauce

¼ cup flour
1 teaspoon salt
¼ cup butter
1½ cups asparagus juice

¼ cup extra butter
2 hard-boiled eggs
Parsley
Paprika

Make a drawn butter sauce of the flour, salt, ¼ cup butter and asparagus liquor, beating in the last ¼ cup of butter after sauce is taken from fire. Add asparagus, spread between and on cake. Garnish with quartered hard-boiled eggs, parsley, and paprika. Serve hot.

From The Louisiana Plantation Cook Book, *by*
Mrs. James E. Smitherman, Shreveport, La.

BOILED BUTTER BEANS—LIMA BEANS
Serves four to six

Butter beans and lima beans are cooked in the same manner. The lima bean is larger and more mealy. They may be seasoned with butter, ham, or salt meat.

2 cups fresh butter beans, or lima
    beans
4 cups water
1 teaspoon salt
1 teaspoon sugar

2 tablespoons butter, or piece of
    boiling meat about 2 inches
    square, 1 inch thick
½ cup milk or cream, optional
Pepper to taste

Wash and pick over the beans; cover with water in a saucepan with lid. Add salt and sugar. Boil for about 10 minutes, then add the butter; or if meat is to be used, add the meat. Boil slowly until beans are tender, about 45 minutes to

1 hour. If pan becomes too dry, add a little warm water. There should be a little broth left with the beans. If desired, just before serving add the milk or cream and season to taste with pepper; reheat.

GLORIFIED LIMA BEANS
Serves four to six

This recipe was given to our contributor by Mrs. Calvin Dyer of Pan American Airways; it has a definite "Pan-American" flavor.

2 tablespoons chopped onions
2 tablespoons chopped green peppers
1 tablespoon butter

2 cups cheese sauce
2 cups cooked lima beans
Bread crumbs
Strips of bacon

Sauté onions and peppers in butter and add to cheese sauce. Pour over limas in casserole; top with buttered bread crumbs (or use plain bread crumbs with strips of bacon on top). Bake 30 minutes in moderate oven (350 degrees). Some prefer this without the bacon—delicious either way.

Mrs. Oliver Smith, Raleigh, N.C.

NOTE: To make cheese sauce, add ¾ cup cheese, grated or cut in small pieces, to medium white sauce (see p. 431).

BARBECUED LIMA BEANS
Serves eight to ten

2 cups dried lima beans
¼ lb. salt pork, cut into ½ inch cubes
Cold water to cover
1 small onion, sliced
1 clove garlic, peeled, chopped
¼ cup fat
1¼ tablespoons prepared mustard

2 teaspoons Worcestershire sauce
1½ teaspoons chili powder
1 teaspoon salt
1 10-oz. can condensed tomato soup
⅓ cup vinegar
1½ cups reserved bean liquid
¼ lb. salt pork, sliced

Soak lima beans overnight. Drain and add cubed pork. Cover with cold water and cook slowly for about 2½ hours, or until tender. Drain, reserving 1½ cups of the liquid. Sauté onion and garlic in fat until golden. Add mustard, Worcestershire, chili powder, salt, tomato soup, and vinegar and reserved liquid. Cook 5 minutes. Alternate limas and sauce in greased casserole. Top with sliced pork. Bake at 400 degrees for 30 minutes.

Mrs. F. M. Talbot, Shreveport, La., from The Junior League of Dallas Cook Book, *Dallas, Tex.*

PINTO BEANS (*Frijoles*)

The pinto, or frijol, is the Mexican staff of life, meaning to the masses what rice does to the Chinese. Affectionately called "el frijolito," the dried bean is boiled like any other dried bean. Then it may be fried, made into fritters, or combined with tomatoes and onions. In areas where Mexican herbs are used, it is highly seasoned with oregano, comote seed, etc. In border and other Southern states, the pinto is a dependable part of the daily diet. It is a favorite dried bean in many sections of North Carolina.

A common way to cook the parboiled bean is to mash and fry in hot fat and serve with chopped onion and cheese. Minced onion and garlic are often browned in the fat, the beans added, and the whole served with grated cheese sprinkled over. A Mexican saying is, "The six-time-fried frijol is the best."

PINTOS WITH CHILIS
Serves four to six

1 lb. frijoles (Mexican beans)   Salt
Cold water

Soak beans overnight; drain. Put on with cold water (as much water as beans); boil until tender; season with salt. Add:

2 chilis   ½ teaspoon dried mustard
1 can tomatoes   Button of garlic
1 lump of brown sugar   2 tablespoons olive oil
1 onion sliced

Boil 2 hours, or simmer slowly 5 to 6 hours.

Mrs. E. H. Booth, from How We Cook in El Paso, *El Paso, Tex.*

STRING BEANS WITH ALMONDS AND MUSHROOMS
Serves four to six

1 lb. string beans, fresh or   2 tablespoons flour
  canned, French style   Salt, white pepper to taste
½ teaspoon sugar   2 cups thin cream or whole milk
Salt, pepper to taste   Juice ½ lemon
1 extra tablespoon butter   Cayenne pepper
½ lb. fresh mushrooms, or 1 cup   ¼ lb. blanched, chopped almonds
  B & B canned   Cheese or bread crumbs
2 tablespoons butter

If fresh beans are used, wash, French, and boil until tender. Season to taste with sugar, salt, and pepper; drain. If canned, drain; heat until tender, season; add the extra tablespoon of butter to hot beans; mix thoroughly.

In a separate saucepan, sauté fresh mushrooms, cut into desired pieces, until tender. Mix with drained, seasoned beans. If canned are used, heat for several minutes, in butter, and stir into beans. Now make a sauce as follows:

Melt butter in pan; blend in flour; season with salt and white pepper to taste, blending in salt and pepper before adding milk; add cream or milk; stir until thickened. Remove from fire; add lemon juice and dash of cayenne pepper. Just before serving, combine beans and mushrooms with sauce, and, lastly, stir in the almonds, whole or chopped. Reheat to boiling point, serve hot. This may all be put into a casserole and baked in moderate oven, 25 minutes. Top with crumbs or cheese if desired. (For a quick dish, blend beans and almonds with 1 can condensed mushroom soup.)

Mrs. Lewis F. Schenck, Macon, Ga.

BARBECUED STRING BEANS
Serves four

These beans are known also as "Sweet and Sour Beans."

1 lb. green beans or 1 No. 2 can wax beans, cut French style or "snapped" into sections
Water to cover
1 teaspoon salt
Pepper, cayenne to taste
4 slices white fatback
2 onions, sliced
1 whole peeled apple, sliced
1 tablespoon butter if needed
1 tablespoon flour
2 tablespoons brown sugar
¼ teaspoon dry mustard
Extra salt and pepper to taste
1 cup bean liquor
2 tablespoons good garlic or apple vinegar

Boil the beans in water to cover until tender. Season with salt, pepper, and a little cayenne; drain, saving 1 cup of bean liquor.

In a heavy pan, fry out the salt fatback; remove meat. In the fat, fry the onion and apple slices until tender, but not brown; remove apple slices and onion to separate dish; keep hot. In the fat (if necessary add 1 tablespoon butter), add the flour mixed with the brown sugar, mustard, and extra salt and pepper to taste; blend quickly, or it will scorch. Add the cup of bean liquor and vinegar; stir constantly until slightly thickened. Add the drained beans and reheat, stirring constantly.

Serve on platter garnished with the onion and apple rings, with apple chutney as an accompaniment. [French rolls and fresh horseradish are suggested accompaniments.—M. B.]

Mrs. Trevor Bevan, St. Petersburg, Fla.

BUCKHEAD BEANS
Serves four

2 cups cooked string beans (fresh, frozen, or canned)
1 medium-size onion, minced
2 tablespoons bacon drippings
1 cup canned tomatoes

¼ teaspoon powdered cloves
2 tablespoons sugar
¼ teaspoon salt
¼ teaspoon black pepper

Place the cooked beans in a saucepan. Add remaining ingredients; stir. Heat to boiling point. Serve.

Or, heat the sauce and pour over the cooked beans.

From The Cotton Blossom Cook Book, *Atlanta, Ga.*

CREOLE GREEN BEAN CASSEROLE
Serves six

1 cup chopped onion
2 tablespoons bacon drippings
2 cups canned tomatoes
1 cup diced celery
½ cup chopped green pepper
1 tablespoon sugar
1 teaspoon salt
½ teasoon black pepper
1 bay leaf

1 tablespoon chopped parsley
1 crushed clove of garlic
1½ lbs. fresh string beans, cut French style (or 3 10-oz. packages frozen French-cut beans)
¾ cup grated sharp cheese
1 cup buttered bread crumbs

In a large skillet, sauté the onion in the bacon drippings until onion is light brown. Add remaining ingredients, except the beans, cheese, and bread crumbs. Simmer the sauce for 30 minutes, stirring often. Remove the bay leaf and garlic clove.

Cook the beans in water until tender; drain. In a 1½- to 2-qt. buttered casserole, place alternate layers of the beans, sauce, and grated cheese. Top with the bread crumbs. Bake in a preheated 325-degree oven for 25 minutes. Serve hot from the casserole.

Mrs. Albert A. Stoddard, Burlington, N.C.

STEAMED OCTOBER BEANS
Serves four to six

This recipe came from Miss Bailey's cousin who was a chef. For years the recipe was kept a secret. After the chef's death, our contributor decided it was "too good not to give to those who want it."

1 lb. October beans (sometimes called "Roman beans," or "shellouts.")

Water

⅛ lb. country ham or smoked bacon

2 cups green corn cut off the cob (fresh)

1 green pepper, seeded, quartered

⅛ teaspoon nutmeg

Salt to taste (no pepper)

Put the beans in the top of a large double boiler; cover them with cold water (just enough to cover); add the ham. Cover and cook over boiling water until the beans are tender. Add the corn, green pepper, and seasoning. Cover and cook for about 10 minutes, or until corn is tender.

Miss Martha S. Bailey, New York, N.Y.

WAX BEANS AND MUSHROOMS
Serves four to six

½ lb. white wax string beans, fresh

½ lb. fresh lima beans

½ lb. fresh button mushrooms

2 tablespoons butter

2 tablespoons lemon juice

Salt and pepper

Fresh parsley sprigs

In a saucepan, combine the string beans and lima beans; add enough water to barely cover the beans. Cook until beans are tender. Add the mushrooms (add a little more water if necessary), and continue to boil about 5 minutes. Drain off the liquid; add the butter, lemon juice, and salt and pepper to taste. Garnish with fresh parsley sprigs.

Miss Martha S. Bailey, New York, N.Y.

HICKS'S BAKED BEANS
Serves about twenty

These are baked each year for Mr. Hicks's Church Bazaar.

2 lbs. small navy beans, dried

2 large onions, chopped fine

1 lb. salt pork (streak-of-lean)

½ of 14 oz. bottle tomato catchup

1 cup Grandma's brand unsulphured molasses

2 teaspoons dry mustard

1 teaspoon ground ginger

½ cup brown sugar

1 teaspoon black pepper

2 teaspoons Worcestershire sauce

Soak the beans overnight in a 1-gallon earthen bean pot. Next morning chop the onions; cut the pork into bite-size pieces. Pour all ingredients into the bean pot with the beans; fill the pot with water. Cover the pot with lid. Bake in a 275- to 300-degree oven "all day" (about 8 hours). Check the water level and keep water to just cover the beans. "Will serve all the family, plus all the neighbors recently transferred from Boston."

Dick Hicks, Greensboro, N.C.

NU-WRAY BAKED BEANS

This is the true Southern baked bean. Parboil yellow-eyed beans to which a piece of salt pork has been added. Be sure to pour off first water, and cook in second water until soft. Drain off water and mix small amount of freshly chopped tomatoes, green pepper, and onions. Add molasses, salt, and pepper to taste. Let salt pork remain in baking dish and place in oven. Cook until done.

From Old-Time Recipes from the Nu-Wray Inn, *by Esther and Rush T. Wray, Burnsville, N.C.*

BEETS
Serves four

The usual Southern way of preparing fresh beets is to leave enough top on whole beets so that they will not "bleed," and boil until tender in water to cover. Plunge them into cold water and skin. Serve whole or sliced, with salt, pepper, and butter to taste, or serve cold with a vinegar marinade made by combining enough good vinegar to cover, with salt, sugar, and pepper to taste. This gives a piquant sweet-sour flavor. Or the whole beets are delightful if glazed in an orange or lemon glaze. To do this:

4 medium-large beets, boiled, whole or sliced in ⅛ inch slices, slightly salted

¼ stick butter, more if desired
3 tablespoons brown sugar
½ cup orange juice

Melt butter in heavy frying pan, add sugar and orange juice, let simmer until sugar is dissolved. Add beets and stir around in pan until coated. Keep heat on low and let beets cook until sauce becomes a thick syrup and beets take on a glazed appearance; serve hot, pour pan sauce over beets.

The boiled beets may be stuffed with a variety of meats and vegetables.

SPICED BEETS IN SOUR CREAM
Serves four

2 cups canned beets, sliced (reserve ½ cup beet juice)
½ cup red wine vinegar

½ teaspoon salt
1 tablespoon mixed pickling spices

2 tablespoons sugar
1 tablespoon fresh horseradish

Sour cream

Drain the beets; set aside in a bowl; reserve ½ cup beet juice. In a saucepan put the beet juice, vinegar, spices, salt, and sugar. Bring to a boil and simmer several minutes. Pour the hot mixture over the beets. Let beets set in refrigerator for at least 6 hours. Drain off the syrup. Mix together the horseradish and enough sour cream to well coat the beets. Stir the sour cream mixture into the beets. Serve with beef. The beets may be served in a bowl as a side dish, or on lettuce leaves as a salad.

SPICED BEETS OVER SPINACH
Serves four to six

1½ tablespoons sugar
2½ tablespoons cornstarch
⅓ cup red wine vinegar
¼ cup beet juice (or water)
1 rounded tablespoon butter
¼ teaspoon ground cinnamon
¼ teaspoon salt
½ teaspoon orange extract

1½ cups sliced canned or fresh-cooked beets
1 pkg. frozen spinach (leaf or chopped) cooked according to pkg. directions, or fresh cooked spinach
Sour cream for garnish, optional

In a saucepan combine the sugar, cornstarch, vinegar, beet juice, butter, cinnamon, salt, and orange extract. Simmer over low heat until the mixture is thickened and clear, stirring constantly. Add the beets and heat thoroughly. Serve the beets over hot spinach. Serve sour cream in sauce boat; spoon a little cream over each serving.

This is a good two-vegetable course to serve with beef or any meat.

Miss Florence Anderson, Jessup, Md.

BROCCOLI

"Brockala" was served in Colonial Virginia as early as 1774 and "dressed," according to Mrs. Hannah Glass (*Williamsburg Art Of Cookery*), with butter "in a little cup." Mrs. Mary Randolph, in *The Virginia Housewife* (1831), added little to the recipe except to enlarge on the method of choosing between the kind that bears flowers around the stalk and the kind "that heads at the top like cauliflowers."

The usual way to cook broccoli (fresh) is to tie it into bundles (after it has been washed) and drop into boiling water; cook uncovered for about 20 minutes. Remove, season with salt and pepper, serve with Hollandaise sauce,

French dressing, cheese sauce, or other sauces. It may be baked like asparagus in a casserole with cheese sauce making it an au gratin. Lemon sauce brings out the flavor. It is often combined with chicken, ham, or other meats and poultry into fancy dishes.

BROCCOLI AND CHEESE CASSEROLE
Serves four to six

2 10-oz. pkgs. frozen chopped broccoli, cooked according to directions, except cut down cooking time by 3 minutes
2 tablespoons butter
2 tablespoons flour
1 cup milk
½ teaspoon each of salt and sugar
Black pepper to taste

1 teaspoon Worcestershire sauce
1 tablespoon tomato catchup
1 3-oz. pkg. cream cheese, broken into small pieces
2 tablespoons crumbled bleu cheese
Buttered bread crumbs (about 1 cup soft crumbs mixed with melted butter)

Cook the broccoli until it is just beginning to get tender. Drain and spread in a 1½-quart greased casserole. In a skillet melt the butter; blend in the flour to make a smooth paste. Stir in the milk, seasonings, sauce, and catchup. Add the cheeses; cook until smooth, stirring constantly. Pour cheese sauce over broccoli; sprinkle the top with crumbs. Bake at 350 degrees until sauce bubbles and top is browned, about 20 minutes.

Mrs. A. F. Soutar, St. Petersburg Beach, Fla.

SWEET AND SOUR RED CABBAGE
Serves four to six

Red cabbage is considered quite a delicacy. It may be boiled and served plain, like other cabbage, but it blends well with a sweet and sour combination of seasonings.

This old recipe instructs that boiling water should be poured over the cabbage several times to take out some of the red color, but I like the color.

1 qt. red cabbage or white
Salt and pepper
2 sour apples, sliced
2 tablespoons fat

Boiling water
2 tablespoons flour
4 tablespoons brown sugar
2 tablespoons vinegar

Shred cabbage fine and add salt and pepper to taste; add apples cut in slices. Heat the fat in a spider (frying pan); add cabbage and apples. Pour boiling water over and let cook until tender; sprinkle the flour over, and add sugar and vinegar. Cook a little longer and serve hot with potato dumplings.

From The Settlement Cook Book, *compiled by Mrs. Simon Kander*

CAILLETTE (*Stuffed Cabbage or Swiss Chard*)
Serves eight

In and around Valdese, North Carolina, the Waldensians have founded a charming settlement based on the traditions of their Italian forefathers. The old-world influence is perhaps more pronounced in the cuisine than in any other phase of living, unless it is the manufacture of superior textiles. The famous Waldensian breads, wines, and daily dishes bear the same names as in Italy and are prepared just as they have been for centuries. Mrs. John D. Guigou (who came to Valdese from northern Italy with her parents, the David Gaydous, in 1911), gives the following favorite vegetable recipe:

Large cabbage or Swiss chard leaves	2 eggs, slightly beaten
Boiling water	1 cup grated cheese, any kind
1 cup warm sweet milk	Salt and pepper to taste
3 cups (old stale) bread crumbs	Dash of nutmeg may be used
	Chicken or beef broth

Have ready the cabbage or chard leaves. (To prepare leaves, slice or shave off thick ribs of leaves, carefully, so as not to break leaves. Pour boiling water over leaves, or let stand in boiling water until pliable.)

Pour the warm milk over bread crumbs; add eggs, cheese, and seasoning. Mix well. Place 1 heaping tablespoon of mixture on each leaf. Fold in sides first; then roll and fasten with toothpick or tie string around the leaf. Drop in boiling chicken or beef broth. Boil gently for ½ hour, or until leaf is cooked tender.

Instead of boiling, the leaves may be baked in a slow oven with the broth, or tomato sauce, in a covered dish.

A good substitute for the cup of cheese would be: 1 cup sausage, 1 egg, only, and very little seasoning. This is better boiled.

Mrs. John D. Guigou, Valdese, N.C.

GLAZED CARROTS

Try adding 2 tablespoons orange or lemon juice to the following "glaze" to give a piquant flavor.

Boil whole scraped carrots until tender. Drain. Meanwhile, melt a large lump of butter in a heavy frying pan. Sprinkle carrots with sugar. When butter is hot, add carrots and roll in mixture until evenly glazed. Serve as main dish or as a garnish for meats.

Mrs. Roger Gant, from Soup to Nuts, *Burlington, N.C*

CREAMED CARROTS AND TURNIPS
Serves four to six

Serve with pork or game.

2 cups carrots, diced
2 cups turnips, diced
Salt and pepper to taste
1 teaspoon sugar

1 tablespoon butter
½ cup light cream (or sour cream)
Paprika

Peel and dice the carrots and turnips; measure. In a saucepan put the vegetables and just enough water to cover. Season to taste with salt, pepper, and the sugar. Cover the pan and cook vegetables until they are tender and the water has evaporated. Add the butter and cream to hot vegetables; let remain on low heat for a few minutes, or until vegetables are reheated. Sprinkle with paprika; serve hot.

Miss Florence Anderson, Jessup, Md.

CARROT RING MOLD
Serves six to eight

This carrot ring may be filled with green peas and mushroom sauce; creamed celery with chopped hard-boiled eggs; sautéed chicken livers mixed with green peas; or other sauces. Substitute almonds or peanuts for pecans if desired.

3 eggs, beaten
4 to 6 grated raw carrots, about 2 to 2½ cups
¼ teaspoon grated nutmeg
½ teaspoon salt
¼ teaspoon white pepper
1 tablespoon minced green pepper if desired
1 tablespoon minced onion

½ cup heavy cream or evaporated milk
½ cup chopped pecans, almonds or peanuts
2 tablespoons butter, extra butter for mold
Parsley or mint
Hot White Cream Sauce, see p. 341

Beat the eggs. Add carrots and seasonings, then milk, nuts. Melt the butter and add. Grease mold well with butter. Pour mixture into the mold and set in oven in pan of water. Bake at 325 degrees for about 35 minutes, or until firm.

Unmold carefully, garnish with parsley or sprigs of fresh mint leaves. Fill with hot sauce.

Mrs. Sidney L. Paine, Durham, N.C.

VARIATION: Green corn or yellow squash may be substituted for the carrots, using same quantity. Squash should be boiled, mashed to pulp, green corn cut off cob, or canned corn.

GARNISHED CAULIFLOWER SUPREME
Serves six to eight

Place 1 head of cauliflower in a cheesecloth bag (to hold the shape); boil in salted water to cover and cook until tender—20 to 30 minutes. Boil a few whole carrots until tender. When cauliflower is done, place on a platter; cut carrots lengthwise and stand the strips on end around the cauliflower. Pour cream sauce around this (over if desired), and garnish with sprigs of parsley.

Boil 2 eggs hard; cream with a fork and sprinkle over the head of the cauliflower and a little over the sauce. Season with white pepper and salt.

Miss Anna Wilson, York, S.C.

CAULIFLOWER WITH ALMONDS
Serves four

1 medium cauliflower, boiled in salted water (1 teasoon salt)	White pepper and paprika
¼ cup butter, melted	¼ cup blanched almonds, chopped and toasted

Boil the cauliflower in water to cover; add 1 teaspoon salt to the water. When cauliflower is tender, but not mushy, drain thoroughly and set back on low heat for a few minutes until all liquid has evaporated. Place cauliflower in serving dish; pour over the hot butter; sprinkle with white pepper and paprika. Sprinkle with the almonds. Serve hot.

If desired, a cheese sauce may be served in place of the butter, using 1 cup of sauce. Sprinkle pepper, paprika, and almonds over the sauce.

Mrs. F. M. Talbot, Shreveport, La.

FRIED CAULIFLOWER
Serves six

1 medium-size head cauliflower, washed; drained	1 egg, beaten
Cracker meal	Deep hot fat

Break the cauliflower head into flowerlets. Roll in cracker meal, then dip into egg. Roll again in cracker meal. Fry in deep hot fat (375 degrees), and fry until golden brown. Drain on absorbent paper. Serve with any desired tart sauce.

CAULIFLOWER AU GRATIN WITH ALMONDS AND CHEESE
Serves four

Mrs. Farish serves this "Arabian" (Southern) dish with Quail-on-Toast, acorn squash with apples and chutney, avocado and grapefruit salad, and flaming plum pudding.

1 small or medium head of cauliflower
1½ cups standard cream sauce

¾ cup grated cheese
½ cup blanched, toasted almonds
Cayenne pepper or paprika

Boil cauliflower in salted water until tender, about 20 minutes. Drain. Make cream sauce; if desired, add part of cheese to sauce; reserve other to sprinkle over top of cauliflower. Place whole, or cauliflower broken into flowerettes, in baking dish. Pour over the sauce. Just before serving, sprinkle with grated cheese, almonds; add cayenne pepper or paprika. Brown in moderate oven (350 degrees) for about 10 minutes. [For cream sauce see p. 431.]

Mrs. John O. Farish, Franklinton, N.C.

CAULIFLOWER CUSTARD
Serves six

"Mrs. Hedgpeth's" is known for its excellent cuisine and the elegant manner in which the meals are personally supervised. This custard is one of Mrs. Hedgpeth's original dishes.

1 cauliflower
2 eggs, slightly beaten
½ teaspoon salt

½ teaspoon white pepper
1 tablespoon melted butter
1 cup evaporated milk

Boil cauliflower in salted water 10 minutes. Drain and chop fine.

Mix together the slightly beaten eggs, salt, pepper, butter, and milk. Stir in cauliflower. Pour into greased custard cups and set in pan of hot water. Bake in moderate (350-degree) oven for 30 minutes, or until firm. Serve hot.

Mrs. J. C. Hedgpeth, Owner, "Mrs. Hedgpeth's," Greensboro, N.C.

THE CHESTNUT

Blight and other diseases have virtually killed the American chestnut trees, but imported chestnuts (Italian, etc.) are to be found in almost any market.

These are prepared and served in the same manner as the American chestnut, which once was the basis for many delicious Southern dishes. Whole, or chopped, the chestnut is a flavorful addition to poultry dressing, vegetables, fruits, and meats. The light, fluffy purée seasons soup; it is delectable when served (flavored) with whipped cream; it makes exquisite soufflés, custards, ice creams, and many other desserts.

Before use in a dish, the chestnut must be precooked, by roasting or parboiling. The roasted chestnut has perhaps the more nutty flavor and the meat is of dry, creamy consistency. But it is tedious and tricky to prepare. If not watched carefully the nuts will explode. If roasted, they should be placed in a slow oven and cooked about 30 minutes. It is advisable to take one out every now and then to split and test. When the meat is creamy and dry, they are done.

The simpler way is to put the nuts on in cold water, bring to a boil, and boil 30 minutes. Dump into cold water; then shell. They may then be riced or sieved. Often they are boiled again in milk to give extra flavor and lightness.

One pound of chestnuts should make from 2 to 2½ cups of purée.

CHESTNUT SOUFFLE

1 cup cooked puréed chestnuts
4 egg yolks, well beaten
½ cup sugar
1 tablespoon butter, melted
1 teaspoon vanilla

1 to 2 tablespoons whiskey or rum or kirsch, or more to taste
4 egg whites, stiffly beaten
Few grains salt

"Boil about 25 large chestnuts for half an hour. Peel, skin, and put through the ricer or food mill. There should be 1 cup of purée. To this add the well-beaten egg yolks, sugar, melted butter, vanilla, and liquor. Add egg whites beaten stiff, few grains of salt, and pour into a greased baking dish. Set in a pan ¼ full of water and put in a moderate oven (375 degrees) until mixture sets. Do not cook stiff—the soufflé should be light, the consistency of baked custard. Serve hot, with Hot Fudge Sauce and sweetened whipped cream flavored with whiskey, rum, kirsch, or vanilla, if preferred."

From Out of Kentucky Kitchens, *by Marion Flexner, Louisville, Ky.*

PUREFOY CHESTNUTS WITH BRUSSELS SPROUTS
Serves six to eight

½ lb. chestnuts
1 qt. Brussels sprouts

Cheese cream suace
Bread crumbs

Boil chestnuts; peel, and cut in half. Boil sprouts in salted water (20 to 25 minutes after having been soaked in cold water for 1 hour) until done. Place a layer of sprouts, layer of chestnuts in a casserole until filled. Cover with cream sauce to which cheese has been added as desired. Sprinkle with bread crumbs and bake ½ hour in moderate oven (350 degrees).

From The Purefoy Hotel Cook Book, *by Eva Purefoy, Talladega, Ala.*

SOUTHERN COLLARDS WITH CORN MEAL CAKES
Serves four to six

1 large bunch fresh collards
2 teaspoons salt
1 teaspoon sugar
3 tablespoons bacon drippings
1 small ham hock

1 pod dry red pepper
1 cup corn meal
1 teaspoon salt
Hot liquor from collards

Wash and trim the collards; chop in coarse pieces. In a saucepan place the collards and cover them well with water. Add the salt, sugar, bacon drippings, and ham hock. Cover and bring to boil. Add the red pepper; simmer until collards are tender.

Combine the corn meal and 1 teaspoon of salt; add enough hot broth to make a stiff batter. Shape the batter into thick little cakes (about ½ inch thick). Add enough hot water to again cover the collards; stir; bring to boil. Lay the corn cakes on top of collards, boil until they are cooked inside. Turn with a spatula once. Serve the collards and cakes together, with any pieces of meat that should be on the ham hock.

VARIATION: The collards may be cooked with seasoning and the ham hock until tender. Drain collards; fry them in 3 tablespoons of bacon fat. The corn cakes may be fried in fat to serve with the collards.

BOILED CORN-ON-THE-COB

In no section of the country is tender green corn more appreciated than in the South, where the housewife serves it in dozens of ways ranging from corn-on-the-cob to the rich Creole *Maïs Roti à la Crème* (Corn Pudding).

To many, boiled corn-on-the-cob is the best and only way to serve corn. Boil only tender young corn. Shuck and silk, drop into boiling water to cover and boil 3 to 4 minutes, *no longer*. Drain and serve with lots of melted butter, salt, and pepper. A Deep South method is to leave a thin layer of shucks on the corn, boil as above, serve in the shucks. One or 2 minutes may be added to boiling time to counteract the covering by the shucks. Or boil the corn; cut off the cob; and season to taste.

CORN OR SHRIMP PIE
Serves six to eight

6 ears corn, grated	Salt, pepper to taste
4 eggs	3 tablespoons butter, melted
1 tablespoon sugar	1 qt. milk

Grate corn and scrape remaining pulp off the cob with a knife. Add eggs beaten with sugar; add salt and pepper to taste, butter, and milk. Bake at 350 degrees for 30 to 40 minutes, or until a knife inserted in center comes out clean.

For shrimp pie add about 2 cups of cooked shrimp.

Mrs. E. S. Pegues, from Mt. Pleasant's Famous Recipes, *Mount Pleasant, S.C.*

SUCCOTASH (*Butter Beans or Limas with Corn*)
Serves six to eight

Succotash is an old, old Southern dish. From a manuscript of Mrs. Labbe Cole, Williamsburg Recipe, *ca.* 1837, is this:

"For a change I cook these butter beans or lima beans and sweet corn together, cutting the corn from the cob and cooking with the beans until tender and about dry. Season with butter, cream and pepper, salt being added when they are put on to boil" (Use: 1 pint beans, 1 pint corn, 3 tablespoons butter, 1 cup milk or cream, pepper to taste. Boil the beans until almost tender before adding the corn. Cook the corn about 10 minutes.)

From The Williamsburg Art of Cookery, *by Helen Bullock*

HARDIMONT CORN "FLITTERS" (*Fritters*)
About twelve "flitters"

These "flitters" are so light they literally flitter from the dish.

About 2 cups fresh corn pulp	2 egg yolks, well beaten
1 cup flour	½ cup milk
1 teaspoon baking powder	2 egg whites, stiffly beaten
Salt, pepper to taste	Hot fat

Cut corn from the cob. Mix flour, baking powder, and seasoning; add to corn and mix. Beat egg yolks; add to mixture; then add milk. Beat the whites stiff; fold in. Drop by spoonfuls into hot fat (deep or shallow) and fry until golden brown.

From manuscript cook book owned by Mrs. J. Crawford Biggs, Raleigh, N.C.

CORN OYSTERS

Grate raw corn from cob, or use canned corn. To 1 cup of corn pulp, add 1 well-beaten egg, ¼ cup flour. Season to taste with salt, pepper and sugar. Drop by spoon into deep fat.

Mrs. C. B. Pearce, from Mt. Pleasant's Famous Recipes, *Mt. Pleasant, S.C.*

CORN WITH CHEESE SOUFFLE
Serves six

½ cup chopped green peppers
1 tablespoon butter
¼ cup flour
2 cups milk
1 cup grated cheese

3 egg yolks, beaten
1 cup corn
1 teaspoon salt
Dash paprika
3 egg whites, stiffly beaten

Brown the chopped peppers in the butter; add flour, then milk, gradually, stirring constantly. Then add the cheese, beaten egg yolks, corn, and seasoning. Fold in stiffly beaten egg whites. Turn into buttered baking dish and bake 30 minutes in moderate oven (350 degrees).

Mrs. H. B. Hardy, from The Guild Cook Book, *Portsmouth, Va.*

VIRGINIA GREEN CORN PUDDING
Serves six

2 cups fresh corn
1½ tablespoons flour
Salt, cayenne pepper to taste
¼ teaspoon mace or little grated nutmeg
1 tablespoon sugar

1 tablespoon minced green pepper (optional)
2 large eggs or 3 small ones, beaten
1 cup thin coffee cream
4 tablespoons butter, melted

Cut corn off cob, being sure to scrape all pulp out with knife as this helps thicken pudding. Mix corn with flour, seasonings, and green pepper (if used). Beat eggs very light; add to corn mixture; add cream. Melt butter and add, saving out a little to grease baking dish. Pour mixture into baking dish; set in a pan of warm water, bake in moderate (350-degree oven) for about 30 minutes, or until custard is firm. Serve hot.

Mrs. J. P. Batt, McKenney, Va.

MRS. ALLEN'S STUFFED EGGPLANT
Serves eight

1 large well-shaped eggplant
Black pepper
¾ cup cracker crumbs
½ cup whipping cream

2 tablespoons butter
2 tablespoons grated onion
4 tablespoons grated cheese
Paprika

Cut eggplant in half lengthwise. Scoop out inside being careful not to break shell. Cook pulp in small amount of salted water until done. Mash and season well with black pepper to taste. Add cracker crumbs, cream and butter, mixing well. Pour into shells and sprinkle with grated onion, then grated cheese and paprika. Place in a shallow pan containing about ¼ inch water. Bake 30 minutes at 350 degrees.

To serve 4, use only 1 shell and halve all ingredients except meat of eggplant.

Mrs. L. B. Allen, Jr., Macon, Ga.

BAKED EGGPLANT
Serves six to eight

1 2-lb. eggplant
Salt
Butter
1 tablespoon Worcestershire sauce

Ripe tomato, sliced
½ lb. grated Cheddar cheese, or
any sharp cheese
Paprika

Peel the eggplant and slice crosswise into ¼-inch slices. Sprinkle the slices with salt and let set for about 30 minutes; drain off the liquid. Grease a shallow baking dish with butter. Lay the eggplant slices in pan with edges touching, but do not crowd in the pan. Generously dot the eggplant slices with bits of butter. Broil in a 400-degree oven for around 12 minutes, or until the eggplant is tender. Sprinkle the Worcestershire over the eggplant. Cover the eggplant slices with slices of ripe tomatoes. Sprinkle the cheese over the tomatoes. Bake in a 325-degree oven for 20 to 25 minutes, or until cheese is melted. Sprinkle with paprika.

Mrs. Colin Dunn, Mineral Wells, Tex.

HALLIE'S ESCALLOPPED EGGPLANT
Serves six

Toasted bread crumbs
Pulp from 1 medium-size egg-
plant
Salted water

1 medium-size onion, grated
½ cup heavy cream or evaporated
milk
1 egg, beaten

3 slices bread, crumbled fine	1 green pepper, chopped fine
3 tablespoons melted butter	½ cup sharp cheese, grated—
1 teaspoon salt	extra cheese for topping

Line a 1½-qt. greased casserole with toasted bread crumbs. Cut the pulp out of the eggplant and boil it in slightly salted water with the onion until vegetables are tender. Drain. Add the milk, egg, slices of crumbled bread, butter, salt, green pepper, and cheese. Mix well. Pour the mixture into casserole and cover with toasted bread crumbs. Bake in a 325-degree oven until the mixture becomes puffy and is set. Just before removing from the oven sprinkle over a layer of grated cheese and continue baking until cheese has melted.

This recipe may be doubled. A larger quantity of onion and green pepper may be used.

Mrs. Herbert Long, Graham, N.C.

EGGPLANT BEEF CASSEROLE
Serves four to six

This is a good simple lunch.

1 medium-size eggplant, peeled, sliced	Basic Tomato Sauce (see Isabella's Chicken Marengo sauce, p. 202)
Ground beef (ground round steak or good cut meat)	Parmesan cheese

Peel and slice the eggplant. Place it in layers in a well-buttered casserole. Cover with a layer of ground beef (make layer thick as desired—from 1 to about 2 inches). Pour over a thick layer of Basic Tomato Sauce. Bake in 350-degree oven for 1 hour. Serve with grated Parmesan cheese.

Mrs. Lambert Davis, Chapel Hill, N.C.

SPANISH PISTO
Serves six to eight

Sheila Kelly Pardo is a native North Carolinian now living in New York. This is one of her favorite "company" casseroles, or "skillet" dishes.

¼ cup olive oil	2 cups diced eggplant (unpared)
1 cup diced, cooked ham	1 9-oz. pkg. frozen artichoke hearts, unthawed
2 large Spanish onions, sliced (about 3 cups)	1 1-lb. can tomatoes, not drained
2 cloves garlic, minced	2½ teaspoons salt
4 to 5 pimientos, diced	⅛ teaspoon pepper

Slowly heat the oil in a large skillet. Sauté the ham in the oil until lightly browned. Add the onions, garlic, pimientos, and eggplant. Cook over medium heat, stirring occasionally, until onion and garlic are tender but not browned. Add frozen artichoke hearts, tomatoes, salt, and pepper. Cook covered until artichokes are tender and tomatoes have lost their shape (about 15 minutes).

Serve hot as a main dish or as an accompaniment to meat or fish. This may be placed in a casserole and kept warm in oven, or served from the skillet.

Mrs. Joseph A. Pardo, New York, N.Y.

TURNIP GREENS AND OTHER GREENS
Serves six

The South has an abundance of greens for cooking: turnip, kale, mustard, chard, collard, spinach, water cress, beet tops, poke, and others. The most popular is the turnip. This is often mixed with kale and/or mustard greens, and these are boiled in more water and cooked longer than the other greens. The most usual meat for seasoning is the streak-of-lean salt pork. Ham and "hog jowl" are also considered fine. Often turnips are boiled with turnip greens and served with them.

Plain Turnip Greens

½ pk. fresh greens; turnip or a mixture of mustard or kale	1 to 2 pods red pepper (optional)
	Salt and pepper to taste
¼ lb. boiling meat	1 tablespoon vinegar (optional)
Boiling water	

Pick over the greens, break off the stems, and wash several times to remove grit. Place in a large pan or colander and pour boiling water over them; drain. Place the meat in large kettle and add just enough water to cover the meat. Bring meat and water to boil. Add the greens, pepper pod. Bring the whole mixture to a rapid boil; reduce heat to low and boil slowly until greens are tender—about 1½ to 2 hours—and the liquid has been reduced to about 1 cup. When done, the greens should have a glazed but not greasy look. Drain and serve with the meat, sliced. Serve the liquid as "pot likker" to be poured over corn bread, if desired.

Spinach, Swiss Chard

Spinach and Swiss chard need no water for cooking, as there is enough natural juice in the leaves. Wash (½ pk.) greens several times, lifting the leaves carefully or they will bruise. Place greens in deep vessel over medium heat.

When juices begin to seep from leaves, boil more briskly for 25 to 30 minutes until liquid is reduced. Remove; drain. In a separate pan, fry out several strips of bacon or boiling meat. Remove meat; add spinach or chard; simmer for few minutes; chop and serve. If meat is not cooked out, season chopped greens with butter, salt, and pepper. I always add 1 tablespoon of vinegar to greens.

About Water Cress ("Cresses")

I feel that water cress is too piquant to cook but should be served as a raw green salad; however, if it is cooked, soak for several hours in cold water to remove bitter taste; cook as turnip greens.

Pokeweed Greens

To cook, prepare by stripping leaves from stalk; rinse and cook quickly in same manner as spinach.

TURNIP GREENS WITH HOG JOWL
Serves four to six

1 lb. mustard greens	Water to cover
½ lb. salt pork or fresh hog jowl or ham hock (less if desired)	1 lb. or more young tender turnip tops
	Spring onions

Wash and drain mustard greens; put in pot with meat with barely enough water to cover. Cook until meat is tender. Wash and drain turnip tops; boil in separate pot until tender. Add to meat pot and simmer a few minutes. Drain. Arrange meat over greens. Cut over all several young spring onions. Serve the pot likker in cups. Serve with corn pone.

Mrs. W. E. Diehl, Eureka Springs, Ark.

HOMINY GRITS (*Corn*)

From corn the South obtains nourishing staple dishes such as Grits, Big Hominy, Little Hominy, Lye Hominy, or Samp.

The most served is grits, the delicate, finely ground white small hominy made from the inner white corn. Yellow grits, while tasty, is not considered so elegant, for it is ground from the husk of the grain. Large hominy is the whole dried grain with the husk removed either by the old method of threshing, or by being soaked in lye. The latter process gives to the grain the well-known title of Lye Hominy, or Samp. Grits is considered a winter dish, while large hominy is more of the vegetable variety and served as such.

Grits, the favorite Southern breakfast dish, is always first boiled. Then, if left over, it may be baked, fried in cakes like potatoes, or turned into other appetizing dishes.

Hominy is often served with sugar and cream, or pounded and made into bread. Hominy, in its dry form, differs from lye hominy, which is dried and then brought back to a puffed state by boiling, then soaking in cold water. Lye Hominy is canned and shipped to market, where it is served in many ways.

BAKED GRITS SHERRY
Serves six

1 cup uncooked grits
½ lb. sharp cheese, grated; or garlic cheese
3 eggs, beaten

¾ cup milk
½ teaspoon Worcestershire sauce
Dash Tabasco sauce
2 tablespoons sherry

Cook the grits according to package directions. Keep heated; stir in the cheese; blend thoroughly until cheese melts. Remove from heat and add the egg-milk mixture. Add the sauces and wine; stir. Pour into a greased 1-qt. casserole. Bake at 350 degrees for around 25 minutes, or until mixture is set and browned slightly on top. Serve hot.

Alfred G. Lea, St. Petersburg, Fla.

GARLIC CHEESE GRITS
Serves six to eight

1 cup grits (long-cooking grits)
3 cups water
1½ cups milk
¼ teaspoon salt

1 6-oz. roll garlic cheese
2 eggs, beaten
Cayenne pepper to taste

Boil the grits in the water, milk, and salt in a heavy saucepan, stirring often until grits mixture is stiff. Break up the cheese and stir into hot grits. Allow grits to cool. Beat the eggs and blend into the cheese-grits mixture. Add cayenne pepper to taste. Pour into buttered 1- to 1½-qt. casserole and bake in a preheated 450-degree oven until bubbly hot.

Mrs. Albert A. Stoddard, Burlington, N.C.

A SET OF GRITS ALABAMA
Serves five

4½ cups water
1 teaspoon salt
¾ cup grits

1 tablespoon butter
½ cup cream

Pour water in the top of a double boiler. Put in level teaspoon of salt. Bring this to a boil and, when boiling, add (slowly) the grits. Keep boiling and stirring until it begins to thicken. When it thickens so that the steam bubbles pop, set this saucepan in the double boiler. Let cook 15 minutes, then stir. Let cook for another 15 minutes; then put in butter and cover. Do not stir. In about 10 minutes add cream; stir vigorously. Let cook in double boiler for about 15 or 20 minutes, or as long as you want to. When ready to serve, beat in small pat of butter. This will make about 5 generous servings.

Walter Gayle, from Old North State Cook Book, *Charlotte, N.C.*

KALE LOAF
Serves four to six

2 tablespoons minced onion
½ cup chopped celery (chop a sprig or 2 of celery leaves to mix with celery stalk)
3 tablespoons butter or margarine; or bacon fat
1 tablespoon flour
¼ cup of the liquid kale was cooked in
1½ cups cooked kale (turnip greens or other greens), fresh or frozen

1 egg, beaten
2 small carrots, cooked, diced
1½ cups cooked rice
1 teaspoon salt
½ teaspoon black pepper
⅛ teaspoon curry powder
3 strips bacon

Sauté the onions and celery in the butter, margarine, or bacon fat. Stir in the flour. Add the kale liquor; stir well. Add remaining ingredients except the bacon. Chill mixture. In a greased baking dish, form the mixture into loaf shape. Lay the bacon strips across loaf. Bake at 400 degrees for 30 minutes.

VARIATION: Use equal quantities of kale and broccoli if desired. Garnish with rings of hard-cooked egg, or wedges of tomato.

Mrs. Douglas Moore, Fort Lauderdale, Fla.

MIRLITON (*Vegetable Pear*) STUFFED WITH SHRIMP
Serves six

3 mirlitons, halved
1 tablespoon butter
1 onion, chopped fine
1 clove garlic, minced
1 tomato, chopped
1 sprig parsley, minced
1 sprig thyme, minced
1 bay leaf, minced

Salt and pepper to taste
¾ cup bread crumbs, soaked and squeezed out
Butter for frying
1½ doz. boiled or canned shrimp, halved
Grated crumbs, butter

Cut mirlitons, or vegetable pears, in half and boil in salted water until tender. Take out and cool. Scoop out the tender insides, mash, and leave the shells in a nice condition to stuff.

Melt butter in a frying pan; sauté onions and garlic until tender. Add tomato, parsley, thyme, and bay leaf. Season to taste with salt and pepper, making all taste snappy.

Next take the mashed mirliton pulp and mix with soaked and squeezed bread crumbs. Season well and fry in butter for 5 minutes. Add the shrimp to the pulp. Mix mixture with the tomato-onion mixture and fill mirliton shells. Sprinkle grated crumbs over tops; dot with butter, and bake in a 375-degree oven until browned.

From New Orleans Recipes, *by Mary Moore Bremer, New Orleans, La.*

BAKED MUSHROOMS

This quaint recipe has survived from the hearth-cooking era. "Place some large, flat mushrooms, nicely cleaned and trimmed, on thin slices of well-buttered toast, putting a little nudgel of butter in each, and also a snuff of pepper and salt; lay them on a baking tray and cover them carefully; heap the hot ashes upon them (on the cover of tray) and let them bake on the hearth for 15 to 20 minutes."

From an early nineteenth-century unidentified cook book owned by Mrs. Norman Riddle, Burlington, N.C.

FRESH MUSHROOMS SOUS CLOCHE
Serves four

These are wine-flavored mushrooms served under a glass bell dome.

1 lb. fresh mushrooms, washed
1 cup water

½ cup white wine

3 tablespoons butter
Mushroom stock
1 tablespoon flour
Juice ½ lemon

1 egg yolk, beaten
½ cup light cream
4 buttered toast rounds, cut to fit
    into bottom of bell

Wash the mushrooms; rinse. Combine the water, wine, and 1 tablespoon of the butter in a saucepan. Add the whole mushrooms. Bring to boiling, reduce heat, and let simmer for 10 minutes. Drain; reserve the stock. Melt the 2 remaining tablespoons of butter; stir in the flour; add the mushroom stock and cook, stirring constantly, until the sauce thickens. Slice the mushrooms thin; add them to the sauce with the lemon juice. Cook slowly for 5 minutes. Beat the egg yolk until thick; add the cream. Gradually add the egg-cream mixture to the mushrooms, mix well, cook until heated thoroughly. Place each round of toast into a heated porcelain shirred egg dish (or any heated dish). Divide the mixture and pour over the toast. Fit a heated bell glass over each serving. Serve immediately. The bell is removed at the table. Or serve the mushrooms on toast, omitting the bell.

From Antoine's Restaurant, New Orleans, La., special permission,
Roy Alciatore, Proprietor

MUSHROOM SOUFFLE
Serves eight to ten

¾ lb. mushrooms
1 tablespoon chopped onion
6 tablespoons butter
6 tablespoons flour
2 cups scalded milk

½ cup grated American cheese
Dash Tabasco
Salt and pepper
6 eggs yolks, well beaten
6 egg whites, beaten stiff

Wash mushrooms well. Chop both buttons and stems fine and combine with onion. Sauté in 3 tablespoons of the butter until lightly browned. Cover and steam over low heat for 5 minutes.

Push mushrooms aside. To the liquid and fat in the pan, add the remaining 3 tablespoons butter. Blend in the flour; add hot milk gradually, and cook, stirring constantly, until thick. Mix in cheese until melted. Add Tabasco and season highly with salt and pepper. Cool.

Stir egg yolks into mixture; then fold in egg whites. Pour into a greased 2-quart casserole and place in a pan of warm water. Bake at 325 degrees for about 1 hour, or until firm. Serve at once. If you wish to hold back the soufflé, reduce heat to 275 degrees or 300, during the last portion of baking.

Mrs. J. Barnett Smith, from The Junior League of Dallas Cook Book,
Dallas, Tex.

OKRA

Okra is said to have been brought in slave boats from the Congo regions to the West Indies and thence to the United States. One of the most simple to prepare, yet among the highly prized Southern vegetables, okra is used in many ways. Boiled, it is served with a variety of sauces. It is famous as a gumbo ingredient in sections where Gumbo Filé is unobtainable; it is delicious fried or combined in stews or with other vegetables. (See Soups, Stews.) Okra may be fried whole or cut into pieces. Annie, our cook for many years, slices the okra into sections about ½ inch long, dredges the sections in flour, and fries them in hot fat. This okra tastes surprisingly like oysters.

My mother makes an okra fritter by chopping fresh tender little pods into thin slices, mixes in enough flour to bind, and seasons with salt and pepper. The mixture is patted into little thin cakes about the size of a jelly glass top, and the cakes are fried in butter. They are served crisp and hot.

Mrs. W. E. Walker, of Burlington, North Carolina, parboils the pods, rolls them in corn meal, and fries them in either shallow or deep fat. Or, she cuts the raw okra into sections (like Annie), dips them into egg batter and fries them in shallow fat. Season to taste.

STEAMED OKRA

Wash young okra pods leaving the stems on. Place in colander over boiling water. Cover and steam for about 15 minutes or until okra is tender. Serve hot, allowing each person to dip okra pod into individual containers of hot melted butter.

Mrs. Robert W. Traynham, Burlington, N.C.

ONION SOUFFLE
Serves four to six

5 large onions, boiled, mashed to
    pulp (about 2 cups)
1 cup salted water
1 tablespoon butter
2 tablespoons brown sugar
Salt to taste
1½ tablespoons extra butter

1½ tablespoons flour
¾ cup onion stock
⅓ cup cream
3 egg yolks, beaten
3 egg whites, beaten stiff
¼ lb. grated cheese, or more
Dash cayenne pepper

Slice the onions; put on to cook in about 1 cup of water, slightly salted. Add the 1 tablespoon of butter, and let onions simmer slowly until liquid is absorbed. Force onions through a colander, or mash finely with fork; add brown sugar, season.

Melt butter in saucepan, stir in flour and onion stock, adding the stock gradually, and being careful that the mixture does not scorch. Add the cream and stir; add onion pulp. Beat the yolks and add; remove from fire and fold in the stiffly-beaten egg whites. Pour into a heavy (earthen) baking dish which has been thoroughly greased with butter. Bake in a moderate oven (350 degrees) for 25 minutes. Just before removing, sprinkle over the grated cheese and light sprinkling of cayenne pepper. Allow cheese to cook to form a nice browned crust.

Mrs. Van MacNair, Berkeley Plantation, Westover, Va.

FRANK HOLT'S FRENCH FRIED ONION RINGS
Serves two

2 large Bermuda onions
Flour
2 well-beaten eggs

1 cup milk
Cracker meal
Deep fat

Slice the onions (about ⅛ inch thick); separate into rings. Roll each ring in flour; then dip into a mixture made of the well-beaten eggs and milk; roll in cracker crumbs and fry in wire basket in furiously boiling deep fat. Remove; drain; and hide while the steaks are broiling.

Frank Holt, Burlington, N.C.

ONIONS IN SAUTERNE
Serves six

1½ doz. small white onions, peeled (or canned onions, drained)

Sauterne
1 tablespoon butter
Cayenne pepper

If fresh onions are used, parboil them in slightly salted water for about 10 minutes, using a covered pan. Drain the onions. Put into a skillet and barely cover with sauterne. Add the butter. Simmer until the onions are tender but not mushy. Drain and sprinkle with cayenne pepper. Serve warm as a side dish or as an hors d'oeuvre.

These are nice to garnish a meat platter.

Mrs. Mollie Boren, Greensboro, N.C.

BLACK-EYED PEAS

Black-eyed peas are esteemed in the South as an appetizing basic dish (traditionally served on New Year's Day for good luck). When possible they are boiled fresh with pork, but are very good in the dried bean.

From black-eyed peas combined with rice comes the famous "Hopping John" (called "Hopping Jack" in some sections), a type of Jambalaya, said to be of Spanish origin. (Jambalaya consists of many combinations of rice and meats or vegetables, or both.) Cowpeas often substitute for the black-eyed peas. This combination is known to the Creoles as *Jambalaya au Congri*.

"Hopping John" is made several different ways. The most common is to boil the peas with pork until tender. Steam rice separately until dry, then add rice to the peas and let simmer until the consistency is of flaky moistness. Many add tomatoes, green peppers, and onions to the peas and serve as a sauce over dry rice.

BOLLITOS (*Black-Eyed Pea Fritters*)
Serves eight to ten

The steward of the Pass-a-Grille Yacht Club boasts that he cooks from *The Southern Cook Book*. We are proud to add this Yacht Club recipe to our collection.

2 cups dried black-eyed peas, soaked over night in cold water
1 small clove garlic

2 bird peppers (small red hot peppers)
Salt and pepper to taste
Hot fat

Soak the black-eyed peas over night in cold water. Rub between palms to loosen husks, while water is running into bowl, floating off as many husks as possible.

Put through a meat grinder with the garlic and peppers, from which the seeds have been scraped, along with salt and pepper to taste. Save the drippings from grinding mixture. When thoroughly ground and mixed, put in electric mixer bowl and beat until fluffy, adding drippings if mixture is too dry. Heat fat in a deep kettle to 365 degrees. Drop black-eyed pea mixture by tablespoons into the hot fat and fry until golden brown. Drain on absorbent paper. Serve hot.

Buddy Borrensen, Club Steward, Pass-a-Grille Yacht Club,
St. Petersburg Beach, Fla.

HOPPING JOHN
Serves four to six

1 pt. (or 1 lb.) fresh black-eyed, or cowpeas
¼ lb. good salt pork meat, "streak of lean, streak of fat"

Cold water, equal to bulk of peas
Salt, pepper
1 onion, optional
1 cup raw rice, boiled separately

Boil together the meat (sliced or diced) and the peas in enough water to double the bulk in deep vessel, until peas are tender. Leave some of the liquid from the peas in the pan. (An onion may be cooked with the peas, whole or chopped.)

In a separate vessel, boil the rice until dry and flaky and each grain stands apart (see rice recipes). When both are done, add rice to the peas and add:

1 tablespoon butter
1/16 teaspoon red pepper

Additional salt and pepper to taste

Let simmer on stove, until flavors blend, about 10 minutes. The liquid should all be absorbed but not dry. Serve hot. Pour over Creole Sauce, optional.

Mrs. Margaret Rolf, Columbia, S.C.

BLACK-EYED PEAS IN VINEGAR-OIL DRESSING
Serves eight to ten

A new New Year's Day dish.

1 lb. fresh or dried black-eyed peas, boiled in salted water, or water seasoned with little ham or fatback
2 large purple Spanish onions or any sweet onions
1 cup salad oil
1 cup cider vinegar

¼ cup sugar
2 cloves garlic, mashed to pulp
1 small hot red pepper, seeded, minced
Black pepper to taste
Salad garnishing: lettuce, tomato, olives, etc.

Boil peas until tender but not mushy; drain. Arrange vegetables in alternate layers in a deep bowl or large jar. Make a dressing of the oil, vinegar, sugar, and seasonings by blending well. Pour over vegetables. Let stand at least 24 hours before serving. Serve as a salad in lettuce cups with wedges of tomato and olives, or serve as vegetable dish.

Mrs. Graydon Pugh, Atlanta, Ga.

GREEN PEAS, ORIENTAL
Serves six

1 lb. (shelled) fresh green peas, boiled, drained, or 1 10-oz. pkg. frozen peas, cooked, drained
1 1-lb. can mixed Chinese vegetables, drained

1 tablespoon butter
Salt and pepper to taste
1 cup sour cream

Mix the peas and Chinese vegetables in a saucepan; add butter; salt and pepper to taste. Cover and heat the vegetables over slow heat. Just before serving, stir in the cream and salt and pepper to taste; reheat. Serve hot.

GREEN PEA TIMBALES WITH MUSHROOM SAUCE
Serves six

2 cups purée made from cooked green peas
4 eggs
4 tablespoons thick cream
1½ teaspoons salt
½ teaspoon white pepper
2 tablespoons melted butter

Onion juice—few drops, or to taste
1/16 teaspoon cayenne pepper
Individual ring molds, buttered
Mushroom Sauce (see Mushrooms Sous Cloche, p. 270)

Make a purée of cooked peas by forcing them through a sieve or food mill. Beat the eggs; stir into the purée; add cream, salt, pepper, butter, onion juice, and cayenne. Pour into 6 individual ring molds. Set molds in a shallow pan with a little water in it. Bake at 350 degrees for 30 minutes, or until mixture is firm. Fill the centers of molds with hot mushroom sauce. Serve hot.

Mrs. Nelson Cheney, from The Monticello Cook Book,
Charlottesville, Va.

NOTE: The green pea mold centers may be filled with creamed chicken, creamed sea food, creamed eggs, or any desired filling.

"OLD SOUTHERN" STUFFED BELL PEPPERS
Serves six

From The Old Southern Tea Room at Vicksburg, Mississippi, is this delicious stuffed pepper.

8 bell peppers
2 small onions

2 tablespoons butter
1 No. 1 can tomatoes

2 cups cracker crumbs
½ cup chopped ham

Salt and pepper to taste

Chop 2 peppers and 2 onions. Sauté in butter until well done. Add tomatoes; cook and add cracker crumbs and chopped ham. Season to taste with salt and pepper. Stuff peppers which have been previously scalded, and sprinkle with cracker crumbs. Brush with butter and bake.

Mrs. W. I. McKay, Owner, The Old Southern Tea Room,
Vicksburg, Miss.

PEPPERS STUFFED WITH SAUSAGE AND RICE
Serves six

6 medium-size sweet green bell peppers
Boiling water
1 teaspoon salt
3 tablespoons finely chopped onions
1 clove garlic, crushed
1¼ lbs. pork sausage
2 cups cooked rice
2 tablespoons finely minced parsley

¼ teaspoon pepper
¾ cup beef consommé
Pinch of salt
1 cup soft bread crumbs
3 tablespoons melted butter or margarine
¾ cup V-8 juice
1½ cups any good hot tomato sauce

Cut the stem ends off peppers; wash and seed them. Place in a large saucepan and pour over boiling water to cover. Add the salt. Parboil peppers for 5 minutes. Remove from pan; invert and drain. In a skillet combine the onion, garlic, and sausage. Stir over medium heat until sausage browns. Add the rice, parsley, pepper, and consommé. Add a pinch of salt if desired. Blend the mixture and stuff the peppers. Arrange peppers in a greased baking dish. Mix the crumbs with the butter and sprinkle over tops of each pepper. Pour the V-8 juice in the pan around the peppers. Bake in a preheated 350-degree oven for around 40 minutes, or until crumbs are browned. Remove peppers to a serving dish. Pour the tomato sauce into the baking dish and stir; heat. Pour the hot sauce around the peppers.

Mrs. H. P. McKay, Onancock, Va.

BAKED PLANTAIN PIE
Serves six to eight

The plantain is a variety of banana that cannot be eaten raw.

3 plantains mashed with
1 cup milk

½ lb. beef, cut into small cubes or sliced

⅓ cup butter
¼ cup minced onion
¼ cup minced green pepper

2 hard-boiled eggs, sliced
12 olives
2 tablespoons raisins

Boil and mash the plantains with the milk. Sauté the chopped meat in the butter. Add the onions, pepper, sliced hard-boiled eggs, olives, and raisins. Cook 5 minutes more. Grease a pyrex mold and put in half the mashed plantains. Then put in the meat mixture and cover with the other half of the plantains. Brown in a 350- to 375-degree oven for 20 minutes. A good luncheon dish.

From Puerto Rican Cook Book, *by Eliza B. K. Dooley, San Juan, Puerto Rico*

IRISH POTATO

The Irish ("Buckra," "white") potato is not so widely served in the South as in the North and West, perhaps because of the popularity of the potato's arch rival—rice. Even so, there are numerous tempting potato dishes served in the South which are generally simple and economical to prepare. The most respected every-day potato dish is the creamed or mashed potato, from which is evolved the richer Duchess variety served as a decorative border for planked meats, sea food, or vegetables. Then there are the "French Fries," boon companion of broiled steak, and dozens of other forms, familiar to all.

BIBBA'S POTATOES "ANNA"
Serves four

4 medium-size potatoes, peeled, sliced thin
4 medium-size onions, peeled, sliced thin (optional)
Buttered oval-shaped casserole (earthen, pyrex or enameled ware)

1 teaspoon salt
Fresh ground black pepper
½ cup butter (¼ pound), melted

Peel and slice the potatoes and onions very thin. Butter the sides and bottom of a casserole (or a pyrex loaf pan) well. Arrange the slices of potatoes and onions alternately up on edges in the dish, packing them close together so the vegetables will not topple over. Sprinkle the salt and pepper over all. In a saucepan melt the butter. Dribble the butter generously over the vegetables. If more butter is needed, add it as potatoes bake. Bake in a preheated 400- to 425-degree oven for around 45 minutes, or until potatoes and onions are browned and tender. Serve hot.

Mrs. W. H. May, Jr., Burlington, N.C.

VARIATION: The potatoes (with or without the onions) may be baked as above in a square 8″ × 8″ × 2″ pyrex buttered dish. Place layers of potatoes on bottom and around sides of dish, standing the potatoes around the sides. Fill the center with layers of potatoes. Bake as above, turn out on a baking sheet. Place under the broiler for a few minutes for bottom potatoes to brown. Serve hot.

Cheese may be sprinkled over Potatoes Anna. Use finely grated cheddar, Romano, or Parmesan. Sprinkle cheese on just before removing from the oven.

DUCHESS POTATO CROQUETTES
Twelve croquettes

3 cups Duchess Potatoes (see recipe)
2 eggs, beaten with 2 tablespoons water

1 cup fine dry bread crumbs
Deep fat for frying

Cool the Duchess potato mixture. Shape equal portions into round or cylindrical croquettes (2½ inches long and 1½ inches in diameter for the cylinders). Beat the eggs with the water. Dip the croquettes in the beaten eggs; then roll them in the bread crumbs. Preheat fat to 375 degrees. Fry a few croquettes at a time until golden brown. Drain on absorbent towels. Serve hot to garnish meat platters, and/or as an accompaniment for meats, sea food or poultry.

CREAMED OR MASHED POTATOES
Serves four

Allow 1 medium potato for each serving:

4 medium-sized potatoes, peeled, halved or quartered, boiled in slightly salted water to cover
2 tablespoons butter

Pure cream or top milk, ½ cup or more
Dash cayenne pepper
Nutmeg if desired

Boil potatoes in a deep heavy pan with top, until tender but not mushy. Drain thoroughly. Set the pan with the potatoes back on heating unit turned to *low;* add the butter, and with a potato masher beat the potatoes with sweeping strokes, mashing at the same time, until mixture is smooth and creamy. Add the milk and cayenne pepper and more salt if necessary, but I like a faint salty taste to potatoes to be counteracted by gravy or sauce. Try to prepare potatoes 10 to 15 minutes before serving; turn heat down to "warm" or set vessel in pan of boiling water. Close tightly with top, and allow to steam until serving time. The potatoes will be as light as meringue. Serve at once with sprinkling of nutmeg or cayenne over to garnish.

Duchess Potato Roses

To the above mixture add **1 egg**; beat all together. Place in a pastry bag with tube having a star-shaped opening. Press mixture through bag; guide it around in small circles winding it around until it comes to a peak in the center of each circle. The little mounds will resemble roses. Brush lightly with brush dipped in **beaten egg**, place **dot of butter** on each "rose." Brown them for several minutes in the oven; the edges touched by butter will brown first giving a "natural" look. To make a plain border around plank or dish, guide mixture in plain or scalloped edging. Brown as for roses.

From The Century Cook Book, *by Mary Ronald*

ANTOINE'S POMMES DE TERRE SOUFFLEES

This famous "French Fried Potato" is a puffed finger-sized delicacy, hollow on the inside with golden brown exterior. The complicated method of cooking involves two kettles of hot grease with infinite care being given to the boiling process. The results are worth the care, as the dish was first made for a king.

The *Pommes Soufflées* originated in Paris in 1837 when a chef named Collinet was preparing French fried potatoes for King Louis Philippe. The King was late and the potatoes had to be refried. The outcome of the King's tardiness was a delicious puffy potato. Collinet gave the secret to Antoine Alciatore, who in 1840 opened his first American "Antoine's" in New Orleans. This is the original recipe, with a modern potato substituted.

Peel Burbank, California, potatoes. Cut into ⅛ inch lengthwise slices, place in a wire basket and run **cold water** over to remove extra starch. Dry thoroughly.

Have **2 frying kettles of fat ready**—one at moderate temperature (330 degrees), the other very hot (380 degrees). Place several sliced potatoes in frying basket in moderately hot fat and cook until they rise to the surface and the edges show faint signs of puffing. (If the puff does not develop, start over.) If the faint puffing appears, then immediately transfer potatoes in basket to the very hot kettle of fat; cook until fully puffed and browned. Drain on absorbent paper; sprinkle with salt and serve immediately. If desired the potatoes may be set aside after the second cooking and given a final dip in the very hot fat, then rushed to the table. If this is to be done, do not fully brown the potatoes in the second fat pot. Finish them in the third cooking.

From Antoine's Restaurant, New Orleans, La.
Special permission, Roy Alciatore, Proprietor

POTATO CROQUETTES
Serves six

3 cups hot mashed potatoes
1½ tablespoons butter
1 teaspoon salt
¼ teaspoon celery salt
Few grains cayenne

1 egg
Creamed chicken or any meat
Bread crumbs
Raw egg, beaten
Hot fat

Mix the first five ingredients; add onion juice to taste and 1 egg. Shape well-beaten mixture into balls. Fill the center with creamed chicken or any meat, shaping the ball in the form of a potato. Dip in crumbs, raw egg beaten, back into crumbs and fry in hot fat.

IRISH POTATO SOUFFLE
Serves four to six

4 large Irish potatoes
1 cup sweet milk
½ cup butter
Salt, white and red pepper to
taste

4 egg yolks
4 egg whites

Boil the potatoes and rub them through a sieve. Take the milk and butter and let come to a boil in a separate saucepan. Add the potatoes and seasonings and beat to a cream. Then put in, one at a time, the egg yolks, beating the mixture well after each egg. Drop a pinch of salt into the egg whites and beat to a stiff froth. Add this to the potato mixture, stirring it lightly, and pour into a well buttered baking dish. Bake 20 minutes at 375 degrees. Serve with meats that have gravies.

Mrs. E. T. Pullen, Winston-Salem, N.C.

RAW POTATO PANCAKES
Serves twelve

This is an old Southern way of making potato cakes.

2 cups raw, grated Irish potatoes
2 eggs

1½ teaspoon salt—pepper, shak-
ing of
2 tablespoons flour

Beat eggs; add salt, pepper, and flour. Grate potatoes quickly (because they will darken) into a bowl of water. Drain and add to batter. Drop by spoonfuls on a hot well-greased griddle or spider and brown on both sides.

"Katch" (Mrs. DeForest Goodell), from Katch's Kitchen, *West Palm Beach, Fla.*

SWEET POTATOES MARGHERITA (*Candied Potatoes*)
Serves six to eight

Slice 5 boiled sweet potatoes and arrange in layers in a buttered baking dish alternating with brown sugar, dots of butter and slices of orange with the peel left on. Add enough water to make a thick syrup. Be careful not to add too much water, for the syrup should be quite rich. Bake in a moderate (350-degree) oven for 1 hour, basting occasionally with the syrup in the dish.

This is especially nice to serve with duck or game. Slices of lemon may be mixed with the orange, or lemon only may be used if preferred.

Leize Dawson, Villa Margherita, from 200 Years of Charleston Cooking, *by Blanche S. Rhett, Lettie Gay, and Helen Woodward*

SWEET POTATO SOUFFLE IN ORANGE BASKETS
Serves eight

6 sweet potatoes, medium or small
½ teaspoon salt
2 tablespoons butter
1 egg
Raisins
Grated rind 2 oranges
Orange baskets
Marshmallows

Boil potatoes; peel and mash with potato masher or ricer; season with salt and butter; add beaten egg, raisins to taste, and the grated orange rind. Make little baskets of scooped out orange shells and fill with potato mixture. Top with marshmallow and bake until light brown.

Mrs. John S. Montgomery, from Favorite Recipes, *Terrace Tea House, Thomasville, Ga.*

SWEET POTATO PUFFS DEMERE

1 small sweet potato for each person
⅓ stick butter
Brown sugar
½ teaspoon nutmeg
Allspice, cloves to taste
Raisins as desired
Few cut pecans

Marshmallows   Hot fat
Corn flakes

Cook and mash the sweet potatoes (allowing 1 small potato for each person), and add a large lump of butter. While still hot, season with brown sugar, spices, raisins and a few cut pecans. When well mixed, take marshmallows and mold the potato mixture around each marshmallow to form balls. Roll in corn flakes and fry in deep fat.

Mrs. Raymond Deméré, Harrington Hall, Savannah, Ga.

PINEAPPLE AND LOUISIANA YAMS FLAMBEE, A LA GERMAINE

This luscious dessert which was quite popular during the "Potato" or "Yam" Session, is one of five of Mrs. Wells's creations.

"Boil **yams**, then slice.

"Roll sliced yams and **sliced pineapple** in **flour**, then in **milk**, then roll back in flour again.

"Fry pineapple and yams in **oil or shortening** until golden brown. Place **cherry** in the center of pineapple. Then put the pineapple and yams in a silver platter, and cover freely with **sugar**.

"Bake in oven 5 minutes, pour **cognac** over it, light with a match, then serve, and add **sherry**."

Mrs. Germaine Wells, Owner, Arnaud's Restaurant, New Orleans, La.

GLENWOOD PLANTATION SWEET POTATO PONE
Serves eight

4 large sweet potatoes, raw   ½ teaspoon nutmeg
Grated rind 1 lemon   ½ teaspoon ground cloves
Grated rind ½ orange   ½ cup New Orleans molasses
2 eggs   1 cup milk
½ cup brown sugar   ½ cup butter
½ teaspoon cinnamon

Grate the potatoes (raw); then the lemon and orange peel. Beat eggs, sugar; add potatoes, spices, molasses, milk, and butter. Put mixture into buttered baking dish and bake slowly at 325 degrees 1 hour. Serve hot with meat course, or cold cut in slices for supper.

Mrs. Edward P. Munson, Glenwood Plantation House,
Napoleonville, La.

FRIED PUMPKIN BLOSSOMS

This is an old recipe taken from a yellowed scrapbook, dated 1832.

1 pt. young pumpkin blossoms,
fresh from the vines; rinsed,
dried
Salt and pepper

1 egg, beaten
Flour or bread crumbs (fine
crumbs)
Bacon drippings

"Take your young pumpkin blossoms, fresh from the garden, with dew on them is the best time. Rinse them and shake them dry. Put on your salt and pepper lightly. Dip them gently into your beaten egg. Dredge them then in flour or bread crumbs. Have some bacon drippings hot in a skillet. Fry the blossoms until brown on both sides. Drain them and serve them crisp and hot with morning eggs and bacon."

RED BEANS AND RICE WITH SMOKED SAUSAGE
Serves ten to twelve

This is from the Wise Cafeteria of New Orleans, a famous establishment serving since 1930.

3 lbs. red kidney beans
1 lb. diced ham (raw)
½ lb. chopped onions
1 teaspoon garlic powder
1 gal. water
Seasonings: salt and pepper, Accent used in measure ratio of
5 parts salt to 1 part pepper
to 5 parts Accent (or to
taste)

3 tablespoons shortening (butter
or margarine)
⅓ cup finely chopped parsley
Cooked rice
Smoked sausage

Soak beans overnight and discard soak water. Combine beans, ham, onions, and garlic powder in the water. Boil slowly until beans are tender but *whole*. Add seasoning, shortening, and parsley; blend in. Serve over steaming rice and smoked sausage.

Mrs. Joseph E. DuBois, Metaire, La.

SOUTH CAROLINA DRY RICE
Serves four

Charles Mason Crowson, famed young Southern portrait painter, says the secret of this rice is lemon juice and butter added to the boiling rice.

1 cup white rice
1½ cups water
Salt to taste

Juice ¼ lemon
1 large lump butter (about ¼ stick)

Put all together in a heavy saucepan and let come to a boil; then stir *just once* with a long-pronged fork. Turn down flame low and let cook until water has cooked out, about 20 minutes. Dish out of pan with a fork and toss lightly into serving dish. The rice will be light, dry, and flaky.

Charles Mason Crowson, Atlanta, Ga.

CHARLESTON RED RICE
Serves eight to ten

6 slices bacon, or left-over ham chunks
1 6-oz. can tomato paste
1 No. 2 can tomatoes
2½ cups raw long grain rice
1 medium-large onion, chopped

6 or more stalks celery, diced
Pinch sage
Pinch thyme
1 small green pepper, chopped fine
Salt, pepper to taste

Fry the bacon or ham in heavy saucepan. Add tomato paste and all other ingredients and let cook until vegetables are tender. Then put into a steamer and cover and let steam until dry. Put in a double boiler, if you want, with the top on and let dry. Takes about 45 minutes to get good and dry. Serve hot. [This is a one-dish meal.—M. B.]

Mrs. David Battle Verner, Charleston, S.C.

WILD RICE WITH MUSHROOMS BAKED IN CONSOMME
Serves four to six

1 cup wild rice, raw
10 oz. can condensed consommé

½ lb. mushrooms
1 tablespoon butter

Wash rice thoroughly, removing husks and foreign particles. Place in wide shallow 1½ qt. casserole and cover with the consommé. Allow to soak 6 hours. Bake, covered, in moderate oven (350 degrees) for 45 minutes, adding a little water if rice becomes too dry.

Meanwhile, sauté the washed, sliced mushrooms in butter until tender. Stir lightly with a fork into the rice. Leave rice uncovered and allow to dry out a little but not to crust on top, in slow oven. Rice should be moist, but all liquid absorbed.

Clara Bond Anderson, Burlington, N.C., and New York, N.Y.

WILD RICE RING MOLD WITH MUSHROOMS
Serves four to six

To make a ring mold, follow the above recipe; pack rice and mushrooms, mixed with little butter if too dry, into a greased ring mold. Unmold and fill center with mushroom sauce.

Sauce

Two cups medium (or as desired) **rich cream sauce** (see Sauces, p. 431), blended with 1½ cups fresh mushrooms, sautéed in 2 **tablespoons butter**. Season with **salt, pepper, a pinch of cayenne**.

OKRA PILAFF (*Pilau*)
Serves four to six

4 or 5 slices bacon
4 cups tomatoes, canned, either purée or strained

4 cups okra, cut up
2 cups washed rice
Salt and pepper

Fry bacon; add tomatoes and cut-up okra. Bring to boil, and add rice, salt, and pepper. Put in steamer and cook until dry, about 1½ hours.

Mrs. E. S. Pegues, from Mt. Pleasant's Famous Recipes,
Mt. Pleasant, N.C.

SHRIMP PILAFF
Serves four to six

Follow the above recipe, substituting 1 lb. cooked shrimp for okra and adding a little red pepper and chopped bell pepper.

Mrs. E. S. Pegues, from Mt. Pleasant's Famous Recipes,
Mt. Pleasant, S.C.

SPINACH SOUFFLE
Serves six

1 cup of cooked spinach, mashed fine, cooked frozen or canned, or fresh
½ cup butter

¼ cup flour
⅓ cup liquid from the cooked spinach
⅓ cup light cream or milk

2 egg yolks, beaten well
2 egg whites, beaten stiff
Salt and pepper to taste

½ cup grated cheese, optional

Boil and drain the spinach; mash or chop fine. Heat the butter in a skillet; stir in the flour; then add the spinach liquid and cream. Cook over low heat, stirring, until mixture thickens. Add the spinach to the sauce. Stir in the beaten egg yolks; fold in the egg whites. Pour into a greased 1½-qt. baking dish. Set in a pan with 2 inches of water. Bake in a 350-degree oven for 35 to 40 minutes. If desired, sprinkle the top of soufflé with the cheese before putting it in the oven. Serve immediately or it will fall.

Mrs. Richard Gwathmey, Wilmington, N.C., from
Soup to Nuts, *Burlington, N.C.*

SPINACH AND MUSHROOMS IN SOUR CREAM
Serves four to six

2 lbs. fresh spinach, boiled (or 1 10-oz. package frozen cooked)
Water, salt
4 tablespoons butter
1 tablespoon Worcestershire sauce

2 teaspoons lime or lemon juice
½ teaspoon fresh ground black pepper
¼ lb. fresh mushrooms, or 1 cup canned, sliced
½ cup sour cream (little more if necessary)

If fresh spinach is used, wash it well in tepid water, then several times in cold water; pick out any wilted leaves. Place spinach in large saucepan; pour over about ½ cup water and 1 teaspoon salt. Cover and steam the spinach over medium high heat until spinach is tender—about 10 minutes. Drain. Put the spinach through a ricer or food mill; pour spinach in a saucepan. Add two tablespoons butter, the Worcestershire sauce, lime juice, and black pepper.

In a second small saucepan, sauté the mushrooms in the remaining 2 tablespoons butter until tender.

Mix the mushrooms with the spinach and stir. Add the sour cream and mix lightly. There should be enough cream to well coat the vegetables and bind them together. If more is needed, add 1 to 2 tablespoons. Reheat the mixture, but do not let boil. Serve hot.

Mrs. John Chester, Memphis, Tenn.

NOTE: If frozen spinach is used, cook until tender; proceed as for fresh spinach.

FRENCH FRIED SPINACH BALLS
Serves six

2 cups chopped cooked spinach
2 tablespoons butter
Salt, pepper
2 eggs, 1 beaten (in spinach) 1 saved
1 cup bread crumbs

2 tablespoons grated onion
2 tablespoons grated cheese
¼ teaspoon allspice
¼ cup water
Bread crumbs

Combine chopped spinach, melted butter, salt, pepper, 1 well-beaten egg, bread crumbs, onion, cheese, and allspice and mix well. Allow to stand 10 minutes; then make into balls. Combine the other egg with the ¼ cup water and beat until well blended. Roll the spinach balls in bread crumbs; dip in egg mixture (from the extra egg); then again in bread crumbs. Fry in hot deep fat until a golden brown. Drain on absorbent paper. Serve hot. [These are delightful served with a cheese cream sauce, tomato cheese sauce, or plain; garnish dish with parsley and wedges of lemon.—M. B.]

From Cooking Round the World and at Home, *Eureka Springs, Ark.*

SPINACH ROVEN
Serves six

4 lbs. fresh spinach
⅓ lb. butter, melted

1 cup heavy cream
Salt and pepper to taste

Wash and boil the spinach in slightly salted water until it is tender. Chop it very fine or put through a food mill; drain. Pour over the melted butter. Pour into a 1½ quart baking dish. Bake in a 400-degree oven for 20 minutes, or until quite dry. Stir in the cream, salt, and pepper. Replace in the oven and heat.

Mary Sams, from The Cotton Blossom Cook Book, *Atlanta, Ga.*

ACORN SQUASH

Cut acorn squash in half; scoop out seed. Rinse, and sprinkle with salt, 1 teaspoon brown sugar, and dash of cinnamon. Put small piece of butter in each center and place on butter a little sausage cake which has been lightly browned in its own fat. Place in open baking dish; pour in small amount of water; bake at 350 degrees until pulp is tender, about 1 hour. These little squash may be served without the meat; if so, use more butter.

Mrs. Don Holt, Concord, N.C.

ACORN SQUASH STUFFED WITH APPLE AND CHUTNEY

Unusual and delicious is this squash prepared to garnish a platter of quail-on-toast.

Allow 1 squash and 1 apple for each person. Peel, quarter, core, and boil squash in salted water until tender. Remove; season each with ½ teaspoon of brown sugar and sprinkling of paprika. Bake apple quarters in a covered baking dish, seasoned to taste, in 325-degree oven until tender. Place a quarter of apple in each quarter of squash. Pour over each 1 teaspoon of chutney. Just before serving heat in 400-degree oven, or under the broiler. [See Apple-Tomato Chutney, p. 419.]

Mrs. John O. Farish, Franklinton, N.C.

SQUASH AND CORN PUDDING
Serves six

1 lb. yellow squash (5 or 6 medium squash)	1 cup creamed-style corn
	1 cup bread crumbs
1 small onion	Salt, pepper to taste
1 egg	Butter

Boil squash and onion together. Mash. Add egg, corn, bread crumbs (save some crumbs for top), salt, and pepper. Dot with butter. Put rest of crumbs on top. Put in greased casserole and bake in 350-degree oven for about 1 hour, or until brown. [Grated cheese may be added to this mixture or used as a topping to substitute for bread crumbs.—M. B.]

Mrs. Gaston Randman, from What's Cookin' in Birmingham?,
Birmingham, Ala.

RIP'S SQUASH CASSEROLE
Serves four

1 lb. summer squash	½ teaspoon celery salt
2 medium-size onions, cut into quarters	Devonshire bread crumbs
	4 tablespoons butter
1 cup sour cream	

In a saucepan, cook the squash with just enough water to barely cover until squash is tender; drain out all free liquid; mash. Boil the onions in a small amount of water until tender; drain off all liquid and mash. Combine squash and onions; mix with the sour cream and celery salt. Pour into a shallow (9-inch round) baking dish (ungreased). Sprinkle generously with Devonshire crumbs. Dot the top with bits of butter. Bake at 325 degrees until the crumb topping becomes brown and pasty. Serve hot.

Ray Cooper Euliss, Burlington, N.C.

SQUASH-PEANUT CASSEROLE
Serves six to eight

1 cup dry bread crumbs
2 lbs. yellow squash, fresh or canned
½ teaspoon salt
1 teaspoon instant chicken bouillon
2 tablespoons butter
1 small onion, grated

1 cup heavy cream or sour cream
Pepper to taste
1 cup salted, toasted peanuts, crushed
5 strips bacon, cooked crisp and crumbled
Parmesan cheese

Butter a 9-inch baking dish or casserole generously, and sprinkle the dish with the bread crumbs (bottom and sides).

Trim the squash and cut it into chunks (if canned squash is used, drain it well but do not cook it). Put the squash in a saucepan with a top; add just enough water to cover squash; stir in the instant bouillon. Cover and boil until squash is tender and all water evaporated. Mash the hot squash in a mixing bowl; stir in the butter, onion, cream, and pepper to taste. Pour mixture into the prepared dish. Bake in a 350-degree oven for 40 minutes. Sprinkle the top with the peanuts and bacon. Sprinkle Parmesan cheese over all. Continue baking until cheese melts. Serve hot.

Mrs. James Lea, Atlanta, Ga.

BAKED ZUCCHINI, ITALIAN
Serves eight

8 zucchini squash (5 to 6 inches long)
Water
¼ teaspoon salt
Pepper to taste
¼ teaspoon each of basil and oregano
½ teaspoon curry powder
1 cup bread crumbs
2 tablespoons butter, melted

½ cup canned mushrooms, chopped
1 6-oz. can tomato paste
1 cup grated sharp cheese
¾ cup evaporated milk
1 tablespoon Worcestershire sauce
1 tablespoon prepared mustard
1 teaspoon brown sugar

Cut the zucchini (unpeeled) into thick slices (about 3 inches long). Simmer in a small amount of water for 10 minutes. Drain well; stir in the salt, pepper, basil, oregano, and curry powder. Place ½ of the squash in a buttered casserole; add a layer of bread crumbs which have been mixed with the melted butter. Add remaining squash, the mushrooms, and remaining bread crumbs. Bake at 350 degrees for 30 minutes. In a saucepan heat the tomato paste; add cheese and stir until cheese is melted. Add the remaining ingredients. Serve the sauce hot, over the squash.

Mrs. Henry F. Hurdle, Marysville, Calif.

ZUCCHINI PANCAKES
Serves four

2 large zucchini squash, unpeeled, grated
2 eggs, unbeaten
4 tablespoons flour
1 teaspoon baking powder
1½ teaspoons sugar
1 teaspoon salt
Ground black pepper to taste
Vegetable oil or butter for frying
Parmesan cheese, optional

Mix all ingredients together except the oil. In a skillet heat to bubbling enough oil to well cover the bottom of the pan. Drop squash mixture by tablespoons into the hot fat and fry as for pancakes, turning to brown on both sides. While cakes are hot, sprinkle with Parmesan cheese. Serve hot.

Mrs. John Chester, Memphis, Tenn.

CINNAMON BAKED TOMATOES
Serves four

1 greased loaf pyrex baking dish, 1½ to 2 qt. size
3 cups canned tomatoes and juice
1½ cups sugar
½ teaspoon salt
3 thick slices cinnamon bread (bakery bought Dolly Madison preferred) or plain white bread
¾ stick butter or margarine
Ground cinnamon

Pour tomatoes in a bowl and mix with sugar; should be very sweet. Pour into baking dish. Break the bread into fourths and stick down in the tomatoes so no part of bread shows. Dot with the butter and, if cinnamon bread is used, sprinkle lightly with cinnamon. If white bread is used, sprinkle generously with cinnamon. Bake in a 300 degree oven for 1½ to 2 hours, punching down the bread often to keep it from scorching. When done the mixture should be set like a thick pudding, and edges should be candied and chewy.

MRS. FALLIN'S CREOLE TOMATOES
Serves twelve

Mrs. Fallin, a former Charlestonian, was a descendant of General Francis Marion. Years ago she gave her recipe for "Creole Tomatoes" to Mrs. Eugene E. Gray of Winston-Salem, North Carolina. This is the famous dish, given me by Mrs. Gray's daughter, Mrs. Don E. Scott.

6 slices bacon	Bread crumbs
2 onions	¾ cup butter
2 doz. large, firm tomatoes	Salt and pepper to taste
8 hard-boiled eggs, mashed	2 tablespoons parsley, minced

Cook bacon until crisp; drain, chop, and set aside. In the pan, leave just enough bacon grease to tenderize the chopped onion. Add to this the pulp, scooped carefully with teaspoon, from the tomatoes. Do not scrape shells too thin. To the above mixture add the mashed eggs, and enough bread crumbs to make a firm mixture. Season with butter, salt, pepper and parsley; if necessary add a little canned tomato juice. Add bacon last and stuff tomatoes. Sprinkle tops with buttered bread crumbs.

Place stuffed tomatoes in a pan and bake in moderate oven (350 degrees) until thoroughly heated and buttered bread crumbs on top are browned. Do not cook long enough for tomatoes to lose shape. Serve hot.

Contributed by Mrs. Don E. Scott, Graham, N.C.

CORNY TOMATOES
Serves six

6 firm ripe tomatoes	¾ cup sliced mushrooms
Salt and pepper	1 cup cooked corn
2 tablespoons onions, chopped	1 egg, slightly beaten
2 tablespoons chopped green pepper	1 teaspoon salt
3 tablespoons butter or margarine	⅛ teaspoon pepper

Wash tomatoes; cut slices from tops of each. Cut out center pulp and reserve. Sprinkle tomato shells with salt and pepper. Sauté onion and green pepper in butter or margarine; add tomato pulp, mushrooms, corn, beaten egg, salt, and pepper and mix well. Fill tomatoes with this mixture. Place in greased baking dish and cover bottom of dish with water. Bake in moderately hot oven, 375 degrees, for 20 minutes.

Mrs. Lester S. Corrick, from What's Dat Cookin'?, *Point Pleasant, W.Va.*

TOMATOES STUFFED WITH CHICKEN LIVERS
Serves six

6 large, firm tomatoes, ripe
1 tablespoon lemon juice
Salt, pepper to taste
Cayenne
2 tablespoons minced onion
2 tablespoons butter
½ lb. chicken livers, chopped, sautéed
½ cup fresh cooked mushrooms, chopped

Buttered bread crumbs (about ½ cup)
2 hard-boiled eggs, sieved
2 tablespoons chopped parsley
2 tablespoons cold water
Cheese sauce
Paprika
6 strips crisp bacon

Wash, but do not peel tomatoes. If possible select them with bit of stem left on top. Cut off top about ½ inch thick; save. Scoop out insides of tomatoes; sprinkle each with a little lemon juice, salt and pepper, and dash of cayenne.

In a saucepan brown the minced onion in the butter. Add the chicken livers; season to taste, and cook for 3 to 4 minutes. The mushrooms may be sautéed with the livers and onion, or cooked separately, so that measuring is more accurate. Blend livers, mushrooms, and onions; add the bread crumbs, sieved hard-boiled eggs, the scooped out inside of tomatoes and chopped parsley; simmer for 3 minutes. Remove mixture and let cool. Then stuff the tomato shells; place the tomato top over to act as a cover. Place tomatoes in a baking pan and add 2 tablespoons of cold water. Bake in moderate oven for 20 minutes, or until tomatoes are tender but not soggy. Serve hot with a cheese sauce, and sprinkle with paprika. (Blend cheese with a cream sauce, if desired.) Garnish with parsley and bacon strips.

Mrs. Eugene Clyde Brooks, Jr., Durham, N.C.

TOMATO-PARMESAN SOUFFLE
Serves eight

2½ cups drained tomato pulp (fresh or canned)
3 tablespoons minced onion
1 clove garlic, minced
3 tablespoons salad oil, or olive oil
Salt and pepper to taste
½ cup dry red wine
1 tablespoon butter

1 cup milk
2 tablespoons flour, mixed to paste with a little of the milk
2 tablespoons butter
5 egg yolks, beaten
⅛ teaspoon salt
⅛ teaspoon cayenne
½ cup grated Parmesan cheese
5 egg whites, beaten

Drain the tomatoes. In a skillet sauté the onion and garlic in the oil; add the tomato pulp. Add salt and pepper to taste. Add the wine and simmer the mixture, stirring often, until all free liquid has evaporated. Add the butter and stir. Set mixture aside.

In a saucepan, combine the milk, flour paste, and butter. Bring the mixture to a boil, stirring constantly. Beat the egg yolks until thick. Stir several table-spoons of the hot sauce into the egg yolks; then stir the egg yolks into the white sauce. Season the sauce with salt and cayenne. Add the grated cheese and allow mixture to cool slightly. Beat the egg whites until stiff but not dry; fold the whites into the cheese sauce.

Pour the tomato sauce into a 1½-quart buttered soufflé dish. Pour in the cheese sauce mixture. Tie a buttered paper collar around outside of dish. Bake in a preheated 425-degree oven for 30 minutes, or until soufflé is puffed up and browned. Serve at once.

Mrs. John F. Schoonmaker, Freeport, Grand Bahama

MRS. HILL'S FRIED GREEN TOMATOES WITH CREAM GRAVY

Slice firm green tomatoes into slices about ⅛ inch thick; roll in flour seasoned with salt and pepper. Fry out in a heavy frying pan strips of bacon, allowing 1 strip of bacon and about 1 tomato for each person. Remove crisp bacon; in the grease fry the tomatoes until golden brown on both sides. Remove to heated platter. To each tablespoon of fat left in pan, add 1 tablespoon of flour and stir, making a brown roux. Season with salt; add 1 cup of sweet milk to each tablespoon of flour and fat. Stir until thickened; pour over tomatoes, or around. Garnish dish with strips of bacon.

FRIED RIPE TOMATOES

Slice firm ripe (not too ripe) tomatoes in about ¼ inch slices; roll in flour seasoned with salt, pepper, and 1 teaspoon of sugar (optional) for each cup of flour. Fry in butter or bacon fat; make cream gravy as above. Serve tomatoes on heated dish and gravy in separate sauce boat.

Mrs. A. L. Hill, Burlington, N.C.

TURNIPS

The turnip, which is essentially a companion of English mutton, is not so popular in the South, but, if "fancied," it is an appetizing vegetable to accom-pany lamb or any other meat. Stuffed, it is delicious.

To boil: the turnip (allow 1 large to each person) is peeled, boiled in covered vessel with salt and pepper and a little sugar to season. When tender, mash and season with butter or salt-meat drippings, or fat from fried bacon.

BLANCHED TURNIPS
Serves four

8 small white turnips
Salt water
Chicken broth, or canned consommé to cover
½ teaspoon sugar
¼ stick butter

3 egg yolks
Salt, pepper (white pepper)
Dash cayenne
1 tablespoon minced onion
2 tablespoons sherry

Peel turnips and blanch by parboiling in salt water for about 10 minutes. Rinse and return to a saucepan with enough rich, seasoned chicken broth or consommé to cover; add sugar and cook until turnips are tender. When tender, stir in butter. Just before serving, beat the egg yolks and blend until smooth with 3 tablespoons of the chicken stock. Gradually pour the egg mixture into turnips, adding a little at a time and stirring with wooden spoon to prevent curdling. Season with salt, pepper, cayenne, and minced onion. Bring to a boil. Just before serving, pour in the sherry.

Mrs. Garvin May, from Soup to Nuts, *Burlington, N.C.*

TURNIP CUPS WITH GREEN PEAS
Serves eight

1 lb. pkg. frozen peas, or fresh
  shelled
8 medium-sized turnips
2 tablespoons butter
1½ tablespoons flour

¾ cup milk
Bread crumbs
1 small can mushrooms, if desired
  (½ cup)

Cook peas in salted water until tender. Pare the turnips and cook in boiling salted water until just tender. Drain and cool slightly; then scoop out insides to make a cup. Drop a little butter into each turnip cup. In a saucepan, melt 2 tablespoons butter; stir in the flour until well blended. Add milk and stir until sauce is thick and well cooked. Add drained hot peas and mushrooms. Fill turnip cups with mixture; sprinkle buttered bread crumbs on top. Place in greased baking dish; bake until brown.

TO COOK FROZEN VEGETABLES

"When cooking frozen vegetables, I have found that it is better not to follow the directions on the package, but merely to rinse the vegetables in cold water, and cook them in the top of a double boiler. Any vegetable loses flavor when cooked in boiling water, and frozen ones more so. This method takes a little longer, but it is especially good with vegetables such as frozen peas, etc."

Mrs. Lambert Davis, Chapel Hill, N.C.

11. Breads, Biscuits, and Waffles

SOUTHERN BREADS

"Take two and butter them while they're hot," is an expression long associated with the Southerner's fondness for hot bread. Although the exigency of time has somewhat modified his taste and made radical changes in the family bread basket, the real Southerner still cherishes such excellent breads as Sally Lunn, Hot Potato Rolls, Popovers, Beaten Biscuit, Light Bread; Spoon Breads, Batter Breads, Egg Breads; the many distinctive breads peculiar to the Creoles: the Brioches, Babas, Calas, French Loaves, French Rolls; the famous Baker's Bread (Pain de Boulanger), the Sweet Potato Breads, and others.

MRS. BRANSON'S HOMEMADE BREAD
Two and a half loaves

Mrs. Branson's bread is a famous Southern "Baker's Bread." The recipe was given me for this book by her daughter, Mrs. George Osborn of Murfreesboro, Tennessee.

2 medium-sized Irish potatoes	2 yeast cakes
1 cup potato water	¼ cup lukewarm water
½ cup melted shortening	2 eggs with milk enough to make
¾ cup sugar	1 cup liquid
2 teaspoons salt	6 cups of sifted enriched flour

Boil the potatoes until very tender; mash. Measure 1 cup of the water in which the potatoes were cooked. Combine the potatoes and water in a bowl and add the melted shortening, sugar, salt, and mix well. Dissolve the yeast in the lukewarm water; when ready, add to the potato mixture; blend well. When the mixture has cooled, add the eggs and milk, which have been well mixed.

Into another bowl sift the flour; add the liquid a little at a time and blend to make a soft dough. Place the dough on a lightly floured board and knead 10 minutes. Place the dough in a large lightly greased bowl, turning once to grease top, and cover with a clean dry cloth. Place in a warm dry corner and allow to rise until double in bulk. Put again on the floured board and knead. Make into loaves and place in well-greased loaf pans. Put in a warm place to rise. When doubled in bulk, bake in a 400-degree oven for 20 minutes. Now turn the oven back to 300 degrees (do not open the door) and bake for another 25 minutes. Remove and turn onto wire racks to cool. Store in waxed paper in a bread box. If you wish to keep the dough overnight, place it in the refrigerator right after the second kneading and the first rising. When ready to bake, make into loaves and allow to rise once. Bake as directed.

Contributed by Mrs. George Osborn, Murfreesboro, Tenn.

CORNISH SAFFRON BREAD

The custom of making Saffron Bread was introduced into Frostburg, Maryland, by settlers from Cornwall, England, about the middle of the 19th century. In Cornwall, Saffron Bread is made on special occasions throughout the year, but in western Maryland it is distinctively associated with Christmas. Here is the recipe:

Set a rising consisting of:

4 cups sifted flour	2 tablespoons sugar
3 cups warm water	3 cakes yeast

Mix until smooth and set in warm place to rise until double in bulk. In a large bread pan measure the following:

18 cups unsifted flour	2 cups sugar
1 tablespoon salt	2 lbs. high grade shortening
2 tablespoons nutmeg	

Blend dry ingredients with the shortening. Add the following:

½ lb. chopped lemon peel	2 lbs. currants
½ lb. chopped citron	1 lb. raisins
½ lb. chopped pecan meats	

Hollow a space in the center of the entire mixture and add:

10 well-beaten eggs	2 cups warm milk
Saffron tea	

(Saffron tea is made from ¼ ounce of Spanish saffron and 1 cup of boiling water, and then cooled to lukewarm.)

Add the rising [sponge—first mixture] and knead together gently until the dough works clean from the hands and the sides of the pan. Set in a very warm place until it doubles in bulk again, before baking for 1 hour in oven at 350 degrees. This recipe makes four large loaves and two 9″ × 12″ pans of buns. The buns should not be baked as long as the loaves. Cut the recipe in half, if desired.

Elizabeth Spitznas for Sarah Goldsworthy Spitznas, Frostburg, Md.
from Maryland Cooking, Maryland Home Economics Assoc.

ORANGE NUT BREAD
One loaf

2 cups all-purpose flour
1 teaspoon baking soda
¾ teaspoon salt
½ cup sugar
1 egg, well beaten
¾ cup strained orange juice

2 tablespoons lemon juice
1 teaspoon grated orange rind
¼ teaspoon grated lemon rind
¼ cup shortening, melted
¾ cup coarsely cut pecan meats

Sift, then measure flour. Sift again with soda, salt, and sugar. Combine well-beaten egg, orange juice, lemon juice, grated rind, and melted shortening. Add the dry ingredients, stirring only until well mixed. Add cut nut meats. Turn into a small sized bread tin lined with waxed paper which has been greased. Cover and let stand 20 minutes. Bake in moderate oven, 350 degrees, for 1 hour.

Mrs. E. L. Gore, Pensacola, Fla.

FINE LOAF BREAD
Five loaves

2 envelopes active dry yeast, or 2
  cakes compressed yeast
1 cup lukewarm water
1 cup Crisco
1 cup sugar

1 cup boiling water
3 eggs, beaten
8 cups flour
2 teaspoons salt
Butter for glazing bread

Dissolve the yeast in the cup of lukewarm water in a mixing bowl. Place the shortening and sugar in a separate bowl; pour the boiling water over, and stir to dissolve. Beat the eggs and mix with the dissolved yeast. In a large mixing bowl, combine the egg mixture and shortening mixture. Add the flour and salt. Stir to mix and knead until the dough is smooth. If bread with "holes" is desired, knead just long enough to blend the dough well. The longer the dough is kneaded, the finer the texture. Cover and let rise until double in bulk (2 to 3 hours).

Divide the dough into 5 equal parts. Place each part in a greased

$7\frac{3}{8}'' \times 3\frac{5}{8}'' \times 2\frac{1}{4}''$ loaf pan. Cover the loaves and let rise for 2 to 3 hours, or until light. Bake in a 350-degree oven for 40 minutes. Remove the loaves from oven and glaze the tops of the hot loaves with butter. Remove the loaves and cool on racks. Wrap in plastic or foil. Store or freeze.

Mrs. Staley P. Gordon, Burlington, N.C.

BANANA-NUT BREAD
One loaf

1 cup light brown sugar
½ cup vegetable shortening
2 eggs, well beaten
4 tablespoons buttermilk
3 ripe bananas, mashed to purée

2 cups flour
1 teaspoon soda
¾ cup chopped pecans
Honey for glaze

Cream together the sugar and shortening; beat in the eggs; stir in the remaining ingredients except the honey. Pour into 1 greased loaf pan ($8\frac{1}{2}'' \times 4\frac{1}{2}'' \times 2\frac{1}{2}''$). Bake at 350 degrees for 1 hour. Ten minutes before removing from oven, glaze the top with strained honey. Serve hot or cold, sliced.

DILL BREAD
One loaf

1 pkg. dry yeast, or 1 cake compressed yeast
¼ cup warm water
1 cup cream cottage cheese, or ¾ cup buttermilk
2 tablespoon sugar
1 tablespoon instant minced onion

1 tablespoon shortening
2 teaspoons dill seed
1 unbeaten egg
2¼ to 2½ cups sifted flour
¼ teaspoon soda
1 teaspoon salt
Melted butter and salt

Soften the yeast in the warm water. In a metal mixing bowl place cottage cheese, sugar, onion, shortening, and dill seed; heat over low heat until shortening melts. Cool to lukewarm temperature. Add the yeast mixture and egg. Add the dry ingredients all at once, beating well. This makes a sticky but firm dough. Cover and let rise in a warm place until light and double in size (about 30 to 40 minutes). Stir down and turn into a very well-greased 1½-quart loaf pan. Let rise until light (about 30 to 40 minutes). Bake for 40 to 50 minutes until dark-brown crust forms. Brush the top with melted butter, and sprinkle lightly with salt.

This bread is much better served after several hours of cooling so the flavors will be mingled. It also makes excellent ham and cheese sandwiches.

Mrs. T. L. Tolbert, from The Chapel Hill Cook Book,
Junior Service League, Chapel Hill, N.C.

VIOLA'S STEAMED BROWN BREAD
Eight to nine cans

1 cup sugar
½ cup raisins
3 cups (Kellogg's) bran
3 cups flour
1 teaspoon baking powder
1 teaspoon salt
3 teaspoons soda

6 tablespoons dark molasses
3 cups buttermilk (if lactic acid milk is used, use 2 cups buttermilk and 1 cup water)
1 large steaming vessel with top
Cans

Mix together the sugar, raisins, bran, and flour in a large mixing bowl, mixing in order given. Add the baking powder, salt, soda and molasses. Stir in the buttermilk. Grease 8 to 9 soup cans or any can of approximate size. Fill the cans ¾ full with batter. Set the cans in a large flat-bottomed kettle on a rack (a canning kettle is fine). Add water to come up about half way on the cans. Tie a circle of foil over the top of each can. Place cover on kettle and steam on top of the stove over medium heat for about 3½ hours, or until the batter is set. Do not let water boil rapidly; reduce heat to low after water comes to rolling boil. When bread is done, remove the foil tops, and set the cans in a preheated 300-degree oven for 20 minutes. Remove bread from the cans and let cool. Wrap them in plastic and store. These may be kept in the refrigerator for several weeks, or frozen. Slice crosswise to serve.

Mrs. John Rich Ireland, Burlington, N.C.

BROWN NUT BREAD WITH HONEY GLAZE
One loaf

3 cups whole wheat flour
2 tablespoons sugar
3 teaspoons soda
1 teaspoon salt
¼ teaspoon nutmeg
½ cup molasses

2 cups buttermilk
1 tablespoon honey
1 tablespoon melted butter
1 cup chopped pecan meats, or nuts desired

Mix dry ingredients well. Blend molasses with milk and mix into dry ingredients. Grease 1 loaf pan and pour in mixture. Bake in 350-degree oven for

45 minutes or until done. Just before taking out, glaze top with 1 tablespoon honey mixed with 1 tablespoon melted butter. Sprinkle over chopped pecans. Return to oven and let glaze for 5 minutes.

Mrs. Stewart B. Cline, Tuscaloosa, Ala.

SOUTHERN CORN BREADS

Southern Corn Bread is subdivided into a number of categories: the corn cake or pone, baked or fried; the breakfast fried "batter cake"; the biscuit-pan-type baked corn bread which is cut into servings (the most commonly served); and then the more elegant deep-dish "spoon breads," (soufflé, batter bread, or egg bread). There also are a number of muffins and gems; the combinations of meal-hominy, meal-flour, meal-rice in breads; and so on.

The first corn bread is said to have been a pone, baked in camp-fire or hearth ashes in Jamestown as early as 1608. This was known as "ashe" cake. Similar was the "hoe" cake, baked in front of the fire on a board or, later on the metal part of a hoe. The pones were made by the Indian method of mixing Indian meal with water.

NORTH CAROLINA CORN PONE

Baked to serve with fish.

1 cup water-ground meal
1 tablespoon lard
½ teaspoon salt

1 teaspoon baking powder
½ cup milk
Enough water to make soft batter

Mix the ingredients well; bake or fry in pones (small cakes) until light brown. (Bake at 400 degrees for 15 minutes.)

W. T. Cheatham, from Soup to Nuts, *Burlington, N.C.*

CORN DODGERS (*Modern Style*)
Thirty small cakes

The Corn Dodger is said to have been so named because, when originally made with only meal and water, it was baked so hard that if it were thrown, the intended victim dodged to keep from being hit. The modern corn dodger may be baked or fried. If baked in pone form, the imprint of four fingers are made across the middle of pone.

This is a small drop cake, baked. Larger cakes may be made if desired.

1 cup white water-ground corn
    meal
1 cup boiling water
1¼ teaspoons butter

⅛ teaspoon salt
2 tablespoons cream
2 egg whites, beaten stiff

Stir water gradually into the corn meal. Mix until smooth; add the butter. Let cool for 10 minutes. Blend in cream, then the egg whites. Drop from a teaspoon onto a greased cookie sheet. Bake in a 350-degree preheated oven for 40 minutes. Serve at once.

Mrs. W. M. Lingo, Jr., from The Junior League of Dallas Cook Book,
Dallas, Tex.

THE HUSH-PUPPY

Tall tales have been told about the origin of the "hush-puppy" and its name. The most widely accepted anecdote is that the little golden-brown puff was created by a group of fishermen holding an al fresco fish fry. Hungry, yapping dogs annoyed the men. An understanding cook threw a few spoonfuls of prepared corn bread batter into the deep fat, tossed the golden-brown cooked puffs to the dogs with an admonishing, "Hush, puppies." In Florida the story is that workers watching the sugar cane syrup vats held the famous fish fry from which evolved the hush-puppy. In Maryland, the inventors were women, holding a combination quilting party and fish fry. Many regions of the South make similar claims to its inception. The truth seems to be that the hush-puppy has been with us a long time, and the manner in which it acquired its intriguing name is still a matter for speculation.

The old Southern type of "puppy" was a little corn bread fritter made with meal, flour, baking powder, and salt, or with just meal and the other usual ingredients. They were mixed with milk or water. Fried in deep fat, the dab of corn bread became a fritter; baked, it was a corn dab.

MOREHEAD CITY HUSH-PUPPIES
Forty to fifty

Years ago The Sanitary Fish Market owners started out in business by selling the superior fish caught off the near-by Atlantic coast. For their own use, they often fried hush-puppies on a small stove in the market. Soon customers began begging a few to take home to serve with their fish. The hush-puppy business eventually outgrew its restricted bounds; so the obliging owners branched out into a combined sea food market and restaurant. Here, their famous little dabs of fried corn bread bring visitors from near and far.

5 lbs. fine corn meal
4 eggs
4 tablespoons salt
1 tablespoon sugar

1 level teaspoon soda
1 qt. buttermilk
Water to make thick batter

Mix all ingredients, adding water last to make batter a thick consistency. Drop into deep fat, preferably Wesson Oil. Cook at 375 degrees until golden brown.

From The Sanitary Fish Market and Restaurant, Morehead City, N.C.

CORN STICKS
One dozen

1 heavy iron "corn stick" pan, well greased
2 cups water-ground corn meal
1 whole egg
1 cup milk

1 teaspoon sugar
½ teaspoon salt
2 teaspoons baking powder
1 rounded tablespoon lard, melted

Beat all together, adding melted lard last. Preheat oven to 450 degrees. Pour batter into corn stick forms. Bake for about 20 minutes, or until brown and flaky when picked with fork.

MISS ROSA'S CORN CAKES

1 cup plain corn meal
1 tablespoon flour
2 teaspoons baking powder
1 teaspoon sugar
½ teaspoon salt

¾ cup sweet milk, or buttermilk
(If buttermilk is used, add ½ teaspoon soda to milk)
Shortening for frying

Mix the dry ingredients; stir in the sweet milk, or the buttermilk with the soda added. Heat ½ inch shortening in a skillet. Drop by tablespoons into the hot fat. Fry until golden brown on both sides. Drain on absorbent paper; serve hot.

Mrs. E. H. Morris, Jr., Raleigh, N.C.

TENNESSEE SKILLET CORN BREAD
Serves six to eight

This is an old-fashioned skillet-baked corn bread. The recipe was brought by Mrs. Hopkins' mother from Clarksville, Tennessee.

Melt 3 tablespoons bacon grease in a skillet.

2 handfuls white corn meal
(about 1½ to 2 cups)
1 cup buttermilk

½ teaspoon soda (level)
1 teaspoon salt (level)
1 egg, beaten

Mix corn meal with the buttermilk, soda, salt, and add beaten egg. Have skillet hot. Pour most of the hot grease melted in the skillet into the bread batter. Pour mixture into skillet and bake in 375-degree oven about 25 minutes. Cut into wedges to serve.

Mrs. Cutler Hopkins, Chapel Hill, N.C.

VIRGINIA GREEN-CORN SPOON BREAD
Serves six to eight

This is a Virginia recipe for one of the most delicious deep-dish corn breads. The soft bread is delicately flavored with the sweet green corn which should always be young and tender. It is a combined bread and vegetable. Serve with fried country ham and hot red gravy.

4 cups sweet milk
2 cups tender young green corn,
cut from cob
1 cup water-ground or white meal
1 teaspoon salt
½ cup butter

1½ teaspoons sugar
3 egg yolks, beaten
¼ teaspoon grated nutmeg
Dash cayenne pepper
3 egg whites, stiffly beaten

Use a heavy saucepan standing in a larger vessel of boiling water. Pour into saucepan 2 cups of milk and bring to boiling point. Add the corn which has been cut down through the middle of the grain, then cut, and the pulp scraped out; let come back to a boil; add the corn meal mixed with salt; and stir constantly until mixture begins to thicken—about 5 to 7 minutes. Remove from heat; add the butter and sugar; stir in the other 2 cups of milk, and beat. Beat the egg yolks and add to meal—corn mixture along with nutmeg and cayenne, and mix well. Now fold in the stiffly beaten egg whites. Grease a large casserole or earthen baking dish and pour in mixture. Bake slowly for about 1 hour (325–350 degrees). Serve at once.

Mrs. R. D. Lea, Chesterfield Co., Va.

MARY PACE'S CORN CRISPS
About two dozen

Scald 1 cup of corn meal with boiling water (about ¾ cup). When cold, beat in the stiffly beaten whites of 4 eggs. Salt to taste. Drop by spoonfuls on buttered tins. Cook in a 325-degree oven 30 minutes.

Mary B. Pace, Louisville, Ky.

COMMONWEALTH CLUB CORN CAKES

These are made to be served with the Commonwealth Broiled Oysters and Ham (see p. 134).

2 cups corn meal, water-ground
½ teaspoon salt
1 tablespoon sugar
1 teaspoon baking powder

2 eggs
4 tablespoons melted butter
3 cups milk

Combine dry ingredients; add eggs, melted butter, and milk. Fry on a medium-hot greased grill. Pour the batter thin, about 4 inches in diameter. Should have lacey edges when done. Six cakes are served to a portion.

W. W. Lamond, Jr., Manager, The Commonwealth Club, Richmond, Va.

"BATTY CAKES" WITH LACY EDGES
Serves six

"For many years, until his death in 1929, Anthony Woodson, brilliant Kentucky wit, editor of the 'Home Folks Column,' was host at an annual celebration known as the 'Batty Cake Brekfus.' This affair was sponsored by his paper, the *Louisville Courier-Journal,* and was usually held on the opening day of the spring racing meet at historic Churchill Downs. Many celebrities were invited to talk and when the 'speechifying' was over they and the other guests sat down to a 're-past' of 'sawsidges, batty cakes with lacey aidges, 'lasses, sputterin' coffee, and fried apples, toothsome style.' Since this meal has become the model for many a Derby Breakfast and Sunday morning 'brunch'," here is the recipe for the "batty cakes."

1 cup white corn meal (water-ground if possible)
½ teaspoon soda
½ teaspoon salt

1 egg, well beaten
1¼ cups rich buttermilk (from which no butter has been removed)

Sift dry ingredients. Slowly add well-beaten egg mixed with milk, beating batter until very smooth. Drop by tablespoons on a well-greased iron skillet (allow 1 teaspoon of lard or substitute for every 4 cakes). When brown on one side, turn with a pancake turner and brown on the other side. If batter gets too thick (and it has a tendency to do this), add a bit more milk, a tablespoon at a time. Serve with molasses or maple syrup.

From Dixie Dishes, *by Marion Flexner, Louisville, Ky.*

HOTEL ROANOKE SPOON BREAD
Serves six to eight

1½ cups corn meal
1 teaspoon sugar
1⅓ teaspoons salt
1½ cups boiling water

4 tablespoons butter, melted
5 eggs
2 cups milk
1 tablespoon baking powder

Mix corn meal, salt, and sugar together. Scald with boiling water. Add melted butter. Beat eggs and add milk to eggs. Put the two mixtures together. Add baking powder. Pour into baking pan and bake 30 to 40 minutes in oven, at 350 degrees.

Fred R. Brown, Chef, Hotel Roanoke, Roanoke, Va.

JOSEPHINE'S BATTER BREAD
Serves four to six

Josephine was for years the cook for the A. P. Cucullu family of Lynchburg, Virginia. This is the recipe for her delicious old-fashioned batter bread.

1 cup meal, sifted once; if water-ground meal is used, sift twice
1 teaspoon sugar

1 teaspoon baking powder
2 cups sweet milk
3 eggs
Butter the size of an egg

Mix the dry ingredients; add milk and eggs beaten together. In a deep baking dish, melt the butter and swish fat around in the dish so that the sides will be evenly coated. Pour the above mixture into the baking dish. Bake for around 30 minutes in 350-degree oven, or until a knife comes out clean from center of bread. Do not let cook until too dry. Serve with butter.

From the Cucullu family recipes, Lynchburg, Va.

SOUTHERN HOMINY BATTER BREAD
Serves four

1 egg
½ cup cold cooked hominy grits put through potato ricer
½ cup meal
1 teaspoon salt

1 teaspoon baking powder
1 teaspoon sugar
Milk
1 tablespoon lard

Beat egg and mix with cold hominy, meal, salt, baking powder, sugar, and milk. Make batter using enough milk to form consistency of custard. Put lard in deep baking pan and heat until it smokes; then pour in batter. Bake about 40 minutes in moderate 350-degree oven. Double recipe will serve about 8. [This is also known as Awdena Corn Bread.—M. B.]

Mrs. R. C. Harrison, Savannah, Ga.

MRS. DIEHL'S EGG BREAD (*for Muffins, etc.*)
One dozen

This is combined meal and flour mixed with sour milk.

2 cups corn meal
2 teaspoons baking powder
½ cup flour
1 teaspoon soda

1 teaspoon salt
2 cups sour milk
2 tablespoons melted fat
1 unbeaten egg

Mix all but fat and egg. Just before pouring into sizzling hot muffin tins or pans (square biscuit pan), stir in the unbeaten egg and melted fat. Bake in a quick oven (400 degrees) until browned and done, about 15 minutes.

Mrs. W. E. Diehl, Eureka Springs, Ark.

CRACKLING BREAD (1)
Twelve 4″ × 4″ squares

This is an old and delicious bread. To make the cracklings more tender, soak in hot water, and drain.

3 cups meal
1 teaspoon salt
1 teaspoon soda

¼ cup shortening
2 cups cracklings
Buttermilk

Use enough buttermilk to make a stiff batter which is made into flat cakes with the hand and baked in the oven; or spread in square biscuit pan; bake at 350 degrees for 25 to 30 minutes, and cut into squares.

CRACKLING BREAD (2)
Serves six

1 cup of cracklings
Hot water

Salt
2 cups meal

Soak cracklings in a small amount of hot water; mash cracklings; add a little salt and combine with the meal; make into a pone; put in hot oven near top of unit, and brown. Then put on bottom rack and let bake until done.

Or add cracklings to ready-prepared corn-bread mix; bake in square biscuit pan at 400 degrees for 25 to 30 minutes.

Mrs. James Arthur Brown, Mobile, Ala.

DAVID HARMAN'S BUCKWHEAT CAKES
Twelve large cakes

1 cup plain flour
1½ cups pure buckwheat flour
¼ teaspoon salt
Buttermilk

1 cake yeast dissolved in water to cover
Pinch soda in ¼ cup water

Make a batter of first three ingredients with enough buttermilk to mix, not too thick. Pour dissolved yeast cake into batter. Let rise overnight. In the morning punch down like—everything! Stir in the soda mixed with water, stir *hard*. Pour onto hot greased griddle. Serve with little pig sausages and maple syrup.

David Harman, from Soup to Nuts, *Burlington, N.C.*

CHRISTMAS TEA RING
Two rings

4 envelopes dry yeast
1 cup lukewarm water
1½ cups sugar
1 teaspoon salt
3 large eggs, beaten
1 teaspoon each of vanilla and almond extract
Grated rind of 1 lemon

1 cup milk or light cream, warmed
5 cups flour (more if needed)
½ cup butter, softened
Extra butter
Chopped red and green candied mixed fruits and nuts

Dissolve the yeast in the warm water; pour into a large mixing bowl. Add the sugar and salt; stir to dissolve. Add the beaten eggs, vanilla and almond extract, and grated lemon rind. Alternately stir in enough milk and flour to make a soft sponge dough. Use a little extra flour if necessary. Add the butter. Place on a floured board and knead until the dough crackles. Place in a bowl which has been dusted with flour. Let remain in a warm place until double in bulk. Punch down the dough; knead it and replace it in the bowl. Cover and refrigerate. Punch down the dough several times. It will stop rising when it is cold. Cover and leave in the refrigerator for at least 3 days. Take out pieces of dough and use as desired for a loaf, rolls, or make a tea ring as follows:

Take half of the sponge dough and roll out on a floured board to make an oblong form about 4 by 10 inches. Brush with softened butter; sprinkle with candied fruits and chopped nuts. Form into a roll and seal the dough with wet fingertips. On a baking sheet, form the roll into a circle. Glaze the top with butter and sprinkle with candied fruits and nuts. Cut through the ring at intervals of about 3 inches on outside of roll. Let rise for 1 hour in warm room, or until it has doubled in bulk. Bake at 350 degrees for 30 minutes, or until golden brown.

These may be wrapped while warm in plastic and frozen. Thaw and heat.

SOUR CREAM COFFEE CAKE

½ cup butter	1 teaspoon baking soda
½ cup sugar	½ teaspoon salt
2 eggs	1 cup sour cream
2 cups flour	1 teaspoon vanilla
1 teaspoon baking powder	

Cream butter until soft; add sugar. Cream the mixture until light and fluffy. Add eggs, one at a time, beating well after each addition. Sift dry ingredients together and add to the butter mixture, alternating with the sour cream. Stir in the vanilla. Pour half of the batter into a greased 9″ × 13″ baking pan. Cover the batter with half of the following filling:

Mix together:

⅓ cup brown sugar	1 teaspoon ground cinnamon
¼ cup granulated sugar	¼ cup finely chopped pecans

Pour the remaining batter over the filling and sprinkle the remaining filling over the batter. Bake at 325 degrees for 40 minutes.

NOTE: This recipe can be halved very successfully and baked in an 8″ × 8″ pan for 30 minutes.

Mrs. L. C. Neville, from The Chapel Hill Cook Book,
Junior Service League, *Chapel Hill, N.C.*

IRISH POTATO DOUGHNUTS
Eighteen doughnuts

This recipe is from the "Old West." The doughnuts are excellent with any meat, game, or poultry.

Shortening for frying
3 tablespoons shortening (Crisco)
¾ cup sugar
3 eggs
1 cup unseasoned mashed potatoes (instant potato mixes may be used)
3 cups enriched flour
2 teaspoons baking powder

1 teaspoon soda
1½ teaspoons salt
1 teaspoon ground nutmeg
½ cup soured milk (Put 2 teaspoons vinegar or lemon juice in a measuring cup; fill to ½ cup level with sweet milk. Let stand 5 minutes before using.)

In a heavy skillet heat enough shortening or fat to measure about 2 inches deep. Heat shortening to smoking heat or 370 degrees.

Cream together the 3 tablespoons shortening and sugar. Blend in the eggs thoroughly, beating to a smooth consistency. Beat in the mashed potatoes. Mix together the remaining dry ingredients; add alternately the soured milk to potato mixture. Roll out the dough on a floured board to ⅜-inch thickness. Cut into rings with a 3-inch floured doughnut cutter. Fry in the hot fat until golden brown on both sides. Drain on paper towels. Serve hot. If desired sprinkle doughnuts in sugar or glaze them.

Mrs. Ruby Thompson, Mountain Home, Idaho

ALAMANCE COUNTRY CLUB ROLLS
Thirteen to fifteen dozen

¾ cup shortening
1 cup boiling water
2 teaspoons salt
1 cup cold water
2 eggs, beaten
1 cup sugar

2 envelopes dry yeast, or 2 yeast cakes
¼ cup lukewarm water
1 teaspoon sugar
8 cups flour (2 lbs.)
½ cup melted butter

Melt the shortening in the boiling water; pour into a large mixing bowl. Dissolve the salt in the cup of cold water. Beat the eggs; slowly beat the sugar into the beaten eggs. Place the yeast, lukewarm water, and sugar in a tall glass; let set until it foams up.

Add the dissolved salt and water to the shortening mixture; stir in the eggs and sugar, then stir in the yeast mixture. Gradually stir in the flour and beat with a wooden spoon until flour is well blended and all lumps disappear. This will make a soft batter. Turn the batter into a second large greased bowl; cover with a cloth and refrigerate overnight. When ready to bake rolls, divide the dough into four or five sections; make into balls. Working quickly, roll out 1 ball at a time on a floured bowl to about ⅛-inch thickness. Cut out with a small cutter (frozen orange juice can or fruit juice glass); with fingertips glaze each side of roll with melted butter. Fold and place on cookie sheets: cover and let rise for about 3 hours at room temperature, or until double in size. Bake in a 400-degree oven for 12 minutes, or until browned as desired. If rolls are to be frozen, brown only slightly; pack lightly while warm in plastic bags; cool; freeze.

Mr. and Mrs. Talmage Scroggs, Managers, Alamance Country Club, Burlington, N.C.

ALABAMA BUTTERMILK LIGHT ROLLS
Seven to eight dozen

This is an old, old recipe brought from Alabama by Mrs. Clary Holt, a native of Eufaula. The wonder characteristics of this dough are that it is practically fool-proof, improves with age, and can be made into rolls, buns, breakfast cake, or little cartwheels.

2 tablespoons sugar	4 to 6 cups flour
4 tablespoons shortening	1 teaspoon soda
1 yeast cake or 1 pkg. dry yeast	1 teaspoon baking powder
Warm water	1 teaspoon salt
2 cups buttermilk	

Cream sugar and shortening. Dissolve yeast in cup with the same quantity of warm water as yeast; fill rest of cup with buttermilk, and set aside. Sift four cups of flour with dry ingredients. Alternate adding flour, buttermilk, and yeast mixture, and the second cup of buttermilk and shortening. Work in enough flour to make a soft dough; this should take between 4 and 6 cups. Put dough in bowl and place in refrigerator. The longer the dough is kept there the better, and the unusual feature of it is that it will rise quickly (in about 1 hour) once it has been thoroughly chilled. If desired, the rising can be forced by placing the made-out dough in around 80 degrees temperature. Bake at 400 degrees for 15 to 20 minutes.

Mrs. Clary Holt, Burlington, N.C.

EASY POTATO ICE BOX ROLLS
Five dozen

¾ cup shortening	1 cup cooked, mashed potatoes
1 cup milk, scalded, or 1 cup boiling water	(cream potatoes well)
½ cup sugar	6 to 7 cups flour
1 teaspoon salt	2 eggs, beaten

Place the shortening in a mixing bowl. Pour the scalded milk or boiling water over it. Stir in sugar, salt, and mashed potatoes. Add enough of the flour to make a stiff sponge. Cover and let stand at room temperature until sponge has doubled in bulk. When dough has risen, add the eggs and remaining flour. Mix and knead.

"You may store in ice box until ready to make rolls, one hour before cooking them. I prefer to allow the second rising of dough to double in size. Immediately roll out on floured board and cut with a biscuit cutter. Fold rounds over and arrange on a cookie sheet. Brush with melted butter and allow rolls to rise again (double in size). Bake in preheated 425-degree oven 12 to 15 minutes until browned to desired stage. Place while warm in plastic bags and freeze if desired."

NOTE: If rolls are to be frozen, bake no more than 12 minutes.

Mrs. E. M. (Tom) Zackary, Graham, N.C.

SOUTHERN IRISH POTATO "BOX" BISCUIT
Four dozen

This quaint concoction is a double-decker raised biscuit often known as "tea biscuit," "split-opens," etc.

3 medium Irish potatoes cooked, mashed
2 tablespoons lard, melted
½ cup butter
⅓ cup sugar
1½ teaspoons salt
1¼ cups sweet milk, scalded, cooled to tepid
1 yeast cake, dissolved in little warm milk
1 egg plus 1 egg yolk, beaten
6 to 7 cups flour

Cook and mash the Irish potatoes fine. Add melted lard, butter, sugar, and salt. Add milk which has been scalded, and dissolved yeast. Add the 1 whole egg beaten with the 1 extra yolk; fold in the flour. Knead and place in a large greased bowl to rise. When double in bulk, remove to floured board and work into smooth dough. Roll out about ½ inch thick; cut with biscuit cutter. Brush each biscuit with melted butter; place one on top of another and put in buttered pans. Bake in quick oven (450 degrees) for 20 to 30 minutes. These are delightful party biscuits. Other rolls may be made from same dough.

Mrs. Franklin P. Harrison, Greenville, S.C.

CHEESE ROLLS
Four dozen

1 cup hot water
¼ cup sugar
1 teaspoon salt
1 yeast cake

2 tablespoons lukewarm water
1 teaspoon sugar
1 well-beaten egg

2½ cups grated cheese
3½ or 4 cups flour

Combine hot water with ¼ cup sugar and the salt; let cool. Soften the yeast in the lukewarm water; add 1 teaspoon sugar; then stir into first mixture. Next add well-beaten egg and cheese and as much flour as can be stirred into dough without kneading. Knead until it can be easily handled. Make out into rolls and let them rise; bake in moderately hot oven, 350 degrees for 12 to 15 minutes.

Mrs. N. F. Dixon, from The Belmont Book of Recipes, *Belmont, N.C.*

POPOVERS THAT POP
Eight

1 cup sifted all-purpose flour
¼ teaspoon salt
¾ cup plus 2 tablespoons milk

2 eggs
½ teaspoon melted shortening

Sift flour and salt. Add milk gradually to make a smooth batter. Beat eggs until light and add eggs to batter mixture. Add shortening. Beat 2 minutes with beater. Fill greased muffin rings ⅔ full. Place in very hot oven (450 degrees). Bake 30 minutes. Lower heat to 350 degrees and bake 10 minutes longer.

Miss Laura Reilley, Hostess, The Governor's Mansion, Raleigh, N.C.

JOSEPHINAS (*for Soups*)

1 cup butter, softened
1 cup green chilis, rinsed and chopped
1 clove garlic, crushed

1 cup mayonnaise
½ lb. Jack cheese (or Cheddar), grated
Hard dinner rolls

Combine the first five ingredients. Split the rolls; toast lightly on the hard side. Spread the split sides with the chili mixture. Broil a few inches from broiler flame until brown and puffy. Serve with soup. Store this mixture in a jar in refrigerator, use as required. Makes about 1¾ pints.

Mrs. Phillip H. Dougherty, Henderson, N.C.

ORANGE-CORN MUFFINS
Ten to twelve muffins

This contributor has won national, regional, and local honors for the 4-H club. This is one of her prize recipes.

1 cup corn meal
1 cup sugar
2 cups flour
½ teaspoon salt
1 teaspoon soda

½ cup salad oil
2 eggs, beaten
2 tablespoons grated orange rind
⅔ cup buttermilk

Preheat oven to 375 degrees. Mix all ingredients in a large bowl. Pour into greased muffin tins and bake 12 minutes. While muffins are still hot, place 1 tablespoon of the following sauce on each.

Sauce

Juice of 2 oranges
1 cup confectioners sugar

Grated rind of 1 orange

Mix all together in a small bowl. Garnish top of each hot muffin.

Miss Linda Rumbley, Burlington, N.C.

COLLEGE INN BLUEBERRY MUFFINS
Fifteen muffins

3 cups sifted flour
4 teaspoons baking powder
½ cup sugar
½ teaspoon salt
1 cup blueberries, canned or frozen

2 eggs, beaten
¼ cup melted shortening
1 cup milk

Sift dry ingredients together and mix in blueberries. Mix eggs, shortening, and milk together. Combine the 2 mixtures. Stir gently just to dampen the flour. Fill muffin pans ⅔ full and bake in 400-degree oven, 20 minutes.

Ernest Coker, Owner, Ye Old College Inn, Houston, Tex.

FLOUR MUFFINS
Eight muffins

1 cup flour
1 teaspoon salt
1 teaspoon sugar
3 teaspoons baking powder

4 tablespoons shortening
2 eggs, well-beaten
⅔ cup milk

Sift flour, salt, sugar, and baking powder together. Add shortening and blend thoroughly; add well-beaten eggs; then add milk. Put in greased muffin rings and bake until browned in 450-degree oven, about 12 to 15 minutes.

Mrs. Lewis Powell, from Christ Church Cook Book,
Petersburg, Va.

VIRGINIA HAM OR BUTTERMILK BISCUITS
Two dozen small

In these you have your "meat and bread," too.

2 cups flour	½ cup ground Smithfield ham
4 teaspoons baking powder	2 tablespoons shortening
Pinch salt (as ham is salty)	¾ cup milk or buttermilk

Sift flour and baking powder; mix with salt and ham; cut in shortening with knife until all is consistency of meal. Add milk; handle as little as possible. Pat out with hands or roll on floured board. Cut out and bake in hot oven (400–425 degrees) until brown, about 12 to 15 minutes. If buttermilk is used, add ½ teaspoon soda and omit ham.

From De Virginia Hambook, *by F. Meredith Dietz, Richmond, Va.*

CREAM BISCUITS
Four to five dozen

For state occasions.

2 eggs, beaten	½ yeast cake, dissolved
2 cups cream	Flour enough to make stiff dough

Beat eggs; add cream and yeast; stir in enough flour to make a stiff dough. Make into biscuits and let rise for 5 hours. You'll feel like ascending when you have sampled one of these delicacies.

From The Savannah Cook Book, *by Harriet Ross Colquitt, Savannah, Ga.*

SOUTHERN BAKING POWDER BISCUITS
Eight

1 cup flour	2 rounded tablespoons Crisco, or
¼ teaspoon salt	lard
2 teaspoons baking powder	Milk (about ⅓ cup)
¼ teaspoon sugar	

Sift together the dry ingredients. Work in the shortening, using hands. Add enough milk to make a workable soft dough, about ⅓ cup. Knead the dough until smooth. Roll out on floured surface to desired thickness and cut with biscuit cutter. Preheat oven to 400 degrees, and bake biscuits for 15 minutes, or until golden brown and puffy.

Mrs. W. W. Brown, II, Burlington, N.C.

BRIDE'S BISCUITS
Twelve to fourteen

This recipe has been passed down to a number of brides, finally coming to our contributor. It was originated by a family cook in Greenville, South Carolina.

½ cup butter, softened	1 cup flour
1 3-oz. pkg. cream cheese, softened	

Blend together the butter and cheese. Mix in the flour and knead mixture to make a dough. Roll out on a floured board and cut with a small biscuit cutter. Bake in a preheated 350-degree oven until the biscuits are lightly browned and puffy, about 12 to 15 minutes. Serve hot.

Mrs. W. H. May, 3rd, Chapel Hill, N.C.

MRS. GRAY'S BEATEN BISCUIT
Four dozen

4 cups best flour	¾ cup lard
1½ teaspoons salt	Ice water

Sift flour and salt together twice and mix thoroughly with the lard. Moisten with iced water added slowly until a stiff dough is formed. Knead until the dough blisters, or beat. Then roll to the thickness of about ½ inch. Cut with a small cutter (about 1-inch round) and bake in a steady, strong oven (450 degrees) about 12 to 15 minutes.

Recipe of Mrs. Eugene Gray, Winston-Salem, N.C., contributed by her daughter,
Mrs. Don E. Scott, Graham, N.C.

ANNIE LEIGH HARDEN'S CHEESE BISCUITS
(With Variations)
Four dozen

½ lb. butter	2 cups cake flour
½ lb. sharp cheese	¼ teaspoon salt

Cream butter and grated cheese; add salt and flour to make soft dough. Chill and use as desired. This dough may be rolled thin and cut with various small shaped cutters to be served on tea plates. Some of the cutters available are hearts, bells, leaves, stars, and circles.

To vary, sprinkle with powdered sugar when cold. They are good when garnished with nuts which should be firmly indented into the dough before baking. Marmalade used on a round biscuit and topped with a doughnut-shaped circle makes a splendid party biscuit.

To make cheese straws, add ¼ teaspoon of cayenne pepper to the original mixture. Roll thin; cut into strips 3 inches long and ¼ inch wide; sprinkle with paprika, and bake at 400 degrees for 10 minutes.

Mrs. Robert Harden, Burlington, N.C.

SWEET POTATO BISCUITS
Two dozen small

2 cups flour
2 cups boiled, mashed sweet potatoes
1 tablespoon butter

1 tablespoon sugar
1 teaspoon salt
¼ teaspoon soda
Buttermilk

Mix flour, sweet potatoes, butter, sugar, salt, and soda. Mix with good buttermilk (to desired consistency). Roll out; cut; bake in quick oven 400–425 degrees for 15 to 20 minutes.

Mrs. W. H. Carroll, from Choice Recipes, *Burlington, N.C.*

SALLY LUNN

The Cowan family figured prominently in the history of Salisbury, North Carolina. The following recipe for Sally Lunn, a bread that was often eaten in the past, was first used by Mrs. Thomas L. Cowan, and has been handed down for five generations in that family. Our contributor is the great-great-granddaughter of Mrs. Cowan.

3 large eggs, or 4 small
3 tablespoons sugar
2 teaspoons salt
4 cups flour

1 cup lard, and butter mixed
1 cup milk, tepid
1 yeast cake, dissolved in ½ cup
lukewarm water

Beat eggs separately. Add the sugar and salt to the flour. Melt the shortening and pour into the beaten egg yolks. Add the milk, yeast, shortening mixture, flour, and stiffly beaten egg whites. Beat thoroughly and set aside in a warm place until risen to double in size (about 3 hours). Then beat, beat, beat. Pour into a greased cake pan (funnel), and let rise again (1½ to 2 hours). Bake in a moderate oven about 45 minutes and serve with melted butter. (Start oven at 325 degrees and, when half-done, increase to 375 degrees.)

Mrs. Charles Lambeth, from Old North State Cook Book, *Charlotte, N.C.*

SALLY LUNN MUFFINS
Three dozen

A rather sweet Sally Lunn.

½ cake yeast, dissolved in a little warm water
¾ cup butter
¾ cup sugar
2 teaspoons salt
4 eggs, well beaten
4 cups flour
1 cup sweet milk

Dissolve yeast cake in warm water to cover well. Cream butter and sugar well; add salt, well-beaten eggs, flour, milk, and dissolved yeast cake. Have the batter smooth by hard beating. Pour into greased muffin tins and let rise to top of tins. Bake in a quick hot oven (450–475 degrees) about 12 to 15 minutes.

Mrs. R. Brentwood Sanders, Newport News, Va.

TURTLE EGG PANCAKES

Serve these with sea food.

15 whole turtle eggs
¾ cup flour
1 small teaspoon salt
2 heaping teaspoons baking powder
1 tablespoon cane syrup

Beat turtle eggs with slotted spoon. Add the flour and salt. Just before cooking, add baking powder and beat well. Add the cane syrup to help brown if desired. The best results will be obtained from cooking on soapstone griddle.

Claude Reese, from Katch's Kitchen, *West Palm Beach, Fla.*

GEORGIA CORN MEAL PANCAKES
Eight to ten cakes

A specialty with fish.

1 cup water-ground corn meal (if available)
½ cup flour
½ teaspoon salt
1½ teaspoons sugar
2 teaspoons baking powder
1 whole egg
Sweet milk

2½ tablespoons melted shorten-   1 tablespoon minced onion
ing

Sift together the dry ingredients; then stir in the unbeaten egg. Slowly add sweet milk to make a smooth medium-soft batter. Add the melted butter and stir again. Add the onion and mix well. Heat a heavy frying pan and pour in enough shortening or fat to cover bottom of pan well. Fry cakes until well browned on both sides. Cakes should be thin.

Mrs. Graydon Pugh, Atlanta, Ga.

"SMACK YOUR LIPS" WAFFLES

Pass the syrup and "smack your lips!" says Blanche Manor, who writes the witty "Chatter" in Sunday's *News And Observer* (Raleigh, North Carolina).

2 cups sifted cake flour   2½ cups milk
¼ teaspoon salt   2 eggs, separated
4 teaspoons baking powder   8 tablespoons melted butter

Mix flour, salt, and baking powder. Add milk and beat until smooth; then add beaten egg yolks and stir. Fold in stiffly beaten egg whites, and, last, the melted butter. Bake to a crisp, golden brown.

Blanche Manor, Raleigh, N.C.

CHOUX PASTE (*Cream Puffs*)
Thirty-six small puffs

1 cup flour, sifted then measured   1 cup boiling water
¼ teaspoon salt   4 eggs
½ cup butter or margarine

Add salt to the sifted flour; sift again. Combine shortening and boiling water in a saucepan; keep on low heat until butter is melted. Add the flour all at one time; stir vigorously over low heat until mixture forms a ball and leaves the sides of the pan. Add the unbeaten eggs, one at a time, beating thoroughly after each addition. Continue beating until a thick dough is formed. Drop by tea-spoons onto a greased baking sheet about 2 inches apart. Bake in a hot (400 degrees) oven for 30 to 40 minutes, or until puffed and golden brown.

Cool and fill the puffs with chicken salad, crab salad, any creamed mixture; custards, ice cream, flavored whipped cream, etc.

Mrs. E. H. Morris, Jr., Raleigh, N.C.

CHICKEN DUMPLINGS

2 cups flour
⅓ cup shortening
2 teaspoons baking powder

1 teaspoon salt
Enough sweet milk to make soft
    dough

Make up and let stand for a while. Roll as thin as possible and cut in squares. Use large container for chicken broth. Drop layers of dumpling squares in boiling broth and allow to boil over each layer before adding another layer. Cover and cook 12 minutes. Season with milk and butter if desired.

Mrs. H. W. Oldham, Eureka Springs, Ark.

GRUMBER POTATO DUMPLINGS *(for Poultry)*
Serves twelve

8 slices bread, dipped in water,
    squeezed out
Salt, pepper to taste
1 small onion, grated
Parsley

4 cups cold potatoes, grated
    (cooked)
2 eggs, well-beaten
Flour
Boiling water

To the bread and seasoning, add potatoes and well-beaten eggs. Form into balls and roll in flour delicately. Drop in salted boiling water or on top of stewing chicken. Cover well and cook for 15 minutes. Try as an accompaniment to stewed chicken on a cold, frosty day.

Mrs. F. G. Hoddick, from The Alexandria Woman's Club Cook Book,
Alexandria, Va.

12. Desserts

THOMAS JEFFERSON'S ICE CREAM
Two quarts

"George Washington is said to have possessed the first ice cream freezer in the United States, but Thomas Jefferson later owned one, too. He called it a 'cream machine for ice,' and it was purchased in May, 1784. Although we remember Jefferson now for other talents, he was known in his day as one of the world's great epicures, and it was he who introduced macaroni and vanilla into the United States."

6 egg yolks	1 qt. cream
1 cup sugar	2 teaspoons vanilla
Pinch salt	

Beat the yolks of the eggs until thick and lemon colored. Add the sugar and the salt gradually. Bring the cream to a boil and pour it over the egg mixture. Put it into the top of a double boiler and cook it until it thickens. Remove and strain through a fine sieve. When it is cold, add vanilla. Freeze as usual.

This recipe is in Thomas Jefferson's Cook Book, *lent by Legette Blythe.*
From Old North State Cook Book, *Charlotte, N.C.*

FRENCH VANILLA ICE CREAM
One gallon

4 eggs	1 qt. whipping cream
3 heaping cups sugar	1½ tablespoons vanilla
2 qts. milk	

Beat eggs in large mixing bowl; add sugar and mix well. Heat 1 quart of the milk to scalding point and pour over eggs and sugar, beating constantly. Pour into freezer and add the other quart of sweet milk. Beat the whipping cream and add to mixture in freezer; add vanilla last. Freeze in hand-turned freezer. [This is often served in meringue shells.—M. B.]

Claiborne Young, Burlington, N.C.

322

CHOCOLATE MOUSSE (*Ice Cream Supreme*)
Serves ten to twelve

7 egg yolks
1¼ cups sugar
1 cup sweet milk
2 to 3 1-oz. squares bitter chocolate, melted

1 teaspoon gelatin, softened in ¼ cup cold water
Pinch salt
2 cups heavy cream, whipped
1 teaspoon vanilla

Beat egg yolks with sugar until lemon colored. Scald milk. Melt chocolate over boiling water or mixed with several tablespoons of hot water. Pour the hot milk slowly into egg-sugar mixture. Return to double boiler and cook over boiling water until custard thickens; add melted chocolate and softened gelatin to mixture. Stir until well mixed; remove; add pinch of salt. Chill in bowl of cracked ice or ice water, stirring constantly. When cold, fold in the whipped cream; add vanilla. Freeze in a mold or in refrigerator tray, or hand freezer.

PEPPERMINT ICE CREAM
Serves four

¾ teaspoon gelatin
1 cup milk

¼ lb. peppermint stick candy
1 cup heavy cream

Dissolve gelatin in about 2 tablespoons of milk. Scald remainder of milk in double boiler. Add dissolved gelatin to scalded milk and stir until dissolved; then add the candy broken into small pieces. Remove from fire; add cream. Cool to 50 degrees and freeze, using 1 part salt to 8 parts ice.

Mrs. J. C. Wilbourne, from Bon Appétit!, *Baton Rouge, La.*

MRS. BIGGS'S CARAMEL ICE CREAM
Three quarts

A never-to-be-forgotten occasion is one of Mrs. J. Crawford Biggs's "Bride's Luncheons"—a traditional party given often for the season's brides—at Hardimont. On these occasions in the spacious dining room, course after course of exquisite creations is served. Each dish is memorable. One I shall always think of happily is her Caramel Ice Cream served as the dessert course at a luncheon given for my daughter-in-law-elect. With little hot lemon cup cakes as an accompaniment, the cream was served by William—long, lanky and adroit—from a huge silver bowl. Here is the recipe for the ice cream.

2 cups sugar
6 whole eggs, slightly beaten
1 cup sugar
Pinch salt
1 qt. cream

1 extra qt. cream, half-whipped
Vanilla
Coarsely chopped toasted almonds

Caramelize 2 cups granulated sugar in a thick pan and let boil until a good brown. In the top of a double boiler combine the beaten eggs, 1 cup sugar, salt, and the first quart of cream. When the custard has thickened, add the caramelized sugar while very hot. Strain and cool. Add vanilla to taste; then add the extra quart of cream just half-whipped. Freeze in hand freezer—I mean freeze by agitation. Serve with coarsely chopped toasted almonds sprinkled over. [This cream is also known as Burnt Sugar Cream.—M. B.]

Mrs. J. Crawford Biggs, Hardimont, Raleigh, N.C.

MACAROON ICE CREAM
One and one-half quarts

A wonderful dessert and extremely easy to make.

2 doz. fresh macaroons
¾ cup sugar
2 cups thin cream

2 cups thick cream
2 teaspoons vanilla
Little brandy, optional

Dry fresh macaroons in oven; crush with rolling pin to make 2 cups crumbs. Add the sugar; then stir in the cream, thin first, thick last. Add the vanilla or, if you wish to bring out the macaroon flavor, add a very little brandy. There should be no real brandy taste at all. Freeze as usual. Some of the macaroons rise to top (if frozen in icebox tray) and make a crust.

Mrs. Oliver Smith, Raleigh, N.C.

MANGO ICE CREAM IN MERINGUE CUPS
One and a half gallons

1 gal. can seeded and sieved mangoes
Juice of 6 lemons
Juice of 6 oranges

1¾ cups sugar
Milk
1 qt. cream

Add fruit juices and sugar to the 1 gallon can of seeded and sieved mangoes; let stand until sugar melts (1 hour). Add all milk possible, saving room for the quart of cream. Stir milk and fruit juices well. Freeze to a mush; add cream, and freeze. Serve in meringue cups.

Meringue Cups

4 egg whites	1 teaspoon vinegar
2 cups sugar	1 teaspoon vanilla

Beat egg whites with sugar and vinegar for 20 minutes. Add vanilla and beat 30 minutes more. Drop by tablespoonfuls on cookie sheet lined with waxed paper; bake in a very slow oven for 40 minutes (250–300 degrees). [These cups may be served filled with any cream or fresh fruits topped with whipped cream.—M. B.]

Una Chapman Dowd, from What's Cookin'?, *Corpus Christi, Tex.*

KING'S ARMS TAVERN GREENGAGE ICE CREAM
(Successor to Travis House)
One gallon

Greengage Ice Cream is served at the King's Arms Tavern in Williamsburg just as it has been for generations. Here is the recipe:

Skin, seed, and mash 1 pint of preserved greengage plums; add the juice of 2 lemons, 2 cups sugar, 1½ quarts of milk, 1 quart of cream with a pinch of salt. Freeze in hand freezer.

From The King's Arms Tavern. Special permission, John D. Green, Vice-President, Williamsburg Restoration, Inc., Williamsburg, Va.

FRESH COCONUT ICE CREAM
Three quarts

In Key West, Florida, they make a wonderful ice cream from the fresh coconut picked at the "jelly stage." This is a recipe using the jellied coconut.

1 pt. coconut water	1 pinch salt
1 large can unsweetened evaporated milk	2 eggs, beaten
	1 pt. sweet cream
1 tablespoon flour	5 coconuts (jelly from)
1 cup sugar	

Scald coconut water and evaporated milk in double boiler. Mix flour and sugar and add beaten eggs and salt. Stir this mixture slowly into hot milk until it thickens. Set aside to cool. Just before freezing, add coconut jelly and sweet cream. (Coconut has a "jelly" texture before it attains the hard, firm consistency commonly found in commercial coconuts. It is coconut in this jellied stage which is used for the best Key West coconut ice cream.)

From The Key West Cook Book, Key West, Fla.

MRS. GRAY'S GINGER PEACH ICE CREAM

This ice cream is from an old recipe originated by the late Mrs. Eugene E. Gray, Winston-Salem, North Carolina. This is the first time the family has given it for publication.

1 qt. of sweet milk
3 qts. of rich cream
1 tablespoon sugar to each cup of cream and milk
1 qt. of peach preserves, chopped into small pieces and the juice from preserves

½ lb. crystallized ginger, chopped into small pieces
Juice of 1 orange
1½ pts. of best sherry

Mix milk, cream, and sugar first, then other ingredients, adding the sherry last. Add more sugar if needed. Freeze in an "old-fashioned" hand-turned freezer. Serve "sticky" Sponge Cake with this cream.

Contributed by Mrs. Don E. Scott, Graham, N.C.

OLD VIRGINIA FRESH PEACH ICE CREAM
One gallon

Pare and stone 1 quart of very soft peaches. Add to them 2 cups of sugar, and mash them thoroughly. When ready to freeze, add 2 quarts of rich cream. (Freeze in hand-turned freezer.) When frozen, this will fill a dish holding 4 quarts.

Mrs. J. E. Timberlake, Stevenson's Depot, Va.

LEMON-ORANGE ICE CREAM
Three quarts

1¼ cups lemon juice
Juice 1 lime
1 cup fresh orange juice

3 cups sugar
1 qt. sweet milk
½ pt. whipping cream

Add sugar to juices and let stand until well dissolved. Pour milk and cream into freezer (hand-turned), and add juice mixture. Stir and freeze at once. This makes a 3-quart freezer of ice cream.

Mrs. Frank M. De Friese, Knoxville, Tenn.

PINEAPPLE SHERBET
One quart

The true Southern sherbet has no milk but is made with a sweetened water base to which fruit juices are added, and then the whipped white of egg.

20 marshmallows
1 cup unsweetened pineapple juice
½ cup water

2 tablespoons lemon juice
2 teaspoons sugar
Pinch salt
2 egg whites, stiffly beaten

Combine marshmallows, pineapple juice, and water in double boiler and heat until marshmallows melt. Cool; add lemon juice and 1 teaspoon sugar. Freeze to a mush. Combine remaining sugar, salt, and beaten egg whites. Stir into sherbet. Freeze.

Mrs. Lyttleton Harris, from Bon Appétit!, *Baton Rouge, La.*

LEMON OR ORANGE SHERBET
One-half gallon

Sugar to taste (2 to 3 cups)
2 qts. water
2 egg whites, stiffly beaten

Juice of 10 lemons if for lemon sherbet, and juice of 2 oranges; if for orange ice, juice of 10 oranges and 4 lemons

Boil the sugar in part of the water until sugar dissolves. Cool; add remaining water and fruit juices, and pour into freezer. Freeze to mush; then add beaten egg whites. Complete freezing.

Mrs. Jackson K. Stewart, Atlanta, Ga.

COFFEE MOUSSE
Serves eight to ten

½ cup milk
6 egg yolks, beaten
¾ cup sugar (sweeten according to strength of coffee)
1 tablespoon gelatin, soaked in little cold water, dissolved over boiling water

2 tablespoons powdered coffee (or to taste) dissolved in ½ cup hot water
1 teaspoon vanilla
2 cups cream, whipped

Heat milk; pour slowly over beaten egg yolks, whipped with the sugar; cook over boiling water until thick. Add gelatin to coffee; dissolve; and chill. Add coffee to custard; stir well. Add flavoring and fold in whipped cream. Pour into greased mold and congeal. Serve with whipped cream. Add extra teaspoon gelatin if stiff mousse is desired. The above makes a tender mixture.

Mrs. Chilton Grandle, Fort Worth, Tex.

ZABAGLIONE (*Wine Custard*)
Serves six to eight

6 egg yolks
1 cup sugar
1 tablespoon flour
¾ cup sherry
2 tablespoons rum
1½ to 2 tablespoons lemon juice

Grated rind of 1 lemon
3 to 4 egg whites
Pinch of salt
3 tablespoons sugar
Grated nutmeg

Beat the egg yolks until light. Add the cup of sugar mixed with the flour (use an electric mixer or rotary beater). Add sherry, rum, and lemon juice. Beat to blend well. Add lemon rind and cook in the top of a double boiler over boiling water. Use a wooden spoon to beat the mixture constantly while it is cooking. Cook until the custard is thick. Remove from heat and allow to cool slightly. Beat the egg whites with the salt until stiff. Add the 3 tablespoons sugar and blend. Fold the egg whites into the custard. Pile the Zabaglione into sherbet or parfait glasses. Sprinkle with a little grated nutmeg.

VARIATION: To make a congealed dessert of the above:

Add to the hot custard, just before taking it from the stove: 1 tablespoon of granulated gelatin softened with 2 tablespoons cold water. Stir until there are no lumps. Pour into individual molds lightly greased with salad oil, or into a 1-quart mold. Chill until set. Loosen the edges of the Zabaglione with a knife, and turn out on the plate on which it is to be served. Serve plain or with a sauce.

From Out of Kentucky Kitchens, *by Marion Flexner, Louisville, Ky.*

FLAN (*Caramel Custard*)
Serves six to eight

The Spaniards are excellent flan- or custard-makers. It has long been considered to be one of their most elegant desserts. The dish has been adapted by many other countries. Made in various ways, the object is to obtain a baked custard of a firm, creamy consistency. The flan is baked either in its own sauce, or served with a sauce over it. It is flavored with vanilla and/or almond extracts, rum, or orange and lemon juices, and grated rinds. Slivered almonds or broken pistachio nuts may be added to the custard or the sauce. Puerto Ricans usually flavor the sauce with rum and use dark brown sugar to make the sauce.

1¾ cups sugar
3 egg whites
8 egg yolks
2 13-oz. cans evaporated milk
2 teaspoons vanilla or almond extract

6 tablespoons brandy or rum, warmed
Slivered, toasted almonds

Use a heatproof baking dish (or square baking pan) that may be placed on direct heat. Put 1 cup of the sugar in the dish and set over high heat for several seconds. Reduce heat; stir constantly until the sugar melts and turns golden. Tilt the pan back and forth until it is entirely coated with the syrup. Set aside to cool. (The syrup will harden.)

Beat the egg whites and egg yolks together until foamy; add the milk, remaining sugar, and flavoring. Beat until the sugar dissolves. Strain the custard into the coated vessel. Cover the vessel; set it in a larger pan containing 1 inch of hot water. Bake in a moderate (350 degrees) oven for 1 hour. While still hot, turn out on a serving platter. When ready to serve, pour warm brandy or rum over the custard and ignite. Send to the table flaming. Sprinkle almonds over and around the custard. This may be served warm or cold.

El Gordo Restaurant, St. Petersburg Beach, Fla.

LEMON ICEBOX PUDDING
Serves eight

This and the following pudding are from an inviting Tennessee hotel where Miss Allie Rogers is the owner-hostess. These are her favorite pudding desserts.

3 egg yolks
½ cup sugar
⅛ teaspoon salt
¼ cup lemon juice

½ cup Pet milk, whipped (chill thoroughly before whipping)
3 egg whites, beaten
¾ cups vanilla wafer crumbs

Cook yolks, sugar, salt, and lemon juice in top of double boiler until mixture begins to thicken. Cool; add whipped milk and egg whites. Line a pan with the wafer crumbs; pour in custard mixture, and sprinkle crumbs on top. Freeze, slice, and serve.

ORANGE ICEBOX CAKE
Serves ten

1 cup sugar
½ cup butter
3 egg yolks, beaten
Juice of 1 large orange
1 tablespoon grated orange rind

Juice 1 lemon
1 teaspoon grated lemon rind
3 egg whites, stiffly beaten
1½ doz. ladyfingers
1 cup heavy cream, whipped

Cream sugar and butter as for any cake. Beat yolks; add to creamed sugar and butter; then add fruit juices and grated rind. Beat egg whites; add last.

Separate ladyfingers; place 6 halves in desired platter; add mixture, then more cakes alternately until there are 5 layers. Place in refrigerator overnight. Before serving, whip the ½ pint of cream, and ice the cake. Garnish with cherries.

Mrs. Edgar B. Fergerson, Paducah, Ky.

FRESH STRAWBERRY ICEBOX CAKE
Serves eight to ten

2 cups strawberries, sliced fine be-
    fore measuring
1 cup sugar
2 envelopes unflavored gelatin
½ cup cold water
1 cup hot water
4 teaspoons lemon juice
½ teaspoon salt
4 egg whites, stiffly beaten
½ cup sugar
1 cup heavy cream, whipped
Halved ladyfingers

"Mix berries and 1 cup sugar together and let stand five to ten minutes, stirring several times, to draw out juice. Soften gelatin in cold water and dissolve in hot water. Add dissolved gelatin, lemon juice, and salt to berries and stir well. Cool, and when mixture begins to thicken, fold in stiffly beaten egg whites to which remaining one-half cup sugar has been added, and whipped cream. Line sides of glass baking dish or large mold with halved lady fingers. Pour in half the filling; cover with layer of halved lady fingers. Chill for 24 hours, or until thoroughly congealed. Put onto platter and garnish with whipped cream and fresh strawberries. Pieces of stale cake may be used in place of lady fingers if desired."

Mrs. Benzie T. Rice, from The Columbia Woman's Club Cook Book, *Columbia, S.C.*

MRS. BARKLEY'S PINEAPPLE-MACAROON ICEBOX CAKE
Serves sixteen

This rich Kentucky recipe was a favorite of the first Mrs. Alben W. Barkley. It is contributed here by her daughter-in-law.

1 cup butter
1 cup sugar
4 eggs
½ cup shredded pineapple
    (canned)
½ cup nut meats, chopped fine
2½ doz. lady fingers, split
1 doz. macaroons, broken into
    small pieces
Sweet cream

Cream butter and sugar; add 1 of the eggs; beat 5 minutes; repeat until the 4 eggs are used. Add the pineapple and nuts. Then cover bottom of a pan (square is good) with ladyfingers, flat side down; spread ½ of butter mixture over ladyfingers; add macaroons, then remainder of butter mixture. Cover with the rest of the ladyfingers. Let stand in refrigerator for 48 hours. Serve with sweet cream, sweetened and flavored to taste.

Mrs. David M. Barkley, Washington, D.C.

KENTUCKY ICEBOX EGGNOG CAKE
Serves six to eight

A treat for the beau monde.

1 cup butter	5 egg whites, stiffly beaten
1 box confectioners sugar	1 cup chopped nuts
6 tablespoons bonded whiskey	2 to 3 dozen ladyfingers
5 egg yolks, well beaten	Whipped cream to ice the cake

Cream together butter and sugar. Add whiskey to well-beaten egg yolks. Mix well so that the yolks are cooked. Add this to the butter and sugar. Next add the stiffly beaten egg whites and nuts.

Line a mold or square cake pan with waxed paper, bottom and sides. Open ladyfingers and cover bottom of pan with them, top side of cake down. Cover with a layer of cake mixture. Do this until there are 3 layers of cakes and 2 of mixture. Last layer should be ladyfingers with top side of cakes up. Place in refrigerator for 12 hours. Serve iced with whipped cream, flavored as desired.

Mrs. Harris W. Rankin, Paducah, Ky.

MACAROON-STRAWBERRY PARFAIT

Mrs. Allsbrook is from Birmingham, Alabama.

3 doz. macaroons, crumbled, soaked few minutes in wine	½ cup sherry wine
Strawberry or red raspberry preserves	½ cup blanched almonds, chopped
	Whipped cream
Boiled custard or vanilla ice cream	

Arrange in layers in a transparent bowl or individual parfait glasses; top with whipped cream; garnish with fresh strawberries (or raspberries) or crystallized cherries. Any number of parfaits may be made from this recipe. Use fresh peaches or peach preserves, plum preserves, pineapple conserve, or crushed pineapple. Make a rainbow parfait by combining the macaroons with several flavors and colors of ice cream, etc.

Mrs. Raleigh Allsbrook, North Bergen, N.J.

MRS. MC LLWAIN'S FROZEN FUDGE CAKE
Serves eight to ten

This Frozen Fudge Cake is a joy, not only because of its wonderful taste, but because it can be kept in the ice tray for days and sliced as needed.

1 cup vanilla wafer crumbs
1½ boxes confectioners sugar
½ teaspoon salt
1 egg, beaten
1 teaspoon vanilla

3 1-oz. squares Baker's chocolate, melted
Cream or milk
1 cup broken pecans
2 cups heavy cream, whipped

Line refrigerator tray or loaf pan with vanilla wafer crumbs. (Grease pan with butter first; crumbs stick better.)

Sift 1 box of sugar and the salt into large mixing bowl. Stir in beaten egg, vanilla, and melted chocolate. Add small amount of cream or milk and sift in extra powdered sugar until mixture is the consistency of soft dough. Add nut meats and spread in pan on top of crumbs.

Whip the cream; sweeten and flavor to taste (vanilla). Spread cream over the chocolate mixture; sprinkle wafer crumbs on top. Place in freezing compartment until cream is frozen hard. Slice and serve—and do *not* count the calories!

If pan is lined with double thickness of waxed paper extending well above ends of pan, the frozen loaf can be removed from pan and sliced more easily.

Mrs. Gene McLlwain, Hartsville, Tenn.

MRS. KILLEBREW'S ENGLISH PLUM PUDDING

Mrs. Killebrew's English Plum Pudding is known throughout Tennessee—and beyond. The authentic recipe given here has been in her family for more than 125 years. She says the pudding is not so hard to make as it sounds!

1½ lbs. suet
2 lbs. raisins (plain)
1½ lbs. Sultana raisins
1½ lbs. currants
1½ lbs. mixed peel, chopped (candid orange, lemon)
½ cup citron, cut up
2 lbs. bread crumbs (in slices before drying bread and rolling)

Little flour
16 eggs
4 cups sugar
1 teaspoon soda
1 teaspoon salt
1½ teaspoons mixed spices
6 lemons, rind (grated) and juice
3 glasses whiskey or wine
Melted butter
Almonds to garnish

"Chop the suet very fine and be sure and get all the little fibers out of it. Have all the fruit cleaned and picked over. Dry the bread slices and roll them into fine crumbs. Sift a small quantity of flour over fruit and suet. Beat the eggs very light and add sugar, soda, salt, spices, bread crumbs, lemon, rind and fruit; last of all the whiskey or wine.

"Take a large cloth of unbleached domestic which has been well soaked in boiling water, squeeze dry. Have a little melted butter to rub all over it (inside); then shake a little flour over it (the butter). Put the cloth in a big bowl; put in the pudding; then gather it all up and leave a little room for the pudding to expand after the tying. Put in a little bit of flour and tie it again (double knot). I have a large kettle with an old plate or flat pan in the bottom to keep it from sticking. Have water about half way up pudding and pat it slowly so water won't stop boiling over pudding. Boil for five or six hours; then take it out and hang up on a stout nail till you are ready to serve it. You can keep it a long time, but it takes about 2½ hours to reheat. Have plenty of blanched almonds to stick all over into pudding and a wee bit of holly in the top. Just as it is ready to be put on table, pour a little whiskey over it and set it on fire for a few minutes to look pretty. I hope you can understand all this."

Mrs. A. B. Killebrew, Clarksville, Tenn.

JEFF DAVIS PUDDING, THE BRIERS

1 cup suet, chopped fine
1 cup molasses
1 cup sour milk in which 1½ teaspoons soda are dissolved
3 cups flour (save ⅓ cup to dredge fruits)

1 cup raisins
½ cup currants
1 teaspoon salt

Take the suet and pour the other ingredients over it. Put into a pudding bag which has been moistened and rolled in flour. Place in a vessel of boiling water and boil 4 hours—3 hours is enough if it boils constantly. Serve with hard sauce seasoned with lemon juice and sherry, or whiskey if preferred. [See Hard Brandy Sauce, p. 455.]

From Recipes Tested and Tried, *by Anne Young White and Nola Nance Oliver, Natchez, Miss.*

OLD SOUTHERN GRATED SWEET POTATO PUDDING
Serves eight

½ cup butter
½ cup sugar
1 cup Georgia cane syrup, or substitute

1 cup sweet rich milk
4 cups grated raw sweet potatoes
1 cup raisins
½ teaspoon cloves

1 tablespoon allspice and cinnamon (mixed)

3 eggs, beaten

In a heavy iron skillet melt the butter. Mix all ingredients, adding the beaten eggs last. Pour into the hot pan with butter; stir until heated. Put in moderate oven to bake (in skillet) at 375 degrees. As a crust forms around the edge and bottom, stir. Do this several times while baking. Bake 40 minutes. Serve with sweet flavored cream or lemon sauce. (This is *the* most delicious pudding. Be sure to follow instructions carefully in order to have the crunchy crust, which gives a flavor similar to candied coconut.—M. B.)

Mrs. George Osborn, Murfreesboro, Tenn.

TYLER PUDDING
Four pies

"This recipe is called Tyler Pudding, although it sounds more like a pie. It was President Tyler's favorite dessert and was given to me by his granddaughter in Richmond, Virginia. Since he had had two wives, and seven children by each, the receipt makes a lot of dessert."

½ cup butter (melted)
5 cups granulated sugar
6 large eggs, well beaten

1 cup thick cream
1 fresh coconut, grated
4 unbaked pastry shells

Cream butter and sugar. Add eggs, well beaten; then add the cream and last the coconut. Pour into pie pans lined with uncooked pastry. Bake at 350 degrees for 30 minutes.

Mrs. Daniel A. Davis, from Recipes from Southern Kitchens, *Augusta, Ga.*

PERSIMMON PUDDING
Serves ten to twelve

3 tablespoons butter
2 cups raw persimmon pulp
3 eggs, beaten
1½ cups milk
2 cups flour
½ teaspoon soda

1 teaspoon each of ground cinnamon and nutmeg
½ teaspoon salt
1¾ cups sugar
¾ cup grated coconut (optional)

Melt the butter in a shallow square or oblong baking dish or biscuit pan. In a mixing bowl, blend the pulp with the beaten eggs. Alternately add the milk with the dry ingredients (mix dry ingredients together) to the persimmon-egg mixture. Add the coconut if desired. Pour into the pan in which the butter has been melted. Bake at 300 degrees for 1 hour. Cut into squares and serve either warm or cold. Top with sweetened and flavored whipped cream.

NOTE: The pudding should be poured in the pan from about 1 to 2 inches in depth, according to the desired thickness.

Mrs. Don E. Scott, Jr., Burlington, N.C.

ORANGE BREAD PUDDING
Serves about six

This was the "State Winner" of the Florida Citrus Recipe Contest.

1½ cups dry bread (break into small pieces)
2 cups milk
3 eggs (2 may be used)
½ cup sugar
1 cup orange juice

Grated orange rind
2 tablespoons melted butter or other shortening
Pinch salt
1 cup pitted chopped dates, if desired

Soak bread in milk for 15 minutes. Beat eggs until creamy and add sugar gradually. Add orange juice, grated rind, melted butter, and salt. Stir into the scalded bread mixture and pour into buttered baking dish. To make a richer pudding add 1 cup of pitted chopped dates. Bake in moderate oven (350 degrees) for 40 to 45 minutes. Serve hot with orange sauce.

Orange Sauce

¾ cup sugar
1 tablespoon cornstarch
Pinch salt
1 cup boiling water

1 tablespoon butter
½ teaspoon grated orange rind
½ cup strained orange juice

Combine sugar, cornstarch, salt, and mix thoroughly. Add boiling water and let boil slowly for 5 minutes, stirring constantly. Add butter, orange juice, and rind.

Mrs. E. P. St. John, Floral City, Fla. (A Florida Citrus Recipe Contest Winner)

QUEEN OF PUDDINGS
Serves six to eight

Queen of Puddings is a Southern dessert, made today in the same manner as it was many decades ago. This is a Charleston recipe from an old cook book in my collection.

1 qt. sweet milk
2 cups bread crumbs
4 egg yolks, beaten
1½ cups sugar
Butter the size of a walnut (1 heaping tablespoon), melted

Juice and grated rind of 1 lemon
Jelly or preserves
4 egg whites, stiffly beaten
4 tablespoons sugar

Pour the milk over bread crumbs; add the beaten egg yolks, sugar, and melted butter. Flavor with part of lemon juice and grated rind. Pour into greased baking dish and bake until done, but not watery—about 40 to 45 minutes or until a knife inserted in center comes out clean (in moderate, 350-degree oven). Should be like a thick custard. Cool slightly; spread over the top a layer of jelly or preserves. Beat the egg whites stiffly; add the 4 tablespoonfuls sugar and remaining half of lemon juice. Spread egg whites over pudding; set into the oven to brown slightly.

From recipe by Mrs. L. P. W. Laurens, Charleston, S.C.

CATHEDRAL PUDDING
Serves six to eight

This is a famous chocolate pudding from the National Cathedral School For Girls (Mt. St. Albans, Washington, D.C.), given me by an alumna.

½ 1-oz. cake chocolate
1 tablespoon butter
1 cup sugar
2 eggs

1 cup milk
1½ cups flour
1½ teaspoons baking powder
1 teaspoon vanilla

Melt chocolate and butter; mix in sugar and eggs. Add milk, flour sifted with the baking powder, and last, the vanilla. Steam (in desired mold or container) for 2 hours. Serve with the following sauce.

Sauce

4 egg yolks
3 cups powdered sugar

4 egg whites, stiffly beaten
1 teaspoon vanilla

Beat eggs separately. Beat the yolks and sugar together 10 minutes; then add whites and beat 5 minutes longer. Add vanilla. This makes a fluffy foamy sauce.

Mrs. W. M. Brown, Jr., Burlington, N.C.

MRS. ORGILL'S CHOCOLATE PUDDING
Serves eight

2 tablespoons gelatin	2 teaspoons vanilla
2 tablespoons cold water	Pinch salt
3 1-oz. squares chocolate	3 tablespoons hot water
1 cup sugar	6 egg whites, stiffly beaten
6 egg yolks, well beaten	Whipped cream

Soak gelatin in cold water. Melt chocolate; add to sugar and well-beaten egg yolks, vanilla, and salt. Add gelatin water to hot water. Dissolve thoroughly, and add to mixture. Fold in stiffly beaten egg whites. Pour into mold and chill. Serve with whipped cream.

Mrs. Joseph Orgill, Jr., Memphis, Tenn.

LOUISE'S MARMALADE SOUFFLE
Serves eight

6 egg whites	4½ tablespoons stiff marmalade
6 tablespoons confectioners sugar	

Beat egg whites stiff. Fold in sugar and marmalade. Place in top of large double boiler which has been very thoroughly greased. Put a piece of greased paper on top and place lid of boiler on tightly. Steam for 1¼ hours. Turn out on serving dish and bring to table immediately. Serve with foamy sauce.

Foamy Sauce

Stir 1 egg yolk in confectioners sugar to make a stiff paste. Thin out with ½ pint whipped cream. Flavor slightly with vanilla. This is a good light dessert to follow a heavy meal.

Contributed by Mrs. Elliott J. Neal, Charlotte, N.C.

MINT SOUFFLE FOR LAMB
Serves eight

This "epicure's delight" is not a dessert, but is a "sweet *entremet*" originated (in Asheville, North Carolina) as a side-dish with lamb, veal, or other meats. It is pretty and adds a cooling note although it is served *hot*.

1 No. 2 can grated pineapple
1 glass (jelly glass) mint jelly
3 beaten egg whites in soufflé
3 scant tablespoons flour

2 beaten egg whites as topping
2 to 3 drops green vegetable coloring

Mix the grated pineapple with mint jelly. Beat the 3 egg whites stiff and dry. Sprinkle in flour and fold mint jelly-pineapple mixture into egg whites. Pour into a greased casserole. Place casserole in a pan of hot water and bake in 350-degree oven for 30 minutes. Just before taking from oven, spread over the top the 2 egg whites beaten stiffly which have been tinted with green coloring. Allow to remain in oven several minutes to brown lightly. Serve hot and immediately. (This will not fall if properly made and served at once.)

Mrs. Katherine Rhea, Rock Hill, S.C.

FRUIT RICE PUDDING WITH LEMON SAUCE
Serves six

1 egg, beaten
½ cup sugar, or according to taste
2 cups cooked rice, dry and flaky
2 cups top milk
½ lb. chopped dates

½ cup chopped figs
½ cup chopped pecan meats
¼ teaspoon ground ginger
¼ teaspoon nutmeg
½ teaspoon vanilla
2 tablespoons butter, melted

Beat egg; add sugar and fold in rice. Add sweet milk, fruits, nuts, and spices; add vanilla; last pour in the melted butter. Pour all into a greased baking dish and bake in moderate (350-degree) oven until custard is set and slightly browned on top, about 30 minutes. Serve with lemon sauce (see p. 454). [Other fruits may be substituted. This is delicious with chocolate or vanilla sauce as well as lemon.—M. B.]

Mrs. John Thomas McBride, Norfolk, Va.

CALAS TOUT CHAUD
About two dozen

Calas Tout Chaud is a fluffy sweet fritter made of rice. Virginia M. Cooper gives a bit of history with her recipe for this delicacy. She says, "This recipe is one of the oldest in the City of New Orleans. The old Negro mammies of 1861 and after the War Between the States, sold on the streets of New Orleans *Calas Tout Chaud* piping hot from their iron sauce pans filled with hot lard. Or they enclosed them in brown paper and filled market baskets that they carried on their heads. The method is written as it was nearly a century ago":

2 egg yolks
1 cup sugar
1 cup boiled rice
2 cups flour

2 teaspoons baking powder
2 egg whites, stiffly beaten
Powdered or granulated sugar

"Mix the yolks of the eggs with the sugar, rice, flour, and baking powder. When they are thoroughly assembled, add the whites of the eggs, well beaten, and give it all a final stirring.

"Have some deep grease at hand, sizzling in your frying pan, and drop the mixture from a spoon into the grease. They emerge golden brown, light and luscious. Drain them on butcher's paper; sprinkle them with powdered or granulated sugar; serve hot."

From The Creole Kitchen Cook Book, *by Virginia M. Cooper, New Orleans, La.*

COLD HEAVENLY RICE PUDDING WITH CARDINAL SAUCE
Serves six

2 cups white rice, cooked and chilled
1½ cups miniature marshmallows
2 cups fresh or canned pineapple chunks, drained

1 cup heavy cream, whipped
¼ cup confectioners sugar
¼ teaspoon almond extract
1 teaspoon vanilla

Mix the rice, marshmallows, and pineapple in a bowl; refrigerate 12 hours. Make the sauce.

Cardinal sauce

1 10-oz. pkg. frozen raspberries, thawed; drained (reserve juice)

Water
1 tablespoon cornstarch
¼ cup currant jelly

In a small saucepan, combine the juice which has been drained from the raspberries, adding enough water to make 1 cup, with the cornstarch. Boil for 1 minute; add the thawed berries and jelly; stir well. Remove from heat and refrigerate 1 hour.

Just before serving the pudding, add the whipped cream, sugar, and extracts to the rice mixture; fold and blend lightly. Serve in dessert dishes; pour the sauce over the pudding.

Mrs. Martha S. Bailey, New York, N.Y.

BOILED BERRY DUMPLINGS
Serves six

1 qt. blackberries, or dew berries
1 pt. water
1 cup sugar
1 teaspoon butter
1 tablespoon flavoring, vanilla, lemon, etc. Sherry gives this a good flavor; use 2 tablespoons just before serving

1¼ cups flour
1½ teaspoons baking powder
1 teaspoon sugar
½ teaspoon salt
1 egg beaten
Sweet milk
1½ teaspoons melted butter

Boil the berries, water, sugar, and butter until berries are tender. Add flavoring. Make dumplings by sifting together other dry ingredients, stirring in egg, and adding just enough milk to make a stiff batter. Stir in melted butter. Drop by teaspoons in the boiling berries and boil for about 5 minutes, or until dumplings are puffy and light. Serve dumplings with the berries and pour syrup over. They may be served with whipped cream or any sauce added.

Mrs. Frank Dandridge, Leesburg, Fla.

MRS. NEAL'S DATE WHIP SOUFFLE
Serves six

Delightful for individual servings.

1 cup dates, cut up
½ cup water
½ cup sugar

½ cup chopped nut meats
½ teaspoon lemon juice
3 egg whites, stiffly beaten

Cook the dates, water, and sugar together slightly. Cool. Stir into the mixture the nut meats and lemon juice. Beat egg whites stiffly and gently fold into the date-nut mixture. Fill 6 small, well-buttered custard or baking cups with mixture. Place cups in a pan of water and bake in slow (325-degree) oven 30 minutes, or until toothpick comes out clean. Should brown slightly on top. Serve with whipped cream.

Mrs. Elliott J. Neal, Charlotte, N.C.

ANTOINE'S FRENCH PANCAKES A LA GELEE
Twelve to fifteen cakes

From this pancake is also made the famous Crêpes Suzette. The consistency is smooth and velvety and the batter pours like cream.

½ cup sifted all-purpose flour
1 egg
1 egg yolk
⅛ teaspoon salt

5 tablespoons milk (about)
3 tablespoons currant or red raspberry jelly
Powdered sugar

Combine flour, egg, egg yolk, salt, and milk. Beat with rotary beater until smooth. If necessary, add more milk to make batter the consistency of light cream. Cover; chill ½ hour in refrigerator. Heat heavy iron skillet; wipe out with waxed paper which has been dipped in butter. Pour in enough batter to barely cover bottom of skillet, tipping while adding batter. Brown pancakes on both sides. Remove from skillet; spread with jelly; roll up jelly-roll fashion. Sprinkle with a little powdered sugar. Place under a broiler to glaze. Serve immediately.

From Antoine's Restaurant, New Orleans, La.
Special permission, Roy Alciatore, Proprietor

DESSERT CREPES
Eighteen to twenty

1 cup sifted all-purpose flour
½ teaspoon salt
1 tablespoon sugar
3 large eggs
1 cup milk

1 cup light cream
2 tablespoons cognac
2 tablespoons butter, melted, extra butter
Confectioners sugar

Sift the flour, salt, and sugar together into a mixing bowl. Beat the eggs and to them add the milk, cream, and cognac. Stir in the melted butter. Let the batter stand at room temperature for about 2 hours. The batter should be thin.

Heat a crêpe pan (or a 6-inch skillet) until hot but not smoking. Brush the bottom lightly with butter, using a pastry brush or wad of absorbent paper towel. For 1 crêpe pour in 2 tablespoons of the batter. Quickly tilt and rotate the pan to spread the batter to edges of pan. Cook over direct moderate heat until the underside is brown and little bubbles have formed on the top—about 1½ minutes. Turn with a spatula and cook the other side about 1 minute or until browned. Repeat until all batter has been used.

As crêpes are cooked, sprinkle the top of each with confectioners sugar, and stack them on a platter which has been covered with a tea towel. When all are done, fold the towel over them. To reheat, place the platter of wrapped crêpes in a 350-degree oven and heat for a few minutes.

NOTE: These may be served as Crêpes Suzette, or rolled and filled with jelly, jam, marmalade; a combination of creamed cheese and jelly; flavored whipped cream, etc.

ELLA'S DOBOSH TORTE (*Frozen*)
Serves thirty-five to forty

This is an original interpretation of the famous Swiss Dobosh Torte. Freeze it for best results. It is not troublesome to make after the first time!

1. Make the whipped butter filling first. Do not make it if kitchen is hot!

Whipped Butter Filling

2 cups milk, scalded
½ cup flour
¾ cup sugar

½ lb. butter
Angel-flaked coconut and finely ground almonds (optional)

Scald the milk in top of double boiler. Mix the flour and sugar together; slowly add to the milk. Continue to cook, stirring, until mixture is thick. This should be cooked until it loses its floury taste. Cool, *very cool*. The mixture should be very stiff and cold to touch. Pour into deep bowl of electric mixer; add the cold butter and beat very hard for 20 minutes to make a fluffy filling. Place in refrigerator until time to fill the cake. Reserve the coconut and almonds.

2. Make the fudge frosting:

Fudge Frosting

2 tablespoons vegetable shortening
2 tablespoons margarine
1 tablespoon light corn syrup
2 1-oz. squares chocolate

7 tablespoons milk
1½ cups sugar
⅛ teaspoon salt
1 teaspoon vanilla

In a heavy saucepan, combine all ingredients except vanilla. Place on direct low heat and cook until mixture comes to a rapid boil. Boil one minute *only*. Cool before adding vanilla. Cool to lukewarm; beat until the consistency is stiff enough for spreading.

3. Make the torte:

Torte

2 11″ × 15″ cookie sheets with sides; greased, and lightly dusted with flour
2 cups sifted cake flour
1 teaspoon soda

¾ teaspoon salt
1¾ cups sugar
¾ cup boiling water
4 1-oz. squares chocolate
½ cup buttermilk (sour milk)

⅓ cup Crisco (vegetable shortening)

2 eggs, unbeaten
2 teaspoons vanilla

Preheat oven to 325 degrees.

Prepare the pans. Sift together the flour, soda, salt, and sugar into a large
mixing bowl. Combine the chocolate and boiling water in top of a double boiler.
Cook slowly over hot water until chocolate is melted and mixture is thick; stir
constantly. Remove from the heat and add the milk; cool. Cream the shortening
in a mixing bowl; add the dry ingredients, chocolate mixture, eggs, and vanilla.
Stir until blended. Beat vigorously (by hand) for 2 minutes. Pour batter into the
2 cookie sheets. Bake on the middle shelf of the oven for about 10 minutes.
Watch this; do not bake too long. Allow cakes to cool in pans. Divide each
cookie sheet into 3 5″ × 11″ layers (making 6 layers in all).

Remove whipped butter filling from refrigerator; quickly spread the filling
between the layers, sprinkling each with coconut and almonds if desired. ("If
you don't give a hoot about calories"). Beat the lukewarm fudge frosting. Spread
gently over the top and sides. Quickly freeze the torte. Wrap in airtight plastic
paper after it is frozen. Cut with serrated knife while cake is frozen. Slice very
thin to serve. This should make 35 to 40 servings. Slice as needed and return the
cake to the freezer.

Mrs. George R. Kerr, Burlington, N.C.

CUSTARD ANGEL CAKE
Serves eight to ten

Cut an Angel Food cake (homemade cake) in half, horizontally. Place
between the two portions the following custard:

3 cups scalded milk, hot
9 well-beaten egg yolks, mixed
with ⅔ cup sifted flour
1⅛ cups sugar

¼ teaspoon salt
Grated (yellow) rind of 2 oranges (large)
1 pt. heavy cream, whipped

Pour hot, scalded milk over the egg yolks which have been beaten and
mixed with the flour, sugar, and salt. Return to double boiler and let cook until
there is no taste of the flour. When cool add the orange rind.

I fit an orange juice glass into the hole in the bottom layer of the cake, then
add the thick custard, then the top layer. The glass holds the top layer off the
custard and prevents its spilling.

After custard has been poured, whip 1 pt. of cream and spread thickly over
top and sides of cake.

Mrs. J. Crawford Biggs, Hardimont, Raleigh, N.C.

FLOATING ISLAND
Serves six to eight

One of the earliest desserts, this dish seems to have originated in England. It is made in several ways; one method is to arrange cake (broken) in a glass bowl, pour over a custard, top with a layer of currant or other tart jelly, and float spoonfuls of meringue which have been steamed in the boiled custard. Still another is to bake a custard with "Islands" of meringue on top. This recipe is a cold dessert.

Almond macaroons, about 1 doz.
3 egg whites, stiffly beaten with 3 teaspoons sugar, 2 drops almond extract
1 qt. sweet milk
1 teaspoon flour

½ cup sugar
Pinch salt
4 egg yolks, beaten
½ teaspoon vanilla
½ teaspoon almond extract
Red jelly, such as currant, etc.

In a large glass bowl, break up the macaroons and press up around the sides of bowl. Prepare egg whites. Heat milk; when it reaches boiling point drop onto it by tablespoonfuls the whipped, sweetened, flavored egg whites. Let simmer 4 minutes. Lift them out and set aside to cool. Mix flour, sugar, and salt, and blend with beaten egg yolks. Pour hot milk slowly into egg yolk mixture and cook in top of double boiler until it thickens. Remove; chill; and add flavoring. Pour into bowl with macaroons. Drop cooked meringue islands on top of custard, and drop dabs of the jelly between the islands. This may be served in individual compotes.

Mrs. Mary S. Peters Cucullu, Lynchburg, Va.

SABAYON DE NARANJA (*Spanish Orange Cream*)
Serves six

4 egg yolks
1 cup orange juice
½ cup sugar
1 whole egg

1 cup whole milk
Juice of 1 lemon
½ teaspoon grated lemon rind

Beat the egg yolks until foamy; add the orange juice; stir in the sugar. Beat the whole egg with the milk. Combine the two mixtures. Add the lemon juice and rind. Place mixture in the top of a double boiler over boiling water and beat it constantly while it cooks. When it has turned into a thick, frothy cream, remove from heat. Serve warm or cold over dessert soufflés or puddings, or in sherbet or parfait glasses for a light dessert.

Mrs. Joseph E. DuBois, Metaire, La.

CHARLOTTE RUSSE
Serves eighteen to twenty

This classic dessert is made by Mrs. Gant as a demand dish for the Burlington Episcopal Church Bazaar, and on many other occasions. It differs from many recipes because it has only the sherry for flavor, and beaten egg whites give it extra lightness.

3 envelopes plain gelatin
3 tablespoons cold water, plus little extra water
1 quart whipping cream, whipped stiff
1 cup sugar
Sherry to taste (use enough to give a good sherry flavor)

5 egg whites, beaten stiffly
Ladyfingers, split
Extra whipped cream, fresh or candied fruits and nuts for garnish
Toasted slivered almonds if desired

Pour the gelatin into a measuring cup; add 3 tablespoons cold water. Allow the gelatin to soften for about 5 minutes. Add a little extra water. Place the container over hot water until gelatin dissolves. In a large mixing bowl beat the cream; stir in the sugar, cooled gelatin, and sherry. Fold in the beaten egg whites.

Line Charlotte Russe pans, molds, or individual dessert glasses with split ladyfingers, turning the crust side to the sides of the containers. Fill molds with the Charlotte Russe. Chill until firm. Turn out on platters and garnish, or serve from containers and garnish each serving. The Russe may be served plain with toasted almonds sprinkled over. Any left-over Russe may be frozen; half thaw to serve. This recipe may be halved.

Mrs. Roger Gant, Burlington, N.C.

SOUR CREAM BRULEE
Serves four to six

1 1-qt. shallow baking dish
2 cups sour cream

1 teaspoon vanilla extract
Light brown sugar

Rinse baking dish in cold water; drain. Mix sour cream with vanilla. Place in refrigerator until cream is cold. Sprinkle top of cream with a heavy coating (about ¼-inch thick) of brown sugar. Set broiler at 450 degrees. Slide cream under broiler unit, about 4 inches from heat. Broil until sugar forms smooth surface. Do not let it scorch. Chill thoroughly. The sugar glaze should crackle; if not, break it with a fork handle. Serve cold.

Mrs. Harris Rankin, Paducah, Ky.

CHOCOLATE SOUFFLE
Serves six

1 1-oz. square unsweetened choco-
    late, grated
2 heaping tablespoons cocoa
1 tablespoon flour
1 cup sugar
4 egg yolks, well beaten

1½ cups milk
2 tablespoons butter
1 tablespoon vanilla (right)
4 egg whites, beaten stiff
Whipped cream, sweetened to
    taste

Combine chocolate, cocoa, flour, and sugar. In a large bowl, beat the egg yolks. Blend the chocolate mixture into the egg yolks. Mix in the milk and butter. Pour into top of large double boiler; cook over boiling water until custard is thick, stirring constantly. Add vanilla; remove from heat and beat as mixture cools.

When mixture is entirely cool, fold in the egg whites. Pour into a greased 1½- to 2-quart soufflé dish or casserole and set in a larger pan of warm water. Bake at 325 degrees for one hour, or until a knife inserted in the center comes out clean. Serve at once with whipped cream, or plain cream.

NOTE: Soufflés may stand about 30 minutes without falling, if they are not removed from the oven. Turn the heat down as far as it will go and open the door for a few minutes to reduce the temperature, but keep the soufflé warm. It may dry out a little, but will not fall.

Mrs. John G. Pew, The Junior League of Dallas Cook Book, *Dallas, Tex.*

POT DE CREME AU CHOCOLAT
Serves four to six

½ lb. sweet milk chocolate
2 cups milk, scalded
3 egg yolks, well beaten
1 teaspoon vanilla extract or
    sherry to taste

Whipped cream, sweetened and
flavored

Shave the chocolate. Scald the milk in the top of a double boiler over boiling water (do not let milk boil). Stir the chocolate shavings into the milk; bring to a boil. Cook the mixture until smooth, stirring constantly. Stir a small amount of hot chocolate mixture into the beaten egg yolks. Slowly add remaining hot mixture, stirring constantly. Return mixture to double boiler and stir until custard is thickened. If the custard becomes lumpy, beat it with a rotary egg beater. Add vanilla or sherry.

Pour the crème into little "crème pots" or custard cups. Chill; serve in the pots. Garnish top of pot with whipped cream, sweetened to taste and flavored with vanilla or sherry.

Mrs. Mary S. Peters Cucullu, Lynchburg, Va.

APPLE FRITTERS (*with Rum Sauce*)
Serves six to eight

4 firm ripe apples, pared, cored, sliced
Cognac
1 egg yolk, beaten
1½ tablespoons sugar
½ cup milk

1 cup flour
¼ teaspoon salt
⅛ teaspoon ground cinnamon
1½ teaspoons baking powder
1 egg white, beaten stiff

Pare and core the apples; cut them crosswise in circles, about ¼-inch thick. Place in a deep bowl and pour cognac over to make a marinade. Cover the apples and let set for several hours, turning them often.

Combine the egg yolk with the sugar and milk; add the dry ingredients; fold in the beaten egg white. Drain the apple slices, and dip in the batter. Fry in deep fat (360 to 370 degrees) for 3 to 4 minutes, or until golden brown. Serve with rum sauce, or sprinkle them with confectioners sugar.

Rum Sauce

2 eggs, beaten until thick
1 cup confectioners sugar

1 cup heavy cream, beaten stiff
1½ tablespoons rum

Beat the eggs; add the sugar, and beat again. Whip the cream and beat in the rum. Combine both mixtures, and beat again thoroughly. Serve over the hot or warm fritters.

Mrs. Dana T. Moore, Omar, West Va.

WARD-BELMONT BANANA FRITTERS

A famous fritter, from Ward-Belmont, Nashville, Tennessee.

1⅓ cups flour
¼ teaspoon salt
2 teaspoons baking powder
1 egg

⅔ cup milk
Bananas
Powdered or granulated sugar

Sift flour together with salt and baking powder. Beat the egg; add milk and stir in dry ingredients. Add the bananas, cut up into desired pieces (as much banana as batter will thoroughly coat). Drop by spoonfuls into deep hot fat. Fry a delicate brown. Serve with either powdered or granulated sugar sprinkled over. Serve with a vanilla sauce (see p. 453).

Contributed by Mrs. Harris W. Rankin, Paducah, Ky.

NUN'S SIGH
About two dozen

This is an old Creole recipe for a soufflé fritter—light as a "nun's sigh."

"Mix ½ cup of milk and water and put into a saucepan. Add 1 tablespoon of butter, 2 tablespoons of sugar, and, as it boils, stir in ¾ cup of flour, into a smooth paste.

"Remove from fire and when cold, add the grated rind of 1 lemon, the beaten yolks of 3 eggs, then the beaten whites, and a pinch of soda. Have a pan half full of boiling lard, and drop batter in from a teaspoon. When brown on one side, turn and brown the other side. Remove with skimmer, drain, and serve at once, with powdered sugar."

From New Orleans Recipes, by Mary Moore Bremer, New Orleans, La.

SOFT GINGERBREAD
Serves six to eight

¾ cup butter
1 cup sugar
1 teaspoon soda
¾ cup sour milk
1¾ cups light molasses (not syrup)

3 cups sifted flour
1 tablespoon allspice
1 tablespoon powdered ginger
3 eggs, well beaten

Cream butter and sugar until light and fluffy. Divide the soda, putting half into the sour milk and the other half into the molasses. Add the flour to butter mixture, then the spices and molasses. Fold the beaten eggs into batter. Pour into a deep, greased baking dish or deep biscuit pans. Bake in a 350-degree oven for 25 to 35 minutes. When done, the texture should be foamy. Serve warm with Hard Brandy Sauce (p. 455).

Mrs. Angus Craft, St. Petersburg, Fla.

BAKED CURRIED FRUIT
Serves six

1 No. 303 can cling peach halves (6 halves)

1 No. 2 can sliced pineapple (6 rings)

1 No. 303 can pear halves (6 halves)
5 maraschino cherries with stems
⅓ cup butter

¾ cup light brown sugar
4 teaspoons curry powder

The day before baking the fruit, drain the fruit and dry it well on absorbent paper towels. Arrange in layers in a casserole. Melt the butter in a saucepan, and add to it the sugar and curry powder. Stir until sugar dissolves. Spoon the syrup over the fruit. Bake uncovered in a preheated 325-degree oven for 1 hour. Baste the fruit well with the syrup as fruit bakes. Cool and refrigerate. 1 hour before serving, reheat the fruit in a 350-degree oven for 30 minutes. Serve warm.

Mrs. George L. Carrington, Burlington, N.C.

FRUIT MACEDOINE
Serves six to eight

Any fresh fruits in season may be used in this dessert. The following combination is suggested:

1 cup each of:

Fresh pineapple, cut into chunks
Fresh strawberries or raspberries
Melon balls
Banana, cut into slices or chunks
Ripe mango, cut into slices
1 orange, peeled and cut into sections

½ cup sugar
2 jiggers (1-oz. jigger) cognac
3 ozs. Madeira or Cream Sherry
Vanilla ice cream, or lemon or orange sherbet

In a deep bowl, combine the fruits, sugar, cognac, and wine. Chill thoroughly. Serve in sherbet glasses with a scoop of ice cream or sherbet on top of each serving. Serve ladyfingers with the fruit.

Mrs. James H. Viser, Hobcaw, Mt. Pleasant, S.C.

TO MAKE A TRIFLE

This old recipe is from *Court and Country Confectioner*, London, 1770. It was used in the Tucker House, Williamsburg, and proved by Market Square Tavern Kitchen in 1937.

"Cover the bottom of your dish with **Naples Biscuits** [ladyfingers] broken in pieces, **Mackaroons**, and **Ratafia Cakes**, just wet them all with **Sack** [sherry], pour on a **good boiled custard** when cold, then a **whipt Syllabub** over that."

From The Williamsburg Art of Cookery, *by Helen Bullock*

A TRIFLE
Serves five to six

This is an old English recipe which came to Mrs. Patterson from her ancestors. We are fortunate to have the first publication of the recipe.

½ cup chopped pecan meats
½ cup seedless raisins
½ cup blackberry or sherry wine
1 cup of egg whites, stiffly beaten
Pinch of salt

1½ cups sugar
1 teaspoon vanilla
Whipped cream
Sugar

Mix the pecans and raisins together in a small deep bowl. Pour the wine over and let soak overnight. When ready to make the trifle, whip the egg whites and salt very stiff and dry; gradually add the sugar, whipping all the time (use a whisk, if possible, to beat eggs). Add the vanilla. Drain the nuts and raisins well; reserve the wine. Fold the nuts and raisins gently into the egg whites. Pour mixture into a spring-form (torte) pan, spreading it part way up around the sides of the pan. Bake in a preheated 250-degree oven for about one hour. Turn off the oven heat and allow the meringue to cool in the oven. Spread the top of meringue with a thick layer of whipped cream, sweetened to taste with sugar and flavored with the wine which was drained from the nuts and raisins. Cut into pie wedges and serve very cold.

Mrs. Fred M. Patterson, Greensboro, N.C.

CREME DE MENTHE DESSERT
Serves four

This is a refreshing dessert to serve with a game or poultry dinner.

1 pkg. lemon or lime jello (standard-size pkg.)
1 cup boiling water
⅓ cup green crème de menthe
½ cup ice water

½ cup heavy cream, whipped
Sweetened whipped cream to garnish
Green or red maraschino cherries to garnish

In a saucepan, add the jello to the 1 cup of boiling water. Add the crème de menthe and ice water. Allow the jello to cool and chill until it begins to stiffen. Whip in the ½ cup whipped cream. Pour the mixture into 4 large sherbet glasses. Chill until firm. Garnish with whipped cream and a cherry.

Mrs. Allan Umstead, Goldsboro, N.C.

COGNAC-COFFEE DESSERT
Serves six to eight

2 envelopes plain gelatin
¼ cup cognac
3½ cups strong coffee (brewed coffee), boiling hot
⅓ cup plus 1 tablespoon sugar

1 stick cinnamon
Whipped cream, sweetened and flavored with cognac to taste
Candied fruit

Soak the gelatin in cognac until soft. Stir gelatin mixture into hot coffee; stir until melted. Add the sugar and stick of cinnamon. Allow mixture to cool. Remove the cinnamon; pour the mixture into a 1½-quart mold or individual molds. Chill until set. Serve with whipped cream. Garnish with candied fruits.

Mrs. William G. Vetterlein, Tucson, Ariz.

WINE GELATIN DESSERT
Serves six to eight

2 tablespoons plain gelatin
½ cup cold water
1¼ cups boiling water
⅔ cup sugar
⅓ cup lemon juice

¾ cup sherry, or any wine desired
Whipped cream, or vanilla custard for garnish

Soften the gelatin in the cold water. Heat the 1¼ cups water to boiling. Add softened gelatin to boiling water; dissolve gelatin. Add the sugar and stir until it is dissolved. Cool gelatin mixture; add the lemon juice and wine. Pour into a 1-quart mold or into individual molds. Chill until set. Serve with topping of whipped cream or vanilla custard (see "Sauces," p. 453).

PEACHES EN LIQUEUR
Serves eight

4 large fresh peaches (½ peach for each serving)
Brown sugar

Brandy or any liqueur
Butter
Sour cream

Peel and cut the peaches in halves. Pack the hollow of each peach with brown sugar. Pour over the sugar enough liqueur to well saturate the sugar. Place a pat of butter on each peach. Place peaches on a broiler pan and broil 3 or 4 inches below the broiler flame. Broil for around 10 minutes. Serve hot. Top each peach with a blob of sour cream. Serve as a dessert or with poultry or meats.

Mrs. Catherine Rhea, Rock Hill, S.C.

13. Cakes and Icings

There are many cakes long associated with the Southern way of living, some inherited from the Old World, others indigenous or adopted and nurtured as our own. Among them are the classics: the Pound Cake, Fruit Cake, Sponge Cake, Butter Cake; Sweet Breads such as Gingerbread, Coffee Cake, and others. From these have developed the bountiful crop of lesser fruit cakes, nut cakes, layer cakes, cup cakes, and so on. Then there are the "Famous Name" cakes: General Robert E. Lee's Cake, the Lane Cake, the Scripture Cake, the Jeff Davis Cake, the George Washington Cake, the Dolly Madison, Dolly Varden, and Jenny Lind cakes, the One-Two-Three-Four Cake, Coconut-Mountain Cake, Silver and Gold Cake, Marble Cake, Watermelon Cake, Twelfth-Night Cake, James K. Polk Cake, and many others.

The "Famous Name" cake, by its longevity, has become public property and appears in most Southern cook books. I am therefore not reprinting some of them, so that there may be space for more of the recipes which by "a pinch of salt," "a lump of butter the size of a walnut," or "a drop of essence," the Southern hostess has made her own.

TWELFTH NIGHT, OR KING'S CAKE (*Gateau du Roi*)

"This is a Creole cake whose history is the history of the famous New Orleans Carnivals celebrated in song and stories. The 'King's Cake,' or 'Gateau du Roi,' is inseparably connected with the origin of our now world-famous Mardi Gras. In fact, it owes its origin to the old Creole custom of choosing a king and queen on Kings' Day, or Twelfth Night. In old Creole New Orleans, after the inauguration of the Spanish domination and the amalgamation of the French settlers and the Spanish into that peculiarly chivalrous and romantic race, the Louisiana Creole, the French prettily adopted many of the customs of their Spanish relatives, and vice versa. Among these was the traditional Spanish celebration of Kings' Day, '*Le jour des Rois*,' as the Creoles always term the day. Kings' Day falls on January 6, or the twelfth day after Christmas, and commemorates the visit of Three Wise Men of the East to the lowly Bethlehem manger. This day is, even in our time, still the Spanish Christmas, when gifts are presented in commemoration of the Kings' gifts. With the Creoles it became 'Le Petit Noel,' or 'Little Christmas,' and, adopting the Spanish custom, there were always grand balls on Twelfth Night; a king and a queen were chosen, and there were constant rounds of festivities, night after night, till the dawn of Ash Wednesday. From January 6, or Kings' Day, to Mardi Gras Day became the accepted Carnival season. Each week a new king and queen were chosen and no royal rulers ever reigned more happily than did these kings and queens for a week."

This is the celebrated cake served on Twelfth Night. It is a basic cake-bread for which New Orleans is famous.

8 cups sifted flour	1 cup sugar
½ oz. yeast dissolved in	2 cups butter, or shortening
¼ cup lukewarm water	½ oz. salt (2 teaspoons)
Milk or tepid water	Candies to decorate
12 eggs	

Take 6 cups of the sifted flour; put into a wooden bread trough (bowl). Make a hole in the center of the flour, and put in the yeast dissolved in warm water. Add milk or tepid water to make the dough, using milk if you want it to be very rich and delicate. Knead and mix the flour with one hand, while adding the milk or water with the other to make a spongy dough that is neither too stiff nor too soft, and when perfectly smooth set the dough to rise in a moderately warm place, covering with a cloth. (Remember that if you use milk, it must be scalded, that is, it must be heated to the boiling point and then allowed to grow tepid.) Let the dough rise 5 or 6 hours, and, when increased to twice its bulk, take it and add the reserved 2 cups of flour into which you will have sifted the salt. Add 6 of the eggs, beaten very light with the sugar and butter (or shortening), and mix all well with the hands, and adding more eggs if the dough is a little stiff. Then knead the dough by turning it over on itself 3 times and set to rise again for from three-fourths to 1 hour. Cover with a cloth. At the end of this time take it up and work again lightly, and then form into a great ring, leaving a hole in the center. Pat gently and flatten a little. Have ready a baking pan with buttered sheet of paper in it and set the central roll in the middle. Cover the pan with a clean, stiff cloth, and set the cake to rise for an hour longer. When well risen, set in a 350-degree oven; let bake for 1 hour and a half; if medium-sized cake, 1 hour, and if very small, ½ hour. Glacé the Brioche (cake) lightly with a beaten egg, spread lightly over the top before placing in the oven; decorate with dragees, caramels, etc.

From The Original Picayune Creole Cook Book, *New Orleans, La.*

MRS. MERRILL'S LANE CAKE
Four Layers

Many Southern states claim the famous Lane Cake, which is similar to the "Rocky Mountain Cake." The difference is in the filling. The Lane Cake has a rich egg-yolk filling with coconut, raisins, and nuts, while the filling for the Rocky Mountain Cake is generally white.

It is said that this cake originated in Eufaula, Alabama. Our contributor, a resident of Eufaula, isn't certain. Her cook, who really is the cake-maker for the family, has been making the Lane Cake for years.

Batter

3½ cups flour
Pinch salt
2 teaspoons baking powder, more if larger amount of flour is used

1 cup butter
2 cups sugar
1 cup sweet milk
1 teaspoon vanilla
8 egg whites, stiffly beaten

Sift flour, salt, and baking powder together 4 or 5 times—the more the flour is sifted, the lighter the cake. Cream butter and sugar together until foamy—if sugar is sifted, the cake is better. Add to butter-sugar mixture the flour and milk alternately, using a little of each. Begin with flour and end using flour. Add vanilla and, last, fold in the stiffly beaten egg whites. Bake in 4 8-inch layer-cake pans, or 3 larger pans which have greased brown paper fitted in the bottom. After pans have been greased and floured, bake in 375-degree oven for 30 to 35 minutes, depending on thickness of the layers. Allow cake to set in pans for few minutes; turn out, and fill with the following.

Filling

8 egg yolks
1 cup sugar
Pinch salt
½ cup butter
1 cup raisins, seeded, chopped

1½ cups freshly grated coconut
1 cup chopped pecans or other nuts
1 cup brandy
1 teaspoon vanilla

Beat the egg yolks until lemon colored; add sugar, salt, and continue beating until mixture is light. Melt butter in top of double boiler and add egg-sugar mixture; stir constantly until it thickens. Remove from heat; stir in the raisins, coconut, nuts, brandy, and vanilla. Let cool; spread between layers; then ice the whole cake with a boiled vanilla icing. [Either of Mrs. Smith's white icings on p. 378, or the Angel Food Icing on p. 367, would be good on this cake.—M. B.]

Mrs. William H. Merrill, Eufaula, Ala.

ROBERT E. LEE CAKE

This is one of the most famous Southern historical cakes. No two authorities seem to agree on the egg content (ranging from 8 to 10 eggs). The icing varies with each recipe. Some variants use grated orange rind or lemon in icing; others use a pure lemon filling and white icing. This is a combination of three old Virginia recipes.

10 egg yolks, beaten
2 cups sugar
1 teaspoon lemon juice
1 teaspoon orange juice

Grated rind 1 lemon
10 egg whites, stiffly beaten
2 cups flour
½ teaspoon salt

Beat the egg yolks until lemon-colored; add the sugar, fruit juices, and rind. Fold in the stiffly beaten egg whites; last, add the flour sifted with salt, by sprinkling in the flour gently by the handfuls. Bake in round ungreased pans, making 3 medium layers or 4 thin layers. Ice with a boiled icing. (Or a lemon icing with coconut and orange and lemon rind to flavor. An Old Williamsburg recipe calls for an uncooked lemon and orange juice filling made by combining fruit juices with sugar and grated rinds. Grated coconut is added and sprinkled over cake.)

Boiled Icing

3 cups sugar
1 cup water
3 egg whites, stiffly beaten
1 tablespoon lemon juice

Grated rind 1 orange
Grated rind 1 lemon
1 cup grated coconut

Boil sugar and water until syrup spins a thread. Pour into whites of eggs, stirring constantly. Add lemon juice and grated orange and lemon rind to icing. Spread between layers and on top and sides of cake. Sprinkle the grated coconut all over top and sides of cake.

MRS. LAURENS' LADY BALTIMORE CAKE

Owen Wister once saw at the Charleston Woman's Exchange an exquisite cake which he is said to have named "Lady Baltimore." Since that day every cake of similar ingredients and form bearing this name is said to be from the original recipe, and hundreds of the cakes go out from Charleston each Christmas.

3 cups cake flour
3 teaspoons baking powder
⅛ teaspoon salt
⅔ cup butter

1¾ cups sugar
1 cup milk
1 teaspoon almond extract
5 egg whites

Sift flour; measure, and add baking powder and salt; sift 3 times. Cream butter; add sugar gradually; cream until light. Add flour alternately with milk in small amounts, beating after each addition. Add almond extract. Beat egg whites until they stand in moist peaks; fold in well. Bake in 3 deep greased and waxed-paper-bottom-lined 9-inch layer pans. Bake in 375-degree oven 20 to 30 minutes. Fill and ice as follows:

Filling and Icing

3 cups sugar
⅝ cup water
2 egg whites

¼ teaspoon cream of tartar
1 teaspoon vanilla
1 teaspoon almond extract

with

2 cups seeded raisins, cut up
2 cups English walnuts, cut up

1 cup sherry

Soak raisins and nuts in wine overnight. Squeeze out before adding to icing or filling. Boil sugar and water together until it forms a heavy thread; pour onto egg whites beaten stiff with the cream of tartar; add flavorings and beat until very thick. Add nuts and raisins and cover layers, top, and sides of cake.

Mrs. John Laurens, Charleston, S.C.

THE SALLY WHITE CAKE

The origin of this cake is not definitely known. One theory is that it was named for a beautiful Southern belle who graced an ante-bellum era. Another is that a Southern housewife by that name originated the cake. It seems to be more widely known along the coastal areas of the Carolinas and Virginia than in other sections. I have three or four variants in my files.

2 cups butter
2½ cups sugar
12 egg yolks, beaten

4 cups flour, sifted
2 teaspoons baking powder
1 tablespoon nutmeg

4 tablespoons sherry
4 tablespoons brandy
2 large, or 3 small coconuts, grated

2 lbs. citron, chopped fine
1 lb. blanched almonds, chopped
12 egg whites, well beaten

Cream butter and sugar; add beaten yolks of eggs. Blend with sifted flour, baking powder, and nutmeg. Add wine and brandy slowly. In large bowl, mix coconut, citron, and almonds. Blend thoroughly with batter mixture. Fold in well-beaten whites of eggs. Cook at 275 degrees for 3 hours. Makes 1 large, or 2 small cakes.

Dolores Holt Cheatham, from Soup to Nuts, *Burlington, N.C.*

JENNIE BENEDICT'S RUM CAKE

Miss Jennie Benedict was for years the leading caterer of Louisville, Kentucky. Among the choice recipes she left is this—one of Kentucky's most famous cakes.

1 cup butter
2 cups granulated sugar
1 cup milk, not too cold
3½ cups cake flour, sifted once before measuring

8 egg whites, beaten stiff, but not too dry
3½ teaspoons baking powder
1 teaspoon vanilla
Pinch salt

Cream the butter and sugar, a little at a time. Add ⅓ each of the milk, flour, and egg whites, in the order named, beating after each addition and beating well and long after the last addition. But mark this—keep out 2 tablespoons of flour, into which mix the baking powder and add this when all the beating is over, the pans greased and lined with paper, and the batter is ready to go into the stove. At the very last, add the vanilla and the salt. Bake in two 9-inch, greased and paper-lined cake pans for 20 to 30 minutes, at 350 degrees. Turn out on racks, and allow to cool before adding the filling.

Filling

Take 2½ cups of powdered sugar, ⅔ cup of soft, creamed butter; blend together, and beat until soft and smooth. (Sifting the sugar makes the blending lighter work.) Add ½ cup of rum. Mix well again. Put into the refrigerator until firm enough to spread. The filling should be ½ to ¾ inch thick. After filling is spread on the cake, put cake and filling into the refrigerator until set and the top frosting is ready to cover all.

Frosting

Boil together 2 cups granulated sugar with enough water to moisten the sugar well—until the syrup will spin a thread. Pour slowly in a fine stream over 2 well-beaten egg whites. While the mixture is hot, add 12 marshmallows, a few at a time, and 1 or 2 teaspoons of rum. Pile high on top of cake and spread over the sides.

Contributed by Cissy Gregg, Home Consultant, Courier-Journal, Louisville, Ky.

THE WILLIAMSBURG ORANGE WINE CAKE

This famous Williamsburg cake has been the prototype for many others. It was proved by the Market Square Tavern Kitchen in 1937.

"Chop very fine or grind, one medium-sized, tender orange-rind and one cup of raisins. Add ½ cup of coarsely-chopped English walnuts.

"Cream one half cup of butter with one cup of sugar, add two beaten eggs, one teaspoon of vanilla and chopped mixture. Sift two cups of flour with one teaspoon of soda, one half teaspoon of salt and add alternately with one cup of sour milk. Pour into well-greased square cake pan and bake in moderate oven about thirty or forty minutes. While hot this cake may be glazed by spreading over it one cup of sugar mixed with one third of a cup of orange juice and returning it to the oven. Others prefer this cake served warm with a syllabub of frothed cream and still others serve it with Wine Icing [see following]."

Wine Icing

"Mix well one third of a cup of butter with two cups of confectioners sugar. Add Sherry to this, slowly beating well; add some finely grated orange-peel, and when thick enough, spread on the cake. Beating the white of an egg into this icing much improves its texture."

From The Williamsburg Art of Cookery, *by Helen Bullock*

DR. REAVES'S WHITE FRUIT CAKE

Batter

2 cups butter
2 cups sugar

12 eggs
4 cups flour

2 teaspoons baking powder
1 cup orange juice

1 tablespoon vanilla
1 teaspoon rosewater extract

Cream well the butter and sugar. Break in 1 egg at a time, beating after each egg. Sift together flour and baking powder and add alternately with orange juice. Add the flavoring. Then add the following fruits which have been dredged with 1 extra cup of flour:

1 extra cup of flour
¼ lb. candied orange peel
1 lb. citron
1 lb. shelled nuts
1 lb. candied pineapple

¼ lb. candied lemon peel
1 lb. seeded dates
2 lbs. white candied cherries
2 lbs. white raisins

Pour into paper-lined pans and bake 3½ hours at 275 degrees. The temperature must be even and slow; otherwise, the cake will be ruined. If a dark fruit cake is desired, instead of white, substitute syrup for orange juice; 1 teaspoon of baking powder for the 2 as above; and black raisins to replace the white.

Dr. Nell Le Compte Reaves, Mobile, Ala.

MRS. BROOKS'S WHITE FRUIT CAKE
Five pounds

1½ cups butter, softened
2 cups sugar
4 cups sifted flour, extra flour for dredging fruits and nuts
1 teaspoon baking powder
1 medium-size coconut, grated
1 lb. blanched almonds, chopped

1 lb. citron, chopped
1 lb. crystallized pineapple, chopped
1 lb. crystallized cherries (white if possible), chopped
12 egg whites, stiffly beaten

Cream the butter; gradually cream in the sugar; work in the flour which has been sifted with the baking powder. Lightly dredge the coconut, nuts, and fruits with flour. Stir in the coconut first; then add the nuts and fruits to the batter. This will be stiff batter, but work all the nuts and fruits in well with the hands. Last, fold in the egg whites. Pour into a greased, floured tube cake pan (standard size). Bake in a slow, 250-degree oven for 3 hours.

This cake contains no egg yolks, liquid, or flavoring. It has a rich flavor from the fruits and nuts.

Mrs. Eugene Clyde Brooks, Raleigh, N.C.

NOTE: If flavoring is desired, add 1 teaspoon anise extract and 1 teaspoon of almond flavoring, or add 2 tablespoons brandy.

MRS. TEAGUE'S NORTH CAROLINA BLACK FRUIT CAKE
Ten-pound cake

The late Mrs. Banks E. Teague for years made this steamed dark fruit cake for a select clientele. It is an old recipe inherited from her aunt around the turn of the century.

The cake is steamed on top of the stove and then baked a little while in the oven. To steam the cakes, Mrs. Teague used a large deep oval tin wash boiler fitted with a rack with holes punched in it to allow the steam to escape upward. The cakes were set on the rack, and the boiler was covered with a lid. A similar steamer may be made out of any large vessel which has a cover and will extend over two heating units.

Fruits and Seasonings

5 lbs. raisins
½ lb. candied pineapple
½ lb. candied cherries
1 lb. citron
½ lb. blanched almonds
½ lb. pecan meats
1 tablespoon cinnamon
1 scant tablespoon allspice

1 scant tablespoon nutmeg
1 scant tablespoon cloves
2 tablespoons grated bitter chocolate
1 jelly glass grape jelly
1 glass grape juice
Brandy to taste, optional

The Batter

2 cups butter
2 cups sugar

12 eggs
4 cups flour (1 lb.)

Cut up fruits and nuts into small pieces. Dredge with part of the flour set out for the cake, using enough to make a thin coating. Mix batter by creaming together the butter and sugar; add eggs one at a time, beating well after each egg. Add flour. Add fruits and nuts, spices, all seasonings, and flavorings; mix thoroughly with hands.

Grease, flour, and line with waxed paper 1 large 10-lb. cake pan or small pans of desired size. Pour mixture into pans and put in steamer over cold water. Close steamer and bring water to boil. When water boils, lower temperature, and steam (on top of stove) for 4 hours. Then remove cakes and put into preheated 250-degree oven. Let bake at this temperature for 1 hour. Steam large cake and bake for same length of time as for smaller cakes.

Mrs. Teague's daughters: Mrs. Ruby Gross, Mrs. B. M. Schoner, Misses Katie and Frances Teague, Burlington, N.C., and Mrs. Foster Hughes, Graham, N.C.

TENNESSEE JAM CAKE
Three large layers

Old in tradition is the Tennessee Jam cake which has been served for many years as a Thanksgiving or Christmas cake. Jam and fig preserves enrich the batter. The cake is frosted with *genuine* caramelized sugar icing.

1 cup butter
1 cup sugar
1 cup blackberry jam
1 cup strawberry preserves
1 cup fig preserves (or use 2 cups jam, 1 cup fig preserves or raisins)
5 egg yolks, well beaten

3 cups flour
1 cup buttermilk
1 tablespoon soda
1 tablespoon cinnamon
1 tablespoon allspice
1 cup grated nut meats
5 egg whites, stiffly beaten

Cream butter and sugar; add jam and preserves. Add the well-beaten egg yolks and beat until smooth. Add the flour and milk to which soda has been added alternately, and mix well after each addition. Add the spices and nuts and mix well. Fold in the egg whites which have been beaten until stiff. Pour into well-greased layer pans and bake in a 400-degree oven for 40 to 50 minutes, or until done. Frost with caramel frosting.

Caramel Frosting

Into a heavy iron skillet measure 3 cups of white sugar and add 1 cup of butter; cook over high heat until lightly browned (do not allow to brown too dark; stir constantly to keep from burning). Add 1½ cups milk to the mixture slowly, and cook slowly until slightly warm. Beat until smooth. While still not thick enough to hold shape, smooth 1 tablespoon of icing on each layer. This will soak in and make the cake hold moisture and not become too dry. When the remainder of the icing has been beaten enough to hold shape, smooth between layers and top. (Frost top and sides.) This cake will be better several days after making as it will then be mellowed. Very rich and especially good.

"Nancy Nash" (Mrs. B. Frank Womack), Foods Editor, The Nashville
Tennesseean Magazine, *Nashville, Tenn.*

JENNIE BENEDICT'S FRUIT CAKE
Twelve-pound cake

A prized Kentucky cake.

2 cups butter
2 cups sugar

1 cup New Orleans type molasses
12 eggs, beaten separately

1 lb. flour (about 4 cups)
2 teaspoons baking powder
1 cup light cream or top milk
1 tablespoon cinnamon
1 tablespoon allspice
2 nutmegs grated, or 2 full teaspoons ground nutmeg
½ glass wine (tumbler)
½ glass brandy (tumbler)

½ lb. citron
2 lbs. raisins
1 lb. currants
½ lb. figs
½ lb. candied pineapple
½ lb. candied cherries
2 lbs. blanched almonds

Cream butter and sugar together. Add the molasses; then the eggs which have been beaten separately. Next add the flour which has been browned. [Spread flour in shallow pan, place in slow oven and brown; stir flour frequently.—M. B.] Then dissolve the baking powder in 1 cup of light cream or top milk and add to the mixture. Add the spices which have been dissolved in the tumbler full of liquors (wine and brandy). Chop fruits and nuts and dredge with flour. Put these in the batter last. Bake slowly at 250–275 degrees for 4 hours.

Contributed by Cissy Gregg, Home Consultant, Courier-Journal,
Louisville, Ky.

PEGGY GAINES'S KENTUCKY PECAN BOURBON CAKE
Three-pound cake

1 lb. shelled pecans
½ lb. seeded raisins
1½ cups flour
1 teaspoon baking powder
½ cup butter
1 cup plus 2 tablespoons sugar
3 egg yolks

2 teaspoons freshly grated nutmeg
½ cup bottled-in-bond Kentucky
  bourbon whiskey
3 egg whites, stiffly beaten
Jumbo pecan halves and candied
  cherries for decorating top of
  cake

"Break the pecans in pieces with the fingers or chop very coarsely; cut raisins in half and set aside. Measure the flour after sifting once; then sift twice more. Take ½ cup of this flour and mix with nuts and raisins. To the rest of the flour add the baking powder and sift again. Cream butter and sugar. Add yolks of eggs one at a time, beating until mixture is smooth and lemon colored.

"An electric beater is excellent for this. Soak the nutmeg in the whiskey for at least 10 minutes; then add to the butter mixture, alternating with the flour, and beating as the batter is being blended. When it is finished it looks and tastes a great deal like eggnog. Slowly fold the raisins and nuts into the batter, using a heavy wooden or large metal spoon. Last of all, fold in the egg whites, stiffly beaten with a few grains of salt. Grease a metal tube pan—one large enough to hold 3 pounds of batter. Line it with brown paper previously greased on both sides. Fill the pan with the batter—and here's a secret: Let it stand for 10 minutes, allowing the mixture to settle in the pan. Meantime, decorate the top of the cake with the candied cherries and Jumbo pecan halves. Now put the pan into a warm—not hot—oven; 325 is about right. Let the cake remain 1¼ hours, but if the top seems to brown too quickly put a piece of heavy wrapping paper over the surface. Test the cake by pressing the surface of the dough with the fingers. If it seems firm and the indentation does not show, the cake is ready to remove from the stove. It should always be slightly moist and when the straw or wire test is made, a few crumbs may adhere even though the cake is ready to take out of the oven; but I let it remain the full 1¼ hours before testing at all. Let the cake stand in the pan for 30 minutes before trying to remove it. Then place a plate a little larger than the pan over the surface and quickly turn the pan upside down. Then gingerly turn the cake right side up on another plate, being careful not to disturb the decorations on top of the cake. It makes a beautiful and delicious Christmas gift. Cut the slices with a saw-edged knife, as it crumbles easily."

From Out of Kentucky Kitchens, *by Marion Flexner, Louisville, Ky.*

OLD-FASHIONED POUND CAKE

The extra cup of sugar makes a rich cake.

1 lb. butter
3 level cups sugar
4 level cups flour (1 lb.)
2 level teaspoons baking powder

Pinch salt
10 or 12 eggs
4 tablespoons orange juice

Cream butter and sugar well; add flour sifted with salt and baking powder. Add eggs one at a time until well blended. Add orange juice. Beat one hour (if electric mixer is used, less time is required). Bake in tube pan 1 hour in 325-degree oven. To vary the flavoring, try using 2 tablespoons orange juice with one teaspoon each of vanilla and anise extracts.

Mrs. E. H. Morris, Sr., Asheboro, N.C.

CRUSTY POUND CAKE

When baked, a rich, crusty top forms on this cake.

1¾ cups butter
4 cups flour
8 eggs, beaten
2 cups sugar
⅛ teaspoon salt

1 teaspoon baking powder
1 teaspoon vanilla extract
1 teaspoon lemon extract
1 tablespoon sherry

Cream butter and work in flour until mixture is of a fine, mealy texture. Beat eggs until lemon-colored; combine with sugar. Add to flour mixture. Add salt, baking powder, extracts, and sherry. Beat 15 minutes with rotary beater, or 5 minutes with electric beater. Bake in greased tube pan in slow oven (250 degrees) 40 minutes, then in moderate oven (325 degrees) 40 minutes. Crust will form, making frosting unnecessary.

Mrs. Richard Watts, Rockbridge Co., Va., from
Recipes from Old Virginia, *Richmond, Va.*

"KATCH'S" GINGER POUND CAKE

Ground ginger gives this an exciting flavor.

2 cups butter
2 cups sugar
10 egg yolks
Juice and grated rind of 1 lemon

4 cups flour
1 teaspoon ground ginger
10 egg whites, stiffly beaten

Cream butter and sugar until no grains can be felt. Add egg yolks and grated rind and juice of 1 lemon. Beat and beat and beat. Add flour sifted 3 times and the ground ginger. Fold in stiffly beaten egg whites. Bake at 325 degrees in tube pan for 1¼ hours.

"Katch" (Mrs. DeForest Goodell), from Katch's Kitchen,
West Palm Beach, Fla.

THE BEST PLAIN CAKE (*Mock Pound Cake*)

This is a versatile cake with pound-cake consistency. It keeps moist for weeks. It may be served plain, iced, or glazed.

3 cups sugar
1 cup butter, softened
½ cup Crisco
6 eggs

3 cups flour
1 teaspoon baking powder
1 cup milk
2 teaspoons lemon extract

Preheat oven to 325 degrees.

In a mixing bowl, cream the sugar with the butter and shortening until mixture is light. Add the eggs one at a time, beating well after each addition. Sift the flour and baking powder together. Add the dry ingredients alternately with the milk. Beat in the flavoring. Bake in a greased and floured standard-size tube cake pan at 325 degrees for 1 hour and 15 minutes. Cool 10 minutes in pan, turn out on cake rack and cool. Ice with favorite cake icing, or glaze as desired. This cake freezes well.

VARIATIONS: Chocolate Cake: Add 5 tablespoons of cocoa to batter. Bake as above.

Anise Cake: Instead of the lemon extract, use 1 teaspoon anise extract and 1 teaspoon vanilla extract.

Almond Cake: Use 1 teaspoon almond extract and 1 teaspoon vanilla.

Caramel Cake: Use 2 cups of light brown sugar and 1 cup of white sugar in place of 3 cups white sugar. Add nuts to batter if desired.

Mrs. E. F. Hart, Burlington, N.C.

TARBORO TIPSY CAKE
Serves eight to ten

The Tipsy Cake and its variants have long graced the Southern festive table. One of the most famous is the Tarboro Tipsy Cake, favorite Eastern Carolina dessert. Mrs. Finley L. Williamson, a native of Tarboro, in giving me her mother's method, adds a bit of whimsical history:

"Somewhat akin to this is 'Tipsy Parson,' possibly so called because as the householder's choicest dessert, it was in the old times prepared especially for the feasts spread when the Parson came to dine. Also akin to this is a dessert my daughter-in-law's family served in the West Indies called 'Trifle.' To my taste, my mother's Tipsy Cake was anything but a 'trifle'—rather the choicest of all her desserts, which invariably had cream, milk, eggs and gelatin, as fundamental components—and this is the way she prepared it.

"The day before needed, a **large sponge cake** was baked an even yellow [see following recipe] in a stem pan. Flavored with **grated yellow rind and juice of 1 lemon**. A **quart of boiled custard** was made. About ½ **pound of almonds** were shelled and blanched by pouring boiling water over them. Let nuts stand until cool enough to handle them. Just before meal time, place the whole cake in a large cut-glass bowl or deep platter; thickly stud the cake with the whole almonds; gradually saturate cake with 2 cups of scuppernong or **sherry wine**. Fill the hole in center of cake with **boiled custard** and pour custard over all; then heap over it a **syllabub made of sweet whipped cream** (not too stiff) flavored with the same flavor of wine used to marinate cake, with 1 tablespoon of powdered sugar added." [See Angel Food Cake Custard, p. 343.]

Mrs. Finley L. Williamson, Burlington, N.C.

YELLOW (*Sponge*) CAKE FOR TIPSY CAKE

This cake is made especially for a "Tipsy" dessert.

12 egg yolks
2 cups sugar
2 cups flour, sifted 3 times
2 teaspoons baking powder

Pinch salt
1 cup milk
(Flavoring if desired)

Beat egg yolks until lemon yellow. Add sugar gradually. Sift in flour, combined with baking powder and salt, alternately with milk, adding flour last. Pour into an ungreased angel food cake pan and bake at 400 degrees for 1 hour.

Mrs. C. A. Anderson, Burlington, N.C.

MRS. FERGERSON'S MACAROON SPONGE CAKE

1 cup sifted sugar
3 egg yolks
1 teaspoon lemon juice
7 tablespoons water
1 cup flour sifted before measuring

1 rounded teaspoon baking powder
3 egg whites, stiffly-beaten

Cream sugar and yolks; add lemon juice, then water and flour (with baking powder) alternately. Fold in well-beaten egg whites. Bake in one pan, 9" × 13", for about 30 to 40 minutes in moderate (350-degree) oven. Cut cake in half and ice with the following icing:

Macaroon Icing

½ cup butter
1 cup powdered sugar
2 egg yolks, beaten
Almond extract

1 cup cream, whipped
1 doz. macaroons, rolled finely (save ½ cup crumbs for top and sides)

Cream butter and sugar; add egg yolks, flavoring, cream, and macaroon crumbs (except ½ cup); ice cake and sprinkle top and sides with macaroon crumbs.

Mrs. Edgar B. Fergerson, Paducah, Ky.

ANGEL FOOD CAKE WITH ICING

1 cup Swansdown cake flour
1 teaspoon cream of tartar
1¾ cup egg whites (about 12)

1½ cups sugar
1 teaspoon vanilla
1 teaspoon almond extract

Sift flour and cream of tartar together at least 5 times. Beat egg whites until bubbly and fluffy but not stiff and dry. Sift sugar, a little at a time, into the beaten egg whites, folding in carefully.

Next, sift flour into egg white mixture, folding in slowly and carefully. Do not beat. Last, add flavoring and pour into an ungreased angel food cake pan, dropping pan on the table 3 times to free batter of bubbles.

Put into a cold oven and adjust heat to 325 degrees and bake 45 minutes—no longer. Take out of oven and turn upside down and leave cake in pan until thoroughly cold or it will fall. If cake is to be iced, it then can be iced. If cake is not being iced the same day, it may be left in pan, inverted.

Angel Food Icing

2 cups sugar
½ cup water
1 teaspoon corn syrup

½ teaspoon vanilla
½ teaspoon lemon extract
2 egg whites, stiffly beaten

Boil together sugar, water, and corn syrup until soft ball forms in cold water. Remove and add flavorings. Pour mixture into stiffly beaten egg whites; beat until creamy.

Mrs. Garvin May, Burlington, N.C.

YELLOW ANGEL FOOD CAKE

This is the "chiffon" of cakes.

1½ cups sugar
1 cup cold water
6 egg whites, stiffly beaten
1 teaspoon cream of tartar
½ teaspoon salt

6 egg yolks, beaten
1 cup cake flour
½ teaspoon vanilla
½ teaspoon almond extract

Boil sugar and water until it spins a thread. Pour slowly, beating all the time, over the stiffly beaten egg whites. Beat in 1 teaspoon cream of tartar; add salt. Beat egg yolks thoroughly and add to egg white mixture. Fold in flour which has been sifted six times; add flavoring. Bake in 325-degree oven in loaf pan for 45 minutes. Cool and cover with desired icing.

Mrs. Marion B. Thompson, from The Columbia Woman's Club Cook Book,
Columbia, S.C.

CHOCOLATE ANGEL FOOD CAKE

A really delicious cake.

12 egg whites
1 teaspoon cream of tartar
Dash of salt
1½ cups sugar

¾ cup flour
¼ cup cocoa
1 teaspoon vanilla

Beat egg whites very stiff; add cream of tartar, salt, sugar, flour sifted together, cocoa, and vanilla. Place in a cold oven. Set heat at 325 degrees and bake for 45 minutes.

From Lady Jo's Southern Recipes, *by Lady Jo Kirby Beals, Texarkana, Ark., Tex.*

MRS. DINGLE'S BLUEBERRY CAKE WITH LEMON SAUCE

½ pound butter, softened
2 cups sugar
4 eggs
3 cups flour
2 teaspoons baking powder

½ teaspoon ground mace or ground spices, (more if desired)
½ cup fresh blueberries, picked over and rinsed thoroughly

Preheat oven to 350 degrees.

Blend together the butter and sugar. Add eggs, one at a time, beating after each addition. Mix flour with baking powder and spices. Alternate adding portions of flour and milk to mixture. Beat until well blended. Pour into greased and floured baking pan, 9 × 9 × 2½ inches. Bake at preheated 350 degrees oven for around 45 minutes, or until center springs back when touched. Do not overcook. Cool in pan. Cut in squares and serve with warm lemon sauce.

Lemon Sauce

1 cup sugar
1 tablespoon butter, softened
½ cup water

1 teaspoon corn starch
Grated rind and juice of one lemon

Mix together sugar and butter in a small heavy saucepan. Add remaining ingredients. Cook, stirring constantly over moderate fire until sauce thickens. Serve warm or cool over blueberry cake. Makes about 1½ cups.

Mrs. R. S. Dingle, Tip Top Inn, Pawley's Island, S.C.

WHITE CAKE

½ cup butter
1½ cups sugar
3 cups plain flour
¾ cup cold water
6 egg whites, beaten stiff with

Pinch salt
4 teaspoons baking powder
1 teaspoon vanilla, lemon, or al-
    mond flavoring

Cream butter and sugar until fluffy. Sift flour; then measure three cups. Sift again. Fold gradually into butter-sugar mixture, adding water, then stiffly beaten egg whites and, lastly, the four teaspoons of baking powder and flavoring. Fold eggs and baking powder in; do not beat. Pour into two 9-inch pans which have been lined with waxed paper, but not greased. Bake in a 325-degree oven for 25 to 30 minutes. For an icing, see White Icings, p. 378.

Mrs. James W. Smith, Americus, Ga.

ROSE CREAM CAKE (*Birthday or Wedding Cake*)

This is Frances Parkinson Keyes's "Birthday Cake," of which she says, "The Rose Cream Cake has been in my family for several generations. Its origin is Virginia. I always use this for my birthday with pink candles, and it is extremely pretty when cut, with the contrast between white frosting and pink inside. It is also very attractive made in all white for a wedding cake."

1 cup butter
3 cups sugar
4 cups flour
2 heaping teaspoons baking pow-
    der

1 cup milk
Vanilla flavoring to taste
Enough vegetable coloring to
    make batter delicate pink
10 egg whites, stiffly beaten

Mix all ingredients as for regular cake, except egg whites (fold in last). Bake in milk pans [similar to layer-cake pans]. Frost with boiled icing.

Frances Parkinson Keyes, from Bon Appétit!, *Baton Rouge, La.*

MOSS ROSE CAKE

4 eggs
2 cups sugar
1 cup milk

½ teaspoon almond extract
2 cups cake flour
2 teaspoons baking powder

Break eggs over sugar and beat 12 minutes—this must be done. Take turns with someone else, make the men folks help, or rejoice if you have an electric beater. Heat the milk to boiling point; add the extract; and let milk sit on back of stove. Sift the flour once; then measure and sift again with the baking powder. Add to the egg-sugar mixture. Add warm milk slowly to the batter and beat three minutes. Bake in two layers in moderate oven (350 degrees) for 25 minutes.

Frost with the following:

½ cup water
1½ cups sugar
2 egg whites, stiffly beaten
1 teaspoon vanilla

2 cups grated coconut
1 orange
2 tablespoons sugar

Add water to sugar and boil until it spins a thread. Pour slowly over the stiffly beaten egg whites and beat until thick enough to spread. Add vanilla and spread on cake, but do not put layers together. Mix the coconut (canned may be used) with the pulp, juice, and grated rind of one large seedless, navel orange, and sweeten to taste (2 tablespoons sugar). When the frosting on cake has begun to set, but is not hard, pat the orange-coconut mixture into it and put the layers together. This gives a blending of textures and flavors that is unique.

Mrs. W. H. Pugh, High Point, N.C.

HONEY UPSIDE-DOWN CAKE WITH HONEY SAUCE

This interestingly flavored cake is served often by Mrs. Lowe at lunch or as a buffet dinner dessert.

½ cup honey
¼ cup butter
4 or 5 unpeeled apples

Maraschino cherries
Nut halves

Put honey and butter in a heavy medium-sized iron skillet and let slowly melt on top of stove. Core the unpeeled apples, and cut them crosswise into ring slices ¾ of an inch thick, preparing enough slices to cover bottom of skillet well. Add the apple rings to honey and butter and simmer until apples are partly cooked, turning once. Place a maraschino cherry in center of each apple ring, and nut meat halves (pecans) in the spaces around the apples. Pour the following batter over the hot mixture:

½ cup butter
¾ cup honey (or part sugar, part honey)
1 egg
½ cup milk
1½ cups flour

1 teaspoon baking powder
¼ teaspoon soda
¼ teaspoon cinnamon
½ teaspoon nutmeg
⅛ teaspoon ginger

Cream together the butter and honey; add egg and beat until smooth. Add milk alternately with sifted dry ingredients. Bake in heavy skillet at 350 degrees 30 to 35 minutes. Turn upside-down cake onto a large platter. This may be served hot or cold with sauce made of ½ cup of honey combined with ½ cup butter, heated. I frequently use ¼ cup light brown sugar and ½ cup honey in skillet instead of proportions given above.

Mrs. M. L. Lowe, Cookeville, Tenn.

MERINGUE SPICE CAKE

¾ cup shortening
2 cups brown sugar
2 beaten egg yolks
2⅓ cups flour
1 teaspoon baking powder
¾ teaspoon salt

1 teaspoon soda
1 teaspoon cinnamon
1 teaspoon cloves
1¼ cups sour milk
1 teaspoon vanilla

Thoroughly cream shortening and sugar; add egg yolks and beat until fluffy. Add sifted dry ingredients, alternating with milk and vanilla. Beat vigorously after each addition. Pour into greased 9″ × 13″ pan. Cover with brown sugar meringue. Bake at 325 degrees about 50 minutes.

Brown Sugar Meringue

1 cup brown sugar
2 stiffly beaten egg whites

½ cup broken nut meats

Slowly add sugar to egg whites; beat until smooth. Fold in nuts. Spread over batter and bake as directed.

Margaret D. Tomlinson, from What's Cookin'?, *Winston-Salem, N.C.*

PENTHOUSE CHEESE CAKE WITH ZWIEBACK CRUST
Serves twelve

The Neiman-Marcus Tea Room in Dallas, Texas, is famous for just such dishes as this:

1 cup sugar
1 tablespoon flour
8 3-oz. pkgs. cream cheese
6 egg yolks, well beaten
1 tablespoon vanilla

1 tablespoon lemon juice
½ lemon rind, grated
1 cup heavy cream
6 egg whites, stiffly beaten

Cream sugar, flour, and cheese. Add egg yolks, well beaten; add vanilla, lemon juice, and rind. Add the cream and then fold in the stiffly beaten egg whites. Pour mixture into spring-form cake pan lined with zwieback crust. Bake one hour in a moderate oven, about 350 degrees. Turn oven off. Open oven door and let cool for 1 hour.

Zwieback Crust

Roll 1 box of zwieback into fine crumbs. Mix with ½ cup sugar and ⅓ lb. butter. We line our pans with the zwieback crust and put them in the refrigerator the night before. This insures a solid crust that does not mix into the cake.

Time and patience is what it takes to make any recipe turn out well. This one takes a lot of both and much careful handling. Each Friday, 15 cakes from this recipe are baked in our kitchen; so we speak from experience.

From the Neiman-Marcus Tea Room, Dallas, Tex.

BANANA CAKE WITH CARAMEL ICING

½ cup butter
1½ cups sugar
3 large bananas, mashed
2 eggs

½ teaspoon soda
½ cup buttermilk
2 cups flour
½ teaspoon baking powder

Cream butter, sugar, and bananas together; add eggs one at a time. Add soda dissolved in buttermilk; then add flour and baking powder sifted together. Bake in a 350-degree oven, in layers or loaf pans, about 30 minutes for layers, 45–50 minutes for loaf cake. Ice with caramel icing:

¾ cup granulated sugar
¾ cup brown sugar

½ cup cream
1 tablespoon butter

Cook sugar and cream together until it forms soft ball when dropped in cold water; remove from stove. Add butter and beat well before spreading on cake. This cake keeps moist for several days.

Mrs. R. E. Donnell, from Home-Tried Recipes, *Americus, Ga.*

CHATTANOOGA CHOCOLATE CAKE
Two layers

½ cup butter (1 stick)
1¼ cups sugar
2 eggs
2 1-oz. sqs. chocolate, melted in
 top of double boiler

1¾ cups flour
1 teaspoon soda
1 teaspoon salt
1 cup sour milk

Cream butter and sugar. Add 1 egg at a time and beat after each. Add melted chocolate. Next add flour which has been sifted 3 times with soda and salt, alternating with the sour milk. (Start adding with the flour, and end with flour.) Bake as 2 layers, or bake in a greased and floured square pan, in a preheated oven at 350 degrees. Bake 30 minutes for the layers and 45 minutes for a deeper pan.

Fudge Icing

2 cups sugar
⅓ cup cocoa
¼ teaspoon salt

½ cup milk
½ cup Nucoa (margarine)
1 teaspoon vanilla

Let all (except vanilla) come to a rolling boil and boil 2 minutes. Remove from stove, and, when cool, beat and add the vanilla.

Mrs. Ambrose S. Ringwald, Chattanooga, Tenn.

CHOCOLATE CUSTARD DEVIL'S FOOD CAKE
Two layers

3 1-oz. sqs. unsweetened chocolate
 (melted)
½ cup milk
1 beaten egg
⅔ cup sugar
½ cup shortening
1 cup extra sugar

2 beaten egg yolks
2 cups cake flour
¼ teaspoon salt
1 teaspoon soda
1 cup milk
1 teaspoon vanilla

Combine chocolate, ½ cup milk, whole egg, and ⅔ cup sugar. Cook over low heat until thick. Cool. Cream shortening and remaining cup sugar. Add egg yolks and mix well. Add sifted dry ingredients alternately with 1 cup milk and vanilla. Stir in chocolate custard mixture. Bake in 2 waxed-paper-lined 8-inch layer cake pans in 350-degree oven for 25 minutes.

Mrs. William A. Hanger, from The Cotton Blossom Cook Book, *Atlanta, Ga.*

MRS. BOST'S DEVIL'S FOOD CAKE

One of the best Devil's Foods.

2 cups sifted cake flour
1 teaspoon baking powder
1 teaspoon soda
¼ teaspoon salt
½ cup butter
2 cups brown sugar
2 eggs beaten light

1 cup sour milk
3 or 4 squares chocolate, melted over hot water, or ½ cup cocoa (3 sqs. chocolate preferred)
1 teaspoon vanilla

Sift flour; measure; and add baking powder, soda and salt. Sift 3 times. Cream butter, and add 1 cup of the sugar gradually. Add second cup of sugar to the beaten eggs; mix well. Combine egg and creamed mixtures. Add flour along with the milk; add chocolate and vanilla. Pour into 2 9-inch cake pans and bake at 325 degrees for 30 minutes. I always use square cake pans. Ice as desired.

Mrs. R. W. Bost, Chapel Hill, N.C.

FROSTED APPLE SAUCE CAKE

1½ cups thick, unsweetened apple sauce
½ cup butter, or other shortening
1 cup brown sugar
1 cup raisins
1 teaspoon cloves

1 teaspoon cinnamon
1 teaspoon nutmeg
½ teaspoon salt
2 cups flour
2 teaspoons soda
½ cup nut meats, chopped

Put shortening, sugar, and raisins into hot apple sauce. When cool, add spices, salt, flour, and soda. Mix; then add chopped nuts. Turn into greased bread pan (loaf) for loaf cake, or 9″ × 9″ cake pan and bake 1 hour at 350 degrees. Cover with the following frosting:

2 cups confectioners sugar
4 tablespoons hot milk

3 tablespoons melted butter
½ teaspoon vanilla

Mix together and spread on while cake is warm. I often bake this cake as a Christmas gift.

Mrs. R. W. Bost, Chapel Hill, N.C.

BABA AU RHUM OR SAVARIN BATTER
Serves eight

This batter may be baked in small ring molds or muffin tins and served with a sauce, filled with fruit, ice cream, or whipped cream. It may be baked in a large ring mold and served in the same manner or glazed with fruit glazes.

1 envelope of active dry yeast
¼ cup lukewarm water
4 teaspoons sugar
¼ cup lukewarm milk
2 cups sifted flour
2 eggs, beaten
½ teaspoon salt
⅔ cup butter, melted
3 tablespoons raisins

3 tablespoons currants
½ cup sugar
¾ cup apricot nectar (juice)
2 teaspoons lime or lemon juice
¼ cup dark rum
Fillings and garnishings: fruits,
  ice cream, whipped cream, or
  Crème Chantilly

Dissolve the yeast in the lukewarm water; stir in 1 teaspoon sugar. When yeast foams, add the remaining sugar (3 teaspoons) and the milk. Stir in the flour and the eggs and beat several minutes. Cover the bowl and let the dough rise in a warm room until it has doubled in bulk. Punch down the dough and add the salt, butter, raisins, and currants. With the fingers work these ingredients into the dough. Divide and place the dough into 8 individual buttered ring molds or muffin tins (large muffin size), filling them ¾ full. Or place all the dough into an 8½-inch ring mold (buttered). Cover and let the dough rise until it fills the molds. Bake the small molds in a preheated 400-degree oven for about 15 minutes, or until when tested with a toothpick the pick comes out clean. Bake the large mold for around 30 minutes. Remove from oven and unmold. Keep the Baba hot.

Meanwhile, make the Rum Sauce:

Rum Sauce for Babas

Mix the ½ cup sugar, apricot nectar, and lime juice in a saucepan. Stir and cook until mixture boils. Continue simmering without stirring for about 5 minutes. Remove from the heat and add the rum.

Invert the large Baba, or the small ones, on serving dishes; pour the Rum Sauce over them.

The center of large Baba, or ring mold small ones, may be filled with fruits (soaked in brandy if desired); ice cream; or whipped, sweetened flavored cream (Crème Chantilly), or any desired filling.

Savarin Cake

Make the batter as for Baba au Rhum, except leave out the currants and raisins. Pour into an 8½-inch ring mold, well buttered. Let rise and bake as for the large Baba. Turn out the cake top side up; prick in a few places with a fork. Pour over the Rum Sauce; let stand 30 minutes. Glaze with an apricot purée. Fill the center as for the large Baba. If individual Savarins are made, garnish as for the large one.

Rum Sauce for Savarin

Bring to boil in a saucepan 2 cups of water and 1 cup of sugar. Cool and add ½ cup cognac, rum or kirsch. Pour over the hot cake.

Apricot Glaze

Heat a 12-ounce jar of apricot jam or preserves in the top of a double boiler. Strain it through a sieve, or mash to make a purée. Glaze the entire surface of the cake with the purée.

Crème Chantilly

Whip 2 cups of heavy cream; stir in 2 tablespoons confectioners sugar, and 2 teaspoons of vanilla. Fill the centers of ring mold cake.

Miss Linda Rumbley, Burlington, N.C.

CHOCOLATE LOG
Serves eight

4 medium eggs, or 3 large ones
1 cup sugar
2 teaspoons vanilla extract
5 tablespoons water
1 cup sifted all-purpose flour
¼ teaspoon salt
1 teaspoon double-acting baking powder

Butter-cream filling (see Ella's Dobosh Torte Filling)
Fudge icing (see Ella's Dobosh Torte Icing)
Chopped toasted almonds

Line a greased jelly roll pan (15½" × 10½" × 1") with greased waxed paper. Beat the eggs until thick; gradually beat in the sugar. Beat in the vanilla and water. Sift together the dry ingredients and add to the egg mixture; beat until batter is smooth. Pour the batter into the cake pan. Bake in a preheated 375-degree oven for 15 minutes. Turn out the cake on a towel; trim off the crust. Roll up cake and towel together. Cool. Unroll the cake and spread with butter-cream filling. Roll up again. Ice with fudge icing. With a fork, curl up a few "knots" in the icing and run the fork tines down to make streaks. Sprinkle the log with almonds to make "bark."

This may be frozen and sliced while frozen. Keep it refrigerated or frozen.

Mrs. Ray Taylor, Greensboro, N.C.

BUTTER-CREAM FILLING OR FROSTING
Two cups

2 tablespoons water
½ cup sugar
¹⁄₁₆ teaspoon cream of tartar
2 egg yolks, beaten

½ cup butter (1 stick)
2 teaspoons vanilla or other flavoring

Combine the water, sugar, and cream of tartar in a small saucepan. Place over medium heat and bring to boiling point, stirring constantly until sugar is dissolved. Cook rapidly without stirring until syrup spins a thread (244 degrees on candy thermometer). Let syrup cool 1 minute. In the small bowl of an electric mixer, beat the egg yolks until they are very thick. Gradually pour in the syrup, beating well after each addition. Add 1 tablespoon of the butter at a time and beat after each addition until all butter has been used. Add the vanilla. Beat until frosting is cool. Chill in refrigerator until mixture is thick and beat again with a spoon. Chill again until cream is thick enough to spread. Use to frost or fill cakes, pastries, etc. Anything frosted or filled with this cream should be kept in a cool place because the cream will melt if allowed to get too warm. It may be stored in refrigerator and kept until needed.

NOTE: 2 ounces of melted chocolate may be added to the cream along with the vanilla to make a chocolate cream. To make a mint cream, add 2 tablespoons of crème de menthe along with the vanilla. Other flavors may be added.

Mrs. John Rich Ireland, Burlington, N.C.

VANILLA CREAM ICING OR GLAZE
Three and one-fourth cups

For hermits, loaf cake, muffin cake, drop cookies, etc.

1½ cups powdered sugar
2 tablespoons butter
1 teaspoon vanilla

⅛ teaspoon salt
2 tablespoons cream, or enough to make a smooth paste

Sift sugar; add all other ingredients and beat until smooth and creamy. Spread on cakes or cookies. When this icing is used for a glaze, it must be spread very thin on the hot cookies. It will form a glaze when cool.

From Dixie Dishes, *by Marion Flexner, Louisville, Ky.*

FLUFFY WHITE ICING

Very good for Spice or Chocolate Cake.

1½ cups light brown sugar (pack the sugar well into cup)

⅓ cup water
1 teaspoon vinegar

2 egg whites, unbeaten   1 teaspoon vanilla
⅛ teaspoon cream of tartar

In a saucepan combine the sugar, water, and vinegar. Bring to a boil. When syrup begins to boil, boil 3 minutes (no less, no longer).

In an electric mixing bowl, have ready the unbeaten egg whites and cream of tartar. Pour in the hot syrup and beat until frosting is fluffy and holds to a spoon. Add vanilla and stir. Will frost and fill 1 2-layer cake.

Mrs. Darrell Springer, Seminole, Fla.

MRS. SMITH'S ICINGS FOR WHITE CAKE

These two icings may be used for any cake. Mrs. Smith created them for her "White Cake." (See p. 369.)

Ten-Minute White Icing

2 egg whites   5 tablespoons cold water
1½ cups sugar   ¼ teaspoon cream of tartar
1½ teaspoons white Karo syrup   Pinch salt

Put all into top of double boiler; stir well. Cook over hot water for 10 minutes, beating with rotary beater. When done, icing should stand up in peaks.

Another White Icing

2 cups sugar   2 egg whites, stiffly beaten
2 tablespoons white Karo syrup   Pinch salt
⅔ cup cold water

Cook sugar, water, and syrup until it reaches soft ball stage (in cold water). Pour syrup gradually over stiffly beaten whites, beating with electric mixer until ready to pour on cake. This icing pours, instead of having to be spread on cake.

Mrs. James W. Smith, Americus, Ga.

LÁNE CAKE FILLING (*Variant*)

For 8-egg cake.

8 egg yolks, beaten   ½ cup butter
1 cup sugar   1 cup chopped nuts

1 cup seeded raisins, chopped   1 teaspoon vanilla
4 tablespoons good brandy

Pour egg yolks, butter, and sugar into top of double boiler; stir constantly until thick. Add remaining ingredients and remove at once from fire. Cool and fill cake. Ice with any boiled icing. [See Lane Cake, p. 354.]

MRS. BIGGS'S CAKE FILLINGS

Bitter Chocolate Filling

1 tablespoon butter   ⅛ teaspoon cream of tartar
2 cups sugar   Few grains salt
2 squares Baker's bitter chocolate   1 teaspoon vanilla
½ cup milk

Boil all together until syrup reaches soft-ball stage in cold water. Remove from heat and beat well. Spread on cake.

Caramel Icing For Layer Cake With Toasted Pecans

3 cups brown sugar   ½ lb. butter
¾ lb. maple sugar   Vanilla to taste
1½ cups milk   Toasted pecans
Pinch of soda to prevent curdling

Put brown and maple sugar, milk, and soda in saucepan. When syrup begins to boil add the butter. Remove from heat. Beat a long time, until thick enough to spread. Flavor with vanilla. Sprinkle toasted pecans over top of each layer.

Mrs. J. Crawford Biggs, Hardimont, Raleigh, N.C.

UNCOOKED FILLINGS, SUMMER-TIME CAKE ICINGS

Chocolate Cake Filling

Fills and spreads two layers.

2 tablespoons butter   1 teaspoon vanilla
2 cups sifted powdered sugar   4 squares Baker's unsweetened
2 whole eggs, or 4 egg yolks   chocolate, melted
½ cup milk

Cream butter thoroughly, gradually add sugar, and cream together well. Add eggs, milk, vanilla, and chocolate. Place bowl in pan of cracked ice or iced water and beat until of right consistency to spread—about 3 minutes. Will fill and cover 2 8-inch cake layers.

Orange Filling

Fills and spreads three layers.

Grated rind 1 lemon
Grated rind 1 orange
3 tablespoons orange juice

1 tablespoon lemon juice
½ cup butter
2 pkgs. powdered sugar

Place grated rind, fruit juice, and butter into a saucepan; let heat long enough to melt the butter; then stir in enough sugar to make icing the consistency of heavy cream. Cool 10 minutes; spread.

Mrs. Rodney Coleman, from Soup to Nuts, *Burlington, N.C.*

MOCHA (*Coffee*) CAKE ICING

For two layers.

1 cup butter
2 cups powdered sugar, sifted
2 egg yolks, unbeaten
2 to 3 tablespoons strong coffee
    made from powdered coffee
    if possible, or reduce freshly
    made coffee

1 teaspoon vanilla

Cream butter and sugar until foamy; add egg yolks, one at a time, beating vigorously after each addition. Flavor with the coffee and vanilla. Spread on any plain layer cake. Nuts may be added if desired. [To vary above icing, add 2 tablespoons of cocoa to mixture. Cream the cocoa with butter and sugar.—M. B.]

Mrs. Charles M. Garrett, Chattanooga, Tenn.

ALMOND PASTE FOR FRUIT CAKE

As a rule the Fruit Cake is not iced, but in many sections of the South the icing plays a great part in preserving and enriching the cake. First an almond paste is spread on, especially if the cake is a wedding cake, and then a boiled white icing or just an old fashioned "rubbed" or hard white icing is spread over.

The almond paste is prepared in this manner: To each pound of blanched almonds, ground through a meat chopper, use 1 cup of sugar, 1 stiffly beaten egg white, ⅓ cup of water, and flavoring as desired, either almond extract, vanilla, or rose water.

Boil the sugar with water until it threads a long thread. Pour very slowly into the egg whites and stir in the ground almonds. Add flavoring and spread on the cake. Let cool; then cover with boiled white icing.

14. Cookies and Small Cakes

JENNIE BENEDICT'S LEMON WAFERS TO BE SERVED WITH HER EGGNOG
Five dozen

These little wafers were originated by the late Miss Jennie Benedict, Louisville, Kentucky, to be served with her eggnog (see Eggnog recipe, p. 39).

½ cup butter
½ cup sugar
2 eggs, well beaten

1 cup plus 2 tablespoons sifted flour
1 teaspoon lemon flavoring

Cream the butter and sugar together until light and fluffy. Add well-beaten eggs and beat until the creamed butter, sugar, and eggs are well mixed and the mass is fluffy. Add sifted flour and beat until smooth. Add flavoring. Drop batter from a teaspoon on greased cookie sheet, keeping the cookies at least 2 inches apart to allow for spreading. Bake cookies in a moderate oven, 350 degrees for 7 minutes, or until lightly browned around the edges and done in the middle.

Contributed by Cissy Gregg, Home Consultant, Courier-Journal, *Louisville, Ky.*

MRS. PATTERSON'S ICEBOX COOKIES
About four dozen

1 cup butter, melted
1 cup brown sugar
1 cup white sugar
2 eggs, unbeaten

1 teaspoon cinnamon
½ teaspoon soda
3 cups flour
¼ lb. nuts (pecans), chopped

Melt the butter; add brown sugar, white sugar, and eggs. Sift cinnamon and soda with flour and add chopped nut meats. Work into dough. Roll in waxed paper; place in icebox overnight. Slice very thin and bake at 400 degrees for 10 to 12 minutes.

Mrs. Stuart Patterson, Vicksburg, Miss.

KENTUCKY MACAROONS
Thirty-six drops

3 egg whites, beaten stiffly
¼ lb. confectioners sugar

½ lb. grated coconut, fresh

Mix; drop by teaspoonfuls on buttered pans and bake in slow oven (325 degrees) until slightly browned, about 12 to 15 minutes.

Mrs. Carrie Bell, Eminence, Ky.

ORIGINAL MORAVIAN CHRISTMAS COOKIES
About seven pounds

For many years at Winston-Salem, North Carolina, a little paper-thin spiced cookie has been baked and stored in tins to delight the children at Christmas. The holidays would be incomplete without them. This recipe was given our contributor by an experienced Moravian cake-maker who uses the original method. The weights and measures are given in the original form because if you are going to make this cookie it is best to weigh ingredients as suggested.

¾ lb. butter and lard mixed
¾ lb. light brown sugar
3¾ lbs. flour (4 cups to lb.)
4 cups Porto Rico molasses
1 tablespoon mace
2 tablespoons ground cloves

2 tablespoons ground cinnamon
1 oz. grated lemon peel
1 wineglass brandy (4 tablespoons)
1 oz. soda in small amount of milk to dissolve

Cream butter and sugar; add flour and molasses with mixed spices (in molasses). Mix all together, using the hands. Add lemon peel and brandy and last the soda dissolved in milk. This should make a stiff dough. If more flour is needed to stiffen dough, use it. Roll very thin, cut cakes in shapes of stars, crescents, animals, etc. Bake in moderate oven, 350 degrees, for 8 to 10 minutes until lightly browned. These will keep for weeks if placed in tins and can be made well before Christmas.

Recipe of Mrs. Eugene Gray, Winston-Salem, N.C.
Contributed by Mrs. Don E. Scott, Graham, N.C.

MORAVIAN WHITE CHRISTMAS CAKES
About six dozen

2 cups butter (1 lb.)
3 cups granulated sugar

5 eggs
1 cup sweet cream

1 teaspoon soda dissolved in hot water

Flour to make a stiff dough

Nutmeg, generously
1 tablespoon vanilla

Cream butter with sugar; add eggs, cream, soda, and flour. Add nutmeg and vanilla. Make into roll; keep in icebox for several days and roll very thin. Cut into cookies; bake at 400 degrees for 10 minutes, or until light brown.

Mrs. Howard E. Rondthaler, Winston-Salem, N.C.

FROSTED BUTTERSCOTCH SQUARES
Twelve 2" × 2" squares

This rich butterscotch square with creamed icing and the Bourbon Ball (below) are from the same expert Kentucky cookie maker.

¼ cup butter
1 cup dark brown sugar (pressed down in cup)
1 egg
¾ cup flour

1 teaspoon baking powder
Pinch salt
1 teaspoon vanilla
¾ cup broken nut meats

Melt butter; stir in sugar and cook until melted. Cool. Stir in unbeaten egg and mix well. Sift dry ingredients together and add to sugar-butter-egg mixture; then add the vanilla and nuts. Bake in a greased paper-lined square cake pan, in 325-degree oven for 25 minutes. Cool in pan; cut in squares and ice with following:

Melt 1 tablespoon of butter, add 1 cup confectioners sugar, enough thin cream to spread and vanilla to taste.

KENTUCKY BOURBON OR RUM BALLS
Two dozen small balls

30 vanilla wafers, ground
2 tablespoons cocoa
2 tablespoons white Karo syrup
⅓ cup crushed pecans

4 tablespoons bourbon whiskey or rum
Powdered sugar

Grind wafers to crumbs; add cocoa and Karo; mix. Add pecans and bourbon; form into balls, and dunk into powdered sugar.

Mrs. Harris W. Rankin, Paducah, Ky.

MARGUERITES
Four dozen

The Marguerite is often simply made by melting a marshmallow on a cracker or small round cake. This is more elaborate.

¼ cup water
1 cup sugar
2 egg whites, beaten stiff with
½ teaspoon cream of tartar, or baking powder

1 to 2 cups pecan meats, broken fine
Candied cherries

Boil water and sugar until it spins a thread. Have egg whites well-beaten. Pour the syrup slowly over whites, beating constantly, to avoid lumping. Add nut meats. Spread mixture on little round cakes or crackers. Bake very slowly in a 325-degree oven until a golden brown, keeping the oven door open. Garnish each with cherry. A pretty cake for a child's party.

From The Louisiana Plantation Cook Book,
by Mrs. James E. Smitherman, Shreveport, La.

CATHERINE'S BROWNIES
Two dozen

2 1-oz. squares bitter chocolate
¼ lb. butter
1¼ cups sugar
2 eggs, slightly beaten

½ cup sifted flour
½ teaspoon vanilla
1 cup chopped nuts
Powdered sugar for garnish

Melt the chocolate over hot water; stir in the remaining ingredients, except the powdered sugar, in the order given. Pour into a greased baking pan (8″ × 12″ × 1″ or equivalent). Preheat oven to 350 degrees; bake for only 20 minutes. The trick of making these brownies is not to overcook them. Take out of oven while they are still gooey. Cool slightly; cut into squares. When cold roll in powdered sugar. Should make around 24 squares, or more if small squares are cut.

Mrs. W. S. Chandler, Burlington, N.C.

BENNE SEED COOKIES
Two and a half dozen

The benné seeds which flavor these cookies so delightfully are not available in many sections. They are associated particularly with Charleston and the surrounding areas. These two recipes are from Mt. Pleasant, South Carolina.

¾ cup butter
1½ cups brown sugar
2 eggs
1¼ cups flour

½ cup benné seed, toasted
1 teaspoon vanilla
¼ teaspoon baking powder

Cream butter and sugar together and mix with other ingredients in the order given. Drop with a teaspoon into pan, far enough apart to allow for spreading. Bake in moderate oven, 350 degrees, for 12 to 15 minutes.

Mrs. R. G. Porcher, from Mt. Pleasant's Famous Recipes, *Mt. Pleasant, S.C.*

BENNE ICEBOX COOKIES
Three dozen

½ cup butter or margarine
1 cup sugar
1 egg, well beaten
½ teaspoon vanilla

¼ teaspoon salt
2 cups flour
¼ cup milk
¾ cup benné seed, toasted

Cream together shortening and sugar; add well-beaten egg, vanilla. Sift salt and flour together and add alternately with milk to sugar mixture. Stir in the benné gradually. Roll into cylindrical shape and place in icebox until chilled, or for as long as desired. Slice thin and bake on greased cookie sheet in a 375-degree oven for 12 minutes.

Mrs. Ferdinand Gregorie, from Mt. Pleasant's Famous Recipes,
Mt. Pleasant, S.C.

EDENTON TEA PARTY CAKES
Five to six dozen

Edenton Tea Party Cakes are said to have first been served on October 25, 1774, when a group of indignant Edenton, North Carolina, ladies met at the house of Elizabeth King, under the leadership of Penelope Barker, to express disapproval of the British tax on tea by pledging themselves to abstain from using tea. This recipe, given to Mrs. Don Scott, is a copy of the original cake as it is still served in Edenton.

¾ cup butter
2 large cups brown sugar
3 eggs
1 teaspoon soda, dissolved in little
    hot water

½ teaspoon salt
1 teaspoon vanilla
4 cups flour

Cream butter, sugar, and eggs together; add the soda which has been dissolved in a small amount of hot water. Add salt and vanilla, then enough of the flour to make a stiff dough. Roll out thin; cut into shapes, and bake in hot oven, 400 degrees, for about 12 minutes. [This recipe, which is widely known, is sometimes varied by using ½ butter with ½ lard. Either way is good.—M. B.]

Contributed by Mrs. Don E. Scott, Graham, N.C.

ICEBOX CUP CAKES
Three dozen

½ cup butter, or margarine
1½ squares chocolate (1 oz. square)
1 cup sugar
⅔ cup flour
1 teaspoon vanilla

2 eggs, well beaten
1 cup chopped pecans
36 small paper cup cake liners (about 1½ inches in diameter)
Icing (see recipes)

In top of a double boiler, melt the butter and chocolate. Mix together the sugar, flour, vanilla, eggs, and nuts; add to the chocolate mixture. With a teaspoon fill the little paper cups half full of batter. Set them on a baking sheet and bake for 12 minutes at 350 degrees. Do not bake any longer. Ice the cakes. Keep them in the refrigerator until ready to be served. Freeze them in plastic and serve cold.

Frosting

2 tablespoons butter, or margarine
1 1-oz. square chocolate
¾ lb. box of confectioners sugar

3 to 4 tablespoons strong cold coffee

Melt the butter and chocolate in top of double boiler; add sugar gradually and beat. Stir in just enough coffee to make a stiff mixture. Ice the cakes while they are still hot. Refrigerate.

LITTLE TWO-EGG MUFFIN LEMON CAKES
Sixteen muffins

This little cake is served hot or cold.

2 eggs, beaten separately
1 cup sugar
½ cup milk

1⅔ cups flour
2 teaspoons baking powder
1 teaspoon lemon extract

Beat egg yolks with sugar; add milk and flour sifted with baking powder; fold in egg whites beaten stiffly, and flavoring. Bake quickly in little muffin tins at 400 degrees for about 12 minutes.

From The Louisiana Plantation Cook Book,
by Mrs. James E. Smitherman, Shreveport, La.

MEXICAN BRIDAL CAKES
Sixty

In Mexico no wedding reception is considered proper unless these little pecan rolls are included among the refreshments. Often called Pecan Fingers, Pecan Rolls, or Nutty Fingers, the recipe is basically the same. This has unusual richness and flavor.

1¾ sticks butter
4 tablespoons powdered sugar
1 teaspoon water
2 teaspoons vanilla

2½ cups flour
2 cups pecan halves
Extra powdered sugar

Cream butter; add sugar, water, and vanilla. Cream well; add flour and knead until dough is light and foamy. Place a small round of the dough in the palm of left hand and press out flat. Place 2 halves of pecan meats together and lay in center of dough. Roll dough around nuts encasing them in a finger shaped covering. Place on cookie sheet and bake in 350-degree oven until light brown, about 20 minutes. Remove and roll in powdered sugar. When cool, store in tins; will keep indefinitely.

Mrs. John Rich Ireland, Burlington, N.C.

KING'S ARMS TAVERN PECAN CONFECTIONS (*Successor to Travis House*)
Two dozen

One of the most widely known Southern cookies is this little nut-egg-white confection.

1 egg white, beaten stiff
1 cup brown sugar
1 pinch salt

1 level tablespoon flour
1 cup chopped pecans

Beat egg white to a stiff froth; add gradually the sugar, salt, and flour. Stir in the nuts. Drop on greased tins by spoonfuls far apart. Bake in a very slow oven for 15 minutes. (300–325 degrees.) Remove from tin when partly cooled.

From The King's Arms Tavern, Williamsburg, Va. Special permission, John D. Green, Vice-President, Williamsburg Restoration, Inc.

HERMITS
Thirty to thirty-six

⅔ cup butter
1 cup brown sugar
2 eggs
¼ teaspoon soda
2 tablespoons sour cream
1¾ cups flour, sifted

¼ teaspoon nutmeg
2 teaspoons cinnamon
¼ teaspoon cloves
1 cup nuts
½ cup raisins, or chopped dates
½ cup citron, chopped

Cream butter and sugar. Add eggs, soda dissolved in cream, flour, and spices. Lastly add nuts, raisins or dates, and the ½ cup chopped citron. Drop from a tablespoon onto a well greased pan. Bake in moderate, 375-degree oven until brown—15 to 18 minutes. While still hot, glaze each cookie with vanilla glaze. This is another Christmas gift box favorite.

ROCKS
Three dozen

This is an old, old favorite cookie. Extra nuts or fruits are sometimes added. Each recipe varies slightly; this one seems to include the essentials.

1 cup butter
1¾ cups brown sugar
3 eggs, beaten
½ teaspoon cinnamon
1 teaspoon mace
1 teaspoon nutmeg
1 teaspoon allspice
1¼ cups chopped pecan meats

1 teaspoon vanilla
½ teaspoon rosewater extract
2 tablespoons strong coffee, cool
2 cups raisins, chopped, floured
    with light coating
2 ¾ cups flour
1 teaspoon soda

Cream the butter and sugar; add the beaten eggs, then spices, nuts, flavorings, and the floured raisins; add flour sifted with soda. Mix the dough which should be very stiff. Place by teaspoonfuls on a buttered tin and bake in moderate (350 degrees) oven until slightly browned, about 12 to 15 minutes. If the dough is not stiff enough, add a little flour.

Mrs. T. Perry Chase, Richmond, Va.

SHORT'NIN' BREAD
About three dozen 2″ × 2″ squares

4 cups flour
1 cup light brown sugar

2 cups butter

Mix flour and sugar. Add butter. Place on floured surface and pat to ½ inch thickness. Cut into desired shapes and bake in moderate oven (325–350 degrees) for 20 to 25 minutes.

PECAN MACAROONS
Four dozen

4 egg whites
2 cups sugar
1 teaspoon vinegar

1 teaspoon vanilla
2 cups pecan meats, chopped

Set egg whites and sugar on back of stove (very low heat or just warm surface) to melt, stirring occasionally until melted; then add vinegar and vanilla. Whip until quite stiff; add pecans; then drop by teaspoons on well-greased tins. (Bake in slow oven, 325 degrees, for 15 minutes.)

From The Galveston Souvenir Cook Book, *Galveston, Tex.*

ALMOND MACAROONS
Two dozen

½ lb. sweet almonds, powdered
2 egg whites

1 level cup powdered sugar

Pour boiling water over the almonds to take off the brown skin; then put them in the oven to dry; when cold, pound them to paste. Beat up the eggs and sugar to a stiff froth and add them to the almond paste, mixing them thoroughly with the back of a spoon. Roll the preparation in your hands in little balls the size of a nutmeg, and place them on a piece of white paper an inch apart. Bake them in a cool oven (300–325 degrees) until a light brown, about 12 minutes.

MRS. REID'S SNOW BALLS (*Angel Food Cake*)
About four dozen

1 cup egg whites
¼ teaspoon salt
1 teaspoon cream of tartar
1½ cups sugar

1 cup cake flour sifted 5 times
¼ teaspoon vanilla flavoring
¼ teaspoon almond flavoring
Grated coconut

Add salt to the egg whites. Beat until foamy; then add cream of tartar and beat until stiff. Add sugar, 1 heaping tablespoon at a time, beating at least 20 strokes after each addition. Fold in flour 1 tablespoon at a time. Add flavoring. Pour into an Angel Cake pan which has been rinsed but not greased. Bake 1 hour; the first half of baking time should be at 275 degrees; the second half at

325 degrees. Remove from oven; turn pan containing cake upside down and let stand 1 hour before removing from pan. Take cake from pan and rub off the brown crust. Break off pieces the size of a walnut. Cover lightly with a boiled icing and roll in freshly-grated coconut.

Icing

1 cup sugar	1 egg white
½ cup boiling water	1 tablespoon sugar
⅛ teaspoon cream of tartar	1 teaspoon fresh lemon juice

To sugar add boiling water and cream of tartar. Boil until syrup spins a thread. Then pour the syrup slowly over the egg white which has been stiffly beaten with 1 tablespoon sugar. Add lemon juice.

Mrs. R. M. Reid, Burlington, N.C.

MRS. MURRAY'S ROLLED WAFERS, OR "CALLA LILY" WAFERS

Twenty-eight wafers

One of the most delicate and temperamental little "tea party" confections is this old-fashioned rolled wafer. It should be made only on dry clear days because the humidity affects the rolling. Mrs. Murray says that patience, and careful following of directions are necessary for the success of these wafers.

¼ cup butter	⅞ cup Red Band bread flour,
½ cup powdered sugar, sifted before measuring	sifted before measuring
	½ teaspoon vanilla
¼ cup milk	

Cream the butter well; add the sugar very gradually creaming as you add. When mixture is thoroughly smooth, add the milk—*drop* by *drop* alternating with the flour. Add the vanilla. When mixture is ready to bake, it should be of the consistency of a thick paste (not a batter—it is called a paste or mixture). Have ready a *cool* slightly buttered baking sheet. With a spatula spread the paste very, very thinly over the entire surface of the baking sheet. Place in a moderate (300 degrees or slightly hotter) oven and bake until only delicately browned. You may have to turn the pan several times to see that paste is browning evenly. When done, take out and set on back of stove. With a sharp knife cut into 3 × 3- or 4 × 4-inch squares, cutting through, leaving clean-cut edges.

With the sharp point of a knife, lift out each square and quickly roll it into desired forms; if a calla lily is to be made, roll in cone shape, overlapping the corners to hold form. For a little cylindrical roll, roll evenly, leaving center large enough to hold filling. If the squares become hard and brittle, return baking sheet to oven and the cakes will soften enough to be rolled. When baked, store in boxes covered with waxed paper and set in a cool, dry place. Dampness will cause them to become soft.

To Fill

Powdered sugar	Vanilla, or any flavoring
Cream	Little butter, if desired

Use sugar and other ingredients according to the number of cakes and amount you wish for each. Cream the sugar with enough cream (and butter if used) to make a stiff paste, add flavoring. To make the center for calla lily, tint a delicate yellow, or leave white. Roll into little cylinders and stick down into the center of cake. I once made these little cakes for a graduation party. Each was rolled to resemble a diploma, filled with filling to symbolize class colors and tied with matching ribbon. You may vary your icing according to the seasons; green and red for Christmas, etc.

Mrs. H. V. Murray, Burlington, N.C.

DARK SECRETS
Two dozen

A cookie of the Deep South.

1 cup sugar	Vanilla
3 eggs	5 to 5½ tablespoons flour
2 tablespoons butter, melted	1 teaspoon baking powder
1 cup chopped dates	¼ teaspoon salt
1 cup chopped pecans	

Mix the sugar with the unbeaten eggs; add melted butter; add dates, nuts, and vanilla. Sift together the flour, baking powder, and salt; add to egg mixture. Grease a shallow baking pan; spread cake mixture in. Bake in 325–350-degree oven until set, about 20 minutes, but do not bake too done as they should be chewy. Cut into squares or strips about 1 inch wide; roll in powdered sugar.

Mrs. David Battle Verner, Charleston, S.C.

BISHOP'S CAKE DEVEREUX
One 9½" × 5½" × 2¾" loaf pan

3 eggs, well beaten	1½ teaspoons baking soda
1 cup granulated sugar	¼ teaspoon salt
1½ cups sifted all-purpose flour	¼ lb. semi-sweet chocolate

2 cups coarsely chopped walnuts meats

1 cup coarsely cut-up dates
1 cup halved candied cherries

Combine eggs and sugar; beat well. Sift dry ingredients together. Cut chocolate into size of lima beans. Add with nuts and fruits to flour mixture. Fold into egg mixture. Pour into 9½″ × 5½″ × 2¾″ greased loaf pan with bottom lined with waxed paper. Bake 1½ hours in moderate oven (325 degrees). Cut; serve like fruit cake.

From Recipes Tested and Tried, *by Anne Young White and Nola Nance Oliver, Natchez, Miss.*

OATMEAL SPICED COOKIES
Two and a half dozen

1 egg
½ cup sugar
3 tablespoons milk
1 cup dry rolled oats
1 cup pastry flour
1 teaspoon cinnamon
½ teaspoon nutmeg

⅛ teaspoon soda
½ teaspoon baking powder
½ cup butter, melted
½ cup nut meats
½ cup raisins
2 tablespoons grated coconut
¼ cup chopped dates

Beat egg, add sugar and milk, mix well, then add rolled oats. Mix spices, soda, and baking powder and sift flour into first mixture. Melt the butter and add; then add the remaining ingredients. Stir until well mixed. Drop by teaspoonfuls on greased baking sheet. Bake at 375 degrees for 15 minutes.

Mrs. Claude Vaughan, from The Pee Dee Pepper Pot, *Darlington, S.C.*

RUTH ALDRIDGE'S CHOCOLATE CUP CAKES
Twenty-eight

One of the richest and best cup cakes.

½ cup butter
1½ cups sugar
2 cups flour
1 teaspoon soda
½ cup sweet milk

3 eggs, beaten
½ cup grated chocolate
½ cup sweet milk, extra
1 teaspoon vanilla
1 teaspoon lemon extract

Cream butter and sugar together; sift flour and soda and add alternately with the milk to butter-sugar mixture. Add beaten eggs. Melt the chocolate with the ½ cup extra sweet milk in top of double boiler. Cool chocolate mixture; then add to the batter. Add flavorings last. Pour into greased muffin rings, using about 1 tablespoon plus 1 teaspoon of batter to each ring. Bake in 375-degree oven until straw comes out clean. Ice with the following rich fudge icing:

2 cups sugar
2 squares chocolate
2 tablespoons cornstarch

1 tablespoon butter
⅔ cup evaporated milk
1 teaspoon vanilla

Cook until mixture thickens and forms soft ball in cold water. Beat until creamy and spread top and sides of cakes. Will not take all the icing unless very generously used.

Miss Ruth Aldridge, Burlington, N.C.

CANDIED FRUIT COOKIES
One 9½″ × 5½″ × 2¾″ loaf pan

Will keep for months like fruit cake.

3 eggs, well beaten
1 cup granulated sugar
1½ cups sifted all-purpose flour
1½ teaspoons baking powder

¼ teaspoon salt
2 cups chopped pecans
1 cup coarsely chopped dates
1 cup halved candied cherries

Combine eggs and sugar; beat well. Sift dry ingredients together. Add nuts and fruits to flour mixture. Fold into egg mixture. Pour into 9½″ × 5½″ × 2¾″ greased loaf pan with bottom lined with heavy brown paper. Bake 1½ hours in a moderate, 325-degree oven. Let cool and slice as needed for cookies.

Mrs. Frank M. De Friese, Knoxville, Tenn.

ALMOND-OATMEAL COOKIES
About three dozen

½ cup butter
1 cup sugar
1 egg, well beaten
1¾ cups rolled oats
½ cup blanched almonds, chopped
½ cup raisins, chopped

1½ cups flour
2 teaspoons baking powder
½ teaspoon each of salt, pow- dered cloves, and allspice
¾ teaspoon powdered cinnamon
⅓ cup milk
Halved almonds

Cream the butter; add the sugar slowly and cream. Add the well-beaten egg, rolled oats, chopped almonds, and raisins.

Mix together the dry ingredients. Add the dry ingredients alternately with the milk to the butter-egg mixture. Drop by teaspoons on a well-greased cookie sheet. Press half of an almond into the top of each cookie. Bake in a 350-degree oven for 15 to 20 minutes, or until browned nicely.

These store nicely and may be frozen in plastic bags.

Mrs. Penn Gant, Danville, Va.

NAPOLEONS

1 rectangle puff pastry, 8″ × 12″ × ¼″ (see Puff Pastry, p. 410)

French Pastry Cream (see recipe)
Icing or confectioners sugar

Prepare a baking sheet by lining it with 3 layers of brown paper. Preheat oven to 450 degrees.

Roll out the puff pastry as directed in basic recipe. Cut the ¼-inch thick dough into strips 1½ inches wide and the length of baking sheet. Lay the strips on the pan; prick the tops of the strips generously with a fork. Chill the dough for 1½ hours. Bake for 8 minutes at 450 degrees. Reduce heat to 350 and bake about 9 minutes. Now place a cold baking sheet under the hot baking sheet and continue to bake another 9 minutes, or until puffed and just golden brown. Cool the strips on racks. When cool, cut them with a very sharp knife into 3-inch sections. Take two of the strips and spread French Pastry Cream between them, sandwich fashion. Continue until all strips have been used. Ice them with any cake icing, or sprinkle them with confectioners sugar. Allow 1 Napoleon per serving.

French Pastry Cream

½ cup sugar
4 tablespoons cornstarch
⅛ teaspoon salt
2 cups whole milk

4 large egg yolks
2 teaspoons vanilla, almond, lemon or orange extract

Combine the sugar, cornstarch, salt, and ¼ cup of the milk in the top of a double boiler. Mix well. Heat 1½ cups of the milk, and gradually stir it into the first mixture; cook, stirring constantly. Stir and cook over boiling water until the mixture is very thick. Beat the egg yolks and blend with the remaining ¼ cup of milk; add the eggs to the cooked sauce. Continue cooking and stirring over hot water until the cream is thick like mayonnaise. Remove from heat and stir in the flavoring. Cool thoroughly before spreading on the Napoleons. Stir the custard occasionally to prevent top from crusting. Makes about 2 cups.

Mrs. Norman Riddle, Bluefield, W. Va.

15. Pies and Pastry

WILLIAMSBURG INN SOUTHERN PECAN PIE
Serves eight *

The Pecan Pie is the South's most popular pie, widely varied in ingredients. I am very grateful for this famous recipe.

Pie Crust

¼ teaspoon salt
1½ cups flour

½ cup Crisco
¼ cup ice cold water

Add Crisco to flour and salt, and mix thoroughly with a fork. Add the ice water and blend well. Roll and place in pie pan.

Pecan Filling

3 eggs
1 lb. light brown sugar
¼ cup butter, melted

Pinch salt
1 teaspoon vanilla
1 cup pecans, chopped

Stir eggs lightly. Beat in slowly the sugar and melted butter. Add salt and vanilla. Line pie plate with pastry and sprinkle ½ of the pecans over the bottom. Pour mixture into the unbaked pie shell. Sprinkle remaining pecans over the top of the mixture. Bake in 350-degree oven for 40 minutes, or until the pie is almost set. Reduce the heat to 225 degrees and cook for 15 minutes, or until the pie is thoroughly set. Makes one pie.

From Williamsburg Inn. Special permission by John D. Green, Vice-President, Williamsburg Restoration, Inc., Williamsburg, Va.

* Unless otherwise noted, all pies will serve 6 to 8 persons.

MRS. MOORE'S CHESS PIE

This "just about perfect" Chess Pie appeared in the first edition of the Burlington Episcopal Church's *Soup to Nuts* some years ago, and by popular demand in the revised 1947 edition.

1 cup brown sugar
½ cup white sugar
1 teaspoon flour
2 eggs, unbeaten

½ eggshell milk
1 teaspoon vanilla
½ cup melted butter

Mix together the white and brown sugar and flour. Break the 2 eggs into mixture; add milk and vanilla. Melt butter and pour in last. Bake in slow (325-degree) oven in uncooked pastry shell. If baked around 30 to 35 minutes, it is better than if cooked fast. When done it will look puffed and yellow; when cooled it falls into rich jelly-like consistency. [This mixture makes delicious little tarts. Put tablespoon in each uncooked pastry shell, bake as above. Serve with whipped cream.—M. B.]

Mrs. S. I. Moore, Burlington, N.C.

CHOCOLATE CHESS PIE

Add 1½ squares of baking chocolate to Mrs. Moore's chess pie recipe. Melt the chocolate with butter and add as final ingredient.

Mrs. Marvin Uteg, Siler City, N.C.

LEMON CHESS PIES

Substitute the ½ eggshell of milk in Mrs. Moore's pie with same amount of fresh lemon juice. Or:

Use four eggs instead of two as used in Mrs. Moore's original recipe, and add four tablespoons of lemon juice.

Mrs. Dover Moore, Graham, N.C.

MRS. BROOKS'S CHESS PIES
About forty

Each Christmas Mrs. Brooks makes dozens of delectable little Chess Pies for the family and her friends. They are paper thin and stacked one in the other like saucers. This is her cherished family recipe.

2 cups butter
3 cups sugar
12 egg yolks, well beaten

2 teaspoons grated nutmeg
Rich pastry made with ½ butter,
   ½ lard (see below)

Cream butter and sugar together; add well-beaten egg yolks and nutmeg. Line little muffin or cake rings with pastry; bake at 400 degrees until slightly brown, about 12 minutes. (Put about 1 tablespoon of filling in each shell. When cooked the custard seems like rich cake.)

Pastry

2 cups flour
½ cup Crisco
½ cup butter
⅛ teaspoon salt

Cold water to mix
Well-greased and floured pie pans
   (heavy pans if available)

Pour flour into a mixing bowl; cut in the Crisco and butter. Add the salt and enough cold water to make a stiff dough. Roll out thin on a floured board. Line little (individual) pie pans with the pastry; trim the edges and prick with fork in several places. Bake in a preheated 400-degree oven.

Mrs. E. C. Brooks, Raleigh, N.C.

GLENWOOD PLANTATION SHERRY PIE

Gertrude Munson's delectable pies are among the favorite Glenwood Plantation House desserts. The following are from her personal files.

Sherry
Macaroons
⅔ cup sugar
1 tablespoon flour
Pinch salt

¾ cup sherry
4 egg yolks
4 egg whites, stiffly beaten
Whipped cream
Almonds

Line the bottom and sides of a pie plate with macaroons which have been soaked in sherry. In a double boiler, cook the sugar, flour, salt, ¾ cup sherry, and egg yolks. Remove from heat. When the mixture cools, fold in the stiffly beaten egg whites. Pour over pie shell. Spread with whipped cream and garnish with almonds. Cool in refrigerator before serving.

GLENWOOD COCONUT PIE
Two pies

An unusual feature of this pie is that the coconut is grated with the inner brown "skin" left on, giving a nutty flavor and texture—and think of the time saved!

1 large coconut, grated without removing outer dark rind

1 cup liquid (milk from the coconut with enough water added to fill cup)

3 cups sugar

Crust

3 cups flour
3 tablespoons lard
3 tablespoons butter

¾ cup milk
1 teaspoon baking powder

Cook coconut, liquid, and sugar over slow fire for 30 minutes; make up the pie crust, and line 2 open-faced pans with the pastry. (The dough is very stiff and when baked makes a nutty crust.)

Pour cooked coconut mixture into the unbaked crusts and bake in moderate oven (375 degrees) until brown.

Mrs. Edward P. Munson, Glenwood Plantation House, Napoleonville, La.

ORTON PLANTATION COCONUT AND ORANGE PIES

Coconut Pie

Two pies

1 grated fresh coconut
6 eggs
2 cups sugar

Small lump butter (optional)
Pastry

Beat eggs well together with sugar and butter (if used). Add coconut. Pour in uncooked pie shells and bake until done, about 30 minutes at 350 degrees.

Orange Pie

1 cup sugar
1 tablespoon butter, melted
Juice and grated rind of 1 orange

3 eggs, blended but not beaten
Pastry

Add all ingredients to well-blended eggs. Place in uncooked pie shell and bake at 350 degrees for 30 minutes.

[In Mrs. Sprunt's original recipe there was no butter, which is an old-fashioned method of making coconut pie. We added butter because some think it adds flavor to the pie. The Orange Pie is often made with no butter. Neither pie has extra flavoring. They need none.—M. B.]

Mrs. J. Laurence Sprunt, Orton Plantation, Wilmington, N.C.

LEMON MERINGUE PIE

4 tablespoons cornstarch
4 tablespoons flour
1½ cups sugar
2 cups boiling water
2 teaspoons butter

4 egg yolks
2 grated lemon rinds
6 tablespoons lemon juice
4 egg whites
4 to 8 tablespoons sugar

Mix cornstarch, flour, and sugar, and add boiling water, stirring constantly. Cook 10 minutes slowly. Add butter, egg yolks, rind, and juice of lemon. Cook 2 or 3 minutes. When cool, pour into baked shell. Beat egg whites dry and stiff; add sugar to whites and spread on pie. Bake until meringue is golden brown, about 15 minutes at 350 degrees.

Mrs. W. H. Crenshaw, from The Belmont Book of Recipes, *Belmont, N.C.*

OLD-FASHIONED LEMON JELLY PIE

3 eggs, slightly beaten
1 cup sugar
2 tablespoons butter, melted

Juice of 2 lemons, grated rind of 1 lemon, or 1 cup bottled lemon juice

Beat eggs slightly, enough to blend yolks and whites; add sugar, lemon juice, and rind; add butter last. Pour into unbaked pie shell and bake in 350-degree oven until filling sets (about 30 minutes) and crust is delicately browned. Let cool; the filling will "congeal" like jelly. Serve each slice topped with a scoop of vanilla ice cream—a delicious pie à la mode.

Mrs. John Rich Ireland, Burlington, N.C.

MARY ALLISON'S LEMON TARTS
One dozen

½ cup butter
1 cup sugar
Pinch salt
3 lemons, juice of all, grated rind
   of 2

3 eggs, beaten separately
12 unbaked tart shells

Cream butter, sugar, and salt. Add the juice of the 3 lemons and grated rind of 2 (grate before squeezing). Add the egg yolks and fold in the stiffly beaten egg whites. Pour into unbaked pastry tart shells and bake until set. (Moderate 350-degree oven.)

Mrs. William Allison, Statesville, N.C.

OLD-FASHIONED LEMON-CAKE PIE

In this one has his cake and pie, because it looks like a two-layered pie.

1 cup sugar
1 tablespoon butter
3 tablespoons flour
⅛ teaspoon salt
2 egg yolks, beaten

Juice and grated rind of 2 lemons
1½ cups milk
2 egg whites, beaten
1 unbaked 9-inch pie shell (see
    Rich Pastry)

Cream together the sugar, butter, flour, and salt in a mixing bowl. Add the beaten egg yolks, lemon juice, and grated rinds; stir and add the milk; blend. Fold in the beaten egg whites. Pour the mixture into an unbaked pie shell. Bake forty minutes at 325 degrees, or until a knife inserted in the center comes out clean.

Bert Laws, Pittsburgh, Pa.

"MAYFLOWER" DEEP DISH APPLE PIE
Serves eight

This recipe is said to have "come over in the celebrated ship in the year 1620."

Rich pie crust for deep dish, with
    top crust
1 cup sugar
Tart apples to fill dish, about 3
    cups

½ teaspoon nutmeg
Dash cinnamon
1 tablespoon lemon juice
Handful of chopped citron
¼ lb. butter

Collect and measure ingredients; peel and slice apples very thin, removing cores and seeds—about 3 cups of tart apples. (Eating apples do not make a good pie.) Roll out bottom crust and line in earthen dish neatly. Spread ½ cup of the sugar evenly over the bottom. Arrange sliced apples in the dish, piling them as high as possible to make a pie rich in filling. Sprinkle remaining ½ cup of sugar over the apples, adding the nutmeg, a dash of cinnamon, lemon juice, and finely chopped citron and butter cut into bits. Roll out top crust, making a slit in opening to allow steam to escape. Wet edges of under crust together. Pie is ruined if juices escape. Place in a hot oven (400 degrees) to brown quickly; cover or turn pan over it; reduce the heat to 300 degrees and cook slowly for an hour. When the pie is baked, its apples will be tender, translucent, and juice will be like jelly. A shallow glass dish or earthen casserole with a cover can be used if you haven't an earthen dish.

This recipe came from a Mrs. Brown, whose grandmother was fifth in descent from William Bradford.

Miss Miltie L. McCusker, from St. Anne's Parish Recipe Book, *Annapolis, Md.*

CHEESE CRUST FOR DEEP DISH APPLE PIE
Two nine-inch crusts

Here is a good Cheese Crust for the Mayflower pie or any other apple pie.

2 cups flour
½ teaspoon salt
Dash cayenne pepper, optional
½ cup lard, or ¼ cup lard with
    ¼ cup butter

¼ lb. grated yellow cheese (about
    1 cup)
7 tablespoons ice water
Vegetable oil
Egg white

Sift dry ingredients and cut in shortening until mealy. Mix in the cheese lightly. Add the water gradually, making a stiff dough. (More or a little less water may be added.) Roll out on floured board; place in deep dish or pie pans. Brush inside crust with vegetable oil, very lightly, and top crust with oil or egg white. This makes crust crisp, and it browns nicely.

Mrs. M. J. Lea, Jamestown, N.C.

KEY LIME PIE

"There once was a lime from Key West
Who was used to take rust from a vest,
    Then he flavored a pie
      With merinque so-o-o-high
    And a daiquiri laid him to rest!"

4 egg yolks
½ cup sugar
½ cup lime juice
½ teaspoon salt
1 tablespoon gelatin softened in
    ½ cup cold water

2 tablespoons Angostura bitters
1 lime rind, grated fine
4 egg whites, stiffly beaten with
    ½ cup sugar
Whipped cream

Beat egg yolks. Add ½ of the sugar, and the lime juice and salt. Cook in double boiler until custard coats spoon. Remove from fire and add gelatin which has been soaked in ½ cup cold water. Add bitters and rind. Mix well until mixture begins to thicken. Fold in beaten egg whites to which the remaining ½ cup sugar has been added. Pour into baked pie crust. Spread with whipped cream just before serving.

From The Key West Cook Book, *Key West, Fla.*

FRESH PEACH PIE

8 large peaches, stewed (enough
    peaches to make 3 cups
    stewed)

¼ cup canned peach juice, or
    water
¾ cup sugar (or to taste)

1 teaspoon vanilla

2 tablespoons cornstarch dissolved in ¼ cup water

1 baked 9-inch pie shell (see Pastry, p. 412)

Whipped cream, sweetened and flavored to taste

Peel and cut up the peaches; place in a saucepan; add the peach juice and sugar. Simmer until the peaches are transparent. Stir in the vanilla and cornstarch mixture. Cook until peaches are thickened. Cool. Pour into a baked pie shell. Chill the pie. Serve whipped cream over the pie.

From the late Frank Bryant; contributed by Miss Martha S. Bailey, New York, N.Y.

CANTALOUPE PIE

1 baked pie crust

1 medium-size cantaloupe (ripe)

¾ cup sugar (more if necessary)

⅛ teaspoon salt

2 egg yolks, well beaten

2 tablespoons cornstarch, dissolved in ¼ cup water

1½ teaspoons vanilla extract

2 egg whites, beaten stiff

2 tablespoons sugar

Pinch cream of tartar

1 teaspoon grated orange rind

Scoop out the pulp of the cantaloupe; put into the top of a double boiler and cook over boiling water until pulp is soft; stir and mash pulp as it cooks. Remove from heat and add the sugar, using more if the cantaloupe is not sweet. Add the salt, egg yolks, and the corn starch mixture. Return to heat and cook over boiling water until custard is thick. Stir in the vanilla. Pour into the baked pie crust. Top with a meringue made by beating the egg whites stiff and gradually beating in the sugar and cream of tartar. Fold in the orange rind. Spread the meringue over the pie and bake in a preheated 350-degree oven until lightly browned. Serve cold.

Mrs. C. E. W. Davis, Topeka, Kansas, from How We Cook in El Paso, *El Paso, Tex.*

RUM BITTERSWEET PIE

This is a two-layer pie of chocolate and rum flavored layers.

16 gingersnaps, rolled fine

5 tablespoons butter, melted

1 cup sugar

1¼ tablespoons cornstarch

4 egg yolks, well beaten

2 cups milk, scalded

1½ 1-oz. squares unsweetened chocolate, melted

1 teaspoon vanilla

1 tablespoon unflavored gelatin

¼ cup cold water

4 egg whites

¼ teaspoon cream of tartar
2 tablespoons rum
1 cup heavy cream, whipped

2 tablespoons sugar
Grated bitter chocolate, optional

Roll the gingersnaps to fine crumbs; melt the butter. Line a 9-inch pie pan with the mixture and bake at 350 degrees for 10 minutes. Cool.

Mix ½ cup of sugar with the cornstarch; beat into the egg yolks. Gradually add the milk, stirring constantly. Pour mixture into top of a double boiler and cook over boiling water for 20 minutes, stirring constantly. To 1 cup of this custard, add the chocolate and vanilla; cool and pour into the pie crust and chill.

Soak the gelatin in water; stir it into the remaining hot custard; cool. Sprinkle the egg whites with the cream of tartar; beat until stiff. Gradually add the remaining ½ cup of sugar and beat well. Just before the gelatin-custard mixture sets, fold in the beaten egg mixture and rum. Spread it carefully over the chilled chocolate layer in pie pan. Chill the pie until set.

Top with whipped cream to which 2 tablespoons of sugar have been added. Sprinkle with grated bitter chocolate, if desired.

Mrs. Alex W. Terrell, The Junior League of Dallas Cook Book, *Dallas, Tex.*

CHOCOLATE CREAM PIE (*Similar to John Marshall Cream Pie*)

The recipe for the famous John Marshall Cream Pie is a closely guarded secret of the chef of the John Marshall Hotel. This recipe, given me by the manager, is similar; a luscious congealed cream pie with bitter chocolate grated on top.

1 tablespoon unflavored gelatin
¼ cup cold water
3 slightly beaten egg yolks
½ cup sugar
¼ tablespoon salt
1 cup milk, scalded

1 teaspoon vanilla
3 stiffly beaten egg whites
1 cup heavy cream, whipped
Shredded bitter chocolate
1 baked pie shell

Soften gelatin in water. Combine egg yolks, sugar, and salt; slowly add milk. Cook in double boiler until mixture coats a spoon. Add softened gelatin; stir until dissolved. Cool; add vanilla, and fold in egg whites and the whipped cream. Pour into a deep baked pastry pie shell (2½ to 3 inches deep); sprinkle top thickly with grated bitter chocolate. Set in refrigerator until congealed. Serve as any other pie. [To make an Almond Pie of this, add ½ cup of shredded blanched almonds to custard mixture; sprinkle top with shredded almonds or chocolate.—M. B.]

William W. Hitchens, Manager, The John Marshall Hotel, Richmond, Va.

COLLEGE INN PUMPKIN HOLIDAY PIE
Two pies

This College Inn creation, a pie with layers of spiced pumpkin custard and mincemeat, combines the two traditional Thanksgiving pies.

Pumpkin Custard

Mix thoroughly in the following order:

2 cups sugar ⎱
4 eggs ⎰ Cream together

Then add:

4 cups custard pumpkin, canned
1 teaspoon salt
2 teaspoons cinnamon

2 teaspoons allspice
3 cups milk

Mincemeat Base Filling

Mix ¾ lb. prepared mincemeat with 8 ozs. chopped tart apples (about 1 to 1½ cups).

Line 2 9-inch pie pans with your favorite crust. Build sides up as high as possible; crimp around edges. Spread ½ of the mincemeat filling in each pie shell. Then pour pumpkin custard on top. Bake in 350-degree oven for approximately 45 minutes. This results in a 2-layer pie of unusual taste.

Ernest Coker, Owner, Ye Old College Inn, Houston, Tex.

MRS. FITZHUGH LEE'S MINCEMEAT FOR PIES
About twelve pounds

From an old cook book which bears no identifications as to author, title, or date, is this recipe by Mrs. Fitzhugh Lee:

"The wife of Gov. Fitzhugh Lee, of Virginia, is a famous housekeeper, and this is how she says she makes the mincemeat for her Thanksgiving Pies:

2 lbs. beef
2 lbs. currants
2 lbs. raisins
1 lb. citron
2 lbs. beef suet

1¼ lbs. candied lemon peel
4 lbs. apples
2 lbs. Sultana raisins
2 lbs. sugar
2 nutmegs, grated

¼ oz. cloves
½ oz. cinnamon
¼ oz. mace

1 teaspoon salt
2 lemons, juice and rind (grated)
2 oranges, juice and rind (grated)

"Simmer the meat gently until tender, and when perfectly cold chop it fine. Stone the raisins, shred the citron, pare, core and chop the apples, chop the suet fine. Mix the dry ingredients, then add the juice and rinds of oranges and lemons. Pack in a stone jar, cover close, and keep cool. This mincemeat will keep all winter. The rule is an old one and said to have come from the Custis family in the beginning. According to Virginia tradition, the Widow Custis who became Mrs. Washington, made famous mince pies."

Book owned by Mrs. Norman Riddle, Burlington, N.C.

MRS. HOLDER'S ANGEL STRAWBERRY PIE

4 egg whites
1 cup sugar
¼ teaspoon salt

½ teaspoon baking powder
1 qt. strawberries
1½ qts. whipping cream

Beat egg whites until stiff, but not dry; add sugar, baking powder, and salt gradually, beating after each addition. Pile into buttered pyrex pie pan and bake in 250-degree oven for 1½ hours. When cool, place drained strawberries in pie shell; cover with cream which has been sweetened and whipped. Other fillings might be coconut, lemon, orange, etc.

Mrs. Robert M. Holder, Atlanta, Ga.

GREENGAGE PIE

This is a famous old pie which has been in Mrs. Boren's family for generations.

1 unbaked (9-inch) pie shell
Greengage plums (canned) to
    cover bottom of pie shell
Finely chopped pieces of citron
1 cup butter

1 cup sugar
Yolks of 8 eggs, beaten
Whites of 4 eggs, beaten
3 drops of bitter almond extract

Prepare the pie shell by spreading with drained plums and citron.

Cream the butter and sugar; add the beaten egg yolks. Fold in the egg whites. Add the *bitter* almond extract. Pour the sugar-egg mixture over the greengages and citron. Bake in a preheated 350-degree oven until the custard is set, around 30 to 35 minutes. Serve cold.

Mrs. Mollie M. Boren, Greensboro, N.C.

MOTHER'S SWEET 'TATER CUSTARD PIE WITH PECAN TOPPING

1 cup boiled riced sweet potatoes
1 cup sugar
2 eggs, beaten
2 tablespoons milk
1 tablespoon sifted flour
Dash of salt

¼ teaspoon ground nutmeg, or more if desired
1 unbaked pie shell
½ cup light brown sugar
½ cup melted butter
1 cup broken pecan meats

Mix the riced sweet potatoes, sugar, and eggs; add the milk, flour, salt, and nutmeg; blend. Pour into pie shell. Bake in a 325-degree oven until the custard is set (about 45 to 50 minutes). When pie has baked about 25 minutes, sprinkle the top with a mixture made of the brown sugar, butter, and pecans; continue baking. This makes a rich topping.

The basic recipe for this is an old "Chess pie" family recipe. To make the Chess pie, leave out the sweet potatoes, the brown sugar, and melted butter topping. The nuts may be added if desired. Bake 35 minutes.

Mrs. John O. Farish, Franklinton, N.C.

STRAWBERRY-CHEESE TARTS
About thirty

1 cup grated cheese
1 stick butter, softened
2 cups flour

⅛ teaspoon salt
⅛ teaspoon cayenne pepper
Strawberry preserves

Mix all ingredients except preserves (no liquid is used). Roll and cut into squares about 2 inches square. Place in center of each square 1 teaspoon of strawberry preserves or jam and fold over at corners. Bake at 375 degrees until slightly brown on top. These are delightful tea accessories or may be filled with anchovies, caviar, tuna fish, meat paste, and served as appetizers.

Mrs. W. Clary Holt, from Soup to Nuts, *Burlington, N.C.*

MUERBE TEIG (*Fruit Pie Crust*)

Muerbe Teig is a German type pie crust which makes a flaky and crusty pie. It is very popular in West Virginia and other sections of the South. This crust is particularly adapted to fruit pies as it does not absorb moisture.

The Crust

¼ cup butter
1 tablespoon sugar
1 egg yolk

Salt
1 cup flour

Cream butter and sugar; add egg yolk, a little salt and flour. Pat and press the dough ¼ inch into greased pan. Place in refrigerator overnight. Then fill with any desired fruit mixture and bake.

Apple Fruit Mixture

4 or 5 apples, peeled, cored and
sliced
Sugar

Cinnamon
1 egg yolk
3 tablespoons cream

Lay apples in rows on top of the dough and sprinkle generously with sugar and cinnamon. Beat the egg yolk and add to it the cream; drip mixture around apples. Bake 20 or 30 minutes in hot oven, or until crust is well baked and apples are soft.

VARIATIONS:

Strawberries: 1 qt., 2 eggs, 1 cup sugar
Blueberries: 1 qt., 2 eggs, 3 tablespoons cream, ½ cup sugar
Plums: 1 qt., 3 eggs, 1½ cups sugar
Cherries: Large can, unsweetened, 2 eggs, 1 cup sugar
Peaches: 1 qt., pared, sliced, 1 egg yolk, 1 cup sugar

Mrs. Werner Yunker, from What's Dat Cookin'?, *Point Pleasant, W.Va.*

MRS. HARDY'S TEXAS PUDDING PIE (*Custard Pie*)
Two pies

This is a very old recipe for pies.

5 eggs
3 cups sugar
1½ tablespoons flour

1 cup butter
1 cup sweet milk
2 tablespoons lemon extract

Beat eggs together until light; add sugar, flour, butter, sweet milk, and lemon extract.

Bake on rich pastry in 2 pie plates in moderate oven (350 degrees), until custard is set, about 35 minutes.

Mrs. C. H. Hardy, Blackstone, Va.

SOUR CREAM PIE

This old-fashioned Southern pie has been in the McCue family for generations. It was originated in the mountains of Virginia as a harvest-time dessert.

1 unbaked pie shell	½ tablespoon ground nutmeg
1 cup commercial sour cream	½ teaspoon salt
1 egg	1 tablespoon butter
½ tablespoon vinegar	¾ cup raisins

Prepare the pie shell. In a mixing bowl, mix remaining ingredients. Pour into the unbaked pie shell. Bake in a preheated 425-degree oven for 35 minutes.

Mrs. Albert McCue, Christchurch, Va.

COTTAGE CHEESE PIE

Phillips Russell says emphatically that this is *not* his recipe. He clipped it and sent it to me for this book. Strange as it sounds, it has a delicious flavor similar to cheese cake.

1 unbaked pie shell	½ cup light cream
3 eggs	2 cups cottage cheese, mashed with fork
½ cup sugar	
1 teaspoon grated lemon rind	2 tablespoons flour
⅛ teaspoon salt	1 tablespoon lemon juice

Beat eggs lightly; add sugar gradually and beat well. Pour in rest of ingredients and mix thoroughly. Pour the above into an unbaked pie crust.

Combine 2 tablespoons sugar with ½ teaspoon ground cinnamon and pour over the pie mixture. Bake 40 minutes in 350-degree oven.

Contributed by Phillips Russell, Chapel Hill, N.C.

"AUNT HATTIE'S" BUTTERMILK CUSTARD PIE
Two pies

"Aunt Hattie" Thomaslin was a native of Archdale, North Carolina. She made this old-fashioned custard years ago, passing the recipe along to later generations. The pie tastes very much like coconut custard pie.

½ cup butter, scant
1½ cups sugar
3 egg yolks
4 tablespoons flour

2 cups buttermilk
Vanilla, optional
3 egg whites, well-beaten
2 unbaked pastry shells

Cream butter, sugar, and egg yolks well. Add flour; beat. Add buttermilk and stir well. Add well-beaten egg whites; stir enough to mix. Bake in unbaked pastry shells at 350 degrees for 35 minutes, or until set.

Contributed by Mrs. David Milton Petty, Bethlehem, Pa.

PASTRY FOR TWO PIE CRUSTS

1½ cups flour
½ teaspoon baking powder
1 teaspoon salt

⅓ cup lard
¼ cup cold water

Sift dry ingredients together; cut lard into dry mixture; add water and handle lightly as possible. Roll thin. Makes 2 9-inch crusts.

Mrs. T. Curry Dedman, Sr., Beaumont Inn, Harrodsburg, Ky.

PUFF PASTRY

Puff Pastry (Puff Paste) is used for making patty shells, pastry horns for cream fillings, croissants, many dessert pie shells, etc. It is tedious to make, but worth the effort.

3 sticks of butter (¾ lb.)
3 cups sifted all-purpose flour, extra flour

¾ teaspoon salt
2 teaspoons lemon juice
⅔ cup ice water

Cut each stick of butter into three lengthwise sections. Flour a square of waxed paper lightly; lay the butter strips on the flour. Wrap and refrigerate.

Mix the 3 cups of flour and salt together in a mixing bowl. Combine the lemon juice and water and stir into the flour, using a circular motion. Mix the dough well, and knead it until it becomes smooth and satiny. Cover the dough, and let it rest for about 25 minutes. Roll out the dough on a well-floured board to about ¼-inch thick, making a rectangle about 8″ × 12″. On one-half of the dough place chilled butter strips side by side to within ½ inch of the edges. Fold the other half of the dough over the butter. Seal the edges with fingertips. Wrap in waxed paper and chill.

Bring the dough out of refrigerator and lay it on floured board. Quickly roll out the dough again to an 8″ × 12″ rectangle, ¼-inch thick. Fold both ends of the dough to the center of the rectangle, making sure edges and corners are even. Now fold the dough over in half to make it 4 layers thick. Again wrap in waxed paper and refrigerate. Repeat the same process of rolling to 8″ × 12″ rectangle, chilling for 30 minutes between each rolling. The last part of the process should end with a folded 4-layer section of dough. Wrap and chill it for at least 3 hours.

Finish the dough by using it according to directions given in individual recipes. This pastry keeps refrigerated for days and may be frozen.

NUTTY PIE CRUST
One crust

Use this for any pie filling.

1 cup flour	⅓ cup vegetable shortening
½ teaspoon salt	Ice water
½ cup nuts (pecans, walnuts, almonds, etc.), crushed fine	

Sift together the flour and salt; mix in nuts. Cut in the shortening and add just enough ice water to moisten dough. Roll out on a floured board. Fit into a 9-inch pie pan.

Mrs. Raleigh Allsbrook, North Bergen, N.J.

TO MAKE YOUR OWN PIE CRUST MIX
Ten Nine-Inch Crusts

5 lbs. flour	1½ lbs. shortening
2 tablespoons salt	

Put the flour into a large mixing bowl. Stir in the salt. Cut in the shortening with knives until a crumbly mixture is made. Store in a cannister and keep in a cool place or refrigerator. When ready to use, take out 2 cups of mix and stir in 4 tablespoons of ice water to make one pie crust. Roll out on floured board.

Betty Albertson, from Treasured Recipes, *by The Helen Freeman Guild, Miles Memorial Methodist Church, Norfolk, Va.*

RICH PIE PASTRY
Three nine-inch shells

2¼ cups flour
1 teaspoon salt
1 cup shortening

3 tablespoons ice water
3 tablespoons lemon juice

Mix flour, salt, and shortening; blend until it resembles coarse corn meal. Sprinkle water and lemon juice over, using 1 tablespoon at a time; mix. Roll into a ball and wrap in waxed paper. Refrigerate until ready to use. Roll out on floured board.

Bert Laws, Pittsburgh, Pa.

CREAM CHEESE PIE CRUST
Three nine-inch crusts

7½ ozs. cream cheese (2½ small
packages)
½ cup vegetable shortening

½ teaspoon salt
2 cups plain flour
1 teaspoon sugar

Allow the cream cheese and shortening to soften; mix them together with a fork until fluffy. Blend in the salt, flour, and sugar, using a fork. When mixture is thoroughly blended, roll it into a ball and refrigerate it for 3 to 4 hours. Pinch off desired portion and roll out on a floured board. Keep remaining dough in refrigerator until ready for use.

This crust is especially good for fruit pies, such as strawberry, apple, peach, etc. It should be baked and then filled with cooked filling. Bake at 350 degrees for 20 minutes, or until crusty and browned.

16. Pickles and Preserves

WATERMELON RIND PICKLE
Six quarts

This is an old Virginia recipe, with ginger flavor.

With a sharp knife cut the thick rind of a melon into squares 1 to 2 inches thick. Remove outside green skin, leaving pieces as thick as possible. Cut out ripe inside meat. Cover rind with hot water and boil until easily pierced with a straw. Rind must be firm, not soft. Drain. Boil syrup of sugar, vinegar, and spices until it thickens; add rind and let it boil once. Leave all in saucepan 3 days; then pour off syrup; boil once; pour back over rind and let stand 3 days. Seal at end of three days in jars. A *thick* rind is necessary.

Syrup For 10 Pounds of Rind

10 lbs. sugar
½ pt. vinegar to every lb. rind
   (2½ qts. for 10 lbs.)

2 ozs. ginger root, broken
2 ozs. stick cinnamon
1 oz. whole cloves

Make this pickle in melon season; keep until Christmas; then it is ready to eat.

Mrs. R. C. Harrison, Savannah, Ga.

MAMMY JANE'S FAVORITE WATERMELON RIND PICKLE
Seven pints

7 lbs. watermelon rind
Water
1 11.5-gram bottle Lily's slaked lime
9 cups sugar
3 cups vinegar

3 2-inch sticks cinnamon, broken into small sections
1 tablespoon whole cloves
1 teaspoon whole allspice
1 teaspoon yellow mustard seed

Cut the green peel off rind, and trim off any red meat from the inside of watermelon rind. Cut into squares or any desired shape (not larger than 2 inches square, if squares are made); place in an agate or porcelain vessel; cover with water. Stir in the bottle of lime with your hand, and keep stirring until lime dissolves. Weight down the rind with a heavy platter. Let stand overnight. Drain off the water and let stand 1 hour in ice water. Dump ice cubes in water to keep it cold. Drain thoroughly to remove all lime.

Make a syrup of the sugar and vinegar. Tie the spices in a small *garni* (bag) and drop into the syrup. Bring syrup to a boil in a large agate vessel (dishpan); drop in the rind and cook it over low heat until the rind is transparent and tender when stuck with a toothpick. Pack in sterilized jars; pour the hot syrup over the rind; seal. Chill before serving.

Miss Sadie E. Steele, from Soup to Nuts, *Burlington, N.C.*

ARTICHOKE PICKLE
Five quarts

Once you have tried this marvelous mustard-artichoke pickle, you will keep a jar on your shelf. It is especially good with roast beef.

1 gal. artichokes (Jerusalem)	Vinegar to cover
1 doz. green and red peppers	1 large box dry mustard (2 oz.)
1 hot pepper	2 lbs. sugar
1 doz. large onions	1 oz. turmeric
2 cups salt	1 oz. celery seed
Vinegar	½ oz. white mustard seed
Cold water	

Scrub and wash artichokes. Chop artichokes, peppers, and onions fine. Sprinkle over with the salt. Let stand 12 hours; squeeze. Cover over with ½ part vinegar and ½ part cold water. Let stand 24 hours. Drain; discard liquid.

Make a sauce of vinegar (to cover mixture) in which you dissolve the mustard, sugar, turmeric, celery seed, and white mustard seed. Pour this over vegetables and pack in jars; seal. [I dissolve sugar and other dry ingredients for this sauce by heating slightly, add the spices, and let cool, then pour over. The sugar will dissolve in cool vinegar if stirred long enough.—M. B.]

Mrs. Kate T. Friedheim, Rock Hill, S.C.

DILL ONION PICKLE
One pint

1 pt. Spanish onion rings (peel onions, slice thin, separate into rings)	½ teaspoon dill seed
	2 teaspoons salt
	½ cup white vinegar
½ cup sugar	¼ cup water

Fill a 1-pint jar with rings of Spanish onion. Combine the remaining ingredients in a small saucepan; heat to boiling and pour over the onion rings. Be sure the jar is filled with syrup. Seal jar. These are ready for use in two days. Chill before serving.

Mrs. David Lea, Memphis, Tenn.

DILL PICKLES GARLIC
Two gallons

8 1-qt. jars or 2 1-gal. jars	Whole, firm, small-to-medium cu-
6 cloves garlic per qt. jar	cumbers
1 twig dill per qt. jar	1 gal. water
1 teaspoon mixed pickling spice	1 cup salt
per qt. jar	1 cup vinegar

Fill scrubbed jars with spices and cucumbers. Bring the water, salt, and vinegar to a boil. Pour boiling hot brine over cucumbers in jars. Seal, while hot, with self-sealing lids. Let stand 4 or 5 days to pickle for half-sour flavor, and a week or more for very sour.

Hannah B. Berg, Chattanooga, Tenn., from What's Cookin' in Birmingham?,
Birmingham, Ala.

BREAD AND BUTTER PICKLES
Three quarts

Six qts. cucumbers, washed and sliced (leave peel on); 1 qt. sliced onions, optional; 4 sweet green peppers. Pour over the above 9 cups of water and 1 cup salt. Let stand 3 hours, drain. Combine:

3 pts. vinegar	1 teaspoon white mustard seed
3 lbs. white sugar	1 teaspoon celery seed
1 tablespoon turmeric	

Heat to boiling. Add vegetables. Bring to boiling point again but do not boil. Seal in sterilized jars. Chill before serving. These are called bread and butter pickles because they are delicious when served with just bread and butter. I like to serve them on round slices of buttered bread at a Coca-Cola party.

Constance Spalding Anderson, from The Cotton Blossom Cook Book, *Atlanta, Ga.*

GRANDMA BILLS'S GOLD DUST PICKLES
Eight quarts

This recipe is well over 100 years old. It originated with the contributor's great-grandmother, whose husband, John Houston, went from North Carolina to Tennessee about 1823.

½ pk. green tomatoes
1 large head cabbage
15 large onions
2 doz. small onions
25 cucumbers
Salt (1½ to 2 cups)
Equal parts vinegar and water
2 cups grated horseradish
1 cup white mustard seed
1 oz. celery seed
½ cup ground cinnamon
½ cup ground turmeric

Syrup:
½ gal. vinegar, boiled with
2½ lbs. brown sugar
1 lb. prepared mustard
1 cup salad oil

Cut the tomatoes, cabbage, onions, and cucumbers into small pieces; sprinkle generously with salt; mix well; allow to stand overnight in the salt. In the morning drain off the brine. Put the vegetables in a large enameled vessel and pour over equal parts of water and vinegar to cover. Let set in cool place for 2 days; drain off the liquid; discard the liquid. Mix in the horseradish and spices. Boil together the vinegar and brown sugar. Pour the hot syrup over the vegetables. Repeat this procedure for 3 days (each day drain off the syrup; reheat it and pour it *hot* over the vegetables for 3 days). On the third day, stir in the mustard and salad oil. Pack the pickle in hot sterilized jars; seal.

Mrs. John Chester, Memphis, Tenn.

PICKLED OKRA
Five pints

2 lbs. tender young okra pods

5 1-pt. screw top jars

Wash the okra, leaving short stem on. Pack okra into the 5 jars. Add to each jar the following:

1 teaspoon dill seed
½ teaspoon alum

1 peeled clove garlic
1 small pod hot green pepper

Place the jars in a large vessel of water and heat the water just to boiling point.

Make the following syrup, and pour it over the okra and seasonings while the jars are in the hot water. Seal jars. These should stand from 6 to 8 weeks before serving. Chill before serving.

Syrup for Okra

3 cups white vinegar   6 teaspoons salt
1 cup water

Bring vinegar, water, and salt to boil; pour hot over the okra. Be sure jars are filled with vinegar syrup. If this is not enough, make additional syrup using same proportions.

MRS. INGLE'S FOURTEEN-DAY PICKLE
Two gallons

This fascinating old-fashioned Southern sweet pickle gives the pickler an interesting two weeks.

First day: place **2 gallons cucumbers** in a stone or enamel vessel; cover with **boiling water**; add **3 cups salt**.

Second day: pour off salt water; put ¾ cup powdered alum over cucumbers and cover again with **boiling water**.

Third day: pour off alum water; cover cucumbers with **plain boiling water**.

Fourth day: drain cucumbers. Boil together **1 gallon vinegar** and **1 box of pickling spices** for 20 minutes. Pour over the cucumbers and let stand 9 days, counting from the day after vinegar is poured over. (During this time the pickler may just "peep" each day at pickles.)

Fourteenth day: take cucumbers out of vinegar; slice in rounds (about ¼ to ½ inch) and pack into glass jars alternating a layer of pickles with an equal layer of sugar, until jar is filled. Keep adding sugar until liquid (made by the sugar and juices seeping from cucumbers) completely covers pickle. Put tops on jars, but jars are not necessarily sealed.

Mrs. Ralph Ingle, Alamance County, N.C.

CINNAMON BUD PICKLES
About six pints

This recipe was carried from the South to Ohio, and now it has come back to us.

Select 25 to 30, three- to four-inch long cucumbers. Soak whole for two weeks in water containing enough salt to float an egg. Remove cucumbers and wash; slice into ½ inch rings. Return to crock. Soak overnight in a solution of alum water, using a lump of alum the size of a walnut to each gallon of water. Drain and wash pickles again. Return them to crock.

Make a syrup of two quarts of sugar to one quart of vinegar. Add 2 sticks of cinnamon and one tablespoon whole cloves. Heat to boiling and pour over pickle slices, being sure the syrup completely covers the pickles. Let stand overnight. Next day pour off syrup and reheat to boiling; pour again over pickles. Repeat this process for four days. On fifth day pack pickles in hot sterilized jars. Heat syrup to boiling point; fill jars with syrup and seal immediately.

Mrs. James Gigante, Worthington, Ohio

HOLLY HILL PICKLES
Two gallons

These delicious pickles call for small "pickling size" cucumbers in brine. Our contributor adds that the "spoonfuls" are "rounded," not "level."

Take small or medium cucumbers out of brine and fill a 2-gallon jar about four-fifths full. Sprinkle over them

2 tablespoons salad oil (olive)	1 tablespoon allspice
2 tablespoons white mustard seed	½ tablespoon cloves
2 tablespoons black mustard seed	1 cracked-up nutmeg
2 tablespoons whole black pepper	2 pods red pepper
2 tablespoons celery seed	1 cup horseradish

Boil 5 lbs. sugar in 3 qts. vinegar and pour scalding hot over the above. Cover closely. Will be ready to use in one month.

Mrs. James N. Williamson, Jr., Orlando, Fla.

CUCUMBER-ONION RELISH
About one and one-half quarts

18 medium cucumbers	½ cup water
6 medium onions	2 tablespoons mustard seed
1 cup salt	1 tablespoon celery seed
2 cups cider vinegar	3 hot red peppers, minced
½ cup sugar	4 bay leaves

Peel cucumbers and onions and slice very thin. Add salt and let stand in a covered crock overnight. Drain and press dry.

Combine the remaining ingredients and bring to a boil. Boil for 3 minutes.

Add cucumbers and onions and let come to boil again. Cook for 2 minutes. Pour into sterilized jars and seal at once.

Mrs. William J. Lang, from The Junior League of Dallas Cook Book,
Dallas, Tex.

MRS. FARLEY'S CHILI SAUCE
About two quarts

An unusually good thick chili.

18 ripe tomatoes, ground, or chopped fine
3 large onions, ground
4 large green bell peppers, ground
1 large red sweet pepper, ground
1 pod red pepper, ground
Dash cayenne pepper
½ small clove garlic, ground
2 cups sugar

3 teaspoons celery seed
3 teaspoons white mustard seed
½ teaspoon mixed ground spices
1 tablespoon Worcestershire sauce
3 to 4 tablespoons salt, according to taste
½ teaspoon white pepper
1½ pts. good vinegar

Grind vegetables or chop fine in wooden chopping bowl. Mix with other ingredients; bring to slow boil and let simmer until vegetables are as tender as mush and juice has become thick. Cover for first hour of simmering to tenderize the vegetables. Bottle.

Mrs. Charles Prentice Farley, Norfolk, Va.

DELICIOUS PEPPER RELISH
About six pints

12 green peppers
12 red peppers

12 mild, medium-sized onions
1 hot pepper

Grind the above; pour over all boiling water; let stand 10 minutes. Drain and bring to a boil in:

6 cups vinegar
2½ tablespoons salt

4 cups sugar

Simmer gently about 10 minutes. Seal in sterilized jars.

Mrs. W. E. Diehl, Eureka Springs, Ark.

APPLE-TOMATO CHUTNEY
About eight pints

13 large apples
13 large ripe tomatoes

¼ lb. mustard seed
3 pts. vinegar

1 lb. brown sugar
¼ lb. salt (scant)
½ lb. onions, minced fine
½ red pepper, chopped fine

½ lb. raisins, chopped
1 oz. turmeric
2 ozs. ginger
2 ozs. ground mustard

Boil apples, tomatoes, mustard seed, and vinegar together until cooked. Put through colander. Add other ingredients and boil 2 hours or more. Put into 1-pt. (or smaller) jars.

Mrs. James C. Cresap, from St. Anne's Parish Recipe Book, *Annapolis, Md.*

PEAR CHUTNEY
About ten pints

This is a delightful form of relish or chutney.

4 to 5 large onions, ground
1 doz. green peppers
3 hot red peppers
½ cup salt
Cold water
2 tablespoons turmeric, powdered
2 teaspoons celery seed

2 teaspoons white mustard seed
8 whole allspice
6 whole cloves
3½ cups sugar
2 qts. white or good cider vinegar
½ pk. pears, ground, not peeled

Grind onions and peppers together; mix well with the salt. Put into a large cloth bag and let drain for 12 hours. Then pour in cold water over mixture and squeeze out as much liquid as possible. Make a bouquet of the spices by tying in a cloth. Mix sugar and vinegar and put on to boil with the spice bouquet. When it comes to a boil, put in ground pear, onions, and peppers; let simmer slowly until tender, from 30 to 45 minutes. Pour into sterilized 1-pt. jars and seal either with top or paraffin.

Mrs. Gunther Reid, Chattanooga, Tenn.

MANGO RELISH (*Pepper Relish*)
About three pints

This is a thick different relish from the usual Pepper Relish. Mix it with mayonnaise for sandwiches.

4 large onions, peeled, ground
12 peppers, red and green (bell type peppers), washed, seeded
1 cup sugar

1 cup vinegar
2 tablespoons flour
2 tablespoons butter
2 tablespoons prepared mustard
1 tablespoon salt

Grind the onions and peppers, using a medium blade. In a large enamel vessel, combine the onions and peppers with remaining ingredients. Bring to a boil and cook slowly until mixture thickens. Seal in sterilized jars. Mix with mayonnaise to use as a relish or for sandwich spread.

Mrs. L. D. Martin, Elon College, N.C.

OLD SOUTHERN BRANDIED PEACHES
Two quarts

1 lb. fresh whole peaches	Brandy
¾ lb. sugar (same amount of water as sugar, cup for cup)	Soda

Put ¼ lb. soda to a pail of water; boil. When boiling throw in 2 or 3 peaches at a time, and let them remain for about 5 minutes; then throw them into cold water for a minute and rub the furze and skin off with a towel, after which throw them into another pail of cold water until all peaches have been prepared. Make a syrup while the peaches are preparing using ¾ lb. of sugar to each of fruit with 1 cup of water for each cup of sugar. When syrup boils, add peaches and boil until they may be easily pierced with a fork. Pack into jars, filling with half syrup from peaches and half brandy.

From Excellent Receipts, *Aiken, S.C., 1874, 1929.*

SWEET PEACH PICKLE
Seven pints

7 lbs. peaches, peeled	1 teaspoon salt
Cloves	2 tablespoons each of whole allspice, cloves
3½ lbs. brown sugar	
3 cups vinegar	2 2-inch sticks cinnamon

Peel the peaches. Stick 2 whole cloves in each peach. Combine the sugar, vinegar, salt, and spices in a large kettle. Bring to a boil. Put in a dozen peaches at a time and cook slowly until they are tender enough to be pierced with a straw. Remove the cooked peaches and pack into sterilized jars. Continue until all peaches have been cooked. Boil the syrup over moderate heat until syrup thickens, about 15 minutes. Pour the hot syrup over peaches and seal.

Vesta Blair, from Katch's Kitchen, *West Palm Beach, Fla.*

SWEET PICKLED FIGS
About six pints

"As told by my sister Daisy. Good for generations!"

7 lbs. ripe firm figs	1 pt. good sour vinegar
5 lbs. sugar	⅓ cup whole cloves
1 cup water	1 stick cinnamon

"Wash figs. Put spices, sugar, water, and vinegar in pot. Let boil. Drop figs into boiling syrup. Bring to rolling boil. Cut heat off. Cover and let stand overnight. Repeat 3 times. Can last time. Use slotted spoon to remove from syrup. Reduce sugar one pound for less sweet pickle.

"Figs *must* be handled with care."

Myrtie Keller, from Maryland Cooking, *Maryland Home Economics Assoc.*

SPICED VINEGAR FOR PICKLES
One gallon

1 gal. vinegar	1 tablespoon turmeric powder
1 lb. sugar	1 tablespoon black pepper
2 tablespoons allspice	1 tablespoon mace
2 tablespoons mustard seed	2 nutmegs, grated
2 tablespoons celery seed	3 onions, sliced
2 tablespoons salt	3 tablespoons horseradish

Bring to boil; use over any sweet pickle.

Mrs. Howard R. McLlean, New Orleans, La.

BAR-LE-DUC
Twelve glasses

A famous gooseberry and currant jelly.

2 qts. gooseberries, put through grinder	8 cups sugar
1 cup water	1 qt. currants, picked off stems

Put gooseberries in kettle with 1 cup water and cook ½ hour. Add sugar and continue cooking for ½ hour. Add currants and cook until syrup jells. If a little less water is used, it will jell much faster.

Mary L. McDaniel, Easton, Md., from Maryland Cooking, *Maryland Home Economics Assoc.*

APPLE-MINT JELLY (or *Plain Apple Jelly*)

Wash and cut up desired amount of apples. Cover well with water and boil until apples are tender and juice extracted. (Do not peel.) Pour all through cloth strainer once (or twice for clearer jelly) and let drip until juice has drained off.

To each cup of the juice, add 1 cup of sugar and boil until mixture jells. If pectin is used, see directions with each bottle. Crush fresh mint leaves and add to jelly 5 minutes before taking from stove. Remove leaves before pouring jelly into sterilized jars. To give a nice flavor of the mint, use 1 large sprig for each cup of jelly.

To make a tasty jelly I often use half peaches and half apple. The parings from fruit make good jelly and may be made in small amounts, which is the best way to make jelly and preserves.

Mrs. Frederick S. Cannon, Knoxville, Tenn.

JAPONICA JELLY (*Quince*)

"This is a very old recipe and the product is considered a great delicacy. Collect the quinces from the Japonica bush—Japanese Quince—very late in the season, just before frost.

"Wash; cut up in ¼ sections and cook with seeds and skin, in enough water to cover, until soft. Allow to drip through 3 thicknesses of cheese cloth. Use equal measures of sugar and juice. Boil rapidly until it jells when a drop is cooled. Pour into small glasses and cover with paraffin. Makes a clear amber jelly."

Anna Allen, Baltimore, Md., from Maryland Cooking,
Maryland Home Economics Assoc.

GUAVA JELLY

Select ripe, tart guavas; wash and slice or cut up, using peel and all. Place in preserving kettle; cover with water, and simmer until fruit is tender and all juices cooked out. Strain. To the liquid add 1 cup of sugar for each cup of juice. Cook until it begins to jell. It is best to add pectin to this—add according to amount prepared. (Directions come with commercial pectin.) Place in jars and seal. Delicious.

ORANGE-LEMON MARMALADE
About one pint

6 oranges	Water
4 lemons	Sugar

Slice oranges and lemons (with rind on) paper thin. Remove all seeds. Add 3 times as much water as fruit; let stand 12 hours; then boil about 1 hour. Set aside and let stand another 12 hours and boil again for 1 hour. Measure fruit and liquid. To each cup of mixture, add 1 cup of sugar. Boil until liquid jells and test in saucer—when jelly slides off it is done. Let stand to cool; then pour into jars and seal. You may add grapefruit to this if desired. The whole oranges may be used without lemon, but the lemon gives added flavor.

Mrs. Angus Craft, St. Petersburg, Fla.

GOLD JELLY
About two pints

2 grapefruits	Water
2 oranges	Sugar
2 lemons	

Shred or chop fruit fine after having removed all seeds and fiber. Measure; cover with three times the amount of water. Let stand until next day; then boil three minutes and let stand until next day. Measure and add an equal amount of sugar and boil until it jellies, being careful not to scorch.

Mrs. Lynwood P. Harden, Charleston, W.Va.

CARROT MARMALADE
Two pints

A Governors Island delicacy, with Southern accent.

1 qt. scraped, grated raw carrots	Juice of 4 lemons
Grated rind of 2 lemons	4 cups sugar

Mix ingredients; bring slowly to boil. Reduce heat, and simmer until thick and clear. Pour into hot sterilized jars and seal.

Mrs. Irving Henry, New Hampshire and St. Petersburg Beach, Fla.

RED RASPBERRY OR DEWBERRY JAM

Wash and drain the berries. Put them in a coarse strainer or wire basket. Dip them up and down in a large bowl of water. Mash them thoroughly; put them in a wide-bottomed enamel or aluminum pan and bring quickly to a boil. Rub about ½ of the mass at a time through a strainer to remove seeds. Measure the pulp and the juice, taking ¾ as much sugar. Bring the mixture to a boil and then allow it to simmer for 10 minutes, stirring occasionally. Pour into jelly glasses. When cold, cover with paraffin.

Mrs. A. J. Sykes, from Victuals and Vitamins, *Greensboro, N.C.*

SOUTHERN FIG PRESERVES

Choose firm ripe figs, but not too soft. Drop them into a soda-water bath made by adding 1 tablespoon soda to each quart of water. Let stand 15 minutes. Remove; rub off fuzz and slough skin. Put into wide open kettle.

To each quart of figs, add 1 cup of sugar, 1 cup of water, ½ sliced lemon, and 1 or 2 pieces of ginger root. Bring slowly to boil. Cook slowly until fruit is tender and clear but still holding original form. Let syrup cook down thick. If figs become too done before syrup is thick, remove fruit; pack in jars; and let syrup continue cooking until thick. Pour over fruit and seal at once.

Mrs. Charles Prentice Farley, Norfolk, Va.

MARTHA WASHINGTON'S PEAR PRESERVES

"Here is a dish from Mount Vernon which brings to mind George Washington's visit to Charlotte in 1791. He entered the city on North Tryon Street, riding in 'a snow white coach with gilded springs, with his crest emblazoned upon the door.' Four horses drew this elegant vehicle, and his entourage included, besides the coachman and postilion, his valet de chambre, two footmen, four riding horses, and a baggage wagon."

Pears   **Water**
Boiling lye   **Brandy**
Sugar (½ lb. to every lb. of fruit)

The pears should be very fresh. Wash them and put them into boiling lye for one minute. Remove and put them into cold water. Next, put them into a prepared syrup of sugar and water, using enough water to dissolve sugar. Then cook them for fifteen minutes. Remove and put on plates to cool. Boil the syrup down to one-half the original quantity. Put the syrup and the pears in jars and add some brandy. Seal while hot.

Mrs. W. Frank Sample, from Old North State Cook Book, *Charlotte, N.C.*

MRS. RILEY'S BAKED PEAR PRESERVES

This is an oven-baked preserve. Pineapple may be added if desired.

Weigh equal parts of sliced pears and sugar. Place pears in bowl; cover with ¾ of the sugar. Let stand overnight. Next morning, drain, and boil juice down about ½ hour. Add to this the rest of the sugar; mix well, and add pears. Bake in the oven (in heavy preserving vessel) until right consistency. Just about

5 minutes before taking from the oven, add 1 can crushed pineapple, if desired. Put in jars, seal.

Mrs. Sam Riley, Eureka Springs, Ark.

PEAR CHIPS WITH GINGER
Six pints

An early form of preserves.

2 lbs. pears
¼ lb. Canton ginger

4 lbs. sugar
4 lemons

Wipe pears; stem, quarter, core, and peel; cut into small pieces. Add sugar and ginger; let stand overnight. In the morning, add lemons cut in small pieces, seeds removed. Cook slowly 3 hours. Pour into hot sterilized jars; cover with paraffin. When cool, put on metal covers, label and store.

From Recipes Tested and Tried, *by Anne Young White and Nola Nance Oliver, Natchez, Miss.*

MANGO CHIPS
Four pints

8 lbs. mango chips
4 lbs. sugar

4 lemons
¼ lb. ginger root

Cut lemons in small pieces; mix all ingredients and cook down slowly.

From Puerto Rican Cook Book, *by Eliza B. K. Dooley, San Juan, Puerto Rico.*

PEAR HONEY

Grind good cooking pears fine with food chopper. Use equal parts pears and sugar; cook until thick as honey; then flavor with vanilla or pineapple.

Mrs. Lydia Jordan, from Community Club Cook Book, *Gibsonville, N.C.*

CHERRY PRESERVES 1947

In 1947, Mrs. McConnell made a cherry preserve which pleased her so well that she affectionately added the date to the name. You will mark the date when you make your first jar by this recipe.

"After pitting cherries (red sour cherries) lift them from the juice and measure them. Place not more than 4 cups in a wide kettle. Add ½ as much sugar as cherries and bring slowly to a boil. Cook until the syrup is thickening and 'slipping' from the spoon, about 20 to 25 minutes, or to 222 degrees, if candy and preserving thermometer is available. Pour into glasses immediately and when cool seal with wax or paraffin.

"The juice which was discarded when cherries were pitted may be made into syrup and used in drinks, etc.

"These preserves are ruby red; the cherries taste fresh and the juices jell."

Mrs. D. E. McConnell, Gastonia, N.C.

MRS. HOLT'S STRAWBERRY PRESERVES
One and one-half pints

This is a perfect recipe for strawberry preserves, worked out after many seasons of trial and error.

4 cups fresh strawberries
5 cups sugar

3 tablespoons lemon juice, or ¼ teaspoon cream of tartar

Place in a wide kettle alternate layers of sugar and berries. Bring slowly to a boil. After the whole mass is boiling, cook 9 minutes. Remove from heat. Add the lemon juice, or the ¼ teaspoon cream of tartar. Let stand overnight. The second day, boil 9 minutes. Allow to cool and place in glasses. Seal with wax or paraffin. Cooked this way the preserves are beautiful, and tender jelly surrounds the plump bright red berries.

Mrs. Don S. Holt, Concord, N.C.

WATERMELON PRESERVE
One and one-half pints

8 cups cubed watermelon (cut into 1-inch cubes)
2½ cups sugar
¼ teaspoon salt
¼ cup cider vinegar
1 slice lemon, ¼ inch thick

Spices tied in cloth bag: ½ stick of cinnamon, ½ teaspoon whole cloves
1 1½-pt. jar (sterilize jar, keep it hot)

Pour the watermelon cubes into a colander. With the palms of hands press out as much free liquid as possible without mashing the fruit out of shape. Let drain until no free liquid seeps from colander. Pour the melon and remaining ingredients into a large saucepan. Bring to a boil and boil gently for 1 hour. With a slotted spoon, lift out the melon and pack it into a 1½-pint sterilized jar. Pour over enough syrup to almost fill jar; leave only headspace. Seal the jar. Chill the preserve before serving.

OGEECHEE LIME PRESERVES

The Ogeechee lime, a Spanish type probably left in the section of Georgia along the banks of the Ogeechee River, is very scarce now, and considered a great delicacy when preserved, to be served with meat or game. It is often found by the Negroes of that section and brought into the city markets. Here is a recipe by Harriet Ross Colquitt.

"Cut off blossom end of limes and soak in alum solution (1 tablespoon alum to 2 gallons water) for 24 hours. Take out of alum solution and boil in clear water. Drain and put in a syrup made of 1 cup of sugar to one cup of water, 1 pound of sugar being allowed for 1 pound of fruit. Cook slowly until transparent."

From The Savannah Cook Book, *by Harriet Ross Colquitt, Savannah, Ga.*

WATERMELON PRESERVES (*"Sweetmeats"*)

Watermelon rind, peeled, cut into
   desired pieces
2½ cups sugar to each lb. rind

Lemons, 2 to each 5 lbs. rind
Alum
Salt

Peel and remove all ripe red part from rind. Cut into small squares or desired shapes. Soak 12 hours in salted water, using 1 tablespoon salt to each quart of water. Drain. Cover with fresh water and boil for about 20 minutes, adding a pinch of alum. Drain. Boil sugar with water, using 1 cup of sugar to each ¾ cup water until thin syrup is made. Add rind and sliced lemon, and let cook until rind is tender and translucent. Pour into sterilized jars and seal.

Mrs. J. W. Sloan, Vienna, Va.

PLUM CONSERVE
About four pints

Eastern Shore special.

3 lbs. damsons or plums, seeded
1 lb. seeded raisins
3 oranges, sliced with rind (quarter slices)

Juice 2 lemons
3 lbs. sugar
2 cups walnut meats

Bring to boil slowly. Cook until thick and clear, stirring constantly to prevent sticking. Pour in scalded jelly glasses; seal with melted paraffin.

Mrs. H. P. McKay, Onancock, Va.

GRAPE CONSERVE
Six pints

5 lbs. Concord grapes
4 large oranges

1 lb. seedless raisins
4 lbs. sugar

Wash grapes; separate the pulp from skins, saving the skins. Boil pulp and run through a sieve to remove seeds. Wash oranges; pare, and remove membrane. Run oranges through food chopper with raisins. Put grape skins, pulp, and orange-raisin mixture with juice, orange rind, and sugar in preserving kettle and cook slowly until syrup forms. Cook well, making sure the skins are thoroughly cooked. Add chopped nuts if desired, and pour into hot sterilized glasses and seal.

Mrs. F. G. Hoddick, from The Alexandria Woman's Club Cook Book,
Alexandria, Va.

BEET PRESERVES
Three pints

For many years I have been trying to find a recipe for these fine preserves. Here it is:

Peel raw beets and cut into thin strips. To 2 lbs. of beets, add 3 lbs. of sugar, ½ cup of water, 3 lemons, sliced thin. Cook very slowly, stirring often. When preserves begin to get thick, add 2 cups chopped pecans and ginger to taste.

Mrs. Max A. Sarasohn, Ensley, Ala., from What's Cookin' in Birmingham?,
Birmingham, Ala.

MRS. GANT'S TOMATO CONSERVE
Two pints

2 lemons, sliced thin
Water to cover
1 qt. ripe tomatoes, peeled

1 pt. diced tart apples
1 cup shredded pineapple
4 cups sugar

Cut lemons in thin slices; cover with water. Cook until tender. Add peeled tomatoes, apples, pineapple, and sugar. Cook until thick and clear. Put into glasses and seal.

Mrs. Roger Gant, from Soup to Nuts, *Burlington, N.C.*

CANTALOUPE CONSERVE
Three pints

2 medium-size ripe cantaloupes, peeled, cut into small dice

12 ripe peaches, peeled, cut into small dice

4 oranges, peeled, seeds and pith removed, cut into small chunks	Sugar ¼ teaspoon salt ½ cup chopped pecans

Combine the fruits in a large saucepan; add ¼ inch of water; boil over moderate heat for about ten minutes. Measure the mixture, undrained; return fruit to saucepan. Add 1 cup of sugar for each cup of fruit mixture. Boil slowly, uncovered, for about 45 minutes to an hour, or until mixture is thick; stir in the nuts. Pour while hot into sterilized ½-pint jars.

Mrs. E. F. Kennedy, Hickory, N.C.

17. Sauces and Dressings

TO MAKE A ROUX

"Make a brown or white roux," appears often in this and other cook books. To do so, add 1 tablespoon of flour to each tablespoon of fat (usually in the pan in which meat or vegetables were sautéed). To make a brown roux, brown the flour to a deep brown. To make a smoother roux, sprinkle salt into the browning flour and fat. When well browned, pour in liquid—water, milk, stock, or other sauce. To make a white roux, smooth flour into unbrowned fat to make white paste; sprinkle with salt, and add liquid as for brown roux. From the white roux come many cream sauces such as Béchamel, which is basically a white sauce.

From the brown roux most Southern gravies are made; add tomato to flavor or to make a tomato sauce; chicken gravy and others are usually made from this base.

HOW TO MAKE WHITE SAUCE (*Cream Sauce*)

(1) Thin Sauce

1 tablespoon butter	¼ teaspoon salt
1 tablespoon flour	1 cup milk or cream

(2) Medium Sauce

2 tablespoons butter	¼ teaspoon salt
2 tablespoons flour	1 cup milk or cream

(3) Thick Sauce

3 tablespoons butter	¼ teaspoon salt
3 tablespoons flour	1 cup milk or cream

Melt butter in saucepan. Stir in flour and salt and blend to smooth paste. Add cold milk and cook until it thickens, stirring constantly. Season as desired.

TINO COSTA'S FRENCH DRESSING
One-half cup

While commissioned in Kentucky to paint portraits, Tino Costa gave his French Dressing recipe to Virginia Fergerson Rankin. In passing the recipe on to me, Mrs. Rankin says that this is the only recipe in her files which she has never before parted with. Make it and you will understand her reluctance.

Crush 1 clove of garlic with wooden pestle in a wooden bowl. Mix together the following:

½ teaspoon sugar
½ teaspoon salt

Dash pepper
½ teaspoon dry mustard

Put ½ cube of ice in the following:

6 soupspoons olive oil
3 soupspoons wine vinegar
1 teaspoon Worcestershire sauce

2 teaspoons A-1 sauce
2 soupspoons tomato catchup

Stir both mixtures together with ice for a few minutes. Pour over salad.

Contributed by Mrs. Harris W. Rankin, Paducah, Ky.

WHITE HOUSE DRESSING (*for Green Salads*)
One quart

1 cup white sugar
1 cup white vinegar

1 cup vegetable oil

Stir the above until sugar dissolves.
Grind together the following:

1 green sweet pepper
1 small can of pimiento (¼ cup)

1 medium-sized onion

Mix the first mixture with the ground sweet pepper, pimiento and onion· then stir in:

3 teaspoons prepared mustard
3 teaspoons coarse salt

3 teaspoons Worcestershire sauce

Stir all ingredients together well—let stand 3 hours before using. Keeps indefinitely if kept cool.

Mrs. T. Curry Dedman, Sr., Beaumont Inn, Harrodsburg, Ky.

YE OLD COLLEGE INN POPPY SEED DRESSING
One quart

This and the following dressing are from famous Ye Old College Inn.

⅔ cup honey
1 teaspoon salt
⅔ cup vinegar
6 tablespoons French's prepared
    mustard

5 tablespoons poppy seed
2½ cups Wesson oil
Optional—1 medium-sized onion,
    finely grated

Mix together in order listed. Blend in a Waring blender or electric mixer until oil disappears. Add the onion if desired.

ORANGE SALAD DRESSING
Serves eight

Ideal for frozen or molded fruit salads.

⅓ stick butter
¾ cup sugar
1 teaspoon flour
2 eggs, well beaten

Grated rind and juice of 2 oranges
Grated rind and juice of 1 lemon
Pinch salt
1 cup whipping cream, whipped

Melt butter in double boiler; add sugar, flour, eggs, juices, and salt. Let cook until it thickens. Remove from fire and cool. Add whipped cream when ready to serve.

Ernest Coker, Owner, Ye Old College Inn, Houston, Tex.

MRS. CHANDLER'S SALAD DRESSING
Two cups

1 small onion, grated
2 tablespoons sugar
1 teaspoon salt
Dash cayenne pepper

1 clove garlic
Juice 1 lemon
½ cup each of vinegar, salad oil,
    and tomato catchup

Beat with rotary beater. Serve cold over salads.

Mrs. Albert B. Chandler, Versailles, Ky.

THICK FRENCH DRESSING
Serves eight

This should be made just before serving. The secret is to pour in the oil *drop* by *drop*. It is especially good for fruits.

½ cup sugar
1½ teaspoons salt
1 teaspoon pepper (black)
¼ small box of paprika (enough
    to give a good red color)

2 teaspoons prepared mustard
Dash each of Worcestershire and
    Tabasco sauces
1 cup vegetable oil
½ cup vinegar

In an electric mixing bowl, mix the dry ingredients, mustard, Worcestershire sauce, and Tabasco sauce. Blend on slow speed, adding the oil drop by drop as mixture is blended. Add the vinegar last and beat until blended. Serve at once while dressing is thick, since it tends to become thin if allowed to set long.

Mrs. A. Glenn Holt, Burlington, N.C.

MRS. HATCHER'S FRENCH DRESSING
One quart

¾ cup sugar
1 cup vinegar
2 cups salad oil
1 bottle chili sauce
Juice 2 onions

Juice 2 lemons
4 teaspoons salt
1 teaspoon black pepper
1 teaspoon paprika
¼ teaspoon red pepper

Mix ingredients with egg beater. If desired add grated rind of half a lemon, and 1 onion and 1 green pepper chopped. This dressing can be kept in refrigerator indefinitely.

Mrs. M. Felton Hatcher, Macon, Ga.

MRS. LOWE'S HONEY DRESSING
One pint

This has a tangy taste which makes it a delightful dressing for fresh fruit salads.

⅔ cup sugar
1 teaspoon dry mustard
1 teaspoon paprika
¼ teaspoon salt
1 teaspoon celery seed

⅓ cup strained honey
5 tablespoons vinegar
1 tablespoon lemon juice
1 teaspoon grated onion
1 cup salad oil

Mix dry ingredients; add honey, vinegar, lemon juice, grated onion. Pour oil into mixture very slowly, beating constantly with rotary beater. Will keep indefinitely.

Mrs. M. L. Lowe, Cookeville, Tenn.

PINEAPPLE DRESSING FOR FRUIT AND FRUIT SALADS
Two cups

2 tablespoons butter
2 tablespoons flour
2 cups pineapple juice
⅓ cup sugar

2 egg yolks, well beaten
1 tablespoon grated orange rind
1 cup heavy cream, whipped

In a saucepan, melt the butter and stir in the flour to make a smooth roux (paste). Stir in the pineapple juice, and slowly bring to a boil, stirring constantly. Remove from heat.

In a bowl, beat the egg yolks and gradually add the sugar; beat until creamy. Gradually stir the hot juice mixture into the eggs. Cool the mixture. Stir in the orange rind. Just before serving fold in the whipped cream. Serve over any congealed fruit salad or fruit salads.

Mrs. Douglas Moore, Fort Lauderdale, Fla.

MARSHMALLOW-SOUR CREAM DRESSING
About three cups

For fruits or fruit salads.

2 cups sour cream
Miniature marshmallows

1 teaspoon lemon juice
Paprika

Place the sour cream in a deep bowl. Add ½ cup marshmallows. Stir well. In about one-half hour add more marshmallows, about ½ cup. Stir. Continue adding marshmallows until the cream will not absorb more. The marshmallows will disintegrate making a smooth thick cream mixture. When all marshmallows have been added, stir in the lemon juice. Serve over fruits or fruit salad. Sprinkle dressing with paprika.

Mrs. Alfred G. Lea, St. Petersburg, Fla.

COUNTRY CLUB ROQUEFORT DRESSING
Four cups

½ lb. Roquefort cheese, crumbled
1¾ cups half-and-half cream
2 cups mayonnaise (1 pt.), home-
    made or bought
¼ teaspoon salt

¼ cup lemon juice
1 teaspoon Worcestershire sauce
3 dashes Tabasco sauce
½ teaspoon garlic powder

Place all ingredients in deep bowl of electric mixer. Mix at low speed until smooth and well blended. Pour into a jar and keep refrigerated. Serve over salads, etc.

This is a thin dressing. If thicker dressing is desired, cut down on cream and mayonnaise.

Mr. and Mrs. Talmage Scroggs, Managers,
The Alamance Country Club, Burlington, N.C.

LOW-CALORIE ROQUEFORT DRESSING
About three cups

Make this in a blender.

1 pkg. bleu or Roquefort cheese dressing mix
1 12-oz. carton cottage cheese
¾ cup milk
½ cup mayonnaise
1 tablespoon lemon juice
1 tablespoon Worcestershire sauce
¼ lb. Roquefort cheese, crumbled fine

Combine all ingredients except Roquefort cheese in the blender container; blend at medium speed until mixture is smooth. Stir in the crumbled Roquefort cheese. Blend a second or two to further crumble the Roquefort, or remove from container before blending in the cheese. Store in a glass jar with screw top. Refrigerate. Will keep for several weeks.

HARD BOILED EGG DRESSING
Serves four

3 hard-cooked eggs, yolks separated from whites
1 tablespoon sugar
½ teaspoon salt
½ teaspoon black pepper
½ cup vegetable oil
2 tablespoons prepared mustard
Vinegar

Peel eggs and separate whites from yolks. Reserve whites. In a mixing bowl, mash the egg yolks and mix thoroughly with the sugar, salt, pepper, oil, and mustard to make a thick smooth paste. Add enough vinegar to make a creamy thick dressing. Blend thoroughly. Add the finely chopped egg whites; blend. Serve over shredded lettuce or chopped salad greens. Good for a wintertime dressing.

Mrs. A. Glenn Holt, Burlington, N.C.

BOILED DRESSING FOR CHICKEN OR TURKEY SALAD
About four cups

9 eggs, well beaten
½ pound butter, softened
1 cup vinegar
4 tablespoons prepared mustard

2 tablespoons sugar
1 teaspoon black pepper
Salt to taste
½ cup extra vinegar

Beat the eggs; add the butter, vinegar, mustard, sugar, pepper, and salt. Pour into top of a double boiler over hot water. Stir constantly over boiling water until the mixture is as thick as mush. Chill; then stir in the extra ½ cup vinegar. Pour over chicken or turkey salad, or any dish calling for boiled dressing. This keeps well in refrigerator.

Miss Carrie Bell, Eminence, Ky.

SOUR CREAM DRESSING
About one and one-half cups

For cucumbers, cole slaw, or on hot baked potato.

1 cup sour cream
2 tablespoons vinegar
1 tablespoon lemon juice
1 teaspoon sugar
1 teaspoon salt

½ teaspoon ground pepper
½ teaspoon paprika
1 teaspoon dry mustard
1 teaspoon celery seed
1 pimiento, chopped fine

Beat the cream until it is stiff; add vinegar, lemon juice, sugar, and salt. Stir in remaining ingredients. Place in a jar and keep refrigerated.

NOTE: May be made in electric mixer or blended with rotary beater.

Mrs. E. F. Hart, Burlington, N.C.

BERT'S PEPPER MAYONNAISE
One and one-fourth cups

1 egg yolk
¾ teaspoon salt
1 teaspoon cracked black pepper
(or fresh ground black peppercorns)

1 cup salad oil (corn oil if desired)
1 egg white
2 tablespoons lemon juice

In the small deep bowl of an electric mixer, place the egg yolk, salt, and pepper; blend on high speed until the egg yolk is thick. Begin adding the oil, drop by drop, until the mixture thickens; gradually add the oil in a thin stream. As mayonnaise thickens, gradually add the egg white alternately with the lemon juice. Beat the mayonnaise until it is very thick. It is ready when it will hold its own form when taken up by spoonfuls.

Mrs. A. Glenn Holt, Burlington, N.C.

SOUR CREAM DRESSING FOR FRUITS
One cup

1 cup sour cream
¼ teaspoon salt

1 tablespoon lemon juice
1 tablespoon confectioners sugar

Whip cream with egg beater; add remaining ingredients. Store in a jar in refrigerator to serve over fruits, fruit salads, etc.

Mrs. Eugene Clyde Brooks, Raleigh, N.C.

BOILED DRESSING
(See pages 82 and 437.)

PRIZE MAYONNAISE
Two cups

This recipe won a ten dollar prize in 1932.

1 egg
½ teaspoon dry mustard
½ teaspoon salt

Juice of 1 lemon
2 cups salad oil
Few drops tarragon vinegar

Place the whole egg in a bowl; add dry ingredients and a tablespoon of lemon juice. Beat a few seconds with Dover egg beater; then add small amount of oil. Beat until dressing begins to thicken; then add oil in larger amounts until the two cups are used. When finished, add remaining lemon juice to taste, also tarragon vinegar. If directions are followed, this mayonnaise will always be delicious and a success.

Mrs. H. B. Hardy, from The Guild Cook Book, *Portsmouth, Va.*

VARIATIONS: (1) To make "Garlic Mayonnaise," place 1 peeled clove of garlic in mayonnaise; close the container, and let stand 12 hours. (2) Horseradish added to mayonnaise is a good accompaniment for cold meats. (3) Add chopped chives or fresh chopped mint leaves to mayonnaise and use as a spread or with salads.

BREAD SAUCE
One cup

A good sauce for asparagus and other vegetables.

½ cup butter, melted
¾ cup fine bread crumbs

Salt, pepper to taste
2 hard-boiled eggs, sieved

Melt butter; let brown slightly. Toss in crumbs and brown quickly; season and add sieved eggs. Pour while white-hot over vegetables. Grand over lobster. Minced parsley or shallots give extra flavor.

Mrs. Howard R. McLean, New Orleans, La.

GARLIC-BREAD SAUCE
One cup

½ cup melted butter or margarine, (or vegetable oil may be used)
1 cup toasted bread crumbs

1 clove garlic, mashed
1 tablespoon lemon juice
Salt and pepper

Melt the butter and stir in the bread crumbs, garlic, and lemon juice. Beat until it thickens and reheat. Season to taste and pour over vegetables.

ORANGE SAUCE
One pint

Serve over hot vegetables—asparagus, broccoli, grean peas, string beans, etc. Make either in a blender or electric mixer. This sauce is rather thin and foamy.

4 egg yolks
½ teaspoon white pepper
¼ teaspoon dry mustard
⅛ teaspoon red pepper
Juice of 1 lemon

1 cup butter, heated
Juice of 1 orange
1 teaspoon grated orange or lemon rind

Put the egg yolks, peppers, and mustard in a blender container, or in deep bowl of electric mixer; blend for several seconds. Pour in the lemon juice and blend a few seconds. Have the butter heated to bubbling point. Gradually dribble in the butter while blending the mixture at low speed. When all butter has been added, pour in the orange juice and orange or lemon rind. Blend just long enough to mix thoroughly. Keep the sauce warm over hot water until time to serve, and serve in sauce boat. This may be refrigerated for days; reheat over hot water before serving.

FOOLPROOF HOLLANDAISE SAUCE, CURRY FLAVOR
One and one-half cups

Mrs. Dickinson was largely responsible for assembling the book from which this recipe is taken.

4 egg yolks
1 teaspoon salt
1 teaspoon curry powder (Madras curry suggested)

Juice of 1 large lemon
Few drops of Tabasco sauce
⅓ lb. butter (½ cup plus 3½ tablespoons)

Place all ingredients, except butter, in a small deep mixing bowl. Beat until well blended. Transfer the bowl to a wire strainer that fits over a few inches of boiling water in a sauce pan. Turn heat to high. Drop in the butter. Stir slowly until the butter has completely melted and blended into sauce. Serve hot.

NOTE: This Hollandaise may be kept for weeks in the refrigerator and brought back to life with a tablespoon or two of boiling water and a dash or two of evaporated milk.

Mrs. E. H. Dickinson, Toronto, Canada; from Light in the Kitchen, *in Braille, by the Canadian National Institute for the Blind, Toronto*

BLENDER HOLLANDAISE SAUCE
Two and one-half cups

1 pound butter, melted
4 egg yolks
3 tablespoons boiling water

2 tablespoons fresh lemon juice
¼ teaspoon cayenne pepper, or white pepper

Melt the butter and skim off any top impurities. Pour off the top fat, leaving the milky substance in the pan. Place egg yolks in the blender container; cover and blend on speed 1 (low) for about one minute, slowly adding the water through the center cap opening. (A tiny funnel is good for pouring through the cap opening.) Turn speed to 3 and add clarified butter very slowly through the cap opening. Add lemon juice and pepper. Blend just long enough to mix. Serve at once.

ANTOINE'S HOLLANDAISE SAUCE
Serves four

1 cup clarified butter
2 tablespoons tarragon vinegar
1 tablespoon water
1 tablespoon minced onion

3 peppercorns
4 egg yolks
Juice of ¼ lemon

Clarify butter by melting it slowly; let stand until all sediment settles to bottom; skim off clear portion. Place in a saucepan the vinegar, water, onion, and peppercorns. Cook over very low heat to reduce liquid to 1 teaspoon. Remove peppercorns. Cool. Add egg yolks; beat slightly. Gradually add melted butter, beating constantly. Add lemon juice. Serve immediately.

From Antoine's Restaurant, New Orleans, La.
Special permission, Roy Alciatore, Proprietor

OLD SOUR
One pint

A famous Key West sea food dressing.

"Old Sour is used by Key Westers on all sorts of sea food. It is made by straining 1 pint of lime juice, adding 1 rounded tablespoon of salt, and storing it in a corked bottle until it is fermented. Is it any wonder our English ancestors who sailed the Seven Seas were known as 'Limeys,' or 'Old Sours'?"

From The Key West Cook Book, *Key West, Fla.*

LIME SAUCE
About three-fourths cup

For lobster or shrimp.

½ cup butter   4 tablespoons lime juice
½ teaspoon Tabasco sauce

In a saucepan, heat the butter to bubbling point. Add lime juice and butter. Reheat; stir. Pour into heated sauce boat. Serve hot with broiled lobster, or use as a lobster or shrimp dip.

TARTAR SAUCE
About two cups

For sea food.

2½ tablespoons minced dill pickles

1 tablespoons minced onion

1½ tablespoons minced fresh parsley tops

1½ teaspoons minced fresh thyme (or ½ teaspoon dried)

1½ teaspoons minced fresh tarragon (or ¼ teaspoon dried)

½ teaspoon sugar

¼ teaspoon paprika

½ teaspoon ground black pepper

1 cup mayonnaise

½ cup sour cream

Blend all ingredients in a mixing bowl. Store in a jar in refrigerator 12 hours before using. Serve cold with sea food.

NOTE: If a curry flavor is desired, add ¼ teaspoon curry powder.

Mrs. Blackwell Robinson, Greensboro, N.C.

ANCHOVY COCKTAIL SAUCE
Serves four

This is a basic sauce for oysters, shrimp, lobster, etc.

1 cup mayonnaise
1 tablespoon tarragon vinegar
½ teaspoon Tabasco sauce

1 cup chili sauce
½ tablespoon anchovy paste

Mix well, chill. This is enough for 2 cups shrimp. Use ½ portion for small can of crab meat.

Mrs. Raymond D. York, from The Monticello Cook Book, *Charlottesville, Va.*

PALM BEACH COCKTAIL SAUCE
One and one-fourth quarts

For a very special sea food sauce I recommend this.

2 cups mayonnaise
2 cups chili sauce
½ cup India relish
1 hard-boiled egg, chopped
1 teaspoon chopped chives
½ chopped green pepper

1 pimiento, chopped
2 tablespoons celery, chopped
1 tablespoon prepared mustard
1 tablespoon A-1 sauce
Salt, pepper, paprika

Mix well, serve.

George La Maze, from Katch's Kitchen, *West Palm Beach, Fla.*

SAUCE FOR RAW OYSTERS
One serving

Mix well. Allow for each serving:

Juice ½ lemon
½ teaspoon vinegar
1 tablespoon tomato catsup

Few drops Tabasco
½ teaspoon grated horseradish
½ teaspoon Worcestershire sauce

From Coastal Cookery, *St. Simons Island, Ga.*

FROZEN SHRIMP COCKTAIL SAUCE
Serves eight

1 cup mayonnaise
1 cup canned tomato juice
Salt, pepper

Worcestershire sauce
Onion juice
Dash Tabasco

Blend mayonnaise with tomato juice; season to taste with other ingredients. (Lemon juice or tarragon vinegar may be added.) Freeze in ice tray or individual molds. Serve over shrimp cocktail. [V-8 juice is a good substitute for tomato juice in the above recipe.—M. B.]

Mrs. Carleton Barnwell, from Favorite Foods of Virginians, *Lynchburg, Va.*

LEE ADAMS' BRANDY SAUCE FOR LOBSTER
One cup

Lee Adams, known on the west coast as Dave Lane, is a former South Carolinian (Florence) who concocts strange but wonderful sea food sauces. This is a favorite that he gave me in Hollywood when he was an entertainer on CBS.

½ cup mayonnaise
1 tablespoon chili sauce
1 tablespoon minced celery
2 tablespoons brandy

1 teaspoon minced onion
1 teaspoon minced parsley
1 teaspoon tarragon vinegar
Salt, pepper, cayenne

Blend all; serve over lobster, etc.

Lee Adams, Station KMOX, St. Louis, Mo.

HAWAIIAN SAUCE
Four cups

For red snapper or other sea food.

4 cups drained canned tomatoes,
    or freshly stewed tomatoes
1 cup sliced almonds
2 tablespoons butter
1 cup diced pineapple

2 tablespoons lemon juice
2 tablespoons soy sauce
Pinch of salt if needed
1 heaping tablespoon cornstarch
¼ cup cold water

In a saucepan, bring the tomatoes to a boil. Sauté the almonds in the butter and add to the tomatoes. Add the pineapple, lemon juice, soy sauce, and salt if desired. Dissolve the cornstarch in cold water; stir into the sauce. Cook over medium heat, stirring, until the sauce is slightly thickened. Serve over broiled red snapper, or in a casserole of shrimp with rice. It makes an excellent dip for fried shrimp.

Judge William L. Shoffner, Burlington, N.C.

CRAB LOUIS SAUCE
About two cups

1 cup mayonnaise
1 tablespoon chopped chives or onion or 1 tablespoon of both
1 tablespoon lemon juice
1 teaspoon chow-chow pickle

1 teaspoon minced green pepper
½ cup chili sauce
1 teaspoon Worcestershire sauce
¼ teaspoon Tabasco
Salt, pepper to taste

Mix all; season to taste with salt and pepper. Serve with crab salad.

Lee Adams, Station KMOX, St. Louis, Mo.

NEIMAN-MARCUS REMOULADE SAUCE
Serves six

1 8-oz. jar New Orleans mustard
6 hard-boiled eggs, chopped fine
2 stalks celery, chopped fine
1 clove garlic, chopped fine

3 or 4 sprigs parsley, chopped fine
1 teaspoon paprika
Salt, pepper to taste
2 cups olive or Wesson oil

Combine; blend thoroughly.

From The Neiman-Marcus Tea Room, Dallas, Tex.

BEARNAISE SAUCE
Three-fourths cup

Béarnaise Sauce is a famous classic served often in the South.

½ cup vinegar
2 tablespoons chopped shallots, or minced onion
2 fresh tarragon leaves
4 egg yolks, beaten

4 tablespoons butter
Salt to taste
1 teaspoon chopped parsley
Dash cayenne pepper

Combine vinegar, shallots, and tarragon in a saucepan and reduce by boiling for 2 minutes. Pour slowly into beaten egg yolks, stirring constantly. Place in top of double boiler and cook until it thickens, stirring constantly. Slowly add by the spoonful the 4 tablespoons butter. Stir and let remain over heat until it is melted and blended. Season with salt to taste. Add parsley and dash of cayenne. If fresh tarragon leaves are not available, substitute tarragon vinegar for the other vinegar. Serve hot over meats.

HORSERADISH SAUCE
One and one-third cups

1 cup sour cream
¼ teaspoon salt
Dash red pepper

¼ cup horseradish
2 tablespoons minced parsley

Blend and chill. Serve with cold roast beef.

Mrs. Charles Plummer, from Christ Church Cook Book, *Petersburg, Va.*

GENGHIS KHAN SAUCE
About one cup

1 clove garlic, crushed
1 1-inch piece of ginger root, crushed (or 1 piece of candied ginger about 1 × ½ inch, with sugar washed off)
1 small carrot, scraped, cut in dice

1 small onion, peeled, diced
1 tablespoon lime juice
1 cup soy sauce
½ cup sweet saki (rice wine), or ½ cup sweet sherry

In a small saucepan, combine all ingredients except the wine. Set on the back of the grill and let simmer for an hour. If scum rises to top, skim it off. Ten minutes before serving add the wine. Strain through a tea strainer and return to saucepan. Keep on a warm place on the grill. Dip meat in sauce before serving. Serve this sauce with grilled chicken, pork, beef, or any meats.

Alfred J. Brown, Lincolnton, N.C.

ROQUEFORT STEAK SAUCE

1 4-oz. wedge Roquefort cheese, creamed
2 drops Tabasco or Texas hot
1 teaspoon Worcestershire sauce

2 tablespoons cream cheese
1 teaspoon Heinz 57 sauce
1 garlic clove, minced

Make paste of all ingredients except garlic. Coat the steak with the above sauce and broil it. Let garlic sauté in pan with the steak. Pour drippings over the steak.

PIQUANT MINT SAUCE
One and one-fourth cups

1 cup good apple cider vinegar
3 tablespoons sugar
½ cup chopped fresh mint leaves

¼ teaspoon salt
Dash lime juice

Boil sugar and vinegar until sugar is well dissolved. Pour over mint leaves and let stand to steep until flavor is extracted. While still hot add salt. Cool; add lime juice. Serve with lamb.

Mrs. Taylor C. Cabiness, Chattanooga, Tenn.

CHATEAUBRIAND SAUCE FOR LAMB
One cup

1 cup dry white wine
1 small onion, minced or 1 shallot minced
⅓ bay leaf
⅙ teaspoon ground thyme
2 tablespoons meat extract, or ½ teaspoon Kitchen Bouquet (meat extract or meat glaze)

2 tablespoons butter
¼ teaspoon dried, crushed tarragon leaves
2 teaspoons chopped parsley
Dash Tabasco sauce
Salt and pepper to taste

In a small saucepan, combine the wine, minced onion, bay leaf, and thyme. Bring to a boil and simmer until wine is slightly reduced (about ¾ original amount). Add the remaining ingredients; blend well. Serve hot over lamb.

CAPER SAUCE
One cup

2 tablespoons butter
1 tablespoon flour
1 cup mutton stock

Salt, pepper
1 heaping tablespoon capers

Melt butter in a saucepan; add the flour and cook for a few minutes, but do not brown. Add the stock; season to taste with salt and pepper. Strain and add capers. Serve over lamb chops.

From The Century Cook Book, *by Mary Ronald*

HONEY-ANGOSTURA GLAZE FOR HAM
About one and one-half cups

1 cup strained honey
6 tablespoons lemon juice

2 tablespoons currant jelly
2 tablespoons angostura bitters

Slowly heat the honey over low heat in a small saucepan. Stir in remaining ingredients. Bring to a boil and remove from heat. Set aside at room temperature. Use to glaze any ham—raw, cooked, or pre-cooked. Bake ham according to packaged instructions. Twenty minutes before ham is ready, pour part of glaze on fat side of ham. Increase oven heat to 425 degrees. Every 5 minutes spread additional glaze on ham until all has been used.

This makes a good glaze for a roasted leg of lamb or pork loin roast.

Mrs. R. C. Moore, Graham, N.C.

ORANGE SAUCE FOR DUCK (*or Any Birds*)
Two cups

Juice of 1 lemon
Juice of 2 oranges
Rind of 1 orange, reserve orange (cut rind from orange into strips)
¼ teaspoon dried rosemary

¼ teaspoon dried tarragon
¼ teaspoon poultry seasoning
¼ cup light brown sugar
2 dashes Tabasco sauce
½ cup dry white wine

Place all ingredients except the reserved orange in a small saucepan. Bring slowly to boiling point, but do not boil. Let stand until mixture is cooled to warm stage. Strain. Cut the reserved orange into thin slices and float it on top of the sauce. Serve over roasted duck. This may also be used over chicken or game birds. It is a good basting sauce for Rock Cornish hens. If used as a basting sauce, add 2 tablespoons of butter to hot sauce, and stir.

Charlie Harville, WYPT-TV, High Point, N.C.

MADEIRA SAUCE (*for Pheasant or Other Birds*)
About two cups

Pan drippings from roasted pheasant or other birds
1 cup chicken stock, or 1 cup bouillon made from 1 teaspoon instant bouillon and 1 cup boiling water

2 tablespoons butter, softened
4 tablespoons Madeira
1 boiled pheasant or chicken liver, chopped (optional)
Salt and pepper to taste

Pour chicken stock into the roasting pan in which a pheasant was roasted. Set over medium heat and stir up all the brown bits, scraping from the bottom and sides of the pan. Gradually stir in the melted butter, stirring constantly until well blended. Add the Madeira and stir. Stir in the chopped liver; season to taste with salt and pepper. Serve hot in a sauce boat.

CURRANT JELLY SAUCE FOR ROCK CORNISH HENS
One and one-half cups

1 10-oz. jar currant jelly
1 tablespoon lemon juice
½ cup beef bouillon or consommé
½ teaspoon ground ginger

1 tablespoon grated orange rind
1 tablespoon flour, mixed with 2 tablespoons bouillon or consommé (optional)

Melt the jelly over low heat in a small saucepan. Stir in remaining ingredients except flour. Bring mixture to a boil; reduce heat and simmer for 15 minutes, stirring often. Use as a basting sauce for roasting Rock Cornish hens. Thicken the pan drippings with 1 tablespoon of flour mixture if desired. The pan gravy may be served as a sauce over cooked hens.

Mrs. R. C. Moore, Graham, N.C.

CHILI SAUCE FOR CHICKEN (*for Barbecue Chicken*)
One and one-half cups

1½ cups chopped fresh tomatoes, or 1½ cups chopped canned tomatoes
4 tablespoons butter
3 green chilis (canned hot type), chopped fine
1 teaspoon ground black pepper

¼ teaspoon ground ginger
¼ teaspoon ground cinnamon
1 tablespoon Samson's Sauce (a hot sauce sold in some food stores), or 3 dashes Tabasco sauce

In a saucepan, place the chopped tomatoes and butter; heat and stir. Add remaining ingredients and simmer on the back of a grill while charcoaling chicken, or on a slow heat on stove. Serve hot over Barbecue Chicken Chili, or any poultry or meat.

A. B. Lea, Jamestown, N.C.

HAWAIIAN SAUCE FOR CHICKEN OR STEAK (*Charcoal Broil*)
One cup

½ cup soy sauce
½ cup sugar
2 cloves garlic, mashed to pulp

1 teaspoon ground ginger
1 dash Tabasco sauce

Mix ingredients. Use as a marinade for chicken or steak. Marinate meat at least 2 hours before broiling over charcoal fire. If desired, heat the marinade after meat has been removed. Serve over the cooked meat.

ORIENTAL SAUCE FOR SPARERIBS, PORK, OR BEEF RIBS
One cup

¾ cup soy sauce
1 tablespoon brown sugar
3 tablespoons minced chives, or 1 small green onion, minced

1 teaspoon ground ginger
1 clove garlic, crushed to pulp
⅓ cup dry wine (red for beef, white for pork)

Mix all ingredients in a small saucepan. Bring to boil. Remove from heat at once. Use to marinate meat; then reserve it as a basting sauce.

Mary Farmer, Roanoke, Va.

BARBECUE SAUCE WITH CELERY
One quart

2 onions, chopped
1 tablespoon butter
1½ cups catchup
1½ cups water
3 tablespoons vinegar
1 tablespoon brown sugar

1½ tablespoons Worcestershire sauce
2¼ teaspoons dry mustard
1½ teaspoons salt
1 cup minced celery

Sauté onion in butter until tender and golden. Mix in the remaining ingredients. Bring to a boil. Then simmer until celery is tender. Brown sugar may be increased to taste. Use it to barbecue chicken, spareribs, or anything else desired.

Mrs. Leland F. Henderson, from The Junior League of Dallas Cook Book, *Dallas, Tex.*

TEXAS BARBECUE CHICKEN OR MEAT SAUCE
For six chickens or six pounds meat

1 tablespoon salt
½ teaspoon pepper
3 tablespoons brown sugar
¼ cup catchup
3 tablespoons prepared mustard (brown mustard)

2 tablespoons Worcestershire sauce
1 cup water
2 tablespoons chili sauce
½ cup vinegar
1 cup melted butter or cooking oil

Mix in the order given, using rotary egg beater as oil is added. Simmer slowly until slightly thickened. This makes 3 cups of sauce. Keep hot.

Jane Erwing Barrow, from DAR Cook Book, *compiled by Aileen Lewers Langston*

DILL BUTTER

1 teaspoon lemon juice
2 tablespoons melted butter

½ teaspoon dill seed

Blend thoroughly and serve on hard bread or with any meat. Good to rub on pork chops that are waiting to be broiled.

MAITRE D'HOTEL BUTTER SAUCE

A famous sauce.

½ cup butter
Salt, pepper to taste

2 teaspoons lemon juice
1 tablespoon minced parsley

Melt butter; add salt, pepper, and lemon juice. Add parsley and serve at once over steaks, hot. If a cold sauce is desired, cream ingredients with butter and spread over broiled steak or fish. If a thickened sauce is wanted, add above to a white cream sauce, seasoning to taste.

Mrs. Eugene F. Barker, Atlanta, Ga.

SAUCE DIABLE
One and one-half cups

3 tablespoons finely minced onions
2 tablespoons butter
2 tablespoons flour
1 teaspoon soy sauce
1 tablespoon Worcestershire sauce
2½ teaspoons hot prepared mustard (Dijon, Mr. Mustard, etc.)

1 cup boiling water
1 rounded teaspoon instant beef bouillon (or 2 bouillon cubes)
2 dashes Tabasco sauce
½ cup red wine vinegar
1 chopped canned hot green pepper (Toredo or Spanish pepper), optional

In a skillet, sauté the onions in the butter until they are transparent and soft. Mix in the flour to make a smooth paste. Add remaining ingredients except the hot green pepper. Cook over medium heat, stirring constantly, until sauce thickens. If desired, add the hot green pepper, minced fine. This is a "red hot" sauce to be used with any meat or sea food. Serve hot or cold.

Mrs. W. G. Vetterlien, Tucson, Ariz.

ANNE'S CHILI SAUCE (*for Matambre or Other Meats*)
Two cups

4 tablespoons butter
1 onion, finely chopped

1 green pepper, finely chopped
1 garlic clove, minced

2 tablespoons flour
1 tablespoon chili powder
1 teaspoon salt

Freshly ground black pepper
1 cup tomato juice
1 cup beef broth

Melt butter in a medium-size skillet. Add onion, green pepper, and garlic; sauté for 5 minutes or more, stirring frequently until the vegetables are transparent but not browned. Blend in the flour, chili powder, salt, and pepper. Stir over low heat for 2 minutes. Stir in the tomato juice and beef broth. Cook, stirring, over medium heat until slightly thickened. Serve hot.

Mrs. O. Ray McKenzie, Burlington, N.C.

ITALIAN SAUCE FOR MEAT BALLS
About two cups

2 tablespoons olive oil
1 clove garlic, minced
½ cup chopped onions
1¼ cans (11-oz. can) tomato soup
1½ cups tomato paste
1 teaspoon salt

⅛ teaspoon pepper
½ cup chopped mushrooms (canned)
¼ teaspoon oregano
½ cup water

Heat the oil in a large skillet; add the garlic and onion and cook over medium heat until light brown. Slowly stir in the tomato soup and paste. Add the salt and pepper. Simmer over low heat, stirring often, for about 30 minutes, or until thickened. Add the mushrooms and oregano. Simmer 5 minutes. If sauce becomes too thick, add the water; stir and reheat. Serve over meat balls in a chafing dish.

Mr. and Mrs. Talmage Scroggs, Managers,
The Alamance Country Club, Burlington, N.C.

CHILI COLORADO (*Red Chili Sauce*)
Two cups

"The base for all red and all hot sauces used in Mexico and Mexican cookery is made as follows, and no substitute, such as chili powder or tomato will do:

"Put a pound of dried red chili peppers to soak in hot water for about an hour. Drain and clean out the veins and seeds. Put through the meat grinder with one large onion and a clove of garlic. Strain and put in salt and pepper. Place the resultant pulps and the water in which the peppers soaked in a glass jar and keep in the refrigerator for future use. The flavor of the chili can be varied by the kind of peppers used. Some red chili is hot and some sweet. Most cooks prefer a chili colorado made of half hot (picoso) and half sweet (pasillo) peppers."

Mrs. Manuel Rodarte, from La Cocina Mexicana, *by "Sally Ann,"*
Food Editor, El Paso Herald-Post, El Paso, Tex.

TO MAKE COCONUT MILK
Six cups

Use this to substitute for water in making any curry; add it to red bean dishes (Red Beans and Rice With Smoked Sausage, p. 284), or for making chicken gravies and sauces.

1 large coconut   6 cups cold water
Cheese cloth

Puncture the eyes of coconut; drain off the "milk"; reserve it. Crack the coconut and pry the shell from the meat. Leave the dark outer coating of coconut on the white meat. Grate the coconut, or cut it into small pieces and grind in a blender, using part of the meat at a time. Place a square of cheese cloth in a large bowl. Put the ground nut meat in the cloth and pour over 2 cups of water. Squeeze the cloth to extract all liquid. Pour over another 2 cups and squeeze; add the remaining 2 cups and squeeze the bag again. Add to this the milk from the coconut. Use as directed. Keep refrigerated until ready for use. This may be frozen in plastic containers.

Mrs. Annie Lee McGhee,
Mount Kisco, N.Y.

PEMBROKE PLUM PUDDING SAUCE
About three cups

This is an old family recipe. Mix 1 cup of butter, 2 cups of sugar, 3 eggs and 1 wine glass of wine. Stir well and let all come to a boil. Serve hot.

Mrs. William B. Rosevear, Pembroke Hall, Edenton, N.C.

HARDIMONT BUTTERSCOTCH SAUCE FOR VANILLA ICE CREAM
About three cups

1¼ cups brown sugar   ¾ cup heavy cream
⅔ cup Karo syrup   Toasted, coarsely broken almonds
4 tablespoons butter

Put sugar, syrup, and butter into saucepan and let boil until soft ball is formed in cold water. Then add cream. Good on vanilla ice cream with toasted, coarsely broken almonds sprinkled over.

Mrs. J. Crawford Biggs, Hardimont, Raleigh, N.C.

HOT CHOCOLATE SAUCE, GREENVILLE
Three and one-half cups

Rich, and good over any pudding, cake, or ice cream.

6 1-oz. sqs. chocolate
2 cups sugar
½ cup butter

Dash salt
1 large can Carnation milk
1 teaspoon vanilla

Melt chocolate; add sugar and butter and salt. Boil for few minutes; add milk; bring back to boil. Add vanilla and blend thoroughly. Serve hot.

Mrs. Gaston Jennings, Greenville, S.C.

FRUIT PUREE
Two cups

2 cups ripe peaches, apricots, mangoes, strawberries, etc.

½ cup sugar
½ teaspoon lemon juice

Slice or cut fruit. Put through a sieve or food mill. Add the sugar and lemon juice. Place in covered container and chill. Serve over puddings or congealed desserts.

VANILLA-COGNAC SAUCE
About one and one-half cups

3 tablespoons butter, softened
7 tablespoons confectioners sugar
4 tablespoons cognac

5 tablespoons boiling water (little extra if needed)
1 tablespoon vanilla (right)

Cream the butter with the sugar until fluffy; gradually add the cognac. Gradually add the boiling water; beat mixture very hard. Set the mixing pan in a pan of hot water; stir frequently; do not allow it to boil. Cook for 5 minutes. Remove from fire; add the vanilla; stir. Serve over puddings, ice cream, cake, etc.

Page Aylett Royall, from Gay Nineties Cook Book (The Dietz Press, Inc., Richmond, Va.)

VIOLA'S RUM SAUCE
About two cups

4 tablespoons butter, softened
1 cup brown sugar
2 egg yolks, beaten

½ cup milk, or cream
⅛ teaspoon salt
3 tablespoons rum

Cream butter and sugar together; add beaten egg yolks, milk, and salt. Cook over medium heat, stirring constantly, until sauce is creamy. Remove from heat; add rum. Good over plum pudding, gingerbread, or vanilla ice cream. Store in refrigerator and reheat for serving.

Mrs. John Rich Ireland, Burlington, N.C.

WHIPPED CREAM CHOCOLATE SAUCE
Two and one-half cups

This is an easy way to make a cake frosting or a sauce for hot puddings. It may also be frozen as a mousse.

1 cup heavy cream
¾ cup sugar
4 tablespoons cocoa

1 teaspoon vanilla extract
Slivered toasted almonds or pistachio nuts for garnish

In the top of a double boiler, combine the cream, sugar, and cocoa. Cook over boiling water, stirring often, for 20 minutes. Add the vanilla. Cool mixture; chill it thoroughly. Whip the chilled cream with a wire whisk until the mixture holds a peak. Use it as it is, or as a frosting or sauce. Sprinkle nuts over if desired. If it is frozen, stir in the nuts. After mixture begins to freeze, stir twice. Cover tray with waxed paper. Serve as a mousse.

Mrs. Norman Riddle, Bluefield, W. Va.

LEMON SAUCE
One and one-half cups

½ cup sugar
1 tablespoon cornstarch
1 cup water

1 tablespoon butter
2 tablespoons lemon juice
1 tablespoon grated lemon rind

In a saucepan, mix the sugar and cornstarch. Gradually stir in the water. Cook over medium heat, stirring constantly until the mixture begins to boil. Stir and boil about 1 minute. Remove from the heat and stir in butter, lemon juice, and rind. Serve warm over puddings, gingerbread, cake, etc.

CREPES SUZETTE SAUCE
Two cups (for eight to ten crêpes)

1 medium-size orange, washed, dried, (and juice of orange)
3 blocks of sugar, broken in hunks
4 tablespoon butter

1½ teaspoon lemon juice
¼ cup Cointreau
¼ cup Benedictine or Grand Marnier

Wash and dry the orange. Take the lumps of sugar and rub them as hard as possible over the skin of the orange so the sugar will absorb the flavor. Crush the sugar, using a board and rolling pin, or in a mortar with pestle. Pour the sugar into a heatproof chafing dish inset pan (or similiar dish). Squeeze the orange and pour the juice over the sugar. Add the butter and lemon juice to the pan. Stir well. Cook until the sugar has dissolved; then add the liqueurs. Heat to boiling point and serve with crêpes as follows:

To Serve Crêpes Suzette
Allow 3 crêpes for each serving.

Heat the Crêpes Suzette Sauce in a chafing dish. Place the crêpes side by side in the sauce and spoon sauce over them. When they are well covered, fold the crêpes first into halves, then into quarters. Repeat until the desired number has been folded. In a small heavy saucepan, heat 2 to 3 tablespoons of cognac or Grand Marnier. Ignite the liqueur and pour it quickly over the crêpes. Bring them flaming to the table, or flame them at the table.

NOTE: The crêpes may be made well ahead of time, but make the sauce just before serving.

HARD BRANDY SAUCE

1 cup powdered sugar
1½ tablespoons soft butter

1 teaspoon heavy cream
Brandy or wine to taste

Cream butter and sugar; soften with cream, using it drop by drop so that the sauce will not become too soft. Add brandy in the same manner, tasting to reach desired flavor. Place in refrigerator to harden. Serve on top of hot, or warm gingerbread.

Mrs. Angus Craft, St. Petersburg, Fla.

BRANDY SAUCE
Two and one-half cups

2 egg yolks
3 or 4 tablespoons brandy or
    whiskey
2 cups powdered sugar
2 egg whites, stiffly beaten

1 cup heavy cream, whipped
Pinch salt
1 teaspoon vanilla
Grated nutmeg

Beat egg yolks; add brandy—a little at a time—and sugar. Then add beaten egg whites and whipped cream, salt, and vanilla; sprinkle nutmeg on last.

Mrs. C. H. Hardy, Blackstone, Va.

CHOCOLATE FUDGE SAUCE
About two cups

2 ozs. bitter chocolate
4 tablespoons butter
1 cup boiling water

1 cup sugar
$\frac{1}{16}$ teaspoon salt
1½ teaspoons vanilla

Melt the chocolate over boiling water in the top of a double boiler, and stir in the butter. Stir until butter melts. Slowly dribble in the boiling water, continuing to stir constantly. Then stir in the sugar. Remove the top of the boiler and place it directly over top of the stove heating unit. Slowly bring mixture to a boil and cook for about 5 minutes. Stir in the salt and vanilla. Serve the sauce warm over cake, puddings, ice cream, or any desired desserts.

Mrs. Charles Cardozo, Richmond, Va.

CARAMEL SAUCE FOR FLAN
About three-fourths cup

This caramelized sauce is often called Burnt Sugar Sauce. It may be used under a baked custard such as Flan, or over any custard, pudding, ice cream, etc.

1 cup granulated sugar   ½ cup water

Pour the sugar into a heavy skillet (iron is best). Begin cooking it over high heat and stir constantly until the mixture lumps. When it begins to lump, immediately reduce the heat and slowly pour in the water, being careful that the hot mixture does not sputter out. The mixture will again lump. Continue simmering it slowly over very low heat until it agains forms a syrup. Remove from the heat. Serve as directed above.

Mrs. Alfred G. Lea, St. Petersburg, Fla.

SHERRY SAUCE (*or Vanilla Sauce*)
About one cup

½ cup milk
1 cup sugar
4 tablespoons butter

3 tablespoons sherry, or 1½ teaspoons vanilla extract

In a small heavy saucepan, combine the milk, sugar, and butter. Bring to boil and simmer for 5 minutes. Add the sherry or vanilla. Serve warm or cold over puddings, cake, ice cream, etc.

18. Lagniappe

Scattered throughout this book are recipes taken or revised from *The Louisiana Plantation Cook Book,* compiled by the late Mrs. James E. Smitherman, Shreveport, Louisiana. The final chapter of her book is called "Lagniappe," meaning "extra gift." The word comes from a charming old Louisiana custom still prevailing among the older generation of merchants and shopkeepers. If you make a purchase, invariably you will be presented with a small extra gift—a prized piece of candy, a handful of cakes, or assorted nuts. Just as I have borrowed Mrs. Smitherman's recipes, I think I shall choose her way of ending this volume, with "Lagniappe."

The Praline has been known in New Orleans for more than two hundred years, says Mary Moore Bremer in her *New Orleans Recipes.* "Even the French explorer, Le Page du Pratz, in the early days of French occupation of Louisiana, mentions that they [pralines] were made from 'Wild pecan kernels, and most highly praised.' " Here are recipes from this book for Pralines and Pecan Glacé.

PRALINES AUX PECANS
Two pounds

4 tablespoons water
2 tablespoons evaporated milk
1 tablespoon butter
½ teaspoon salt

4 cups brown sugar
2 cups broken pecans
12 drops vanilla extract (optional)

Put water and evaporated milk into a saucepan; add butter, salt, and brown sugar (measure these exactly; do not round measurements). Melt over a slow fire and boil, stirring constantly. Add broken pecans.

When candy begins to thicken, remove from fire and stir while cooling. While it is still pourable, drop with large spoon onto oiled paper, making cakes 3 or 4 inches in diameter. Add vanilla extract to this recipe if pralines are to be kept for more than a few days.

From New Orleans Recipes, *by Mary Moore Bremer, New Orleans, La.*

PECAN GLACE
Two pounds

3 cups sugar
½ teaspoon cream tartar

1 cup water
Pecan halves

Put sugar, cream of tartar, and water into saucepan; stir as mixture heats until sugar is dissolved. Wipe away any sugar crystals that may form on the sides of pan, and cook syrup without stirring until it threads crisply when dropped from a spoon; and immediately dip perfect halves of pecans, one at a time, using a long sharp pin, and place on buttered dish. Work fast for the glacé hardens rapidly.

This is one of the most delightful ways of using pecans. Dates, almonds, Brazil nuts, Malaga grapes, orange sections, and even violets may be treated the same way.

From New Orleans Recipes, *by Mary Moore Bremer, New Orleans, La.*

COCONUT PRALINES
One-half pound

1 cup sugar
1 cup fresh coconut, grated

½ cup water
½ teaspoon vanilla

Mix sugar with water and let stand until sugar is partly dissolved. Place in saucepan over low flame; let gradually simmer and boil until syrup is slightly thickened. Add coconut; let boil until all forms soft ball in cold water. Remove, and drop by spoonfuls on buttered surface. Let harden.

Miss Jonsey Ann Brittle, Charleston, S.C.

PANOCHA
One-half pound

Panocha, known also as "Pinoce," or Mexican Candy, is a rich fudge, popular in many Southern regions. This is a true Mexican recipe.

1 cup white sugar
1 cup brown sugar
½ cup cream or evaporated milk

2 tablespoons dark corn syrup
1 tablespoon butter
2 tablespoons water

Cook all ingredients together for 5 minutes, *by the clock,* after boiling point is reached. Beat thoroughly and add:

¾ cup broken nut meats

Pour into buttered platter and mark into squares before candy cools.

Mrs. E. D. Raynolds, from La Cocina Mexicana, *by "Sally Ann,"*
Food Editor, El Paso Herald-Post, *El Paso, Tex.*

"SNAP DRAGON"

An old New Orleans custom, and a fascinating party surprise.

Cover a heavy platter (earthenware or heavy, plated silver) with **giant raisins**. Pour over enough **brandy** to soak into raisins. Let set for few minutes. Then light brandy. Guests are supposed to snap at raisins while flame glows.

From New Orleans Recipes, *by Mary Moore Bremer, New Orleans, La.*

PARTY MINTS WITH ROYAL ICING

2 cups sugar	¾ cup cold water
2 tablespoons white Karo syrup	¼ teaspoon cream of tartar
Pinch salt	Oil of peppermint

Put sugar, syrup, salt, and water in top of double boiler. When it starts to boil, add ¼ teaspoon of cream of tartar. Let boil until soft-ball stage is reached. Take up; place vessel in cold pan of water and start beating with electric mixer until creamy. Then add 3 or 4 drops of peppermint. Return vessel to hot water and let melt. Drop mixture by teaspoonfuls on waxed paper. This makes a pretty flat mint to be decorated with the following:

Royal Icing

1 egg white	Vegetable coloring
Confectioners sugar	

Beat egg white lightly; add enough powdered sugar to make mixture stiff enough to put into pastry tube. Tint; put into pastry tube, and decorate—making desired flowers and colors.

Mrs. James W. Smith, Americus, Ga.

THELMA MADRY'S CREAM MINTS
One pound

Thelma Madry's Cream Mints are so in demand that one must speak weeks ahead in order to procure a few. This is the first publication of her recipe, which she modestly says is an open secret. The secret is in learning from experience how to time the cooking, how to pull the "taffy" to the perfect stage—and knowing enough about meteorology to be able to judge good mint-making weather. Yes, on certain days the temperamental mints are likely to become contrary and go back to sugar.

½ cup water   5 drops oil of peppermint
2 cups sugar   Vegetable coloring, if desired
4 tablespoons butter

Put water, sugar, and butter on to cook; bring to boiling point; reduce heat slightly; and boil until syrup forms a hard lump when dropped into ice water. Do not stir at all during entire process. Pour on marble slab; add oil of peppermint and vegetable coloring.

Butter the fingers and begin to pull almost before the candy has had time to cool at all, using the tips of the thumb and two fingers. Pull until a slight crust begins to form on the outside of the candy—practise will determine the length of time required. Twist into a rope and cut with scissors into small pieces. Allow to cool thoroughly on the slab. Pack in airtight tin box for a day or two until they cream. A marble slab is absolutely necessary. [Decorate if desired, using pastry tube. Try using Mrs. Smiths Royal Icing (above) to decorate this mint.—M. B.]

Mrs. W. D. Madry, Burlington, N.C.

PEACH LEATHER

Once this strange-sounding, but delicious, old form of candy was made professionally by an older generation of "Deep" Southern ladies. But it has been no exception to the fact that most secrets (like murders) will eventually out. It is cooked in the sun like "sun-cooked preserves." This is a word-of-mouth recipe, although the facsimile is in many cook books.

Select ripe soft peaches; peel and mash to a purée. To every cup of peaches add ¼ cup of granulated sugar (or brown sugar may be used). Mix sugar with peaches; let simmer over low heat until mixture comes to a good boil; boil only 1 or 2 minutes. Remove. Pour into shallow pans or platters in a thin coating. Cover with mosquito netting; let sit in the sun for several days, bringing in each night, until mixture has cooked down to a good tough "leather." Cut in squares; sprinkle with powdered sugar. Roll, if desired, and resprinkle with powdered sugar. Someone should sit and watch leather, to see that no insects crawl under netting. (Apricots may be used.) 4 lbs. peaches to 1 cup sugar should yield 1 lb. candy.

Mrs. William DeR. Scott, Graham, N.C.

APPLE LEATHER

3 cups apple sauce	¼ teaspoon nutmeg
½ cup sugar	Nuts, optional

Spread ½ inch in shallow pan. Bake in slow oven ½ day. Take out and roll in powdered sugar like a jelly roll. Nuts may be added before mixture is baked. Slice thin. Use as a confection.

Mrs. C. M. Buxton, Loudown Co., Va., from Recipes from Old Virginia, *Richmond, Va.*

LIB HARMAN'S FROSTED GRAPES

Mrs. Harman uses these as a centerpiece, to garnish salads or tea platters, or to encircle molds of any salad.

Wash and thoroughly dry **clusters of any variety of grape.** Dip into **unbeaten egg white,** being careful that each grape is well-coated. Now roll in **granulated sugar.** Place in icebox and allow to chill until the sugar hardens. When ready, the grapes have an exquisite frosting. [Try frosting sprigs of mint leaves by same method—pretty and good, too.—M. B.]

Mrs. David Harman, from Soup to Nuts, *Burlington, N.C.*

WINE DATES, STUFFED

To make an unusual and tempting confection, use **large processed dates;** pit and cover in any good **wine** (sherry preferred) for about 1 hour. Cut **marshmallows** into quarters. Drain the dates; dip marshmallows quickly into the wine, and insert in each piece of marshmallow a **whole pecan meat.** Stuff dates with marshmallow and pecan; press opening together, and roll in granulated sugar. Figs may be stuffed in same manner. Almonds may be substituted for pecans.

Mrs. John Rich Ireland, Burlington, N.C.

PRESERVED VIOLETS—ROSES

A nostalgic reminder of Old-World influence in this recipe which had its inception many years ago, presumably in New Orleans where so many quaint and charming customs have originated.

Make these little "preserves," store them in fancy glass jars, and give them for Christmas gifts, just as our contributor does.

2 cups granulated sugar
1 cup hot water
About 4 cups fresh stemmed violets, washed and drained,

but do not bruise petals. If roses are used, measure 2 cups fresh small buds, washed, drained, stemmed

Dissolve the sugar thoroughly in the hot water. Add the flowers; set on a medium flame and let syrup simmer until it reaches the soft ball stage in cold water. Stir flowers gently with wooden spoon. Remove from flame and continue to stir until the syrup begins to granulate and reaches the consistency of coarse meal. Empty over a wire rack or colander and shake off the extra sugar. Cool and pack into jars, and seal. They will keep indefinitely. Use them to decorate cakes, to garnish fruit salads, tea plates, or to serve in little cut-glass compotes.

Condensed from recipe by Mrs. William Wooton, Baltimore, Md., from Soup to Nuts, *Burlington, N.C.*

SPICED NUTS
About three-fourths pound

1 cup sugar
1 teaspoon cinnamon
⅛ teaspoon cream of tartar
¼ cup hot water

1½ cup nuts (pecans, English walnuts, etc.)
½ teaspoon vanilla

Mix sugar, cinnamon, cream of tartar, and water. Boil until a little of the mixture forms a firm ball in cold water. Add nuts and vanilla and stir until mixture sugars. Turn out on a flat surface and separate the nuts.

Mrs. Addison White, from 100 Favorite Recipes, *Huntsville, Ala.*

EAU SUCREE FOR DYSPEPSIA

After each meal the Creole head of the house mixes a glass of water with 1 tablespoon of sugar. This he passes to each member of the family to take a sip. It is said to be the reason there is no such thing as dyspepsia in New Orleans. (Mothers even give it to their babies.) Just in case you have found our Southern recipes too rich, we pass you a sip of *Eau Sucrée.*

INDEX ⌒